DISTRIBUTED INFORMATION SYSTEMS

From Client/Server to Distributed Multimedia

Errol Simon

The McGraw-Hill Companies

London · New York · St Louis · San Francisco · Auckland
Bogotá · Caracas · Lisbon · Madrid · Mexico · Milan
Montreal · New Delhi · Panama · Paris · San Juan · São Paulo
Singapore · Sydney · Tokyo · Toronto

Published by
McGraw-Hill Publishing Company
Shoppenhangers Road, Maidenhead, Berkshire, SL6 2QL, England
Telephone 01628 23432
Fax 01628 770224

British Library Cataloguing in Publication Data
Simon, Errol
   Distributed information systems
   1. Electronic data processing – Distributed processing
   2. Client/server computing 3. Computer networks
   I. Title
   004.3'6

   ISBN 0 07 709076 4 (pbk)
   ISBN 0 07 709265 1 (hbk)

Library of Congress Cataloging-in-Publication Data
Simon, Errol.
      Distributed information systems : from client/server to distributed
   multimedia / Errol Simon.
         p. cm.
   Includes Index
      ISBN 0-07-709076-4 (pbk) ISBN 0-07-709265-1 (hbk)
      1. Database management. 2. Distributed databases. I. Title.
   QA76.9.D3S56385 1996
   005.75'8—dc20   95–39032
                                                         CIP

McGraw-Hill

A Division of The McGraw·Hill Companies

1234 CUP 99876

Typeset and printed and bound in Great Britain at the University Press, Cambridge
Printed on permanent paper in compliance with ISO Standard 9706.

To Herline, Stuart and Sasha-Louise.
Errol Simon

CONTENTS

TRADEMARK NOTICE

PREFACE

In the past decade the computer industry has been revolutionized. Users are demanding ever more complex applications to meet the need to provide information to support business functions in an increasingly competitive business environment. This has resulted in increasingly diverse requirements for data manipulation and presentation where often the information required is not in a predictable form. Today, applications are being constructed using a wide range of third-party, packaged software to satisfy the need for rapid application development and to exploit the new levels of functionality and ease of use that they provide. Tens of thousands of packaged software are available for the most popular computers and operating systems thus providing an increasingly wide choice. End-users are consequently demanding the integration of a variety of discrete applications available at the desktop to accommodate greater levels of manipulation, integration and ease of use. The combination of powerful packaged software, the availability of advanced communication technologies and rapidly advancing PC architectures has been the stimulus for higher user expectation in terms of what levels of integration and ease of use are achievable.

These forces have created the need for a more flexible IT infrastructure giving greater freedom of design to build information systems. The infrastructure is required to facilitate integration of potentially diverse data sources, a range of media types (text, audio, video, etc.) and in a user environment which allows flexibility of access in a way that hides complexity. Furthermore, the infrastructure must exhibit levels of security, robustness and maintainability at least equivalent to that of the traditional centralized mainframe environment.

To date, many organizations have successfully evolved (some over twenty years) core information systems based on the centralized mainframe computing environment. These (largely transaction processing) systems are gradually being revamped as senior managers see opportunities to create more cost-effective, flexible and easy-to-modify systems. Evidence suggests that there is a large-scale move away from centralized mainframe systems towards distributed systems which is perceived as the key approach to infrastructure design for the foreseeable future. New applications are now much more likely to be developed for execution on UNIX or PC-based servers than on mainframes. Moreover, these new systems are likely to coexist with long-standing core operational systems as many will remain on the mainframe for a long time. It is difficult and costly to re-engineer thousands of lines of difficult program code performance-tuned to support a high transaction rate with low response times.

While distributed systems should not be regarded as a panacea for all the world's computing problems, they can provide an efficient, effective and economical solution to many business requirements, taking advantage of advances in computer and communication technologies.

This book explores the various enabling technologies and components which underpins the design and development of **distributed information systems** (the term distributed system is also used synonymously in this book). The main objective is to provide answers to the following fundamental questions:

1. What is a distributed information system (DIS)?
2. How is a DIS structured?
3. What IT infrastructure is required to support the various types of DIS?
4. What are the design rules relating to the development of DISs?
5. How can a distributed IT infrastructure be implemented and managed to ensure that mission-critical or high-integrity DISs can be implemented successfully?

There are several excellent text books which mostly deal with the technical aspects of distributed *operating* systems. However, there are very few books which look at distributed systems from an *information systems* perspective (although many operating system issues are also relevant in this context). Thus, the book is seen as complimentary to those which provide an operating systems perspective on distributed system. The study of distributed information systems integrates within a single context, a number of key subjects:

- computer networks and communications;
- distributed operating systems;
- database and file systems;
- information systems development and management.

Thus, the book necessarily covers a wide range of topics in an integrated manner, but with references to more detailed coverage of specific topics in the text and in the further reading section of each chapter.

This is not a theoretical book, its primary aim is to acquaint the reader with the most significant concepts associated with distributed information systems and provides a clear yet comprehensive coverage of ideas illustrated by reference to practical implementations. The further reading section of each chapter contains pointers to other relevant literature. This book first examines the driving forces behind the move away from 'centralized' to 'distributed' systems utilizing a high speed internetwork of smaller cheaper computers. A DIS increasingly consists of packaged software components running either on client or server platforms as opposed to expensive bespoke solutions running in a mainframe environment.

Major advances in communications technology facilitate world-wide exchanges of multimedia data streams which are a feature of modern information systems design. This book focuses on relevant developments particularly in high-speed (broadband) networking.

Emphasis is also given to network architectures and network operating systems. Organizations are becoming highly dependent on an information network infrastructure, therefore a section of the book is devoted to internetworking technologies.

Various programming paradigms and software design approaches are relevant to the development of distributed applications and are likely to change significantly the development methods used in the future. Several chapters of the book are devoted to the design of distributed applications and the IT infrastructure required to support them.

One of the major impediments to the widespread implementation of distributed information systems is the complexity of systems management. This book examines the problems of, and solutions to distributed systems management and system security.

TARGET AUDIENCE

The book is intended primarily as a textbook for second or third level undergraduate modules on distributed multimedia, multimedia information networks or distributed information systems (depending on the particular emphasis of the module). It is also aimed at postgraduate students of MSc courses which include a module on distributed information systems or for introductory postgraduate readings. The systems implementation theme of the book will also be useful for systems analysts and consultants who are involved in distributed systems development projects. Systems managers will also find the book useful, in that they will gain awareness of the scope of distributed systems. Systems managers will also find the management and security aspects of distributed systems informative from a practical perspective. The book is also suitable for short courses covering distributed information systems concepts and principles. Prerequisite knowledge of introductory computer communications, databases, operating systems and information technology concepts is assumed.

The book is designed for a year long (two semester) module and is organized in four parts. Part One takes as its theme the concepts underpinning distributed information systems. Chapter 1 gives a brief historical perspective of the evolution towards distributed information systems. Centralized and distributed information systems are compared and contrasted. Chapter 2 introduces the definition of terms and concepts used throughout subsequent chapters of the book. It examines the concepts of information exchange and offers a more formal definition of a distributed IT infrastructure and distributed information systems. Information representations are detailed, with emphasis on multimedia data streams. The important issue of transparency (concealing distribution) is introduced. Various classes of distributed services are also introduced. Chapter 3 turns to the concepts of distributed processing. Various models for structuring a distributed system are examined, including client/server and distributed object models. The message passing and remote procedure call (RPC) mechanisms are detailed as examples of remote inter-process communication. Practical illustrations of distributed programming involving UNIX sockets, OSF/DCE RPC and OMG/CORBA are used to illustrate the basic steps involved in developing a distributed information system.

Part Two is devoted to internetworking issues. The quality-of-service requirements to support multimedia traffic are discussed. Chapter 4 introduces underpinning communications concepts and backbone network technologies. Chapter 5 details access network technologies. Access networks are normally implemented using local area network technologies. Chapter 6 describes the concepts and techniques for implementing large-scale internetworks. The X.25 and TCP/IP routing protocols are detailed.

Part Three focuses on the design and implementation of a DIS. Chapter 7 addresses the issue of building distributed services which are designed to be scalable, responsive and dependable. Chapter 8 describes generic services and corporate application and information services which are utilized when developing a DIS. Chapter 9 focuses on the issue of distributed data. Options for distributing data are explored. Distributed transaction processing issues are examined. Chapter 10 proposes an approach to implementing a DIS from the logical design of the system. The ISO open distributed processing (ODP) reference model is used as the basic development framework.

Part Four looks at management, standards and security. Chapter 11 focuses on the bridge between organizational structure and culture, information systems requirements and management. Standards for distributed systems management are covered. Chapter 12 describes a systematic approach to standards evaluation and selection to form an organizational unit or project architecture for the implementation of a distributed system. Techniques that enable more informed decision-making about standards are described. Chapter 13 covers security issues.

Case studies, modelled on real-life organizations, are used as a vehicle to illustrate practical problems in the design, implementation and management of distributed information systems. End-of-chapter review exercises are used for self-study to reinforce the material in the chapter. Each chapter also includes suggestions for further reading and research.

In an undergraduate programme, the book can for example be used to support two semester-based (15 week) modules:

MODULE 1: MULTIMEDIA INFORMATION NETWORKS (15 WEEKS)

Chapter 1   Distributed systems evolution
Chapter 2   Characteristics of distributed information systems
Chapter 3   Distributed processing
Chapter 4   Network technologies - backbone networks
Chapter 5   Network technologies - access networks
Chapter 6   Internetworking
Chapter 8   Generic services

MODULE 2: DISTRIBUTED INFORMATION SYSTEMS (15 WEEKS)

Chapter 7   Building distributed services
Chapter 8   Generic services
Chapter 9   Distributing data
Chapter 10   DIS development
Chapter 11   Decentralized management and control
Chapter 12   Open systems and standards selection
Chapter 13   Security

Although the book introduces some fundamental concepts that apply to distributed information systems, Module 1 (multimedia information networks) should be underpinned by other modules which provide a basic knowledge of programming, computer architectures, computer communications, operating systems, databases and systems analysis. Module 2 (distributed information systems) should have as a prerequisite Module 1, database systems (incorporating SQL), and systems development. The Further Reading section of each chapter will provide the reader with references to suitable background reading and more detailed coverage of specific topics.

READER SUPPORT

You can receive information about updates and any additional material by subscribing to the mailing list *dis-readers*. To do this, send an email message to majordomo@wlv.ac.uk containing the line: 'subscribe dis-readers'.

   To get help with using the mailing list, send the message 'help' to majordomo@wlv.ac.uk. The anonymous FTP directory pub/disbook is available at host ftp.scitsc.wlv.ac.uk to enable readers to access information. Readers on the World Wide Web can also access the information at URL: http//www.scit.wlv.ac.uk/disbook/

ACKNOWLEDGEMENTS

I would like to express my gratitude to the many people who have contributed to the preparation of this textbook. Firstly, I would like to thank my wife Herline Simon and my children Stuart and Sasha-Louise for once again enduring sustained periods of absence. Secondly, Rob Moreton, Andy Sloane, Peter Bates, Jon Wallis and other colleagues at the university who provided valuable information. Thirdly, to the many classes of students attending relevant undergraduate modules and those on the MSc in advanced software technology at the University of Wolverhampton who provided useful feedback on the scope and content of the book. Finally, my thanks to the people at McGraw-Hill who worked on this book, in particular the unflagging support of editor Rupert Knight.

Errol Simon

PART ONE

Concepts

1

DISTRIBUTED SYSTEMS EVOLUTION

1.1 INTRODUCTION

Organizations today are expanding far beyond their traditional geographic boundaries in the search for new business, new customers, new markets and improved financial and organizational viability. Almost every country around the world has been subject to increased competitive pressures largely arising from a global recession, advancements in the development of free-market economies and the further removal of trade barriers between nations. Increased competition between organizations and the development of the 'global market' involving Europe (eastern, central and western), the United States, Japan, the Third World and the Pacific Basin has brought new challenges and has forced management to adopt more sophisticated corporate strategies. This, in turn, has resulted in the need for a more flexible and productive IT infrastructure to support increasingly innovative information systems.

Organizations are creating IT infrastructures which support the delivery of information, experience and services on demand, in the right form, at the right time, at the right price, to fixed or mobile workstations anywhere (e.g. in the home, office, public area, car, aircraft, etc.). Bandwidth, distance and time will no longer be significant cost elements as service and access become the dominant features of the changing demands of an information focused society (Cochrane, 1995).

The IT industry is experiencing a major evolutionary leap forward. Desktop workstations have been transformed from computation-intensive to communication-intensive (and information-intensive) that use in addition to text and graphics, 'information rich' media types such as audio, animation and video (Dustdar, 1994). Many IT users, who routinely use services such as electronic mail and remote information services, are communication-intensive users already, gaining significant benefits from the success of distributed systems technology

3

without knowing in detail how these systems are designed and implemented. In fact, a fundamental design goal of distributed systems technology is that, where possible, distribution should be concealed, giving users the illusion that all available resources are located at the user's workstation. A *distributed system* in this context is simply a collection of autonomous computers connected by a computer network to enable resource sharing and co-operation between applications to achieve a given task.

Information technology, in addition to supporting internal operational systems such as accounting and order processing, is being positioned as enabling technology in the quest to achieve sustainable competitive advantage. Information technology, correctly harnessed, adds value to an organization which may be so fundamental that it causes long-term changes to the quality and nature of business processes. Table 1.1 summarizes the main types of added value through the use of IT (Darnton and Giacoletto, 1992). IT added value can be achieved through the use of both centralized and distributed systems. Although centralized systems have been the mainstay of IT for about three decades, three driving forces have served to propel distributed computing as a key development for the 1990s and beyond:

1. Advances in computer and communications technology used to implement the IT infrastructure.
2. A growing applications portfolio due to the pervasive application of IT to operational, management control and strategic levels of an organization.
3. Shifting organizational structures to meet a rapidly changing business environment. Organizations are seeking to implement an appropriate balance between centralization for tight co-ordination and decentralization for enhanced organization flexibility and responsiveness to meet a changing business environment.

In this chapter the above driving forces are described. The advantages and disadvantages of distributed systems are also examined.

Table 1.1   IT added value

Type of added value	Description
Space	Activities can be sequenced tightly and co-ordinated in spite of the fact that an organization may be geographically dispersed.
Time	The effects of time barriers and differing time zones are reduced. Many activities can be performed with smaller time gaps than is otherwise possible.
Event sequences	Related events can be tightly sequenced (mainly as a result of the reduced effects of space and time).
Complexity	Many calculations carried out routinely by computers are practically impossible for humans.
Knowledge	The pool of knowledge and expertise encapsulated in computer-based information systems is way beyond the capacity of any individual (or groups of individuals). Therefore, IT has become a means of extending an individual's knowledge base. *Access* to information and knowledge bases is an increasingly important requirement.

1.2 IT INFRASTRUCTURE ADVANCES: POWER TO THE DESKTOP

When it was very expensive for an organization to purchase a single computer system, locating computing capacity, applications and data in a tightly managed mainframe environment was a highly appropriate way to manage computing resources efficiently. Moreover, large organizations were regulated based on traditional views which can be traced back to early twentieth-century management scientists. These views are still widely held today and are commensurate with top-down control where strategy is developed at the top and the rest of the organization is seen as a means of implementation (the 'bureaucratic' or 'mechanistic' principle of control). Thus centralized control of expensive computing resources mirrored the way organizations were typically regulated. Access to remote computers were facilitated by **wide area networks** (WANs) which were developed initially to support access to centralized mainframe computers. WANs are discussed in detail in Chapter 4.

However, the centralized control of computer resources and marginal involvement in application development was not welcomed by user departments. A degradation in flexibility and responsiveness was perceived, coupled with an increasing desire to control their own resources. For many organizations, centralized control of information systems and management was becoming inconsistent with user departments being given an increasing degree of discretion. The pressure to decentralise continued to gather strength and implementing new applications on local resources was considered by user departments as a step in the right direction.

1.2.1 Minicomputer technology

Some of the immediate limitations of the mainframe environment, from the users' perspective, were overcome in the 1970s with the introduction of time-sharing, multi-user minicomputers. Minicomputers were placed in user departments bringing computing resources nearer to the user, heralding the era of decentralized control of computing resources. The minicomputer was sufficiently inexpensive to encourage the use of more than one computer on a site. This encouraged the idea of access (local and remote) to specialist applications on dedicated computers. In addition, the presence of multiple minicomputers locally stimulated the development of data communications technology for local communications – a **local area network** (LAN). LANs are described in detail in Chapter 5. However, one of the major drawbacks of this approach was the loss of centralized control of the organization's data store and the reduced levels of information sharing, though users argued that the central data store was locked away in a highly controlled, fortress-like glasshouse (central computer services) – they could see it, but couldn't access it easily!

The development of affordable microprocessors and local communication technologies were the stimuli for the next major development in computing – the development of the personal computer and associated local area network technologies. By the early 1980s the costs and size of computing and communication technologies reduced dramatically as the use of very large-scale integrated circuitry increased. Also significant improvements in reliability, flexibility and versatility were realized, and the technologies were being used across many application areas.

The Ethernet local area network (Metcalfe and Boggs, 1976) was subsequently developed by Xerox, Intel and Digital partly to meet the need for faster data communication between minicomputers. Later, LANs also became the means by which users accessed resources and applications residing on minicomputers. An unfortunate consequence of this development was that more minicomputers entered the market which was already becoming overwhelmed with an increasing variety of incompatible operating systems and communication protocols.

Planning and controlling the IT infrastructure became difficult due to the increasingly incompatible components being introduced.

1.2.2 Personal computers

The use of minicomputer technology to support single users interacting using a graphical user interface was mainly pioneered by researchers at the Xerox Palo Alto Research Center from the early 1970s. The Apple II computer was one of the first commercially available **Personal computers** (PCs), followed by the ubiquitous IBM PC which developed rapidly throughout the 1980s to become the standard 'dedicated computer on the desktop' technology. At the time of writing, PCs costing under £1000 incorporate support for video, audio, CD-ROMs, a large amount of memory and disk storage, and with processing power equivalent to a powerful mainframe in the 1980s.

Initially, stand-alone PCs proliferated and it was soon realized that a communications facility was required to allow resource sharing at the local level to reduce costs and improve levels of service, management and administration. The development of LAN technologies, at a cost well within departmental budgets, resulted in the integration of minicomputers, microcomputers and LANs which were able to provide most of the computing needs of a typical department within an organization – without the requirement to access a mainframe system. In fact the cost argument for the centralized mainframe environment completely evaporated. Grosh's law (processing power increases according to the square of its cost), which favoured large monolithic computers, was turned upside down as it was now cheaper to take advantage of multiple low-cost processing elements, each capable of supporting data storage, manipulation and presentation using graphical user interfaces – and much more powerful than the mainframes of the 1970s and early 1980s.

In reality, Grosh's law is based on mainframe costs which generally included high profit margins. Mainframe systems are to some extent competing with PC technology by dramatically reducing profit margins. If we were to add up the total computing power represented by the 100s of PCs on desktops in an organization, however, the total figure would suggest that to displace it would require a mainframe which is larger than any available for the foreseeable future! Distributed processors are here to stay. The technical challenge is how to utilize this distributed power effectively. Distributed processing issues are discussed in Chapter 3.

1.2.3 Wide area information services

The 1990s saw a significant increase in the use of the **Internet** wide area network as a global communications infrastructure. The Internet is a web of separate networks interconnected to support communications on a world-wide scale (it is discussed in detail in Chapter 6). Internet technology was developed in the 1960s by a research project commissioned by the US Department of Defense. The technology developed was made widely available to universities and the research community to such an extent that they now rely on the Internet for electronic mail, remote login, access to remote files, etc. In 1980, approximately 100 computers were connected to the Internet, in 1995 there were over one million. In the 1990s, with the increasingly global marketplace, the Internet is now seen as a key foundation technology to support global communications and electronic commerce. Many services are available over the Internet, ranging from electronic mail to distance learning and electronic trading.

The Internet is a powerful example of a successful distributed systems environment. The Internet is also a good example of how autonomous organizations can co-operate for mutual benefit to form a global, scalable facility. This configuration is described as a *federation* of separate (autonomous) systems, each co-operating with others when necessary (by consent of the owning organizations through contract negotiation or legislation for mutual protection) for mutual benefit and to preserve local autonomy. Thus federated systems promote local autonomy while allowing partial and controlled sharing of resources. The principle of federation is widely used to implement scalable distributed systems.

1.2.4 IT infrastructure and application design

In terms of IT infrastructure and application design, three significant trends were observed: advanced, off-the-shelf applications software, client/server computing and multimedia information systems. Firstly, the availability of increasingly sophisticated application software available 'off-the-shelf' with advanced graphical user interfaces (GUIs). This was facilitated by the arrival of standardized bit-mapped displays that became a standard item on a personal computer. GUIs increased significantly application demands for processor power, memory, disk storage and I/O rates. These demands could not be supported economically on a time-shared computer; a dedicated processor per user was necessary. Secondly, a new paradigm was being widely used to structure IT infrastructure components and applications: the **client/server** model (used extensively in the 1970s to structure operating system-level process interactions). Unlike the master–slave model inherent in mainframe systems, co-operating processes in the client/server model interact on an equal footing (i.e. they interact as *peers)*, but with distinct roles. A client process running on a user workstation makes requests to a server process (normally running on another computer in the network) through a well-defined interface. The server process executes the requested operation and generates a reply to the client. Server computers can offer a range of services (or specialized functions). This is illustrated in Figure 1.4. A centralized mainframe infrastructure has been replaced by a **distributed IT infrastructure** consisting of multiple client and server computers connected to a network. The mainframe computer's role is shifting from being the 'central hub' to simply acting as a repository of corporate or 'mission-critical' data and applications. Although for historical reasons most information systems in use today do not fully exploit a distributed IT infrastructure, many new systems and those replacing old systems are being designed to do so. In this book we detail the underlying concepts, mechanisms and technologies for building a distributed IT infrastructure and information systems that exploit it. The client/server model and other models for structuring distributed systems, such as the **group model** which supports communications between groups, are described in Chapter 3.

1.2.5 Multimedia information systems

A third significant trend is the development of information systems which integrate multiple media types (e.g. text, audio, graphics and video) – **multimedia information systems**. For example, many banking organizations are integrating multimedia information systems into the basic automated teller machines transforming them into integrated business transaction and customer services points. There are three main characteristics of a multimedia information system: it is *computer based*, it integrates a *variety* of media types and it is *interactive* (Williams and Blair, 1994). Three main factors have contributed to its wider use: the availability of low-cost desktop publishing and presentation software, reduction in the cost of high-capacity optical storage technologies such as CD-ROM, and the use of multimedia in computer-based entertainment (or 'games') software. The technologies of four main industries are now converging to create the 'multimedia industry, (Dustdar, 1994):

- The computer industry, with expertise in microcomputer-based hardware and software technologies.
- The TV and broadcasting industry, with expertise in global video and audio technologies, and information services.
- The telecommunications industry, with expertise in national and international voice and data communications technologies.
- The printing and publishing industry, with expertise in information services and publishing technologies.

All media types are being digitized so that they can be combined and used in new ways, and **distributed** over information networks. Thus, a new type of information system has evolved: **distributed information systems** (DISs). An example of this approach is the new information services introduced over the Internet using a distributed hypermedia technology known as the **World Wide Web** (Berners-Lee *et al.*, 1992 (a) and (b)), or 'The Web' for short. A Web client (known as a browser) allows a Web document (containing text, graphics and other media types) to be browsed and embedded links to other documents held on Web servers traversed. Another example is a videoconferencing system with information and application sharing facilities. An example of a multimedia information systems access is shown in Figure 1.1. Web technology is described in detail in Chapter 8. Media types and multimedia information representation are discussed in Chapter 2.

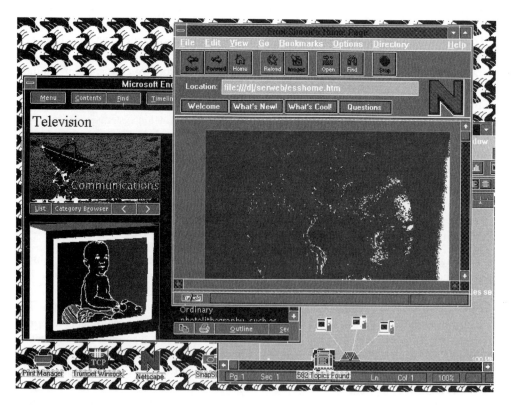

Figure 1.1 Multimedia information systems.

Multimedia information systems introduce special requirements regarding the design of the IT infrastructure. In particular, the real-time synchronization of video and video with other media types requires an infrastructure that is much more sensitive to timing issues and the storage and transmission of large data volumes (a digitized movie requires about one gigabyte of storage, uncompressed). An example system is **videoconferencing** which requires that audio and video data streams are transmitted across networks at a fixed rate with very little delay between successive packets, otherwise a user perceives significantly poor images or distorted sound. Traditional network technologies are being enhanced to take account of these new demands. These are detailed in Chapters 4, 5 and 6.

1.3 APPLICATIONS PORTFOLIOS: FROM EFFICIENCY TO FLEXIBILITY

To provide an insight into the evolutionary changes in application development focus, it is useful to view an organization's information systems (IS) requirements as a hierarchy of three important classes (Anthony, 1965) as illustrated in Figure 1.2:

- operational systems, which support the basic operational activities of the organization (e.g. accounting, stock control, payroll and personnel systems);
- (management) control systems, which support the decision-support needs of middle managers (e.g. budgetary control, production planning, inventory management and quality analysis);
- (strategic) planning systems, which support the (strategic) decision-support needs of senior managers, and provide the means to improve competitiveness by changing the nature or conduct of business.

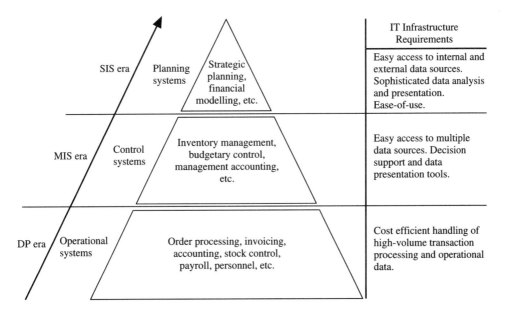

Figure 1.2 The changing application portfolio.

Below is a historical perspective on the development of operational, control and strategic planning ISs.

1.3.1 IS developments in the 1960s

During this generation the main focus was the centralized development of operational systems on a business function by function basis. Typically accounting functions were early candidates for automation. The main design aims were efficient transaction processing and efficient use of IT resources.

1.3.2 IS developments in the 1970s

With the introduction of minicomputers, operational systems could be implemented either as centralized systems or decentralized with some operational functions running locally on minicomputers within the functional department. Automation of operational functions continued. Organizations also began to turn their attention to automating management control functions such as budgetary control, sales analysis and management accounting. This was achieved by consolidating and analysing historical data produced by operational systems and producing predefined reports. Professional staff and middle managers began to interface to computers via terminals as well as receiving printed output. Thus began a demand for decision-support software for management and planning staff. However, the problem with early management control systems was that they were based on automating control procedures demanding largely predefined data requirements. They could not cope with 'on-demand' enquiries and analysis which require flexible (i.e. not predefined) access to data and flexible processing of data with a range of data presentation options.

1.3.3 IS developments in the 1980s

With the development of personal computers and local area networks came local hardware and software (e.g. spreadsheets and presentation software) that were better able to meet the flexible access and processing requirements of management control and planning staff. Furthermore, end-user computing resources were available at a cost affordable by business units without having to seek approval from central IS/IT management. The momentum for more flexible access to data residing primarily on mainframe systems increased. Because the data processing needs of managers were increasingly unpredictable, PC software suppliers soon began to deliver increasingly powerful and sophisticated tools for data collection, management, manipulation and presentation - largely under the control of end-users. Dramatic improvements in reliability, functionality and ease-of-use, and increasing independence from the central IT function made this option increasingly attractive.

It can be seen that for many organizations, there was an increasing danger of a separation between the operational systems environment (tightly controlled by the central computer services function) and the *management information systems* (MIS) environment which was increasingly dominated by hardware, software and applications controlled by user departments.

1.3.4 IS developments in the 1990s

Clearly, both the operational systems and MIS share a common database and IT infrastructure and so it was quickly realized that it was generally not appropriate to separate them. Equally, the central IS/IT function needed to recognize that the deployment of IS/IT passed through a major transition – in some cases unobserved by the central IS/IT function and mostly driven by end-users! Both operational and MIS systems continued to be developed, but many organizations realized that it was critical that IS/IT development and management proceed in a way that recognizes the needs of both camps. Many organizations are still grappling with the problems of transition from the **DP era** (an emphasis on operational systems) to the **MIS era** (Ward *et al.*, 1990). Ward suggests that some organizations are moving into a third era: the **strategic information** systems (SIS) era characterized by the use of IS/IT to improve competitiveness by changing the nature or conduct of business (in addition to its use to improve internal business practices). Many such systems involve tighter linking of the organization to its customers and suppliers, improving customer service. These systems typically use DP and MIS data and applications but in a way that fundamentally changes the way that an organization's business is conducted, and results in significant competitive advantage. Research suggests that strategic information systems can be classified into four types (Ward *et al.*, 1990):

1. those that link an organization to its customers, distributors, suppliers, etc.;
2. those that improve the integration of data relating to an organization's internal processes;
3. those that deliver new or enhance existing products and services based on information;
4. executive information systems that provide executive management with information to support strategic planning.

The main technical challenge of the migration to SIS is that it demands an IT infrastructure that is able to link an organization with its customers, distributors, suppliers, etc. The 'marketplace' is increasingly a global one requiring an IT infrastructure which provides connectivity on world-wide scale. Furthermore, the infrastructure should support enterprise-wide manipulation and integration of data for the delivery of information-based products and services and executive information if it is to facilitate the development of SIS. With such diverse data access, manipulation and presentation requirements (broadly similar to MIS needs), the flexibility of distributed systems makes it well suited to support the needs of SIS.

Many organizations have focused on the use of distributed multimedia technology to create strategic information systems which lead to new products and services, and enables an organization to change delivery channels to reach their customers (Dustdar, 1994). For example, 'self-service' kiosk systems are having an impact on the provision of customer services in retail organizations. Distributed information systems, employed strategically, leads to the following benefits:

- Improved customer penetration, targeting and service (e.g. 24-hour availability).
- More effective use of the workforce (e.g. staff can concentrate on selling).
- Easy updating of information.
- The potential to exploit new delivery channels.

The use of a DIS to support a variety of strategic goals is explored in Chapter 11.

1.4 ORGANIZATIONAL STRUCTURES: BALANCING CO-ORDINATION AND FLEXIBILITY

Organizational structure has become an important parameter in the drive to sustain competitive advantage and to remain responsive to an increasingly complex and dynamic environment. An organization's corporate strategy and organizational structure are closely linked since structure can determine organization efficiency, creativity and how well it can respond to changes in the business environment. Organizational structure and culture are also important factors in designing distributed systems because they shape the system and the structure of administration and systems management functions.

The primary purpose of organizational structure is to facilitate the co-ordination of activities and to enable efficient control of its members so as to achieve corporate objectives. Three important components of structure can be identified (Robbins, 1989):

1. *complexity*: the degree to which the organization's activities are broken up or differentiated;
2. *formalization*: the degree to which rules and job procedures are standardized,
3. *centralization*: the degree to which decision-making authority is concentrated at a single point in the organization.

Thus, organizational structure will vary in terms of the degree of complexity, formalization and centralization. Two extremes of organizational structure can be identified: the *mechanistic structure (hierarchical)* characterized by high formalization, high complexity and high centralization; and the *organic structure* characterized by low formalization, low complexity and low centralization (decentralization). A typical sample of real organizations would reveal that in practice most structures in use would fall somewhere between these extremes, but there is a definite trend towards more organic structures as illustrated in Figure 1.3. Is there an optimum structure for a particular organization? The notion of the 'permanent best-fit organizational structure' has dominated the thinking of management scientists and consultants this century. This thinking continues to the present day and organizations are continually restructuring to arrive at the best-fit organization. Research and notable failures, however, have made it clear that there is no permanent best-fit; particular structures are good for some and bad for others.

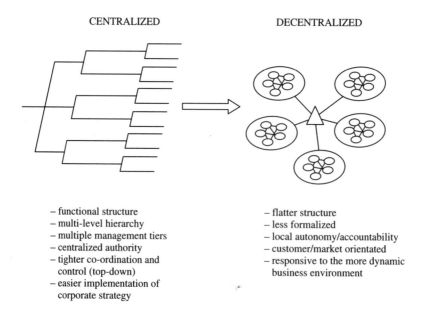

CENTRALIZED   DECENTRALIZED

- functional structure
- multi-level hierarchy
- multiple management tiers
- centralized authority
- tighter co-ordination and
  control (top-down)
- easier implementation of
  corporate strategy

- flatter structure
- less formalized
- local autonomy/accountability
- customer/market orientated
- responsive to the more dynamic
  business environment

Figure 1.3 Decentralized organizational structures.

Until recently, the regulatory mechanisms used to manage IS/IT did not take account of the structure and management approach of the organization which it served. Until the 1980s, the management approach was almost exclusively centralized, relying on a centralized IT infrastructure irrespective of the structure, systems and management style of the organization itself. With the variety of organizational structures in use, the approach to managing IS/IT must take account of such factors to better serve the needs of the organization. For example, is a centralized IS/IT unit appropriate for a highly organic organization? A distributed IT infrastructure, with the flexibility to underpin both centralized and decentralized IS/IT development and management approaches, is likely to be more suited to those organizations with a complex, highly decentralized structure. Moreover, as noted earlier, restructuring is commonplace, causing new demands on the existing IT infrastructure. These changing demands can best be absorbed by a flexible, distributed IT infrastructure.

In the drive to achieve an optimum balance between organization creativity and efficiency, organizations in the 1990s and beyond are seeking a better fit between IS/IT management and organizational structure which will naturally lead to the adoption of a distributed IT infrastructure. Effective deployment of information systems does not depend solely on the availability of computing resources but on the effective use of these resources by people in the organization. Thus, an organization should identify its informational needs and relate them to organizational structure, management philosophy and operational procedures. We will return to this theme in Chapter 11 where the relationship between organizational structure and information systems is examined in detail.

1.5 CENTRALIZED VERSUS DISTRIBUTED SYSTEMS

A historical perspective on the evolution of distributed systems reveals a number of advantages and disadvantages. In practice, both centralized and distributed approaches have a role to play in the future design of the IT infrastructure and information systems. A centralized system can be equally responsive to end-user needs in the right circumstances and can offer superior security, data integrity and systems management functionality.

1.5.1 Advantages of distributed systems

The main advantages of distributed systems is their ability to allow the sharing of information and resources over a wide geographic area, giving a systems designer freedom to optimize the placement of distributed system components such as data and processing. This then supports:

- **Improved flexibility**. Computers and other IT infrastructure components can be flexibly located at points within the organization where they can be utilized most effectively. Components can be added, upgraded, moved and removed (usually in small increments over a wide range of capacities), without impacting upon other components, to meet present and future needs. The ability of an IT infrastructure or application to grow to meet increasing user or application demand while minimizing disruption, is known as **scalability**.
- **Local autonomy**, by allowing **domains of control** to be defined where decisions are made relating to purchasing, ownership, IT budgets, operating priorities, IS development and management, etc. Each domain decides where resources (including manpower and IT infrastructure components) under its control are located. This autonomy is recognition of

the distributed nature of many organizational activities. Domains can be *federated* when necessary for mutual benefit.

- **Increased reliability and availability**. In a centralized system, a component (hardware or software) failure can mean that the whole system is down, stopping all users from getting work done. In a distributed system, multiple components of the same type can be configured to fail independently and (e.g. through replication) provide a level of fault tolerance. Thus, failure of one component may isolate a group of users, but does not necessarily prevent others from operating.

- **Improved performance**. Large centralized systems can be slow performers due mainly to the sheer volume of data and transactions being handled. A service which is partitioned over many server computers, each supporting a smaller set of applications and users with access to local data and resources, results in faster access (response times). Another performance advantage is the support for parallel access (updates and retrievals) to distributed data across the organization.

- **Security breaches are localized**. In distributed system with multiple security control domains, a security breach in one domain does not compromise the whole system. Each security domain has varying degrees of security authentication, access control and auditing.

1.5.2 Disadvantages of distributed systems

Against the above advantages are a number of disadvantages, most of which correspond to the advantages of centralized systems:

- **It is more difficult to manage and secure**. Centralized systems are inherently easier to secure (offering a single security domain, controlled by a single authority) and easier to manage. Distributed systems require more complex procedures for security, administration, maintenance and user support due to greater levels of co-ordination and control required. This usually results in higher costs associated with managing and securing a distributed systems environment.

- **Reduced reliability and availability**. In contrast to the potential improvements in reliability and availability discussed above, a centralized system can often offer more controlled physical, operational and environmental conditions borne out of years of development and improvement. Moreover, a distributed system consists of many more components which can potentially fail, causing loss of availability.

- **A shortage of skilled support and development staff**. In a decentralized operation, scarce support and development can be dispersed, resulting in a loss of economies of scale which, in turn, leads to higher costs. Another issue is the level of support offered by vendors. The commitment and level of support offered by vendors of distributed software and hardware to 'corporate' organizations grappling with the issues of building large-scale distributed systems is not yet comparable to the traditional large mainframe-based vendors. This is due in part to the fact that many vendors are supplying only a small part of the overall system. In practice, whereas in a centralized system the mainframe supplier provided the equipment and integration support as a single package, distributed system implementation commonly involves multiple vendors and therefore requires the skills of a systems integrator. Problem isolation and resolution can be much more difficult and costly when multiple vendors are involved. This is exacerbated by the need for staff to develop a wide range of knowledge and skills.

Thus, distributed systems are not a panacea for all the world's computing problems. Like many innovations, they provide a solution to many problems, but also introduce new ones. With the potentially significant disadvantages highlighted above, why should any organization take the risk of implementing a distributed system? The answer is that, although overcoming the disadvantages represents a significant challenge to any organization, it is often perceived that the advantages (which are generally user-centred) significantly outweigh the disadvantages (which are generally centred around staffing, management and administration). Implementing a distributed IT infrastructure gives an organization the flexibility to choose an appropriate balance between the high levels of discipline and co-ordination associated with centralized control, and the flexibility and local autonomy offered by decentralization. A distributed IT infrastructure supports tight management of corporate data by locating it on a limited number of tightly managed server computers, easily accessible to users via a desktop computer. Data can be duplicated in a controlled manner to improve performance and availability. Thus an appropriate balance between control, efficiency, flexibility and local autonomy can be realized.

1.6 SUMMARY

In this chapter we have described the main driving forces responsible for the evolution of distributed information systems implemented over a distributed IT infrastructure. The main challenge to organizations is how to utilize this new approach to build systems which deploy information technology more effectively to support operational and strategic business goals. For brevity, throughout this book distributed information systems will be abbreviated 'DIS', although the term 'distributed system' is also used. Chapter 2 provides a more formal definition of a DIS and the underlying distributed IT infrastructure.

1.7 CASE STUDY: LIFE INSURANCE COMPANY EMBRACES DISTRIBUTED SYSTEMS

1.7.1 Background

United Life, a US insurance company based in Washington DC, traditionally relied on proprietary mainframes to run all applications. The core operational systems (accounting, payroll, etc.) were developed some fifteen years ago based on an IT infrastructure comprising an IBM mainframe with a wide area network connecting terminals across five major cities. In the increasingly competitive insurance market, companies like United need to develop new customer services quickly to increase its customer base and retain existing customers.

United fastened on to a new distribution strategy to augment its business by establishing a new business unit in the independent insurance brokers' market segment. Administrative staff would process and store data on the brokers themselves and contract information. The timescale to make it all happen was very tight as they intended to maximize competitive advantage. For the 75 strong central IS unit (computer services) this meant a short timescale (eight months) in which to develop an information system to underpin the new business venture; certainly not enough time to develop a mainframe-based system using the traditional highly structured process from design to implementation and testing, etc.

Coincidentally, computer services was experimenting with a small prototype distributed

IT infrastructure consisting of a LAN with ten PCs and two UNIX servers. Twenty developers were trained and demonstrated that client/server technology could be a practical approach for this kind of application development and environment. After much thought it was decided that the new customer administration and service information system (CADSIS) would be implemented using the new technology. The main justification was firstly the wide range of data sources and sinks with a requirement for real-time access to many types and levels of data by a wide range of personnel; and secondly, it provided the potential for rapid development of CADSIS by buying off-the-shelf hardware and software for the system and using third-party systems software to build the infrastructure quickly. It was estimated that the main application would take more than two years to develop on the mainframe, but with seven to ten client/server developers this could be cut to within the timescale required and at the same time offer enhanced application functionality provided by the packaged software and the distributed IT infrastructure.

1.7.2 Systems development

The initial development environment was enhanced to include X-terminal emulation software installed on the PCs and Novell Netware to allow the UNIX server to also act as file servers. A UNIX server also acted as a gateway allowing access to electronic mail and other systems running on the IBM mainframe. A fourth-generation development system was used to develop the application in conjunction with the Oracle DBMS product. Approximately 80 per cent of the programming code was generated automatically by the development system. The application itself incorporates an innovative commission formula compared with its competitors which was designed to attract better staff.

The production environment comprises a UNIX Server which acts as an application server and file server as well as the network gateway. The broker unit managers and staff access applications and data use 25 486 PCs. TCP/IP runs across the wide area network linking development and production environments. The cost of acquisition was estimated at $7000 per seat, with an additional $4000 per seat for training and ongoing support costs. The business unit saw this as an initially high start-up cost that would easily be justified on the basis of no mainframe charges incurred.

Standard PC applications were installed, and the cut and paste facilities under Microsoft Windows are used extensively to allow staff to easily manipulate and correlate data from multiple sources. The overall layout is shown in Figure 1.4. Development, testing and final acceptance was achieved within eight months as planned.

1.7.3 The cultural change

The experience with distributed systems was more than just an experience with new technology. Like most large organizations, United developed a strong mainframe orientation, a culture that consequently did not welcome change from the 'everything's got to be done in one place' approach. It usually reacted to any new developments with 'we've always developed systems this way, it works and we've invested a lot of money in the existing infrastructure'. Meanwhile other client/server projects were initiated and a new mind-set evolved amongst those developers involved in developing the new applications. In these new projects these developers worked virtually hand-in-hand with actual business users, customizing, tailoring and reusing elements of the new distributed IT infrastructure and adding new elements to cater for the

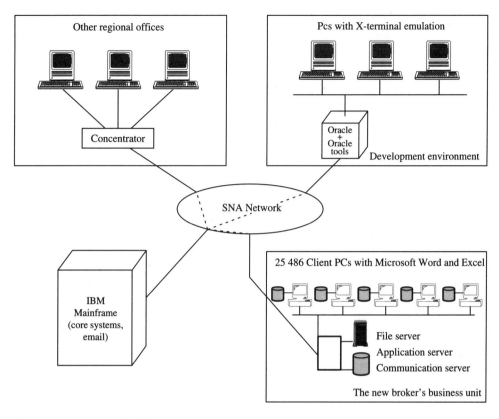

Figure 1.4 Case study: Life's IT infrastructure.

needs of new applications. The infrastructure became more complex as additional UNIX servers were being installed to support new applications. It became obvious that hardly any new development was being written for the mainframe. The 'legacy' core applications are expected to remain on the mainframe for a long time as it would be a difficult and costly exercise to re-engineer thousands of lines of complex application code.

The cultural changes were also on the user department side. The client/server approach has suddenly unlocked the door to a wealth of real-time data and data manipulation and presentation tools, completely replacing the old tradition of largely batch processing and report generation of yesterday's information requests. These users are having to get used to the sheer power and flexibility that was only a dream a year ago.

1.7.4 Future challenges

As the distributed IT infrastructure increased in complexity, the need to engage in strategic planning was realized to avoid the usual problems of distribution – lack of control of data and system management. Questions were raised such as where should we keep all this data? How are we going to manage software distribution and updating? Is the network resilient enough now that the business is heavily reliant on it? To this end, a major review (involving a local consultancy) of the current approach took place with a view to creating an appropriate IS/IT strategy, architecture and infrastructure.

The IT infrastructure allows components from different vendors to be easily slotted in to replace existing components with minimal disruption to users (if it is carefully planned). In this sense they now have a viable open systems environment.

1.7.5 Case study discussion points

1. Can centralized and distributed approaches coexist at Life? What are the likely financial, technological and organizational implications?
2. Suggest and justify how United Life might approach a transition from centralized main-frame to a distributed IT infrastructure. What are the benefits of a complete migration to a distributed IT infrastructure?

1.8 REVIEW QUESTIONS

1. Discuss the driving forces behind the move from centralized to distributed systems.
2. Discuss in what ways distributed systems can add value to an organization's activities and business processes.
3. Compare and contrast centralized systems with distributed systems. Do distributed systems have significant disadvantages?
4. Suggest reasons why some organizations continue to adopted a wholly centralized approach.
5. What is a distributed information system (DIS)? Give reasons why a DIS is becoming an increasingly popular means of structuring a computer-based information system

1.9 FURTHER READING

Darnton and Giacoletto (1992) is a good general text on the potential influence of IT on organization effectiveness, and the relationship between information, IT and organizations. McNurlin and Sprague (1989) provides a useful perspective on the evolution from centralized to distributed information systems. Ward *et al.* (1990) consider strategic IS/IT issues. A technical perspective on multimedia computing trends and technology implications is given in Davies and Nicol (1991) and Buford (1994).

2

CHARACTERISTICS OF DISTRIBUTED INFORMATION SYSTEMS

2.1 INTRODUCTION

A serious obstacle to any in-depth discussion of distributed information systems is lack of an agreed definition of terminology. A wide spectrum of information systems appear to be classified as distributed. It is not possible to provide a universally accepted definition. Instead, in this chapter we define key concepts and terms associated with DISs that will be used frequently throughout this book. The key characteristics of a DIS and the underlying distributed IT infrastructure will be discussed in order to formulate working definitions. The intention is to state assumptions and interpretations so that what follows in subsequent chapters is consistent with the definitions given.

2.2 INFORMATION AND INFORMATION EXCHANGE

In our daily lives we obtain and use information from a variety of sources. Information is obtained from banks, train stations, supermarkets, newsagents, leisure centres, libraries, television, etc., each presenting (or representing) information in different ways. We may not always agree with the information given or find it particularly useful. What is clear is that the right information is a vital resource; we cannot operate effectively without it.

The word 'information' is usually used in a number of different senses. This is because there are perhaps two main schools of thought concerning what information is and the relationship between users and the information they receive and use (Harrington, 1991):

1. The *objective information concept.* Information is thought to be neutral and absolute, that

is, it is a resource of the organization that is predictable, consistent and unchanging. Information therefore exists independent from its receiver; an independent entity waiting to be used. Misinformation or misinterpretation is caused by a lack of understanding of the information itself and can be avoided through better training in how to interpret the information correctly. Users can receive information and manipulate it (by use of standard procedures) without necessarily understanding its meaning.

This concept of information has been the basis for the traditional approach to designing information systems. Most structured design methodologies are underpinned by this concept. Information systems process information to produce new information which is simply added to the 'pool' of information used by the organization. Information does not change during transmission to the receiver, although it can change its 'form'. These forms are usually categorized as *data* (structured numbers and codes); *voice* (coded voice signals); *text* (documents and messages); or *images* (hand drawn, photographic, graphical or video that are coded or scanned electronically). This concept is illustrated in Figure 2.1.

2. The *subjective information concept.* This individualistic viewpoint declares that information is 'in the eye of the beholder'. Here the word 'information' is used to make a distinction between the raw materials (referred to as data which in this case is simply representations of information) and the meaning ascribed to it by someone (usually termed the 'user'). Information and data are distinct. Thus for example, an order item of 10 boxes of A4 paper is a piece of neutral data. It becomes information to a production scheduler when it is used to schedule deliveries for the next day. It also becomes different information to the finance clerk when it is used in computing invoice information. Equally, it may be of no consequence to someone in the research department. Thus what belongs to the organization are the data on its products, personnel, customers, suppliers, etc. Individuals within (and outside of) the organization form their own information by ascribing meaning to this data. Management can promote more effective use of data usually through training on available data sources, formal business rules and other informal knowledge, but it can exert little control over how users turn data into information. Thus information is not seen to exist prior to it being perceived by the receiver (user) and cannot therefore exist as a static organizational resource.

Information is required by people in society (and enterprises within society) in order to plan, monitor and control activities. People learn through the exchange of information in order to gain knowledge from others, and both inform others and are informed by others. However, the results of information exchange may lead to misinterpretation.

Misinformation or misinterpretation is an everyday occurrence in society. This is due to the fact that the informer must express the information (i.e. encode it in a communicable

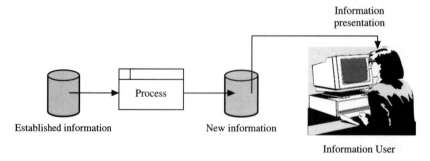

Figure 2.1 The objective information concept.

form as data, where data could be in the form of codes, digital voice, graphical images, video, etc.) in such a way as to ensure that the informant interprets it in the way that the informer intended. Thus successful information exchange is when the intended knowledge has been communicated. Consequently, we define information as any knowledge about things, facts or concepts. Data is defined as representations of things, facts, ideas or concepts in communicable forms that facilitate information exchange. This concept is illustrated in Figure 2.2.

This concept of information implies that an effective information system is one which is designed to produce data relevant to its users and allow users to manipulate it in powerful ways in order to produce information by ascribing meaning to the processed data. While information is dynamic and continuously evolving, data is, in contrast, static and unchanging.

Traditional large organizations are oriented towards the objective information concept. This is perhaps because it complements classical management thinking which seeks to standardize (i.e. make consistent) information and procedures to promote organization cohesion. Staff are viewed as individuals not likely to be trusted to use 'information' for the good of the organization. Smaller organizations, however, particularly those which consist largely of highly technical or professional personnel, tend to subscribe to the subjective information concept, recognizing that these powerful individuals have particular knowledge, skills, experience and insight which demand a freedom or individuality in terms of the use and manipulation of data. In this case, standardization of 'information' would be a negative practice. Thus the information concept that an organization naturally adopts appears to be contingent on the nature of the organization.

In an effort to maintain consistency of definition, in this book we adopt the subjective information concept as a basis for the subsequent definition of terms used throughout. Choice of this concept is consistent with the increasing use of IT by skilled and professional staff, senior and executive personnel who demand a more individualistic perspective on their information needs. In the context of this book, the choice of concept is made to maintain *consistency* of view rather than as a statement about the accuracy of a particular concept.

An *information system* (IS) is thus defined as a system which manipulates data and normally serves to collect, store, process and exchange or distribute data to users within or between enterprises or to people within wider society. Thus the two main characteristics of information systems are *data* and the manipulation of it by means of *actions*. The concept of a system is recursive in that a system consists of components from which the system is composed, but a component may itself be a system (subsystem). Indeed, any system may be a component of

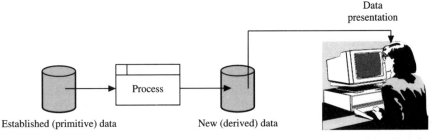

Figure 2.2 The subjective information concept.

some larger system. It is also important to note that in this definition *users* of data supplied by the information system are part of the information system since it is the user that ascribes meaning to the data processed by the system. Indeed, the user often both receives information and is a source of data which is captured and stored in the information system.

2.3 MULTIMEDIA REQUIREMENTS

An effective information system is one which is designed to produce data relevant to its users and allows users to manipulate it in powerful ways in order to produce information by ascribing meaning to the processed data. The data space available to users is growing rapidly with the increased ability to access remote information services. If this data is not carefully filtered and presented in formats easily digested by users then data overload results because users expend most of their effort on the boring task of filtering and trying to interpret data that is not presented in a meaningful way. Presented appropriately, humans can understand data in multidimensional forms very well. The part of the human mind that processes incoming signals is highly tuned to input from our stereoscopic visual system. Thus, appropriate data represented in terms of visual, moving, morphable shapes can greatly enhance a user's ability to ascribe meaning to it.

Almost every type of media (text, data, voice, pictures, animation, video, etc.) has its place in communicating information to users. Each can play a part in communicating information in appropriate and compelling ways. Thus a feature of *multimedia* information systems is the *variety* of media types which can be utilized, the need for the *integration* of sources of media types into a single, coherent highly *interactive* information system. Williams and Blair (1994) provide a useful definition of a multimedia information system as one which supports a variety of media types and which integrates sources of media types into a single system framework thus enabling users to share, communicate and process a variety of forms of information in an integrated manner.

Multimedia information systems can be wholly contained in a single client workstation or, more usefully, make use of media sources available across a network, transforming it into a distributed information system (DIS). A group video conference system is an example of a DIS which operates across a network. A DIS involving real-time voice and video as well as data sharing is usefully modelled as separate (but synchronized) streams of voice, video and data. Each voice or video stream consists of a sequence of frames with well-defined timing characteristics (Herbert, 1994 (a) and (b)). A video conferencing DIS may need to drive each stream separately (e.g. to provide edit and capture operations) or to carry out additional processing on a stream (e.g. to define an operation to search a voice stream for a particular phrase). This leads to the requirement to provide application developers with a 'streams' interface which offers a high level of functionality to manipulate separate multimedia streams (possibly in real time). Also, to meet strict timing characteristics of some media sources (e.g. voice and video) applications require some level of control over how key resources such as processors, memory buffers, network protocols and network bandwidth are allocated so that application quality of service requirements are met. These have important implications in terms of operating system design, network technologies and higher-level services which are explored in subsequent chapters in this book. In general, a DIS demands more stringent timing and resource bandwidth requirements and requires application programming interfaces (APIs) which provide a fine-grained control of underlying resources (Herbert, 1994 (a) and (b)). Another aspect of multimedia information systems is the increased storage requirements. For example, the storage requirement for one second of full-motion digitized video requires approximately 10 to 30 megabytes of storage, digitized voice requires 8 kilobytes per second and compact disk quality audio requires around 90 kilobytes per second. This compares with 12 kilobytes for one full page of text! Multimedia storage requirements can be reduced by employing **compression** techniques prior to storage (or transmission over a network). Obviously, compressed data must be decompressed before use. Modern compression and decompression techniques can be classified as *real-time* or *batched* (non-real-time). An ideal system is one which offers real-time compression and decompression without loss of presentation quality (known as *lossless compression*). In practice, this is technically very challenging and quality is normally compromised to achieve real-time requirements (known as *lossy compression*). The precise requirements, however, are application dependent. For example, batch compression/real-time decompression is ideal where large multimedia documents are involved (e.g. in desktop publishing) and where real-time compression may not be required.

Data and information about things relevant to an enterprise are inherently distributed. For example, a travel organization may receive information about travel requirements and reservations directly from customers as they visit travel agents across the country and through booking forms that are received centrally at head office. The data collected may then need to be moved from one location to another depending on the location of storage and processing facilities that make up the relevant information systems supporting the enterprise. Data collected and used in one location is often needed in another. A general principle underlying the development of a DIS is that media sources are stored close to where it is generated, manipulated where it is held and accessed from any location.

Modern information technologies impose little constraint on the location of storage and processing technologies and application programs required for data processing. However, the complete collection of data handled by its various information systems must be reliable and secure whilst allowing flexible access by users within and outside of the enterprise. Distributing storage, processors and processing provides the potential to enhance reliability, performance and accessibility but increases the complexity of global security and systems management. Thus, security and the complexity of systems management are constraining forces in an enterprise's drive to maximize the benefits of distributed information systems. We defer any detailed discussion regarding management and security issues to Chapter 13.

2.3.1 Multimedia content and storage

Standards for the capture, storage and transfer of multimedia data is a vital factor in the widespread acceptance and growth of multimedia information systems. Unfortunately there are many competing standards in this area, resulting in the frequent need to convert from one format to another using appropriate utilities. There is currently no standardized way to compose a multimedia information system, store it and distribute it over a network so that it can be executed on someone else's computer. In general, standards emerge from three primary sources:

1. Technology or specifications which have gained widespread acceptance in the marketplace. These are known as *de facto* standards.
2. Consortium standards in which a group of companies define a specification and corresponding products in order to stimulate the market towards a widely accepted standard.

3. Regional, national and international accredited (referred to as *de jure* standards) standards organizations. For example, the Organization for International Standardization (ISO).

In this section we will detail relevant multimedia standards.

Digital video and image standards

Video is broadcast as an analogue signal that contains pictures and audio data in a particular sequence. The picture and sound are typically encoded by a video or television camera and decoded by television-type equipment. The decoded video signal is displayed as a sequence of still images or frames. When the frames change at a rapid rate (e.g. 15–30 frames per second) they give the illusion of full motion. When the television receives a video sequence, an electron gun displays each frame one line at a time (known as a *scan line*) beginning at the top of the screen (each odd-numbered line is displayed first, then the electron gun moves back to the top of the screen and displays the even-numbered lines).

Several standards are used for encoding video signals which specify the precise frame rate and scan lines per frame. In the US, the National Television Standards Committee (NTSC) specification (30 frames/s and 525 scan lines per frame) is used; while European countries (except France) use the phase alteration line (PAL) standard. In France, the sequentiel couleur avec memoire (SECAM) specification is used. Both PAL and SECAM use 25 frames/s and 625 scan lines per frame. Analogue video signals contain colour and brightness attributes. These attributes can be output in different formats which affect the resulting quality of video output. The composite video signal format combines colour and brightness attributes into one output signal. The S-video format separates colour and brightness into two signals which results in a better picture quality. The RGB format separates the video signal into separate signals for red, green and blue colour components for even better picture quality. A digital video format is also an alternative.

Digitized video output files can be very large. This is simply because video carries an enormous amount of information. The higher the quality of the video and audio captured, the larger the output file. Digital video quality is determined by:

1. the frame rate of the captured video;
2. the size of the video frame used for capture;
3. the quality of the audio captured with the video;
4. the number of colours used. The number of bits per picture element (pixel) determines how many colours are used per pixel. The more colours used, the more the digitized video resembles the original video. The number of bytes per pixel is normally one, two or three.

We can calculate the resulting uncompressed file size due to video only given the above parameters as follows:

```
Uncompressed video content = frames-per-sec * frame_size
* seconds_of_video_captured where frame_size = frame_height
* frame_width * bytes_per_pixel
```

For example, the video content of a file which contains one minute of video, uses 320-by-240 frames, has a frame rate of 15 frames per second, with 24-bit (3 bytes) per pixel, is:

```
15 * (320 * 240 * 3) * 60 = 198 megabytes
```

Video output file is commonly compressed to reduce its data-storage requirements. Compression methods for compression/decompression are known as **codecs**. No one codec delivers optimum compression and playback quality for all data types and circumstances.

De jure standards for multimedia content have mainly been addressed by ISO in subcommittee ISO/IEC JTC1/SC29 which is responsible for standards for the coding of audio, picture, multimedia and hypermedia information. It currently has three working groups: JBIG/JPEG, MPEG and MHEG.

JBIG/JPEG   The Joint Photo Expert Group (JPEG) developed a lossy compression standard (known as JPEG) for static images (e.g. a photograph or graphic). JPEG can also be applied to moving images (e.g. video), compressing each frame in isolation. The Joint Bi-level Image Expert Group (JBIG) developed a lossless image compression standard (JBIG) for static images.

MPEG   MPEG (Motion Picture Expert Group) is a compression standard established in 1988 for moving pictures, associated audio, and their combination when used to store and retrieve audiovisual data on digital storage media (e.g. a CD-ROM). The emphasis is on handling video and audio as an integrated unit of data, preserving their time relation. MPEG-1, -2 and -3 correspond to encoding at 1.5, 10 and 40 Mbit/s, respectively. MPEG-3 was subsequently dropped when it became apparent that MPEG-2 functionalities made it virtually redundant. An MPEG-4 work item was proposed in 1991 which targets audiovisual coding at very low bit-rates. MPEG-4 codecs will enable real-time motion video over standard voice-grade telephone lines.

MPEG-1 was designed for narrow-bandwidth storage media, such as single-speed CD-ROM drives which provide a 1.5 Mbyte/s data transfer rate. Full playback of an MPEG-1 video stream currently requires additional hardware because the algorithms are very complex. Ideally, a software only solution for playback should be available as an alternative to encourage widespread usage. This requirement has been met by the industry with the introduction of proprietary standards such as Microsoft's Audio Visual Interactive (AVI) and Intel's Indeo video compression standard.

The MPEG-2 standard addresses storage media transmission rate requirements with data transfer rates of up to 10 Mbyte/s. It offers better video quality than MPEG-1 video and facilitates much higher frame sizes, greater frame rates and resolutions. The higher transfer rate reduces the play time accordingly so that a longer play time is achievable on an appropriate CD-ROM drive. This is in keeping with the dramatic increases in storage capacity associated with the next generation of CD-ROM technology (which will offer gigabytes of storage on one CD-ROM). The falling cost of video distribution technology and the adoption of standards such as MPEG-2 and MPEG-4 will facilitate new applications such as multimedia on demand (both for residential and business users), and high-quality business information on demand.

MHEG   Multimedia data may consist of multiple media types with spatial and temporal relationships between them. For example, a multimedia information system may consist of video, audio and text media types, synchronized in a particular way which can be altered by user interactions. The Multimedia and Hypermedia Information Coding Experts Group (MHEG) is focused on developing a standard (known as MHEG) for describing the interrelationships between multimedia structures in a multimedia information system. MHEG objects are in final form (i.e. the recipient cannot easily revise the content or structure).

Hypertext and hypermedia standards

A multimedia data object can contain cross-references (commonly known as *links*) to other objects. Cross-references normally capture associative relationships between data items. Associativity is in fact a fundamental data processing mechanism used by the human mind to connect disparate data items to produce information (Lansdown, 1993). In multimedia presentation systems, cross-referencing text using links (known as *hypertext links*) or any multimedia data object (known as *hypermedia links*) recognizes the interconnectedness of information (Nelson, 1990) and the value of associativity.

Digital speech and audio standards

Speech and audio signals are inherently analogue. Digital storage and transmission of sound involves analogue-to-digital signal conversion. Several methods can be used to change an analogue signal into a representative binary stream. A basic approach is to sample the analogue signal at a specified rate and code the amplitude of the signal at each sample as a binary number. This techniques is known as **pulse code modulation** (PCM). The process of attaching a specific value to a sampled signal is known as **quantizing**. Errors are inherently introduced as a result of quantizing because a constantly changing signal is being represented by a set of discrete values. Clearly, the sampling rate and the range of values used to represent an amplitude value (the quantum step size) determines the accuracy of quantization. PCM systems typically sample at 8000 samples/s and use 256 possible values (i.e. 8 bits) to represent the amplitude value. The resulting bit rate for PCM sound encoding is 8 x 8000 = 64 000 bit/s. In a network which transmits voice signals digitally, for example, a 64 kbit/s channel is required if PCM quantization is used. PCM encoding and coding is carried out by a *codec* device which, for example, is built into digital telephone handsets and video conferencing hardware.

In PCM, signal distortion is proportional to the quantum step size, a technique known as *companding*, compresses the higher amplitude signals to a smaller amplitude range and expands smaller amplitudes to larger values. For historical reasons, two standard (incompatible) companding schemes for PCM are in widespread use: the **mu-law** (a 7-bit companding scheme used in North America and Japan) and the **A-law** (an 8-bit companding scheme used in the rest of the world).

In an effort to reduce the data rates required to encode sound, variations of the basic PCM technique have been developed. In the *differential* PCM (DPCM) technique, the differences between samples are encoded rather than the absolute amplitude values. Since the amplitude values do not vary significantly from one sample to the next, fewer bits are required to represent the signal. DPCM uses a 4-bit quantum step size at a sampling rate of 8000 samples/s giving a total transmission rate of 32 kbit/s. DPCM can be extended to adapt to the dynamic variations in speech signals using the *adaptive* DPCM (ADPCM) technique (ITU-T Recommendation G.721) which introduce variable or adaptive quantization step sizes. ADPCM offers good quality speech transmission at 32 kbit/s.

A further development in digitized speech is the **linear delta modulation** (DM) technique. This technique simply makes a comparison of each sample with the previous and transmits a 1 if it is higher and 0 if it is a lower value. Initially, the quantized digital signal differs significantly from the input (analogue) signal but becomes approximately equal over time. DM is used for low cost encoding of speech signals. Improvements in performance and reductions in the transmission rate can be achieved by using adaptive techniques (known as *adaptive delta* *modulation* (ADM)) which vary the quantization step size to achieve a better fit to the input signal. One ADM technique, known as *continuously variable slope delta modulation* (CVSD) varies the quantization step size almost continuously to achieve a good fit.

PCM and DM techniques are known as *waveform encoding* techniques because they treat the speech signal as an analogue signal and can be used to encode any analogue signal. An alternative approach is to break up the speech input signal into its basic components and waveform characteristics (e.g. frequency, pitch, amplitude, and so on) and model these parameters. This data is then passed to a digital encoder and onto the transmission link. A **vocoder** is a device which models speech signals. A **linear predictive coding** (LPC) vocoder uses a predictive model of the speech signal. Using this technique, the transmission rate for digitized speech reduces to as little as 2.4 kbit/s. The quality of LPC speech can be improved by using adaptive techniques (known as adaptive predictive coding (APC)).

Audio signals (e.g. CD audio) require much higher sampling rates and quantization step sizes. Stereo audio requires two separate audio channels while mono recording require only one channel. Full CD quality stereo audio encoding generally requires a sampling rate of 44.1 kHz (a popular sampling rate established by Philips and Sony as opposed to the 32- and 48-kHz rate established by the ITU for PCM music representation), a quantum step size of 16 bits (2 bytes) and two channels. Thus:

```
Uncompressed audio content = step_size * sampling_rate * no_of_channels
                           * seconds_of_audio

One minute of uncompressed CD audio = 2 * 44 100 * 2 * 60 bytes
                                    = 176 400 * 60 bytes
                                    = 10 584 000 bytes
```

Thus one minute of uncompressed CD audio requires about 10 Mbytes of storage and a transmission rate of 1.4 Mbit/s. Storage volume and transmission rate can be reduced (with reduced quality) by reducing the quantization step size to 8 bits and the sampling rate to 22 500 kHz or 11 250 kHz.

Compression techniques can also be applied to further reduce storage volume and transmission rates. The MPEG-1 standard is a three-part compression standard that addresses video and audio compression techniques for synchronized video and audio at a total bit rate of about 1.5 Mbit/s. The MPEG/audio compression algorithm is in fact the first international standard for the digital compression of high-fidelity audio (ISO, 11172-3). Other algorithms address speech-only applications or provide only medium-fidelity audio compression performance (Pan, 1995). Unlike vocoders which are tuned for speech signals, MPEG/audio compression does not make any assumptions about the nature of the audio source. Much of the compression is as a result of removing perceptually irrelevant parts of the audio signal and offers an assortment of compression modes. The audio sampling rates can be 32, 44.1, or 48 kHz. One or two channels are supported in one of four possible modes (Pan, 1995):

1. mono on a single channel;
2. mono on two independent audio channels;
3. stereo mode with shared bits;
4. joint-stereo mode with shared joint stereo coding.

MPEG/audio offers three compression layers which provide a range of trade-offs between algorithm (and hence codec) complexity, compressed bit stream rates, and audio quality. Layer 1 offers the simplest complexity and is targeted bit rates above 128 kbit/s per channel.

Layer 2 offers intermediate complexity and is targeted at a bit rate of 128 kbit/s. Layer 2 uses the most complex algorithms but offers very good audio quality at 64 kbit/s making it suitable for transmission over an ISDN network. MPEG synchronized audio and video over ISDN networks is giving rise to many new multimedia applications, notably in the news and advertising industries (for example, where it is used to transmit news and advertising items) and in on-demand business and industry services marketing.

The MPEG-2 audio compression standard offers the following enhancements over MPEG-1 which makes it highly suited to digital video broadcasting in consumer and business markets:

1. support for up to five high-fidelity audio channels and a low frequency enhancement channel;
2. support for up to seven additional commentary channels for multilingual audio. Commentary channels have half the sampling rate of high-fidelity channels;
3. lower compressed bit rates (down to around 8 kbit/s);
4. additional, lower sampling rates of 16, 22.05, and 24 kHz.

It is clear that high quality, low bit rate, and low cost synchronized video and audio services will be a reality when MPEG-2 and MPEG-4 codecs are mass produced both as software-only and hardware/software products.

2.4 MULTIMEDIA INFORMATION EXCHANGE

When data is transferred from one process to another it is important for the receiving process to recognize the nature of the data. For example, a process could receive graphical data encoded in a variety of possible formats. Distributed information systems integrate a number of media types which need to be represented in a way which does not restrict the range of media types that can be employed, but provides a uniform method of describing the information representation. This is a standard problem in electronic mail systems. The electronic mail system world has produced two candidates for use in describing media types: ITU-T X.400 (ITU-T, 1988) and the Multipurpose Internet Mail Extensions (MIME) standard (Borenstein and Freed, 1992). Both address the need to facilitate multimedia mail transfer. The MIME standard is described here. X.400 is described in Section 8.13.2.

The original Internet mail standard SMTP (Postel, 1982), and subsequent enhancements (Crocker, 1982; Rose and Stefferud, 1985; Sirbu, 1988), fully describe how to send flat US-ASCII text but not multimedia objects in a single message. The MIME standard was 'designed to provide facilities to include multiple objects in a single message, to represent body text in other than US-ASCII, to represent formatted multi-font text messages, to represent non-textual material such as images and audio fragments, and generally to facilitate later extensions defining new types of Internet mail for use by co-operating mail agents' (Borenstein and Freed, 1992).

MIME defines a special header format (commonly known as a MIME header) which describes the format of the subsequent data. A MIME header has the following fields:

1. A **MIME-version** header field, which specifies which version of the MIME header format this header conforms to.
2. A **content-type** header field, which is used to specify the **media type** and **sub-type**. A

number of content-type/sub-type pairs have been standardized. MIME defines a registration process which uses the Internet Assigned Numbers Authority (IANA) as a central registry to ensure that duplicate pairs with different meanings cannot be created. Standard content-type/sub-type pairs are summarized in Table 2.1. Any new pair may be registered with IANA. New pairs do not need to be registered. Non-registered pairs are known as 'Non-standard pairs' and can be used, but must adhere to a restricted naming convention (names must be preceded with the two characters 'x-'). A content-type may specify a number of optional parameters. For example, the text/plain content type specifies a character set parameter (charset).

3. A **content-transfer-encoding** header field, which can be used to specify any additional encoding that was applied to the data in order to allow it to pass through a communications channel with data or character set limitations or for other reasons. Unlike content-types, the proliferation of transfer encoding options is undesirable. In general, there is a trade-off between the desire for a compact and efficient encoding of large binary data and the desire for a readable encoding of data that is mostly, but not entirely 7-bit (Borenstein and Freed, 1993). Example values are 7bit, quoted-printable, base64, 8bit, binary and x-token (i.e. private transfer encoding). The values 7bit, 8bit and binary all mean that no encoding has been performed on the data but are useful indications of the kind of data contained in the object. Thus for example the header:

```
Content-type: text/plain; charset = ISO-8859-1
        content-transfer-encoding: base64
```

specifies that the data object is a base64 ASCII encoding of data that was originally ISO-8859-1 encoded, and will be in that character set again after decoding.

4. Two additional header fields can be used to further describe the data , the **content-ID** and **content-description** header fields.

This simple header format is widely used outside of the context of Internet electronic mail to describe the contents of any multimedia object. An example of the use of MIME headers is in the World Wide Web system which is discussed in Chapter 8. A simple example of a text message preceded by a MIME header is given below.

```
MIME-Version: 1.0
  Content-type: text/US-ASCII
  This is an example text message encoded with the standard US-ASCII
    encoding standard. Other encoding standards could be used and
  specified in the MIME header using the charset = xxxxx parameter

  Regards

  Errol Simon
```

An equivalent audio message would be sent as follows:

```
  MIME-Version: 1.0
  Content-type: audio/basic
  ------ base64 encoded using 8-bit PCM mu-law goes here------
```

A compound data object containing different media types is coded as a data stream with multiple MIME headers using the multipart content type, as illustrated in Figure 2.3.

Table 2.1 MIME standard content-type, sub-type and parameter definitions

Content-type	Description	Important parameters	Sub-type	Sub-type description
Text	Textual information	Charset	Plain richtext	Unformatted text Formatted text
Multipart	Data with multiple parts of independent data types	Boundary	Mixed alternative parallel digest	Mixed types Same data, multiple formats Parts viewed simultaneously Each part is of type message
Application	Uninterpreted binary data	Type, padding	Postscript	Postscript document
Message	An encapsulated SMTP message	ID, number, total, access-type, expiration, size, permission, name, site, directory, mode, server, subject	fc822 partial external-body	SMTP conformant message Fragmented message External data source
Image	Static image data		JPEG GIF	JPEG encoded image GIF encoded image
Audio	Audio data		Basic	GIF encoded image
Video	Video data		MPEG	MPEG encoded video
X-token	Privately-defined content type			

```
MIME-Version: 1.0
Content-type: multipart/mixed;
   boundary=this-is-boundary-1

Preamble, should be ignored by MIME conformant readers.
   --this-is-boundary-1

Note, this text should be displayed. Note also that the preceding
     blank line signifies that no MIME header information is supplied,
     therefore text/plain charset=us-ascii should be assumed.

Regards

Harry Smith

 --this-is-boundary-1
Content-type: multipart/parallel;
   boundary=this-is-boundary-2

 --this-is-boundary-2
Content-type: audio/basic
Content-Transfer-Encoding: base64

 ---- base64 transfer encoded using 8-bit ISDN mu-law [PCM] goes
   here------

 --this-is-boundary-2
Content-type: image/gif
Content-Transfer-Encoding: base64

 ---- base64 encoded graphics goes here------

 —this-is-boundary-2
Content-type: image/gif
Content-Transfer-Encoding: base64

  ---- base64 encoded graphics goes here------

 --this-is-boundary-2—

 --this-is-boundary-1

Let me know if you agree with the graphic design as described in
   the audio.

Bye for now.
 --this-is-boundary-1—
```

Figure 2.3 A compound data object encapsulating multimedia types.

Thus the MIME header specification is a simple but powerful standard to facilitate the interchange of multimedia objects.

2.4.1 Information retrieval

A related requirement is the ability to search for information in electronic form which meets specified criteria, and to request transmission of, and receive, some or all of the defined information. Individuals are now proactive in seeking out electronic information relevant to their business, social and recreational needs. This has an obvious parallel with the traditional use of libraries for searching for information contained in printed material. Libraries have developed the Z39.2 standard for machine-readable cataloguing of information and is the basis for most current library automation systems and services (Michael and Hinnebusch, 1995). The National Information Standards Organization (NISO) have produced important standards in the area of library systems and services (including the Z39.x standards).

The ANSI/NISO Z39.50 (IR) standard is an information retrieval (IR) protocol for information searching and retrieval in a client/server networked environment. Z39.50 was first introduced in 1988 (Version 1, also known as Z39.50-1988). Version 2 was published in 1992, and Version 3 is imminent at the time of writing. It is generally implemented as an application protocol using TCP/IP as the underlying transport service (see Chapter 6). Thus users can access remote information services without knowledge of the location of information providers (i.e. *where* to search for information), and the details of *how* to search remote information repositories. The type and format of data to be requested and returned is negotiated at connection time. Although originally targeted at bibliographical information, IR standards are being broadened to include access and retrieval of all types of information. This is a challenging requirement since it is not yet clear how we can classify certain types of information (e.g. images and video), what information they contain, or what relevant functions are associated with the information. Standards such as the MIME standard detailed previously can be extended to provide 'meta-information' in addition to content-type and other fields to facilitate searching.

Z39.50 is defined as a set of services: Search, Present, Explain, Delete, Scan, Abort and Extended services. The Search service is at the heart of the IR standard because it specifies the search parameters and the actions to be taken by the server in the process of performing the search. A search produces a **result set** which consists of pointers to database items which satisfy the search criteria. An Explain service provides a location-independent way of discovering database information. Z39.50 accommodates an external query language but also defines its own. The Z39.50 query language uses reverse Polish notation for unambiguously expressing potentially complex variables, constants and operators such as the Boolean operators AND, OR, NOT and exclusive OR (XOR). Other operators are proximity searching, greater than and less than a specified attribute value. The Present service provides the ability to request from a server the results of a previous request. The Delete service supports the deletion of one or more result sets from previous searches. The Abort service is used to break an association with an information service. A Scan service implements a browsing facility.

Z39.50 provides the protocols required for powerful and flexible information search and retrieval. It is being extended to discover and process a variety of different types of information. A more detailed discussion of Z39.50 can be found in Michael and Hinnebusch (1995).

2.5 DISTRIBUTED IT INFRASTRUCTURES

Information technology (IT) is defined as the range of electronic technologies for collecting, processing and distributing data, and consists primarily of computer and communication technologies. The term *information network* is used to refer to IT components designed to facilitate information exchange. An *IT infrastructure* is a set of IT components designed and implemented to satisfy the information needs of a specific community of users. The IT infrastructure comprises the elements that make up the physical system supporting data collection, processing and presentation. Using the human body as an analogy, it represents the physical body with its storage, manipulation, control and communication mechanisms. The IT infrastructure can be described using logical and physical views. The logical view describes it as co-operating processes that manipulate data on behalf of users, and present information to users of the information system. The physical view consists of network equipment, computers, operating system software, database management systems, packaged enabling software and system utilities.

A distributed IT infrastructure exhibits a number of additional attributes (Mullender, 1989; Bal, 1990):

1. **Multiple autonomous processing elements.** This is perhaps the attribute that all would agree is a feature of a distributed IT infrastructure. Multiple autonomous processing elements are now a standard component of today's IT infrastructure. Use of the term 'autonomous' implies that inherently there is no 'master–slave' relationship between processing elements (although the designer has the freedom to choose to implement such relationships). Thus it excludes traditional centralized mainframe-based IT infrastructures.

2. **Information exchange over an information network.** The information network connects the autonomous processing elements. This facilitates parallel information exchanges and processing.

3. **Processes interact via non-shared local memory**. Multiple processor computer systems can be classified into those that share memory (known as *multiprocessor* computers) and those without shared memory (known as *multicomputers*). A hybrid configuration involves separate computers with *distributed shared memory*. Whilst multiprocessor systems are a component of a distributed IT infrastructure (e.g. a multiprocessor computer acting as a single server), in this book we will focus on multicomputer configurations that support process interactions by message exchanges across an information network rather than through distributed shared memory. For a detailed examination of distributed shared memory systems, see Tanenbaum (1995).

The design of the distributed IT infrastructure determines the extent to which an information system can be distributed. In order to ensure that the IT infrastructure continually evolves to meet present and future needs, there needs to be a long-term IS/IT strategy which takes account of long-term requirements. By 'IS/IT strategy', we mean the use and management of IS/IT by an organization to achieve its desired goals in a changing and competitive operational environment. A complete IS/IT strategy has three main elements:

- **The IS/IT architecture**. The IS/IT architecture is 'the practice and process of establishing, and maintaining, a plan or map of what kinds of computer and related technology are appropriate for what kinds of uses. It also addresses where as well as how the various technologies will be linked and will work with each other' (Perley, 1993). Within this, IS/IT infrastructure is the base of hardware, software and communications facilities on which a new DIS is built.

- **IS/IT standards.** IS/IT standards need to be specified by the IS/IT strategy. Decisions need to be made about which type of standards (open, proprietary, *de facto*) should be adopted, and which internal standards should be specified.

- **IS/IT procurement.** The IS/IT strategy needs to specify the policies for procuring new IS/IT facilities which conform to the selected architecture, whether it be hardware or communication systems, application packages, or bespoke software developed in-house.

An IS/IT architecture can be further divided into four constituent architectures:

1. **Production architecture**, which establishes the hardware and software technologies to be used to support the production information systems.
2. **Development architecture**, which establishes the hardware and software technologies to be used to support the information systems development activities.
3. **Information architecture**, which establishes the types and location of information which is utilized by the production information systems, and how (and from where) information is accessed by the users and application processes. Data distribution issues relating to the development of an information architecture are covered in Chapter 9.
4. **Service architecture**, which establishes the type and location of the range of user and application services. Example services are detailed in Chapter 8.

These and other issues relating to the development of IS/IT architectures and the selection of standards are covered in detail in Chapter 12.

Although there is no universally accepted definition of what a DIS is, we can see from our discussion so far that it can be characterized by four principal attributes:

- it is implemented over a distributed IT infrastructure;
- it can access and incorporate a variety of media types;
- it processes data from a variety of media sources in an integrated manner, where possible involving the reuse of existing processing objects. A physical view of processing consists of a web of co-operating processing objects and related data objects (media sources) which may be distributed across the IT infrastructure;
- it provides presentation mechanisms that determine the way data is made visible to the user and provides for a high level of user interaction and control.

2.6 DISTRIBUTION TRANSPARENCY

A major consideration when designing DISs is the extent to which the distribution of components of the information system should be made transparent to application designers and users. Moving to a distributed IT infrastructure enhances flexibility but increases complexity (as perceived both by users and application designers). Users are demanding a simple user interface to this complex world which, in turn, demands functions for concealing complexity. Most users desire a **single system image** where all resources are perceived to be centralized at the desktop computer. This is in fact a design issue and affects the way that both the IT infrastructure and DISs are designed. We use the term **distribution transparency** to describe the visibility of distributed components within a DIS. There are two transparency choices:

1. **Full distribution transparency.** The complexities introduced by distribution are completely concealed. This simplifies application development (from the perspective of the application designer) and improves usability (from the perspective of the user of the infor-

mation system). In addition, it accommodates the incorporation of existing systems based on centralized systems. For example, a database application designed to execute on a single host machine is able to make use of distributed resources without knowledge of whether the resource is local or remote, and with no change to the application. Generic functions for full distribution transparency are generally implemented at the operating system level.

2. **Partial** or **selective distribution transparency**. Full distribution transparency does not allow applications the opportunity to exploit decentralization at the level of the application process. Implementing generic functions for full distribution transparency can also impose significant performance and other overheads that may be avoided if specific mechanisms are incorporated at the application level. The application designer may need to reveal that some DIS components are distributed and therefore requires a development environment that gives some freedom to take account of this. For example, when developing a DIS to allow users to order a pizza, it is useful to establish the location of the user to determine if there is a pizza outlet in the user's locality!

It is the designer who chooses the extent to which users are made aware of distributed components by selecting a level of distribution transparency appropriate to the application. The main drawback is the potential increase in complexity. Some systems allow the application designer to select the level of transparency according to the demands of the application.

The generic functions required to achieve full distribution transparency are well known (ANSA, 1993; ISO, 10746-3) and consist of the following ten transparency functions:

- **Access transparency.** Hiding the use of communications to access remote resources (e.g. programs, files, data, printers, etc.) so that the user is under the illusion that all resources are local (i.e. available at the workstation). Remote resources are accessed using exactly the same mechanism for accessing local resources, for example, clicking an icon in a graphical user interface (subject to appropriate security checks).

- **Location transparency.** Users do not have to know the location of remote resources. Resources are accessed by logical or functional name. At system-level, these names are translated to addresses and access requests communicated to the destination resource. For example, to print a file the printer name may be LPT1. At system-level the name LPT1 could be mapped to a print spooling service located on a UNIX minicomputer attached to the network. Thus, interacting processes can be located anywhere in the distributed systems environment. Resource naming, addressing and routing functions are required to fully implement location transparency.

- **Concurrency transparency.** The user is unaware of the existence of parallel access to remote resources, and inconsistencies are avoided by using concurrency control mechanisms. This is particularly important when remote data is being accessed. In this case, concurrency control ensures that the database image is consistent. Appropriate synchronization and event-ordering functions are required.

- **Migration transparency.** The potential to relocate resources dynamically without users being aware of reconfigurations. This is an important feature as it recognizes that IT configurations continually change due to growth, enhancement and reconfiguration for fault avoidance and load balancing. For example, a high-speed computer could be installed on the network and an existing database application migrated to it leaving the current computer to act as an additional print and file server. User workstations would not need updating, but would automatically adjust to the new location of the database application. Thus dynamic configuration (and reconfiguration) functions are required to implement migration transparency.

- **Replication transparency.** Hiding any differences between replicated and non-replicated resources. A distributed system provides the opportunity to replicate resources to increase availability and performance.

- **Partition transparency.** Hiding any differences between a partitioned and non-partitioned service. A distributed system provides the opportunity to partition over two or more computers to increase performance, availability and scalability.

- **Persistence transparency.** Hiding the deactivation and reactivation of resources. Deactivation and reactivation are often used to maintain the persistence of a resource when a system is unable to provide it with processing, storage and communication functions continuously.

- **Failure transparency.** Hiding the effects of partially completed interactions that fail (partial failures). This is usually achieved through replicating resources and employing recovery mechanisms, and/or ensuring that interactions are transactional (i.e. they either complete entirely or fail with the complete removal of partial effects).

- **Performance transparency.** Minimizing the performance overheads in using remote resources, so that response times and throughput are comparable with the case when all resources are local. Optimization of system performance will be influenced by the chosen combination of transparency functions identified above. For example, by exploiting replication transparency, parts of a database could be replicated and stored locally on a particular user's workstation to enhance performance.

- **Scaling transparency.** Systems constantly change, grow and merge introducing variations in scale. Scale is measured, for example, in terms of speed (slow to fast), size (small to large), geographic scope (local or remote). Scaling transparency is hiding variations in system behaviour due to arbitrary scaling. Scaling should not require significant changes to the system structure and operations in order to accommodate it. For example, migration of an application from a PC to a UNIX-based multiprocessor computer should be transparent if transparency functions such as migration, location and access transparency are implemented.

If all of the above transparency functions are built into the IT infrastructure (usually as software components) then full distribution transparency can be achieved. The *degree of distribution transparency* is a measure of the distributed nature of the IT infrastructure. In assessing the degree of distribution transparency, only the first seven functions are considered. Failure, performance and scaling transparency are achieved through the use of a combination of the other seven functions. This is described in detail in Chapter 7. We can now offer a more formal definition of a distributed IT infrastructure (adapted from Bal, 1990):

> A distributed IT infrastructure is an IT infrastructure incorporating multiple autonomous processors that do not share local memory, but co-operate by sending data messages over an information network. The IT infrastructure exhibits distribution transparency.

2.7 COMPONENTS OF A DIS

The designer of a DIS may be required to choose to what extent *data, processing* and *presentation* components are to be localized or distributed. This is known as *application partitioning*. External services and data sources of interest to the DIS user are naturally distributed since it is unlikely that all data requirements are stored at the user's workstation. We define these components as:

1. **Data.** This is concerned with the structures and functions for information retention and manipulation. It may consist of many data objects, representing many media types. For example a data object could be a relational database, a graphics file, an audio file or a multimedia data stream.

2. **Processing.** This is concerned with processing data objects. It may contain processing objects such as viewers, browsers, search engines, application-specific logic and so on.

3. **Presentation.** This is processing directly concerned with making data visible to users and handling user interactions. There are two levels of concern:

   - **user interface.** The aspects of the user interface that the user physically perceives. It consists of a standardized set of aesthetics in terms of appearance (a common 'look and feel') that visually appears to be the same from application to application. These specifications promote consistency and predictability in user interface behaviour which, in turn, leads to ease of learning and learning retention.

   - **presentation management.** The user interface manager (UIM) that provides the basic operations used to build and control the user interface under application (and user) control. Three key functions are provided by presentation management software: display services, dialogue control and an application programming interface. Display services manages all user interface devices (e.g. a bit-mapped screen, mouse, keyboard, video camera, microphone and speakers). Dialogue control provides mechanisms for creating and manipulating the user interface and event handling functions. An API provides any application with a low- and high-level interface (normally in the form of program libraries) through which application-specific interfaces can be constructed. An example of a UIM is the Microsoft Windows software.

In addition to the above components, four services are required which are normally assumed to be incorporated into the distributed IT infrastructure:

- A **separation mechanism.** This enables the separation and linking (or binding) of data, processing and presentation components.
- A mechanism for the **identification** of target objects. This is concerned with the naming and addressing of components that may or may not be separated, but wish to co-operate.
- **Administration and management** of the overall system. This is concerned with the administration and management of all resources to ensure that functional and non-functional quality of service requirements are continually being met.
- **Security.** This is concerned with the provision of security services so that confidentiality, integrity and availability requirements are continually being met.

2.7.1 Rightsizing

A DIS should seek to exploit the strengths of various elements of the distributed IT infrastructure. A useful approach often used in designing a DIS is to simply match DIS components with the appropriate elements in an IT infrastructure. This approach is known as **rightsizing** and essentially observes that:

1. User workstation platforms are optimized to support the graphical user interfaces that

have become a standard feature of the presentation component of a DIS. These platforms are optimized to support multimedia user interfaces. Thus, presentation components should normally reside on the workstation platform.

2. Any powerful processor configuration, ranging from a uniprocessor PC to multiprocessor configurations, can be used to support processing components of a DIS. The scale of processor should be sized to the processing requirements. This is the essence of the right-sizing approach. **Downsizing** is the case where applications are migrated from a larger processor (e.g. a mainframe) to a smaller processor, usually to improve performance or because it is more cost effective. In contrast, **upsizing** is the migration to a larger processor, for example, due to growth in the number of users connected.

3. Processors with high input/output bandwidth – typical of high-end minicomputer and mainframe sized server platforms – are required to support high-volume data (typical of corporate databases) and batch processing applications. An added attraction is that a high level of management control over corporate data can be exercised when data is concentrated over a small number of large servers.

4. The information network simply provides support for parallel information exchanges between presentation, processing and data components.

A distributed IT infrastructure gives the flexibility required to maximize the utilization of all resources in the infrastructure. An essential aspect of DIS design and implementation is the placement of data, processing and presentation objects to fully exploit the underlying infrastructure. This is explored more fully in Chapter 10.

2.8 CLASSES OF DISTRIBUTED SUPPORT SERVICES

Because many applications require the same high-level services such as services for distributing presentation, processing and data components on to any chosen nodes in the IT infrastructure, much of the functionality required is offered as services as an integral part of the distributed IT infrastructure. For example, Sun Microsystem's Network File Service (NFS) (Sandberg et al., 1985), can be regarded as providing a distributed service for data file storage and access. We can define the following classes of high-level distributed support services which can be built into a distributed IT infrastructure and which supports the implementation of a DIS:

1. Distributed presentation services.
2. Distributed processing services.
3. Remote data access service.
4. Remote file access services.
5. Distributed data management services.
6. Distributed object management services.

Each of the above support services are described in the following sections.

2.8.1 Distributed presentation services

A distributed presentation service allows the presentation component either to be wholly resident on the client or split across client and server elements of the IT infrastructure as shown in Figure 2.4. All other components reside on the server side. In the case when the presentation component is split, a 'presentation' protocol is designed to support communication between the

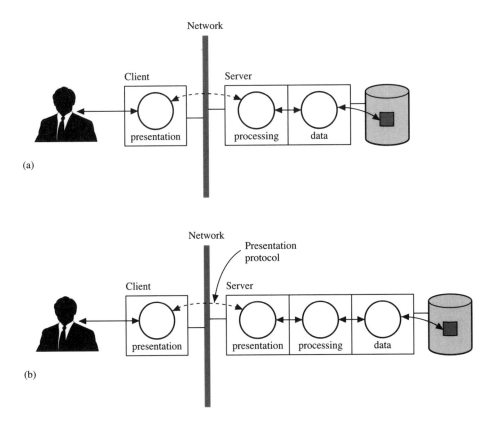

Figure 2.4 Distributed presentation services. (a) Presentation component only on client. (b) Presentation component split across client and server.

client and server components. An example of this configuration is the X-Window system developed jointly by the Massachusetts Institute of Technology (MIT), IBM and DEC, in a project known as Project Athena (Champine, 1991). In this system the presentation management software (known as X-Windows) can be split across a client and a server. An application executing on the server can use the presentation management component on the server to control the client's display elements (e.g. screen, keyboard, etc.) and receive any events generated by a user using the client workstation. The X-Windows systems is described more fully in Chapter 10.

2.8.2 Distributed processing services

In this case, the DIS consists of co-operating processing objects distributed across client and server elements of the IT infrastructure. An increasing number of systems fall into this category. Client processing objects need assistance when identifying the server object and routing requests to the object. On the client side, assistance is provided (transparent to the DIS processing object) by a special infrastructure object called a user agent which conceals the complexity of client/server interactions. At the server side, a special processing object, the **server wrapper**, receives client requests and passes the request to the appropriate server object. Figure 2.5 shows an example configuration.

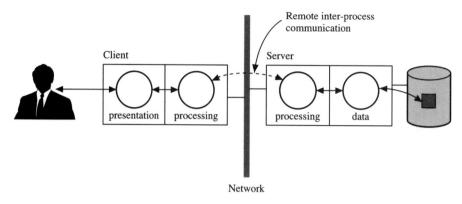

Figure 2.5 Distributed processing services.

To illustrate this, consider a hotel booking DIS which is split between client and server platforms. Client processing is mostly concerned with presentation objects which handle user interactions and presentation data (e.g. a graphic display of available rooms) to the user via a graphical user interface. The client also accesses locally-held data. A client process engages in a dialogue with a server-based processing object that implements the booking service and allows any client object to request a booking. When a booking request is received, the server object executes the appropriate operation and sends a reply back to the client confirming whether the operation was successful. The client object processes the response and feeds back data to the presentation object for output to the user. This configuration is illustrated in Figure 2.6.

2.8.3 Remote data access services

In this configuration the presentation and processing components resides on the client. The data component resides on one or more servers using database management system (DBMS) software. Storage and retrieval of data across the network is at the record level within a database. When a user wishes to access data, the user uses a data manipulation language (e.g. the relational language SQL) to specify the data request and sends it to the server (with assistance from a user agent). The request is transferred to the server on which the appropriate database resides. On the server side, a server wrapper receives (SQL) requests from clients and routes it to the DBMS for processing. The results are sent back to the originating client object. The transport of SQL operations to the server for processing is virtually transparent to the client object due to co-operation between the user agent and server wrapper. User agents and server wrappers are supplied either with the DBMS product or by a third party software product. This configuration is illustrated in Figure 2.7.

This configuration is attractive because it minimizes network traffic, particularly if common and complex queries can be stored in the DBMS (known as stored procedures) and invoked by clients. Only processed data (i.e. the result of an SQL query) need travel across the network. The database server manages the database and maintains data integrity. Large data transfers can be managed by sending back partial record sets rather than all of the data in a single reply message. This method of storing and retrieving data is detailed in Chapters 8 and 9.

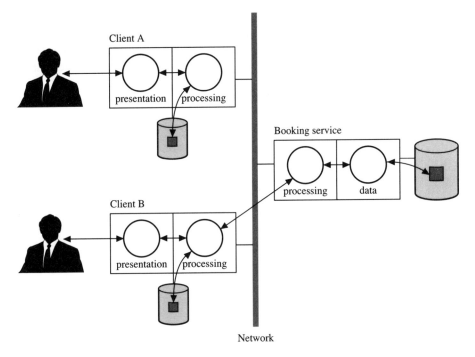

Figure 2.6 An example distributed processing system.

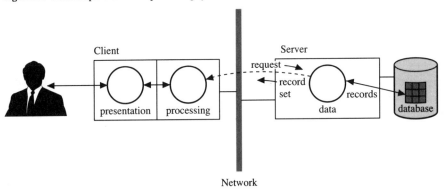

Figure 2.7 A remote data access (RDA) service.

2.8.4 Remote file access services

This describes an environment where presentation and processing components reside on the client side and data objects on the server side. Data objects are stored on one or more servers implementing a file service that can be utilized by users. Storage and retrieval of data across the network is at the file block level within a file system. File servers do not generally support the storage and retrieval of structured data blocks (e.g. records). Whenever a client object requires access to a file data object, it issues a file request such as read( ) or write( ). A user agent (known as a redirector) traps the request and determines whether the file is local or remote. If the file is local, the request is passed to the local operating system. If remote, the user initiates a connection to the appropriate server and sends the request (e.g. to retrieve a data block) to the server wrapper. The request is passed to the server operating system for processing. This functionality is built into most LAN network operating systems and distributed file systems, giving distribution transparency to client objects. This is illustrated in Figure 2.8. Example RFA service implementations such as Network File Service (NFS), are described in Chapter 8.

2.8.5 Distributed data management services

A remote data access (RDA) service provides easy access to a remote database system. When multiple RDA servers are available, each managing a portion of the data objects required by a client object, the processing object must be aware of the location of all relevant data objects and the database tables that they represent. A distributed data management system conceals the location of database tables, presenting client objects with a view consisting of a single, centralized database from which data objects can be defined independent of location. In essence, the transparency functions are integrated into the distributed data management service. An example configuration is shown in Figure 2.9. Distributed data management services are covered in Chapters 8 and 9.

2.8.6 Distributed object management services

The term 'object' has been used in this chapter to describe an entity with a well-defined interface (described by a well-defined set of operations) which can be invoked by sending a message to it. More formally, data and associated operations are closely coupled. An object represents a self-contained unit which encapsulates data and operations (usually known as 'methods') that manipulate the data. Objects interact with other objects using some form of message passing. Objects can both request service and offer services to other objects. In this sense, an object can potentially act both as a client (a consumer of services) and as a server (a service provider). A DIS modelled on the object paradigm, uses the object as the unit of distribution. A distributed object management service manages the distribution of objects across multiple computers, but giving the illusion of a single, global object space. The distributed object model is examined in detail in Chapter 3. An example of an architecture based on the distributed object model; the CORBA architecture developed by the Object Management Group (OMG, 1992), is also discussed in Chapter 3.

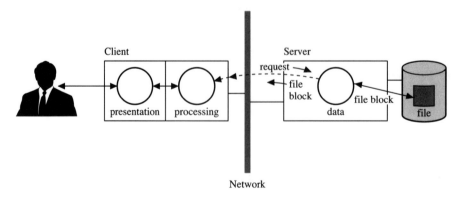

Figure 2.8 A remote file access (RFA) service.

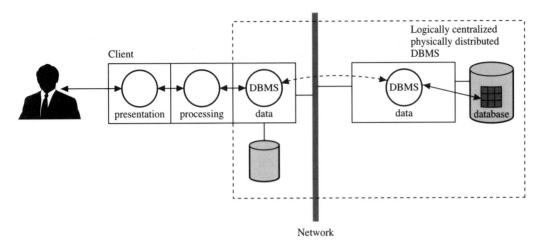

Figure 2.9 Distributed data management.

2.9 SYSTEMS DEVELOPMENT

Use of the above reusable services greatly simplifies the DIS development process since much of the functionality required by an application is already available via well-defined application programming interfaces (APIs) to standard services. The application developer can concentrate on interfacing with existing services as necessary to meet user requirements. This improves programmer productivity, reduces the timescales for application development and reduces the costs of ongoing maintenance of the DIS. Generic distributed services are explored in detail in Chapter 8. An approach to DIS development using ISO open distributed processing (ODP) concepts (ISO 10746), rapid application development (RAD) and object modelling is presented in Chapter 10.

Clearly for a given set of user requirements, several generic services may need to be utilized. For example, an order processing application may be partitioned over several computer systems using a distributed processing service and may access one or more databases using a remote database access service. Systems developers have at their disposal an increasingly wide range of services as building blocks for implementing DISs. Services are selected according to the nature of users' functional requirements and non-functional requirements such as cost, performance, availability, scalability and so on. From a user perspective, the systems environment is viewed as a powerful set of computer applications available at the user's desktop workstation. From the perspective of an applications developer, user applications consist of a potentially complex web of interlinked data, processing and presentation components which exploit reusable services. These perspectives are explored in detail in Chapter 10.

2.10 SUMMARY

This chapter identified the characteristics of distributed information systems, distributed IT infrastructures and distributed services, which serve as a basis for discussing issues raised throughout this book. The notion of a DIS as an information system with distributed components leads to the identification of several key distributed services. Distribution transparency is a desirable goal as it simplifies the distributed IT infrastructure as viewed by application developers and users by concealing distribution. Distribution transparency and the use of reusable distributed services, leads to increased application development productivity and enhanced usability (while maintaining flexibility of access).

2.11 REVIEW QUESTIONS

1. Discuss the differences in definitions of data and information that can arise. To what extent does an organization's interpretation of the meaning of data and information depend on cultural issues?
2. What are the distinguishing characteristics of a multimedia information system? Discuss the implications for the design of the underlying IT infrastructure.
3. Define the meaning of the term 'distributed IT infrastructure'. Discuss the differences between a centralized and a distributed IT infrastructure.
4. What are the ten transparency functions that can be built into a distributed IT infrastructure?
5. Identify the three components of a DIS that can be distributed. What are the advantages and implications of distributing components?
6. What is the difference between the degree of distribution transparency and the degree of component distribution?
7. Identify the types of distributed services which directly assist in the development of a DIS. Give a practical example of the implementation of each class of support service.

2.12 FURTHER READING

An interesting perspective on information, information technology and organizations is found in Harrington (1991). Another perspective on the structure of distributed applications is found in Hackathorn (1993) and Berson (1992). Adie (1993) is a detailed survey of distributed multimedia research projects, relevant standards and example products. Champine (1991) gives an overview of Athena, a large-scale distributed system at MIT of over a 1000 workstations. A number of important *de facto* standards, such as X-Windows (graphical user interface) and Kerberos (security), emerged from this project.

3

DISTRIBUTED PROCESSING

3.1 INTRODUCTION

Distributed processing can loosely be described as the execution of co-operating processes which communicate by exchanging messages across an information network. This implies that the IT infrastructure consists of distributed processors, enabling parallel execution of processes and message exchanges. In this chapter, common models to support interaction between processes executing in a distributed IT infrastructure are considered. The chapter focuses on the most widely used models of process interaction: the client/server model, the group model and the distributed object model. Data exchanges between co-operating processes can be implemented in two ways: using some common but passive resource or memory (a shared memory mechanism), or by supporting message exchanges between them. Discussion is focused on two widely used message exchange mechanisms: message passing and remote procedure calls (RPC). Some practical implementations will be examined to illustrate the above approaches.

3.2 PROCESSES AND THREADS

A **process** is a logical representation of a physical processor that executes program code and has associated state and data (a process is sometimes described as a virtual processor). A process is also the unit of resource allocation and so is defined by the resources it uses and by the location at which it is executing. A process can run either in a separate **address space** (i.e. have a private range of addresses available to it) or may share the same address space. Processes are created either implicitly (for example by the operating system when a program is to be executed) or explicitly using an appropriate language construct or operating system function such as `fork()` in the UNIX environment.

In uni-processor computer systems many processes appear to be running at the same time. In reality there is never more than one process executing on a single CPU; a time slicing technique is used to enable multiple processes to use it, switching between them so rapidly that, under the right conditions, each process seems to be executing continuously. Switching between processes involves saving the state of the currently active process and setting up the state of another process (this is sometimes known as **context switching**). Context switching is carried out by very low-level code in the operating system kernel. Many operating systems (e.g. UNIX) allow programs to create additional processes (other than the one it is running in) thus enabling multiple concurrent 'child' processes to be executing, each competing for CPU and other resources as with other processes. In the UNIX `fork()` mechanism, when a child process is created using `fork()` all the resources belonging to the original program (running in the 'parent' process) are duplicated thus making them available to child processes. Thus child processes have their own address spaces but with duplicated resources.

It is a common requirement for a program to create multiple processes which are required to share memory and other resources. For example, a program may wish to create a sub-process to wait for a particular event. Some operating systems support this situation efficiently by allowing a number of processes to share a single address space. Processes in this context are often referred to as **lightweight processes** or **threads** and the operating system is said to support **multi-threading.** A thread is thus the unit of scheduling and execution in a multi-threaded OS. Memory and other resources are allocated to the address space within which threads are executing (an 'address space' and associated resources are variously known as a task, actor, process, cluster, etc.). Context switching between threads in the same address space is much faster than context switching between (heavyweight) processes in separate address spaces. The main drawback is that because all threads share memory and other resources, there is much more scope for conflicts and programs need to be carefully written to detect and recover from such conflicts. This can be achieved by use of semaphore and locking mechanisms for co-ordinating actions on specific resources as discussed in the next section. In this book, the term 'process' is used to refer to heavyweight and lightweight processes (threads) unless stated otherwise.

In multi-processor systems multiple processes and threads can execute simultaneously (in parallel); one per active CPU without the need to re-write programs. Thus, this approach to implementing concurrent programs is independent of the underlying processor architecture.

3.3 SYNCHRONIZATION OF CO-OPERATING PROCESSES

There are two main reasons why there is a need for synchronization mechanisms (Bacon, 1993).

1. Two or more processes may need to *co-operate* in order to complete a given task. This implies that the operating mechanism must provide facilities for identifying (naming) co-operating processes and synchronization of processes with each other.
2. Two or more processes may need to *compete* for access to shared services or resources. The main implication is that the synchronization mechanism must provide facilities to allow one process to wait for a resource to become available and another process to signal the release of a resource.

When processes are running on the same computer, process synchronization is straightforward since all processes use the same physical clock and can share memory. Synchronization via shared memory is achieved using well-known mechanisms such as semaphores which are designed to provide mutually exclusive access to a non-shareable resource by preventing concurrent execution of the critical region of program code through which the non-shareable resource is accessed. Mutual exclusion is achieved by enclosing each critical section of code by **WAIT**(mutex) and **SIGNAL**(mutex) semaphore operations where mutex is the name of the semaphore and is initialized to the value 1. For example, if a semaphore called mutex has been allocated and initialized to 1, then the program code fragment in Figure 3.1 illustrates how the critical section is coded. Semaphores can also be used to synchronize co-operating processes by ensuring that one process will wait on another based on the occurrence of a particular event, and for the waiting process to be signalled that it can now proceed. For example, Table 3.1 shows the use of WAIT and SIGNAL operations to synchronize two concurrent processes.

```
/* execute non-critical section of code                    */
/* block the current process until it can
    acquire the mutual exclusion lock:-                     */
        WAIT(mutex);
/* execute critical section of code                         */
        critical_section(............)
/* release the mutual exclusion lock:-                      */
        SIGNAL(mutex);
/* execute non-critical section of code                     */
```

Figure 3.1 Mutual exclusion using semaphores.

Table 3.1 Synchronization using semaphores

Process A	Process B
/* synchronize with process B */ **WAIT**(sync)	• •

/* proceed since now synchronized */
  •
  •
	SIGNAL(sync)

Semaphores can be used as a synchronization mechanism in all types of process interactions when processes share memory by using multiple semaphores with appropriate initial values. The initial value of a semaphore is the maximum concurrent usage of a resource. The value of a semaphore at any instance indicates the number of units of resource available.

An alternative approach to synchronization of concurrent server processes is eventcounts and sequencers (Reed and Kanodia, 1979). Eventcounts allow processes to co-ordinate their actions by observing the sequencing of event occurrences. An eventcount is an object that keeps count of the number of events of a particular type that have occurred so far. It is typically represented by a non-decreasing integer variable, initialized to zero, and with the following primitive operations:

ADVANCE(eventcount)　　　– signals the occurrence of an event associat-
　　　　　　　　　　　　　　　　ed with an eventcount by increasing the
　　　　　　　　　　　　　　　　eventcount by 1.

READ(eventcount)　　　　　– returns the current value of eventcount.

AWAIT(eventcount, value)– blocks the calling process until the event-
　　　　　　　　　　　　　　　　count is greater or equal to value.

Sequencers are required to totally order events. A sequencer is also typically represented by a non-decreasing integer variable, initialized to zero, but with the following primitive operation:

TICKET(sequencer)　　　　– returns the current value of sequencer then
　　　　　　　　　　　　　　　　increases the value.

The TICKET operation is analogous to the use of numbered tickets in restaurants and busy shops to control the order of service. Customers are served in the order of the number on their ticket. To illustrate the use of eventcounts and sequencers, suppose a banking service is defined with an operation CreateAC which creates a new bank account so that, for example, unique account and PIN numbers are generated and to ensure that account data consistency is maintained. An eventcount and sequencer can be used to implement a mutual exclusion (mutex) mechanism to ensure that only one CreateAC operation can execute the critical section of code at any moment in time. When a server receives a client request it creates a child process to handle it. Thus multiple child processes may be executing in the non-critical section of the CreateAC operation. An eventcount called CREATE_EC and sequencer called CREATE_SQ are defined and initialized on server startup. A child process about to enter the critical section first acquires a ticket by executing:

$$myturn = TICKET(CREATE\_SQ)$$

which returns a value in the variable myturn to represent the position of the process in the queue of client processes waiting to execute the critical section. An AWAIT(CREATE_EC, myturn) operation is executed which has the effect of blocking the child process until CREATE_EC is greater or equal to myturn. When this occurs, the child process has permission to execute the critical section. When the critical section has been executed, the child process hands control to another process by executing operation ADVANCE(CREATE_EC), which effectively allows the next child process to enter the critical section.

3.4 INTER-PROCESS COMMUNICATION

When processes in the same computer wish to interact they need to make use of an inter-process communication (IPC) mechanism which is usually provided by the native operating system or presentation management components. A number of mechanisms are available. Perhaps the most primitive IPC is a synchronous filter mechanism. Most UNIX and MS-DOS users are familiar with the *pipe* mechanism which is an example of a filter mechanism. for example:

```
ls -l | more
```

The commands ls and more run as two concurrent processes, with the output of ls con-nected to the input of more. This has the overall effect of listing the contents of the current directory one screen at a time. Many processes can be piped together in this way. As a synchronization mechanism, normally the source process will write to the pipe until it is full (the maximum size of a pipe data stream is implementation dependent) then block until some data is read by the target process. If the target process reads an empty pipe which has not been closed by the source process it will block until the source process writes some data to the pipe. If the source process closed its end of the pipe, a read on an empty pipe receives an end-of-file condition. The main advantage of pipes is simplicity. Pipe linkage mechanisms are unidirectional and bound to specific source and target processes, however, and do not offer a secure means of communication.

Named pipes overcome some of these limitations by allowing a pipe link to exist without being bound to source and target objects. Unrelated processes can establish communication using a named pipe facility because the interface is much like an ordinary file, indeed, named pipes are often registered in the operating system's file system with an access control list equivalent to an ordinary file for security purposes. Once named pipes are created they behave in a similar manner to ordinary pipes.

An alternative IPC mechanism is use of the local file. The principal advantages of this method are that it can handle large volumes of data and it is a well-understood approach which has been the basis of online information systems for decades. A database is a collection of data items which can be read from or written to by co-operating processes as a means of passing data or synchronizing. The main drawbacks are that there are no inherent synchronization mechanisms between communicating processes to avoid state data corruption, therefore synchronization mechanisms (e.g. file and record locking) need to be developed to allow many concurrent processes to communicate while preserving data consistency. Secondly, communication is inefficient since it usually relies on a relatively slow, non-volatile disk storage facility.

Since all processes are local, the computer's random-access memory can be used to implement a *shared memory* facility using random-access memory. A common region of memory addressable by all concurrent processes is used to define shared variables which are used to pass data or for synchronization purposes. Processes must use semaphores or other techniques since there is no inherent synchronization mechanism. This is a very efficient mechanism but normally cannot cope with large data transfers. An example of a shared memory mechanism is a *clipboard* facility supplied by most presentation management software.

A common asynchronous linkage mechanism is a *message queuing* mechanism which provides the ability for any process to write to a named queue and for any process to read from a named queue. Synchronization is inherent in the read/write operations and the message queue which together support asynchronous communications between many different processes. Messages are identified by a unique identifier or by message type. Security is implemented by associating an access control mechanism which identifies the owner process and read/write rights permissions for other processes. The main limitation is that these systems are designed to hold relatively small amounts of data.

A common synchronous IPC is the use of normal procedure calls using dynamic link libraries. When a procedure which resides in a dynamic link library is called, the binding between caller and called procedure is resolved at that point. This mechanism is widely used since it is well defined and well understood by application developers and facilitates software component reuse. Data is passed as parameters of the procedure call which means that only relatively small amounts of data can be passed between processes.

3.5 STRUCTURING A DISTRIBUTED SYSTEM

Six main paradigms are commonly used to structure an information system:

- the master–slave model;
- the client/server model;
- the peer-to-peer model;
- the group model;
- the distributed object model;
- the multimedia streams model.

Each of these models is examined in turn.

3.5.1 The master–slave model

A master–slave model may be an appropriate model for structuring a distributed system. In this model, a master process initiates and controls any dialogue with other (slave) processes. Slave processes exhibit very little intelligence, responding to commands from a single master process and exchange messages only when invited to by the master process. The master process defines the command set and appropriate responses associated with the dialogue. The slave process merely complies with the dialogue rules. An example configuration is given in Figure 3.2. This was the model on which online centralized computers running time-sharing information systems were based. The model has limited application in a distributed IT infra-structure because it does not make best use of distributed resources and the master process represents a single point of failure.

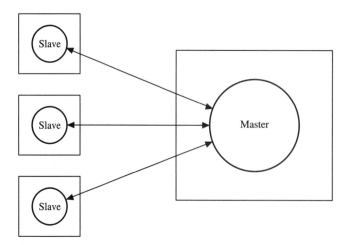

Figure 3.2 Master–slave model.

3.5.2 The client/server model

The client/server model is the most widely used paradigm for structuring distributed systems. A client requests a particular service. One or more processes called *servers* are responsible for the provision of a service to clients. Services are accessed via a well-defined interface which is made known to the client community. On receipt of a valid request, a server executes the appropriate operation and sends a reply back to the client. This type of interaction is known as a **request/reply** or **interrogation**. Alternatively, an interaction could be initiated by a client resulting in the conveyance of information to the server requesting a function to be performed by the server process. This type of interaction is known as an **announcement** and is clearly one-way communication as no reply is sent back to the client. A client can potentially generate a request for service at any time. A server can have multiple interfaces (e.g. a management interface and a separate interface through which client requests are handled).

Both clients and servers normally run as user processes. A single computer may run a single client or server process or may run multiple client or server processes (or both). A server process is normally persistent (non-terminating) and provides services to more than one client process. Clearly, client/server interaction is based on a request/reply protocol as illustrated in Figure 3.3.

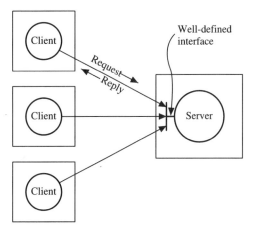

Figure 3.3 Client/server model.

The main distinction between master–slave and client/server models lies in the fact that client and server processes are on an equal footing but with distinct roles. The use of a (small) manageable number of servers (i.e. increased centralization of resources) improves systems management compared with the case where potentially every computer can be configured as client and server. This model, known as a **peer-to-peer** model, is so-named because every process has the same functionality as a peer process as illustrated in Figure 3.4

3.5.3 The group model

Client/server interaction involves two communicating parties: a client and a server. Another model which is appropriate to some types of distributed systems is the **group** model. In many circumstances, a set of processes need to co-operate in such a way that one process may need to send a message to all other processes in the group and receive responses from one or more members. For example, in a video conference involving multiple participants and a whiteboard facility, when someone writes to the whiteboard, every other participant must receive the new image. A second example is a computer conferencing system (e.g. the Internet USENET system). When a subscriber sends a message to a news item, all other subscribers receive it. This is

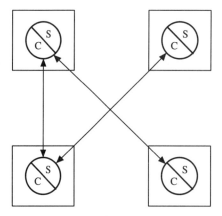

Figure 3.4 Peer-to-peer model: C, client function; S, server function.

modelled conveniently as set of group members which behaves as a single unit called a group. The group model is illustrated in Figure 3.5. When a message is sent to the *group interface*, all members of the group receive it. How does a 'group' message get routed to every member? There are three main approaches (Tanenbaum, 1995), as shown in Figure 3.6:

1. Send a separate copy of the message to be individually routed to each member. This is known as *unicasting*. An implicit assumption is that the sender knows the address of every member in the group. This may not be possible in some systems. In the absence of more sophisticated mechanisms, a system can resort to unicasting if member addresses are known. The number of network transmissions is proportional to the number of members in the group.
2. Send a single message with a *group address* which can be used for routing purposes. This is known as *multicasting* and relies on an underlying multicasting network facility. For example, multicasting is supported in most LAN protocols and the TCP/IP protocol.

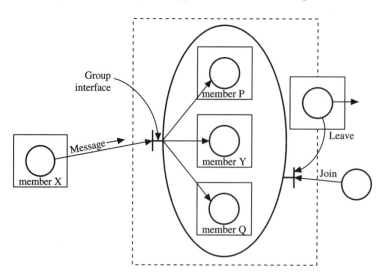

Figure 3.5 Group model.

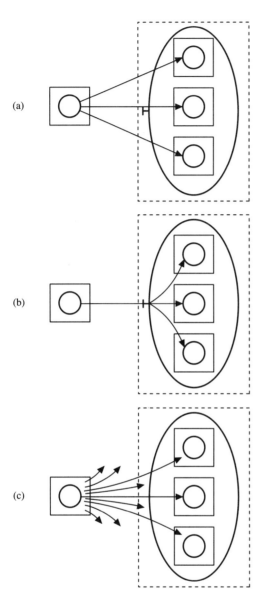

Figure 3.6 Routing group messages: (a) unicast; (b) multicast; (c) broadcast.

When a group is first created it is assigned a unique group address. When a member is added to a group, it is instructed to listen for messages stamped with the group address as well as for its own unique address. This is an efficient mechanism since the number of network transmissions is significantly less than for unicasting.

3. *Broadcast* the message by sending a single message with a broadcast address. The mesage is sent to every possible entity on the network. Every entity must read the message and determine whether they should take action or discard it. This may be an appropriate mechanism in the case when the address of members is not known since most network

protocols implement a broadcast facility. If messages are broadcasted frequently, however, and there is no efficient network broadcast mechanism, the network soon becomes saturated as broadcasts are propagated over an internet (known as a broadcast storm). Therefore broadcast-based group communications do not scale well unless an efficient low-level broadcast facility is available.

In some cases, a group message (e.g. an update request to a group of replica servers) must be received by *all* group members or none at all. Group communication, in this case, is said to be **atomic** or **all-or-nothing**. Achieving atomicity in the presence of failures is difficult, resulting in many more messages being exchanged. Another aspect of group communications is the ordering of group messages. For example, in a computer conferencing system a user would expect to receive the original news item before any response to that item is received. This is known as **ordered multicast** and the requirement to ensure that all multicasts are received in the same order for all group members is common in distributed systems. Atomic multicasting does not guarantee that all messages will be received by group members in the order in which they were sent. Clearly, implementing group communications protocols is non-trivial. An example of a group communication system which addresses ordered multicasts and, to some extent, atomic multicast, is the ISIS system developed at Cornell University (Birman, 1993). In ISIS, broadcast primitives are defined to ensure that all messages arrive in the same order to all parties (e.g. group members) with fault tolerant features. ISIS is described in detail in Tanenbaum (1995); and Coulouris *et al.*(1994).

Often group processes are directly supporting groups of people who are working informally or formally on projects for which co-operation is of mutual benefit. Information system to support computer-supported co-operative (or group) working (commonly abbreviated to CSCW) are commonly based on the group model, and are detailed in Chapter 13.

3.5.4 The distributed object model

The terms *object* and *object-oriented programming* are used ambiguously in the field of computer science which causes much confusion if not appropriately defined. Object technology offers a different programming model from traditional structured programming which is based on the separation of data and the processing of data through functions and procedures. An object is a computational entity which encapsulates both private data describing its state and a set of associated operations (which defines the object's interface to the outside world) as a representation of a real-world object. An object is described in terms of its *attributes* (internal state data) and methods (procedures which operate on the state data).

An object's state is visible only within the object and is completely protected and hidden from other objects as a way of hiding complexity and as a protection from misuse. The only way to examine or modify an object's state data is by sending a *message* to the object which has the effect of invoking one of a well-defined set of methods that define the object's interface to the outside world. Thus without knowing the detail of how an object is implemented, it can be used by simply knowing the methods that define the object's interface. An object may invoke other objects, allowing the creation of a potentially complex web of object invocations, as illustrated in Figure 3.7.

An object-based or object-oriented model is recognized as offering important advantages in the development and maintenance of distributed information systems for the following reasons.

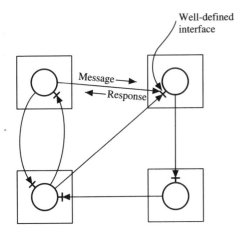

Figure 3.7 Distributed object model.

- Implementation detail is hidden and the use (and re-use) of objects emphasized through the definition of well-defined object interfaces. This can lead to greater development productivity, and reduced software maintenance costs.
- Objects can be written to handle a wide range of media types (including text, voice, animation and video) using essentially the same object interface which provides a consistent approach to handling multimedia objects.
- It provides the foundation for DIS integration into specific line-of-business solutions by re-packaging existing functionality.
- An object is a natural unit of distribution. The message-passing nature of inter-object communications maps easily to a distributed systems environment. A message-passing or RPC remote IPC mechanism can be used to implement the communications channel through which messages can be passed between objects.

A *class* is a template from which objects may be created (every object is therefore an *instance* of some class in as much as a class exists at program compile time, but objects exist at execution time with state representations and associated operations as defined by the class). *Inheritance* is a mechanism that permits new classes to be defined as an extension of another (previously defined) class which provides support for creating new objects by extending existing templates. *Polymorphism* (which means 'many forms') provides the ability for different (but related) objects to share the same method names, thus allowing different objects to be accessed through the same interface. A technique called *overloading* implements polymorphism by ensuring that, even though there may be multiple methods with the same name but different method definitions, the method definition used is one which is appropriate to the type of object involved. The overall effect is, for example, of multiple object types each representing a different media type which can be hidden behind a common object interface (e.g. all objects define open, create, display, print and delete methods but with different method definitions).

Programming languages that support objects as a language feature are known as *object based* and *object oriented* if they also support inheritance. The *sequential* object model is based on the notion of active and passive objects. An object is activated when it receives a message from another object. The object that sent the message becomes passive as control is transferred, and waits for a result. After servicing the message and sending the result, control is transferred to the waiting object which now becomes active and the sender passive. At any instant, only one object in the system is active. This is similar to process activation and passivation.

Current widely-used object-oriented systems usually assume the sequential object model with all objects running in a single name space on a single computer. The distributed object model allows objects to persist in an active state irrespective of whether they have sent a message or received a result. In fact the model allows an object to send messages to multiple objects concurrently and receive results asynchronously.

Programming languages that support distributed objects define an object as the unit of distribution. The distributed object interaction model differs from the client/server model in that an object can both request and provide services (i.e. it can act both as a client and server). In this sense, objects interactions resemble peer-to-peer interactions except that objects can exhibit different functionality. Since each object-to-object interaction is request/reply dialogue, for the purposes of object modelling it can be useful to view an object as a composite client and server assemblage. A popular standard for implementing distributed objects is the Object Management Group's common object request broker architecture (CORBA), which is discussed in Section 3.10.

3.5.5 The multimedia stream model

Modelling of interactions between multimedia objects uses object-oriented and distributed object paradigms. Object-orientation is particularly appropriate as features such as exchanging object references and content-specific operations (using polymorphism) are readily supported. A **multimedia stream** can be described as a continuous medium with a well-defined start and end, which takes place at a defined rate and exhibits unstructured behaviour (Linington, 1994). Thus, *time* is a very important parameter. A stream may be labelled with a set of events which can signify changes in presentation state or used to trigger display actions. A multimedia stream may also have attributes such as the default display size. One important consequence of the encapsulation of potentially diverse, unstructured data is the need to provide the controlling application with more freedom to configure resources to support it. This is covered in Section 3.6.1 where the concept of *explicit binding* is introduced.

A generalized architecture for modelling multimedia data streams is illustrated in Figure 3.8, and incorporates the following concepts (Herbert, 1995; Linington, 1994; ISO, 10746-3).

- A multimedia stream interface is one in which all interactions are **flows**. A flow is an abstraction of a sequence of interactions, resulting in conveyance of information from a

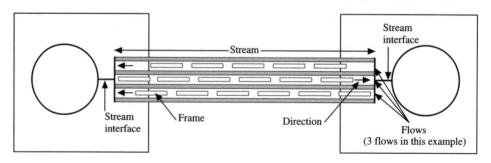

Figure 3.8 Multimedia streams model.

producer object to a **consumer** object. For example, a videoconferencing stream interface may consist of three flows: audio, video and data. In the MIME convention this was modelled as a multipart/parallel content-type (see Figure 2.3).

- Each stream interface comprises a finite set of **action templates**, one for each flow type in the stream interface. Each action template for a flow contains:
  1. the name of the flow;
  2. the information type of the flow (e.g. audio, video or data);
  3. whether it is a consumer or producer (but not both).
- A flow has a set of **frames** (or signals).
- A frame has a name and a set of typed arguments (**attributes**).
- Streams are themselves typed and can be conformance type checked. The analogy here is the content-type field in MIME which can be regarded as indicating the *type* of the MIME stream.
- Frames are transmitted by producer via non-blocking writes and read by consumers via blocking reads. This is analogous to writing frames to a buffer; and application reads from the buffer.

This model provides a flexible approach to modelling multimedia streams.

3.6 REMOTE IPC

In a distributed IT infrastructure, processes interact in a logical sense by exchanging messages across an information network. We refer to this form of communication as *remote IPC*. As with local processes, remote processes are either co-operating to complete a defined task or are competing for the use of a resource. In the physical network remote IPC can be implemented using the message passing paradigm or the shared memory paradigm. Typical remote IPC functions based on the message passing paradigm are:

- process registration for the purposes of identifying communicating processes;
- establishing communication channels between processes;
- reliably routing messages to the destination process;
- synchronization of processes in the case where processes are competing or co-operating in a way that requires it;
- closing down communication channels.

In general, the message passing paradigm is more widely used in commercial systems. Object-oriented concepts naturally embrace the concept of message passing and therefore map easily to message passing or remote procedure calls as remote IPC mechanisms for inter-object communication in a distributed object environment.

3.6.1 Binding

At some point, a process needs to determine the identity of the process with which it desires to establish a connection. This is known as binding. A process generally can be bound to another process at one of two stages:

1. destination processes are identified explicitly at program compile time (and therefore cannot easily be changed). This is known as **static** or **early binding**;

2. source to destination bindings are created, modified and deleted at program run-time. This is known as **dynamic** or **late binding**.

While static binding is the most efficient approach and is most appropriate when a client almost always binds to the same server, in some systems (e.g. accessing external information services) it is often not possible to identify all potential destination processes. Dynamic binding facilitates location and migration transparency when processes are referred to indirectly (e.g. by name) and mapped to the location (address) at run-time. This is often facilitated by a facility, known as a **directory service**, which can be used by the sender to locate a server. When a server is first activated it **exports** information to the directory service regarding the type of service being offered and where it can be located. The sender **imports** its requirements to the directory service, which returns the address of a server which can meet its requirements. This is illustrated in Figure 3.9. This is analogous to finding the telephone number of 'Harry Smith' in a telephone directory and, like the telephone directory enquiry service, is normally implemented as a 'global directory service' that provides this service.

Both binding mechanisms connect source to destination regardless of the quality of connection required by the application. For example, an application may be time sensitive and a slow network link is almost as catastrophic as a network failure. It may be that judicious choice of network connection and protocols and with priority access, a more acceptable quality of service may have been negotiated. This leads to the idea of **explicit binding** which gives applications control over the binding mechanism, allowing negotiation of much more complex configurations to meet a particular application's quality of service requirements. If the requirements cannot be met, the application can take appropriate action. To facilitate explicit binding, each client and server must initiate some negotiation which establishes whether the necessary resources can be marshalled to meet the particular quality of service (QoS) specified (usually by the client). A **binding manager** (also known as a binding object)

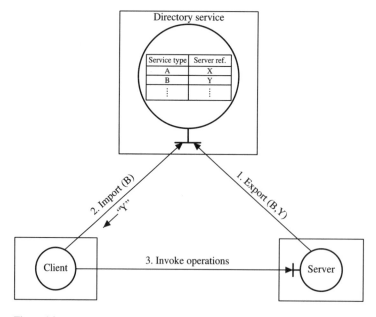

Figure 3.9 Dynamic binding using a directory service.

encapsulates the explicit binding mechanism and is visible to client and server processes. An explicit binding manager: (1) negotiates with other binding managers with a view to matching user quality-of-service requirements to IT infrastructure component capabilities (QoS parameters are crucial as a basis for matching requirements to capabilities); and (2) assists in local resource scheduling and control.

Network-level QoS parameters are discussed in Chapter 4. An example configuration incorporating explicit binding (Herbert, 1995) is given in Figure 3.10.

3.6.2 Connectionless and connection-oriented communication

A consideration when supporting process interactions is whether to establish successful contact first (a connection) with the destination process before any messages are sent. If this **connection-oriented** (also known as *virtual circuit*) approach to IPC is used then it minimizes the overheads of subsequent message transfer by, for example, setting up a routing path during connection which all messages follow avoiding the need to send full addressing information for each subsequent message sent (a connection identifier is used instead which requires fewer bytes). Also it is more straightforward to employ error control, flow control, sequence control and other protocols for enhanced reliability. If the destination process is contacted initially then this is an opportunity for negotiation of some aspects relating to subsequent dialogue. At the end of the dialogue, the connection must be closed down to release network resources. The telephone system is a good example of use of the connection-oriented approach (also known as circuit switching).

However, if a relatively small number of messages are exchanged during a dialogue between co-operating processes then the protocol overhead due to connection establishment and subsequent close down is significant. In this case a **connectionless** (also known as *data grams*) approach is appropriate whereby no initial connection is made; instead, each message

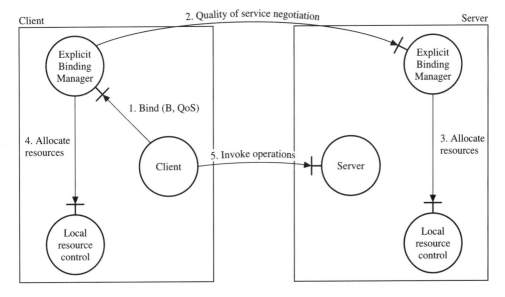

Figure 3.10 An explicit binding mechanism.

is transported as an independent unit of transfer and carries data sufficient for routing from originating process to destination process. The postal system is an example of the use of this approach. The use of elaborate protocols to enhance reliability is normally dispensed with in order to minimize end-to-end transmission delay. Further error control can be achieved using higher-level protocols implemented on the end host computers.

The rule-of-thumb guideline for selecting the most appropriate communication type is to use the connectionless approach when a typical dialogue consists of the exchange of a small number of messages only, otherwise connection-oriented is more efficient. Most practical implementations of message passing support both approaches.

3.6.3 Synchronization

Another consideration in remote IPC mechanisms is whether a process should be delayed (known as *synchronous* or *blocked*) until it receives a response from the destination process. A primitive is *non-blocking* (or *asynchronous*) if its execution never delays the invoking process. Non-blocking primitives must buffer messages to maintain synchronization. Non-blocking clearly maximizes flexibility but often make application development difficult due to the increased complexity of asynchronous time-dependent programs. Synchronization is easy to maintain and programs easier to write when blocking versions of message passing operations are used. When the `send_message` operation is executed, the invoking process is blocked until the receiver actually receives the message. A subsequent `receive_message` operation again blocks the invoking process until a message is actually received. This has the effect of synchronizing sending and receiving processes. Co-operating processes, however, may need to synchronize without using blocking operations. Other more elaborate **distributed co-ordination** approaches are introduced in Chapter 8.

3.7 REMOTE IPC: MESSAGE PASSING

A 'low-level' remote IPC (in as much as the application developer is usually explicitly aware of the message used in communication and the underlying message transport mechanisms used in message exchange) is **message passing.** Processes communicate directly using `send` and `receive` or equivalent language primitives to initiate message transmission and reception, explicitly naming the recipient or sender, for example:

> **send**(message, destination_process)
> **receive**(message, source_process)

This is known as message passing using **direct communication**, and is illustrated in Figure 3.11. Message passing is the most flexible remote IPC mechanism in that it can be used to support all types of process interactions (e.g. client/server, group or distributed object) and underlying transport protocols and can be configured by the application according to the needs of the application.

Another useful technique for identifying co-operating processes is known as **indirect communication**. Here the destination and source identifiers are not process identifiers. Instead, a **port** (also referred to as a **mailbox**) is specified which represents an abstract object at which messages are queued. Potentially, any process can write to a port or read from it. To send a message to a process using this mechanism, the sending process simply issues a send

(a)

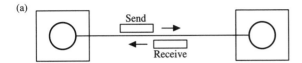

(b)

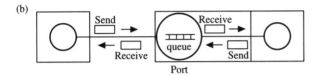

(c)

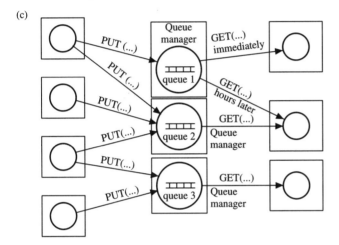

Figure 3.11 Message passing: (a) direct; (b) indirect; (c) message queuing.

operation specifying the **well-known port** number which is associated with the destination process. For example:

```
send(message, destination_port)
receive(message, source_port)
```

Normally, the receiver creates the port (i.e. is the owner). To receive the message, the recipient simply issues a receive specifying the same port number. Security constraints can be introduced by allowing the owning process to specify access control rights on a port. Messages are not lost providing the queue size is adequate for the rate at which messages are being queued and dequeued. Clearly multiple ports can be associated with communication between two processes thus supporting multiple, unidirectional or bi-directional channels. A good example of this approach is the UNIX Sockets IPC which will be examined in the next section. This approach provides the flexibility for programming distributed systems and is used extensively in implementing distributed services.

An extension of message passing by indirect communication is known as **message queuing**. In this higher-level form of message passing, store-and-forward techniques are used to propagate general-purpose messages reliably and asynchronously from a local message queue (usually held on non-volatile storage) to a remote queue associated with the destination process. The creation of message queues and routing of messages is handled by **queue managers**. One significant advantage of message queuing is the ease in which it supports parallel communication with multiple processes. Message queuing also moves much of error handling logic to systems software which is hidden from users.

3.8 CASE STUDY: MESSAGE PASSING USING THE SOCKETS

The sockets programming interface provides a simple way of programming any distributed application using indirect message passing communication. The sockets mechanism is supported by a collection of library functions in popular operating systems such as UNIX. At the simplest level, a socket provides a **file descriptor** object at each end of a communications link. The descriptor can be used with standard operating system read and write primitives in the same way as descriptors are used when reading from and writing to files and pipes. In this way it provides a file-like interface in keeping with the UNIX 'everything is a file' abstraction. Before using the descriptors it is necessary to open the link. The basic operations involved in establishing a link between two applications via a network are:

1. create a socket;
2. bind the socket to a port;
3. connection to the remote program;
4. data transmission.

3.8.1 Creating a socket

A socket is created by the system call socket() and has three parameters:

1. The address format. This specifies, essentially, the addressing domain in which operation is going to take place. Common values almost always supported are AF_UNIX (for local IPC) and AF_INET (for TCP/IP based transport protocols).
2. The communication type. This specifies the type of communications that will be associated with the socket. Common values are SOCK_STREAM (connection-oriented) and SOCK_DGRAM (connectionless datagrams)
3. The protocol to be used. In most cases there is no choice and the parameter is simply set to zero.

    The socket() call will simply return a socket descriptor or an error indication.

3.8.2 Binding to a port

Before a socket can be used sensibly it must be associated with a port. To do this it is first necessary to initialize the components of a suitable structure. If the program is going to initiate a connection (e.g. a client program) then it needs to determine the well-known port number and server address of the associated server process. If the process is a server process then it simply wishes to listen for incoming connections and it issues a bind() call specifying the socket descriptor and the addressing information (including the well-known port number). If the process is a client, the actual binding to the port is performed by the connect() call. In this case, any free port number can be used to make the connection (this is done dynamically by the connect operation when the use of `bind()` is omitted). The only port number that both ends must agree on is the server's.

3.8.3 Accepting client connections

If connection-oriented mode has been set, a server process must accept incoming connections explicitly. Two routines are involved. The first is `listen()` which returns when a connection request is pending on the socket and the second, `accept()`, which returns a new descriptor which is used in all subsequent reads and writes. The listen routine has two parameters, the first is the socket number (socket descriptor), the second is the maximum allowable number of pending client requests (used for concurrency control). The accept routine has three parameters, the first is the descriptor of the original socket associated with `listen()`, the second is the object containing details of the communicating entity (the requesting client), and the third parameter is the size of the object. The return value of `accept()` is the descriptor associated with the socket described by the second parameter.

3.8.4 Data transmission

Once a connection has been established normal `read()` and `write()` calls may be used. Alternatively the remote IPC specific operations `send()` and `recv()` may be used. When data transmission is complete `close()` must be used to close the connection (otherwise the server will very quickly run out of resources). When one end of a communications link is closed then the next read on the other end will return a zero. It is possible (by use of `ioctl()`) to put a socket in *non-blocking* mode. If this is done, a read with no data available (i.e. no message has been received) returns immediately with the value zero and errno is set appropriately. Sample client and server 'C' program fragments are given in Figures 3.12 and 3.13. All global data type definitions and function prototypes are included in the 'bank.h' header file. The client program simply creates a socket and sends a message requesting execution of the *deposit* operation. The server program must listen for requests and service them accordingly. This is carried out in four stages:

1. *Open the well-known port.* This opens the communication channel through which client requests are received.
2. *Wait for client requests.* The server listens for client requests.
3. *Process client request.* A client request is received. The server allocates (subject to authorization and protection rules) a local port for this request and spawns an independent process to execute the program code associated with the request and generate the reply.

```
#include "bank.h"
void main(void)
{
fd = socket(transport, CO, 0);              /* connection-oriented socket*/
connect(fd, &outport, sizeof(outport));     /* connect using dynamic port*/
write(fd, deposit_req, sizeof(deposit_req));/* send deposit request*/
close(fd);
}
```

Figure 3.12 An example client.

```
#include "bank.h"
void main(void)
{
    int  listen_fd;                                    /* descriptor for socket                 */
    int  source_fd;                                    /* new descriptor returned by accept() */
    listen_fd = socket(transport, co, 0)               /* create socket                         */
    bind(listen_fd, &outport,sizeof(outport)           /* bind socket to well-known port 1234 */
    listen(listen_fd,2)                                /* listen for client connection          */
    while (1)  {                                       /* accept client requests forever        */
        source_fd=accept(listen_fd,&newsock,&len);  /* accept client connection                 */
        read(source_fd, msg, MSGSIZE);                 /* read message sent by client           */
        switch(msg.opcode)  {                          /* do request                            */
        case deposit:                                  rlt = deposit(&msg, &opresult);break;
        case withdrawal:                               rlt = withdrawal(&msg, &opresult); break;
        default:
        }
    write(source_fd, opresult, sizeof (opresult));/* send operation result to client      */
    close (source_fd)
    }
}
```

Figure 3.13 A sample server.

4. *Wait for next client request.* The server again listens for the next client request while the independent process is handling the current request.

The number of concurrent client requests being handled is limited only by the capabilities of the native operating system, performance considerations and the nature of the client/server application.

3.8.5 Connectionless (datagrams) communication

The programs shown use connection-oriented communications. This requires the explicit use of `connect()`, `listen()` and `accept()` routines to establish a connection before data transmission. If the socket is of type SOCK_DGRAM then an initial connection is not necessary. If the socket is in the connected state then the routine `send()` may be used, if not, `sendto()` may be used. The `sendto()` routine takes both the message body and the destination address as parameters. If the socket is in the connected state, the routine `recv()` may be used to receive the next incoming data item. If the socket is not connected, the `recvfrom()` routine may be used to receive the next incoming item, optionally specifying that data can only be received from a particular system. As an alternative to the above mechanism for connectionless communication, data structured according to the predefined rules may be used in conjunction with the `sendmsg()` and `recvmsg()` routines.

3.8.6 Multi-threading – support for multiple clients

The sample server program does not handle efficiently multiple simultaneous requests to the port number. This is because the server wrapper that handles incoming requests is suspended while a client request is being handled. A simple solution to this problem is to use another thread, or (in the absence of multi-threading) a process spawning mechanism such as the UNIX `fork()` call. The new thread (or child process) is created each time a new client request is received. It simply executes an `accept()` the connection request, processes the request, sends the results to the client and terminates.

3.9 REMOTE IPC: THE REMOTE PROCEDURE CALL

The client/server model is essentially a request/reply interaction. This interaction is very similar to the traditional procedure call in a high-level programming language except that the caller and procedure to be executed are on a different computer. A procedure call mechanism which permits the calling and called procedures to be running on different computers is known as a **remote procedure call** (RPC) (Birrell and Nelson, 1984). RPC is a popular mechanism for developing distributed systems because it looks and behaves like a well- understood, conventional procedure call in a high-level language (all programmers are familiar with the concept of calling a subroutine or procedure). A procedure call has proved to be an effective tool for implementing abstraction since to use a procedure all one needs to know is the name of the procedure and the arguments associated with it. RPC is therefore a remote operation with call semantics similar to a local procedure call, and can provide a degree of:

- access transparency since a call to a remote procedure may be similar to a call to a local procedure. In practice, there will be differences in semantics due to the need, for example, to handle a wider variety of exceptions;
- location transparency since the developer can refer to the procedure by name, unaware of where exactly the remote procedure is located;
- synchronization between processes since the process invoking the RPC call is normally suspended (blocked) until the remote procedure is completed, just as in a call to a local procedure.

An RPC protocol is implemented in the following way (see Figure 3.14):

1. When a process makes an RPC call (e.g. `RemoteProcX (x,y,z, result)`), the address of the server process is first determined (e.g. via a directory service). The call parameters x, y and z are packed into a data structure suitable for transfer across the network. This is called marshalling. These steps could be carried out by the client process, but to simplify the RPC interface from the perspective of the application developer, the potentially complex steps of name resolution and marshalling are carried out by a special procedure called the *client stub*.
2. The data is then passed to lower level RPC transport protocol (e.g. message passing using `Send` and `Receive` primitives) for transporting the RPC call and call parameters across the network.
3. The server process unmarshalls the call parameters from the data structure in a form suiable for making a local procedure call. The server process has an associated *server stub* that carries this out transparent to the server process.
4. The call is then made to the required procedure (in this case `RemoteProcX(x,y,z)`).
5. The procedure result is marshalled by the server stub and sent back across the network to the client process using the same low-level RPC transport protocol (e.g. `Send`).
6. The client stub unmarshalls the result and passes the result (and control) back to the client process.

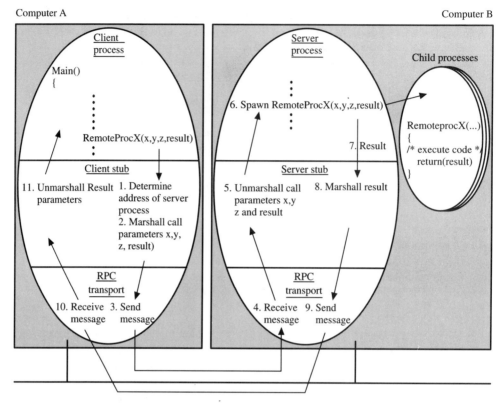

Figure 3.14 The remote procedure call (RPC) process.

3.9.1 RPC exceptions

The above mechanism, however, needs to cope with a wider range of exceptions than is typical of a local procedure call. For example:

- what if parameters x,y and z are either global variables or pointers? Many programming languages can support parameter passing using call-by-value (a copy of data is passed) or call-by-reference (a pointer to the data item is passed);
- what if there are differences in the way that client and server computers represent integers, floating point and other data types?
- what if the RPC call fails? Can the call be recovered?
- is the client authorized to call the named procedure?

Marshalling is complicated by use of global variables and pointers as they only have meaning in the client's address space. Client and server processes run in separate address spaces on separate machines. One solution may be to pass the data held by the global variable or pointed to by the pointer. However, there are cases when this will not suffice, for example, when a linked list data structure is being passed to a procedure that manipulates the list.

Differences in data representation can be overcome by use of an agreed language for representing the data being passed between client and server processes. For example, a common syntax for describing the structure and encoding of data, known as **abstract syntax notation** (ASN.1) (ISO 8824) was defined by as an international standard by the International Organization for Standardization (ISO) for this purpose. ASN.1 is very similar to the data declaration statements in a high-level programming language, and a useful description is found in Tang and Scoggins (1992). Marshalling is then a case of converting the data types from the machine's representation to a standard representation (e.g. ASN.1) before transmission. At the other end, the data is converted from the standard to the machine's internal representation.

3.9.2 Failure handling

RPC failures can be difficult to handle. There are four generalized types of failure that can occur when a RPC call is made:

1. the client request message gets lost;
2. the client process fails while the server is processing the request;
3. the server process fails while servicing the request;
4. the reply message is lost.

If the client message gets lost then the client will wait forever unless a time-out/retry error detection mechanism is employed. If the client process fails, the server will carry out the remote operation unnecessarily. If the operation involves updating a data value (e.g. updating bank account details) then this can result in loss of data integrity. Furthermore, the server would generate a reply to a client process that does not exist. This must be discarded by the client machine's communication system. When the client process re-starts, it may send the request again (as if for the first time) causing the server to execute the same operation more than once.

A similar situation arises when the server crashes. The server could crash just prior to execution of the remote operation or just after execution completes but before a reply to the client is generated. In this case, clients will time-out and continually generate retries until either the server restarts or the retry limit is met.

3.9.3 Execution semantics

The number of times a remote procedure executed can be difficult to determine in the presence of failures. Three kinds of RPC execution semantics are defined which can be guaranteed by a particular RPC mechanism in failure situations:

- At-most-once semantics: the RPC mechanism guarantees that the remote procedure is either never executed or executed partially or once. This requires the server to keep track of invocation identifiers of all procedures previously executed to avoid duplication.
- Exactly-once semantics: the RPC mechanism guarantees that the remote procedure is executed exactly once. This is difficult to achieve given the nature of failures which may occur.
- At-least-once semantics: the RPC mechanism guarantees that the remote procedure is executed at least partially or once. This is easily achieved by re-requesting remote procedure execution if failures occur. Clearly, at-least-once semantics is appropriate only if executing a remote procedure once has exactly the same outcome as executing the same request multiple times. An operation with this characteristic is said to be **idempotent**. An example of an idempotent operation is a `read` operation on a data file. Any operation which does not change the state of remote data can be classed as idempotent.

- Transactional (zero-or-once) semantics: the RPC mechanism guarantees that the remote procedure is either never executed or executed once. This requires the server to keep track of invocation identifiers of all procedures previously executed to avoid duplication. The server must also ensure that state data is either updated permanently by an operation taking it from one consistent state to another, or that it is left in its original state if the operation is aborted. This type of RPC is commonly known as **transactional RPC**. Transactional operations are described in greater detail in Chapter 9.

Ensuring that a remote operation is carried out exactly once is difficult under these circumstances. The server needs to distinguish between new requests and duplicate requests for execution of an operation that has been completed already. This state data must remain consistent despite client and server crashes or lost messages in order to ensure at-most-once RPC semantics. Many servers do not retain state data and are therefore known as 'stateless' servers. In this case, clients are responsible for retaining state data on past requests (e.g. the value of the read-write pointer in file operations). Stateless servers can at best support only at-least-once RPC semantics.

The complexity of error recovery is reduced when it can be assumed that requests are idempotent, since the simpler to implement at-least-once RPC semantics can be implemented effectively. For example, a number of distributed file server protocols (e.g. Sun Microsystems' NFS) are designed to assume that all requests such as file open, read, write, delete, etc. exhibit idempotent behaviour (strictly speaking some operations are not idempotent but can be written to exhibit idempotent behaviour). The stateless servers and at-least-once RPC semantics are implemented to avoid the protocol overhead associated with suppressing duplicate requests after recovering from a failure. However, stateless servers do not cope well with concurrent access as concurrency control requires the retention of state data to facilitate locking.

At-most-once RPC semantics can be achieved only if both client and server reliably detect failure conditions. Use of techniques such as sequence control, connection-oriented RPC transport services and retention of state data to maintain mutual state and so on, implies a significant protocol overhead. However, these techniques must be implemented if non-idempotent requests are to be supported successfully.

In the discussion so far, we have assumed that any client can invoke any remote operation on any server via an RPC mechanism. In practice, before a remote operation is executed by a server, they should authenticate each other. This requires a sub-dialogue that is initiated when the server receives a client request. The sub-dialogue may involve the use of an 'authentication server' and uses encryption techniques for further security. This requires both the client and server to maintain state data for security purposes which means that sophisticated security techniques require stateful servers. Security issues are examined in Chapter 13 where an authenticated RPC mechanism is explored.

3.10 CASE STUDY: DCE RPC

It is clear from the above discussion that there are many problems to be overcome when implementing an RPC mechanism. These problems complicate the basic RPC calls from the perspective of an application developer. This is eased by the use of client and server stubs to hide much of the complexity. However, to enable proper and efficient client and server stub generation, the RPC calls must provide much more information than is associated with a local procedure call. Use of RPC mechanisms is simplified by the use of an **interface definition language** (IDL) to describe the server object interface by specifying the operations, parameters and data types required to implement the interface. The IDL file containing IDL statements is converted into client and server stubs by an IDL compiler. This process is illustrated in Figure 3.15.

DIS development is simplified by concentrating on specifying the interface in the IDL and writing the client-side processing objects to the IDL file interface definition. The client object does not need to know *how* the remote operations are implemented. If the application developer is developing the server objects, each operation implementation must be supplied.

To illustrate the use of an IDL and the process of developing a distributed application at this level, we examine the RPC mechanism defined by the Open Software Foundation's Distributed

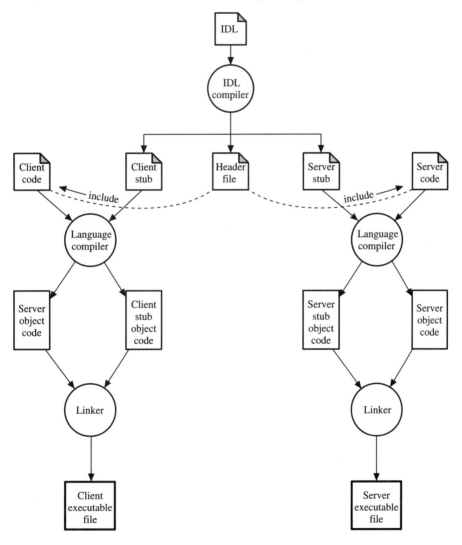

Figure 3.15 Steps to develop client and server programs using an IDL file.

Computing Environment (OSF/DCE). RPC has a strong association with implementing client/server applications, although client/server interactions can equally be implemented using message passing. However, it is usually the case that an RPC mechanism is used by application processing and application support functions, and a message passing mechanism is used to build the RPC mechanism because RPC is at a higher level of abstraction.

Although programming RPC interaction is more straightforward than message passing, it is still a demanding task for an application developer. It is for this reason that application processing functions do not generally use RPC but utilize simpler application programming interfaces supplied by application support functions (e.g. file and print services). The application support functions make direct use of an RPC mechanism to support remote IPC in implementing the various transparency support services. Remote IPC between application processing objects can be largely described using a high level IDL. Most of the complexity of generating the underlying network dependent functions can be automated by the IDL compilation and linking process.

A sample IDL in DCE RPC and client code fragment for the Bank service are shown in Figures 3.16 and 3.17. It is evident that DCE IDL closely matches the C programming language syntax and semantics. A binding handle contains all the information needed to connect to a particular bank server. A bank server is found by executing an import_interface operation which uses a DCE service (the DCE cell directory service) to locate it. Note that the call to the server-based deposit operation is almost like a local function call except for a few extra parameters. In general, an IDL almost gives sufficient information to enable a client to utilize a service described by the interface. Additional information such as the binding mechanisms required and the mapping to a specific language, is not detailed in an IDL and is specific to the RPC implementation.

```
/* Bank.idl  */

interface bank
{
    typedef [string, ptr] char *acct_t          /* define a datatype for      */
                                                    account name
    void deposit(
      [in] handle_t        binding_handle,       /* binding handle to Bank     */
                                                    server
      [in] acct_t          acct,                 /* IN acct parameter:         */
                                                    account number
      [in] unsigned32      amount,               /* IN amount parameter:       */
      [out] float          balance               /* OUT balance parameter:     */
                                                    new balance
};
    void withdrawal(
      [in] handle_t        binding_handle,       /* binding handle to Bank     */
                                                    server
      [in] acct_t          acct,                 /* IN acct parameter:         */
                                                    account number
      [in] unsigned32      amount,               /* IN amount parameter:       */
                                                    amount to deposit
      [out] float          balance               /* OUT balance parameter:     */
                                                    new balance
    };
}
```

Figure 3.16 An example DCE RPC IDL file for the Bank service.

```
#include "bank.h"
void main(void)
{
    rpc_binding_handle_t      binding_h = NULL;      /* binding handle to bank       */
                                                         server
    unsigned_char_t           acct;                  /* acct: account number         */
                                                        supplied by the user
    unsigned32                amount;                /* amount: amount value         */
                                                        supplied by the user
    float                     balance;               /* balance: balance value       */
                                                        returned by the server
    unsigned32                dce_status;            /* status code returned by      */
                                                        DCE
    unsigned32                opresult;              /* status code returned by      */
                                                        the bank server
    int                       option;                /* selection option             */

    do
    {
        printf ("1.  Deposit\n");                    /* display menu                 */
        printf("2.   Withdrawal\n");
        printf("3.    Exit\n");
        printf("\nPlease select an option: ");

        scanf("%d", &selection);                     /* get selection                */
        switch(option)                               /* do request                   */
        {
          case 1:  /*Deposit*/  /* deposit request   */
              import_interface(                      /* bind to any bank server      */
                          "bank",                    /* name of interface            */
                          bank_v1.0_c_ifspec,        /* context                      */
                          &binding_h,                /* will contain the handle      */
                                                        for the bank server
                          &dce_status);              /* DCE return code for the      */
                                                        operation
              get_data(acct, &amount);               /* prompt user for acct and     */
                                                        amount values

              deposit(binding_h, acct, amount, &balance, &opresult, &dce_status);    break;
                      printf ("New bank balance is %d ", &balance);

          case 2:  /*Withdrawal*/                    /* withdrawal request           */
              import_interface(                      /* bind to any bank server      */
                          "bank",                    /* name of interface            */
                          bank_v1.0_c_ifspec,        /* context                      */
                          &binding_h,                /* will contain the handle      */
                                                        for the bank server
              &dce_status);                          /* DCE return code for the      */
                                                        operation
          get_data(acct, &amount);                   /* prompt user for acct and     */
                                                        amount values

        withdrawal(binding_h, acct, amount, &balance, &opresult, &dce_status);    break;
        printf ("New bank balance is %d ", &balance);

      case 3: /* Exit */
            break;
      default: /* any other option */
            printf("Invalid option.  Try again.\n\n");
    }
    } while (option != 3);   /* redisplay menu until                                  */
                                option 3 (exit) is selected
```

Figure 3.17 An example DCE client which calls Bank server operations.

3.11 CASE STUDY: DEVELOPING DISTRIBUTED SYSTEMS USING CORBA OBJECTS

An ideal implementation of a distributed object model provides the programmer with facilities for writing a distributed object-oriented system in the same manner as a centralized object-oriented system but with transparency functions (e.g. a global name service for location transparency) that manage object distribution at run-time (through client and server stub procedures). The transparency and other functions for managing distributed objects are collectively known as *distributed object management*. Distributed object management services must provide support for synchronization of multiple, concurrent object execution, for protecting objects against unauthorized access, for recovery from partial failures, for ensuring the integrity of modification to the state data of persistent objects and so on. Typical object management functions are:

- Class management. Create, modify, delete, copy, distribute, describe, and control definitions of classes, the interface to classes, and relationships between class definitions.
- Instance management. Create, modify, delete, copy, move, invoke, and control objects and the relationship between objects.
- Object storage. The provision of permanent or transient storage for large and small objects, including their state and operations (methods).
- Integrity. To ensure the consistency and integrity of object state both within single objects (e.g. through locks) and among objects (through transaction mechanisms).
- Security. To provide (define or enforce) access constraints on objects and their components.
- Query. The ability to select objects or classes from implicitly or explicitly identified collections based on some selection criteria.

The Object Management Group (OMG), a non-profit industry consortium founded in 1989 supported by major computer vendors, some end-users and some research organizations, aims to promote the use of distributed object technology in software development by stimulating a unified market for products. OMG developed a single architecture which can be used to develop technology for developing distributed object-oriented information systems in a heterogeneous environment. Its charter includes:

- to establish industry guidelines;
- to develop object management specifications to provide a common framework for application development.

Conformance to these specifications will make it possible to develop distributed information systems in a heterogeneous environment consisting of different hardware platforms and operating systems. The OMG defines 'object management' as software development that models the real world through representation of objects. CORBA technology can be used to implement both fine-grained and coarse-grained DISs. The use of object technology (object-orientation) is widespread and growing. OMG's objective is to influence the following:

- standards development, by defining an overall architecture and reference model known as the Object Management Architecture (OMA);
- application programming interfaces (APIs) for objects and applications: across DOS, OS/2, UNIX, etc.;
- distributed object management service standards.

3.11.1 CORBA distributed objects

To an application developer using CORBA-based object technology, logically the world looks like a sea of objects. Physically, an object can potentially be placed anywhere within a distributed IT infrastructure. A special component called the object request broker (ORB) is responsible for making distribution transparent and providing a mechanism for trading. Objects use the ORB to make and receive requests and responses to other objects transparently. Each CORBA object has an *object reference* which uniquely identifies an object regardless of its names (an object can have several names). An object references another object by specifying an operation name, the target object reference and zero or more parameters. In addition, a request context can be passed to give data about the nature of the request which may affect performance of the request. The outcome of a request is either results or an exception. Request parameters may be classed as IN (passed from client to server), OUT (passed from server to client) or IN/OUT. An object's interface is specified by defining a set of operation signatures which defines the type of requests that can be made on an object satisfying that interface. Operation invocations are synchronous, request/reply mechanisms, but a (unreliable) one-way invocation mechanism is also available. An operation signature identifies:

- the operation name;
- parameter types and directions (IN, OUT or IN/OUT);
- a specification of the result of the operation;
- a specification of the exceptions that may be raised and the types of the parameters accompanying them;
- a specification of additional contextual data that may affect performance of the request;
- an indication of the execution semantics the client (requester) should expect when invoking the operation. The OMG object model defines two styles of execution semantics: at-most-once or best-effort (request-only).

OMG defined an interface definition language (IDL) which is used to describe the interfaces that client objects call and object implementations (server objects) provide (OMG, 1994). The CORBA IDL obeys a subset of the C++ language grammar and the same lexical rules with additional keywords to support the object distribution concepts defined in the OMG object model. An example IDL for the Bank example featured in the previous sections is given in Figure 3.18. Pre-processing of an IDL file generates a client stub, a server implementation skeleton (which is used by the ORB to make calls to method implementations) and header file (e.g. bank.h) containing relevant declarations.

The 'C' program code fragment in Figure 3.19 shows how to invoke an operation and recover from a user-defined exception or a standard exception (i.e. a defined set of exception names which may be returned as a result of any operation invocation). Standard exceptions may not be listed in **raises** expressions in an IDL file. Client stubs allow applications access to the IDL-defined operations using a syntax (and semantics) that is easy for programmers to use once they are familiar with the IDL language rules and the mapping for the particular programming language as demonstrated in Figure 3.19. CORBA maps more naturally to an object-oriented language such as C++. Client stubs make calls to the ORB on behalf of the client operation using ORB-specific core operations. The ORB calls the appropriate object operation via the corresponding implementation skeleton. An object implementation

```
interface bank{                               // define interface called BANK
     typedef unsigned long Number;            // define datatype called Number
     exception OpResult {string<80> OpReason;}; // signature for exception operation
     void deposit (                           // signature for deposit operation
                    in string acct,           // IN acct parameter: account number
                    in Number amount,         // IN amount parameter: amount to
                                              //    deposit
                    out float balance)        // OUT balance parameter: new balance
                    raises (OpResult)         // user-defined exception for deposit
                    context (contextX);       // context which may affect
                                              //    performance
     void withdraw (                          // signature for withdraw operation
                    in string acct,           // IN acct parameter: account number
                    in Number amount,         // IN amount parameter: amount to
                                              //    deposit
                    out float balance)        // OUT balance parameter: new balance
                    raises (OpResult)         // user-defined exception for deposit
                    context (contextX);       // context which may affect
                                              //    performance

}
```

Figure 3.18 Bank interface definition using CORBA IDL.

```
#include "bank.h"                             /* contains bank object         */
                                              /*  declarations

Environment              ev;                  /* holds result information     */
Context                  ctxt;                /* context name declaration     */
bank                     bank_ref;            /* holds the bank object        */
                                              /*  reference
bank_deposit (bank_ref, &ev, &ctxt, acct, amount,  /* call the deposit operation   */
     &balance);
switch (ev._major) {                          /* check response               */
     case NO_EXCEPTION:                       /* deposit was successful       */
     /*   process any out and inout arguments                                 */
     printf ("New bank balance is %d ", &balance);  /* print new balance      */
     break;
case USER_EXCEPTION:                          /* an exception was raised      */
/*  handle exception condition                                                */
     break;
default:                                      /* a system exception was raised */
/*  handle standard exception  condition                                      */
     break;
}
```

Figure 3.19 Invoking the Deposit operation of a bank object from a client program.

normally accesses services provided by an ORB through a special object called an *object adapter*. Object adapters provide access to ORB services including:

● generation and interpretation of object references;
● method invocation;
● security of interactions;
● object and implementation activation and deactivation;

- mapping object references to implementations;
- registration of implementations.

When a client sends a message to a remote object server the object adapter on the server needs to invoke the appropriate method. To achieve this, the adapter needs to handle two types of activations: object implementation and object activations. Object implementation is required when no implementation for an object is currently available to handle the request. An object activation is required when no instance of an object is available to handle the request. An object implementation is activated by starting a server process which executes a program containing the object implementation. This is illustrated in Figure 3.20. Several types of CORBA object servers can be implemented which are distinguished by an *activation policy* which defines how object implementation and object activation are handled.

- *Shared server policy*, where multiple objects are implemented by the same program. An object adapter activates a server process the first time one of the objects receives a request. The adapter subsequently delivers method and object activation requests to any active object in the server.
- *Unshared server policy*, where an object implementation can be activated only once per server process. This is commonly used when an object represents a single application or requires exclusive access to a resource.
- *Per-method server policy*, where a new server process is started dynamically for the duration of each method execution in response to a method request. Thus each server process executes a method then terminates.
- *Persistent server policy*, is similar to the shared server policy except that server process start-up is initiated outside of the object adapter followed by adapter registration indicating that it is active. The adapter is still responsible for routing method requests to it. If no server process exists when a request arrives, an error message is sent back to the requesting object.

The type of server implementation therefore determines the type of response a requesting object can expect when a message is sent to another object and determines how object implementations are handled.

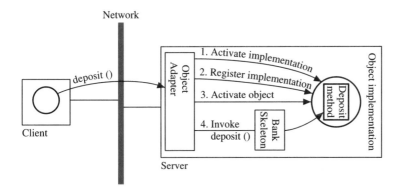

Figure 3.20 CORBA object adapter mechanism.

3.12 SUMMARY

In this chapter the basic concepts of distributed processing have been explored. Six models for structuring a distributed system were identified: master–slave, client/server, peer-to-peer, group, multimedia stream and the distributed object model. The issues of identifying processes, remote IPC, process synchronization and remote operations are all fundamental to the successful implementation of a DIS. The message passing and RPC mechanisms provide the basic techniques for implementing a distributed system according to a specific model (e.g. the client/server model). The distributed object model provides an alternative paradigm for designing and implementing distributed systems. An object is a natural unit of distribution. Implementing a DIS using these mechanisms, however, is very challenging for an application developer. In practice much of the requirements can be specified in an interface definition language from which much of the required program code can be generated automatically by pre-processors much in the same way as visual programming environments which are available for more conventional environments. Message passing and RPC remain the most common underlying (low-level) mechanisms for supporting inter-process and inter-object interactions.

3.13 REVIEW EXERCISES

1. What are the advantages and disadvantages of threads over the use of multiple processes in implementing distributed systems?
2. Describe four commonly used methods of implementing inter-process communication in the case when all communicating processes are executing on the same computer.
3. Compare and contrast five models for structuring a distributed system.
4. What is the objective of remote IPC? Compare and contrast message passing with a remote procedure call (RPC) mechanism.
5. What problems can arise when either the client, network or server fails during a remote procedure call? Discuss the different types of execution semantics an RPC mechanism may offer.
6. Design and implement a simple program which implements two functions called `Echo` and `Reverse` which takes a string and returns the same string or the reversed string, respectively. Test the functions by implementing a test program. Using any message passing facility available to you, restructure the program using the client/server model and implement both the client and server components. Reflect on the additional programmer effort required to implement the client/server based application.
7. Describe the use of an interface definition language in an RPC mechanism. Define the client/server program in Question 6 using the DCE interface definition language described in Section 3.10.
8. Programming languages commonly support global variable declarations and call-by-reference parameter passing. What problems do these pose when implementing an RPC mechanism?
9. Implement the client/server program written in Question 6 using an RPC facility.
10. Why may RPC be a more suitable mechanism for implementing client/server software than message passing?
11. Why is the client/server model more widely utilized than the peer-to-peer model?
12. Give example applications which would benefit from being implemented using facilities which support the group model.

13. What problems arise when implementing group communication mechanisms?
14. Discuss the similarities and differences between the client/server model and the master–slave model.
15. Discuss the similarities and differences between the client/server model and the distributed object model.
16. Describe the program in Question 6 using the CORBA IDL.

3.14 FURTHER READING

For an in-depth treatment of interprocess communication issues see Mullender (1993). Coulouris *et al*. (1994) and Tanenbaum (1995) provide excellent coverage of RPC, distributed operating systems, group communications, and synchronization issues. For a good text on distributed programming see Brown (1994). It covers pipes, shared memory, message queues, semaphores, threads, sockets and RPC. Birman (1993) contains a detailed description of the ISIS toolkit for reliable group communications. Bever *et al*. (1993) and OSF (1992) give a good introduction to DCE, and Shirley (1992) provides a detailed tutorial on writing DCE server and client programs.

PART TWO

Internetworking

NETWORK TECHNOLOGIES – BACKBONE NETWORKS

4.1 INTRODUCTION

In communication of any type we can identify four basic components: a message, a sender, a receiver and a communications channel over which messages are sent from sender to receiver. To illustrate this, consider a telephone connection. In this case the sender and receiver are human beings which utilize a telephone handset as the sending/receiving device. The communication medium is the telephone line. The handsets are required to encode messages in a form suitable for transmission over the communication channel (e.g. copper wire). In any physical system, faults occur due to the imperfections which are inherent in the components which make up the physical system. A **network protocol** defines rules and techniques for successful message transmission, masking (hiding) some failures so that the system behaves as if these failures are not present. In this section we will briefly introduce important concepts underpinning this part of the book. There are many sources for further detail, for example Sloane (1994), Halsall (1992) and Stallings (1994).

Five types of media commonly used to implement a communications channel are illustrated in Figure 4.1 on page 82. In twisted pair copper cable, two single wires, each encased in colour coded plastic insulation, are twisted together to form a pair. Multiple pairs are bundled together surrounded by outer insulation. Twisted pair cable is very susceptible to electromagnetic interference (EMI) from nearby circuits (known as near-end cross-talk) and electrical equipment such as photocopiers and fluorescent lighting. Some twisted pairs, known as **shielded twisted pair** (STP) contain a metal shield for further protection (ordinary twisted pair is known as **unshielded twisted pair** (UTP)). UTP cables dominate buildings, carrying voice and data traffic. **Coaxial cable** consists of four parts: an inner conductor which carries the signal, a protective plastic coating, shielding and outer insulation. This construction

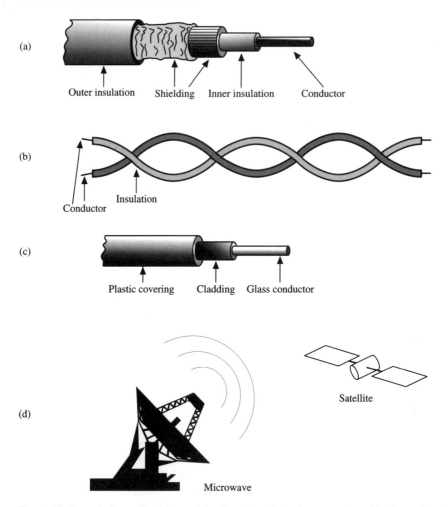

Figure 4.1 Transmission media: (a) co-axial cable; (b) twisted-pair copper wires; (c) fibre optic cable; (d) radio transmission over free space.

results in much better electrical characteristics suitable for high speed transmission over long distances. Various forms and combinations of inner and outer conductor (shielding) is used for different types of connections and speed requirements. **Optical fibre** cable consists of thin strands of transparent and translucent glass through which **light** from a laser or light-emitting diode (LED) is transmitted. The light is guided through the cable by internal reflections caused by the characteristics of the cable. As light rather than an electrical signal is used, the signal is not distorted by EMI. The major drawback of optical fibre is the cost of implementation compared with UTP/STP and coaxial cable. Many networks employ **radio signals** over free space to transfer both voice, video and data messages. Radio transmission provides high transmission capacity without the location inflexibility associated with cabling, but can be blocked by metallic objects or severely affected by interference.

Information networks have matured rapidly from a basic facility to enable remote terminals and printers to be connected to a mainframe, through to complex, multi-protocol, integrated infrastructures. With the move to distributed systems, an information network infrastructure is now a critical facility; the *central nervous system* of an organization.

The term 'enterprise network' is used to refer to an information network (small or large) defined to meet the needs of a specific organization, entity, or user community. Thus an enterprise network could be a multi-segment LAN within a single building, a campus network, or a world-wide network infrastructure for a multinational organization. Whatever its shape, the enterprise network needs to be flexible enough to cope with future growth, possibly operating on a world-wide basis, and freeing workers to work from any location, while providing access to corporate, departmental, workgroup and personal information.

Enterprise networks are not usually designed from a blank sheet in a top-down fashion but evolve over time by interconnecting existing separate networks. The interconnection of separate networks is typically required to enable end-user access to resources and information services not available on the local network. An enterprise network capable of satisfying an organization's long-term needs to exhibit the following characteristics:

- **Accessibility**: all resources required by a user should be accessible.
- **Extendibility**: the network must be designed so that it can be extended easily to incorporate new technologies and features.
- **Scalability**: a scalable network infrastructure is one that can cope easily and efficiently with the addition of users and sites.
- **Reliability**: organizations are becoming increasingly dependent on the enterprise network to support the business.
- **Performance**: the throughput and performance must match end-user and application quality-of-service requirements.
- **Security**: transmission must take place in a secure environment.
- **Ease-of-management**: the network must be manageable.

In this and subsequent chapters the network options available to build an enterprise network are examined. The successful deployment of an enterprise network depends on effective design and implementation of two basic building blocks:

1. **Access networks**, which connect end-user workstations and other local equipment. Access technologies are designed to meet the need for efficient information exchange within a single site, and to provide a gateway to off-site resources and information services.
2. **Backbone networks** that support the interconnection of access networks to facilitate information exchange between user endpoints located on different sites.

Access network technologies are described in Chapter 5. A backbone network interconnects access networks to enable enterprise-level and inter-organizational information exchanges. In this chapter various technology options for implementing backbone networks are examined. A distributed IT infrastructure is commonly structured using the client/server model. The client/server model will be assumed in this book unless stated otherwise.

4.1.1 Communication requirements

The primary purpose of an enterprise network is to enable local client application processes to exchange information with local and remote server processes. Information is exchanged in logical data units called **messages** which are usually of variable length. Sending and receiving devices can be connected together in one of a variety of ways. A **network topology** is a

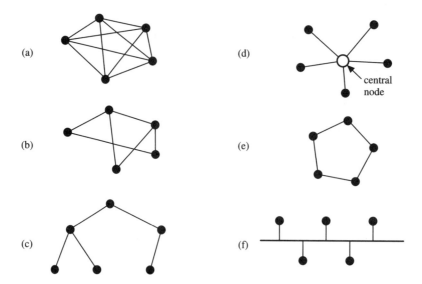

Figure 4.2 Network topologies: (a) Fully connected; (b) partially connected; (c) tree connected; (d) star; (e) ring; (f) bus.

particular arrangement of devices and links between them for the purposes of communication. Some common topologies are illustrated in Figure 4.2. There are three fundamental approaches to message exchange over a particular topological arrangement:

1. A **broadcast** technique, typical of radio and television services, where all devices in the network can receive transmissions regardless of their origin. The sending device simply 'broadcasts' the message on a shared communications channel. Transmissions are received through the channel by all connected devices. With appropriate logic at the destination device, all irrelevant transmissions (e.g. transmissions that do not contain the correct destination address) are ignored. Note that only one sender at a time should use the shared channel to transmit a message, otherwise transmitting signals will collide and the information being carried will be lost. Problems arise if the shared channel is heavily utilized or dominated by a single sender or when there is contention for the use of the channel by multiple senders. These situations must be resolved by additional network protocols. Local area networks generally use a shared communications medium and are referred to as **shared medium LANs**.

2. A **circuit-switching** technique, typical of a PBX and voice networks, where a point-to-point connection between devices is established before transmission. Once connected, both ends have dedicated use of all the bandwidth provided for the connection. In dial-up telephone services, the connection is released when the call is terminated. In private dedicated (or *leased line*) services, the connection is permanent thereby eliminating the need for call set-up and clear down

3. A **packet-switching** technique, typical of data networks, where a message is subdivided into smaller units called packets before transmission. Each packet includes addressing information to enable it to be routed independently across a packet-switching network by packet-switching exchanges (PSE), as illustrated in Figure 4.3. Each PSE stores the

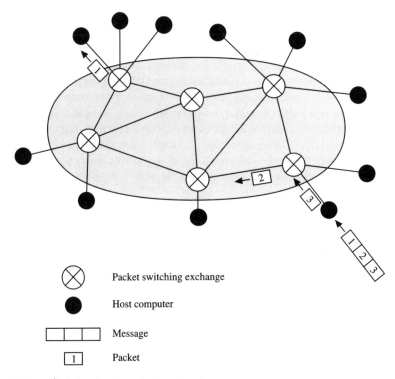

⊗ Packet switching exchange

● Host computer

▭▭▭ Message

☐1 Packet

Figure 4.3 An X.25 packet switching network.

packet in a buffer temporarily and subsequently forwards it to another PSE closer to the PSE to which the destination node is attached. Finally, the local PSE delivers packets to the destination node. This technique is termed 'store-and-forward' and improves trunk line utilization in a network designed to carry bursty traffic typical of data networks. The splitting of messages into smaller 'packets' avoids undue delays arising from long message transmissions. Two types of connection services may be offered by a packet switching network:

- a virtual circuit service which emulates a circuit-switched connection by first establishing a connection with the destination endpoint before data transmissions take place. When the dialogue is complete, the virtual circuit is cleared down. All data packets follow the same route through the network (a route which is established at call set-up). A permanent virtual circuit is permanently set up and the route for all data packets is established at subscription time (eliminating the need for call set-up and clear down).
- a datagram service where each packet contains full addressing information and is routed independently through the network.

4.1.2 Changing bandwidth requirements

Currently, access networks rely heavily on LAN technologies as they have traditionally been the most cost-effective solution to support data and text traffic typical in an office environment. Backbone networks are designed primarily to carry voice or data. For example, a public telephone network is designed to carry voice but is also used to carry data. Similarly, a public data network is designed to carry data but can also carry video and audio streams. Locally, voice information exchange is supported by PBX technology and an associated cabling infrastructure. These technologies are being enhanced to provide better support for DISs which generate large (and sometimes long lasting) multimedia streams. Streams of this type are termed isochronous traffic which require a near constant inter-arrival time between successive transmissions associated with the same dialogue. For example, if success voice transmissions were subject to wildly varying delays, the resulting voice output would include discernible slurs and distortions. Isochronous traffic demand high-bandwidth and low inter-arrival delay (also known as latency or jitter). Applications generating this type of traffic must be underpinned by a network that can guarantee frame transmission and inter-arrival delay within time periods demanded by the application. This means that ideally the underlying network must be able to

- guarantee the throughput demanded by a DIS when it is ready to transmit;
- guarantee a maximum **end-to-end delay** specified by a DIS;
- guarantee a maximum difference in the delay between different packets (known as **delay jitter**) specified by a DIS. This is particularly important for voice streams since widely varying delays has the effect of breaking up continuous speech;
- guarantee specified error characteristics. Voice and video can tolerate relatively high bit and packet error rates. Frequent packet loss will be perceived by users. For example, a bit error resulting in a pixel displayed as blue instead of black is not noticeable, but packet loss results in the loss of a significant amount of pixel information which causes a black box to be displayed on the screen.
- provide a scalable architecture to meet the future growth needs of an organization. Ideally, the network technology should offer a wide range of speed options (limited only by the cable type and associated connection equipment) with low end-to-end inter-arrival delays accomplished by fast switching and routing of packets.

Table 4.1 illustrates the quality-of-service characteristics of various types of traffic streams (Hehmann *et al.*, 1990). A number of parameter values are application-specific, but indicative values are given to illustrate the magnitude rather than absolute values. More flexible bandwidth allocation techniques and user-specific access quality of service mechanisms are required in order to use bandwidth more effectively than is typical of access network technologies in widespread use. A dedicated point-to-point network link of the required throughput and error characteristics is well-suited to support delay-jitter sensitive traffic streams. The use of network switches and other intermediate devices, whilst offering connection flexibility

Table 4.1 Traffic stream quality-of-service characteristics

Stream type	Maximum end-to-end delay (ms)	Maximum delay jitter (ms)	Average throughput (Mbit/s)	Acceptable bit error rate	Acceptable packet error rate
Voice	250	10	0.064	$< 10^{-1}$	$<10^{-1}$
Video	250	10	100	10^{-2}	10^{-3}
Compressed video	250	1	2–10	10^{-6}	10^{-9}
Data file transfer	1000	–	2–100	0	0
Real-time data transfer	1–1000	–	< 10	0	0
Static image	1000	–	2–10	10^{-4}	10^{-9}

and more efficient use of links, introduce additional delays. As well as network QoS requirements, the end devices must also handle packets so as to meet user requirements. Therefore, QoS extends to local resources such as buffer management, flow control, processor scheduling, etc.

4.1.3 Standards

Publication of standard interfaces and protocols and world-wide adoption are important prerequisites to the design and implementation of national and world-wide information network infrastructures. This is true whether a network is public or private. For example if standards were not defined and adopted world wide then the international public telephone system would not have achieved the world-wide compatibility that we all take for granted.

While the telecommunications industry quickly realized the importance of international standards in the development of communications equipment, the computer industry (particularly major computer manufacturers) has not always welcomed or embraced this view. Consequently numerous, manufacturer specific, protocols are in widespread use. Standardization helps to ensure:

- a mass market for products which, in turn, encourages greater competition and the use of mass production techniques which, in turn, leads to lower costs;
- that products from different manufacturers can work together giving purchasers more choice, encouraging competition, and leading to lower costs.

The main disadvantage of international standards designed by standards committees (known as *de jure* standards) is the slowness of the standardization process which often delays the introduction of newer technologies that can bring major benefits to organizations. This is often the reason why industries do not wait for *de jure* standards to develop but adopt *de facto* standards which are regarded as such by virtue of their widespread use in the marketplace.

The main organizations of relevance to *de jure* communications standards are the International Organization for Standardization (ISO), a voluntary organization whose members are representatives of designated national standards bodies; the telecommunications branch of the International Telecommunications Union (ITU-T) whose members are governments, and the Institute of Electrical and Electronics Engineers (IEEE) a professional society which produces standards for use by computer manufacturers. The ITU-T, formerly known as the CCITT, is mainly interested in producing standards for developing national and international public networks. The issue of standards is covered in detail in Chapter 12.

The proliferation of proprietary network architectures in the 1970s helped to stimulate demand for communication standards which were 'open' or 'non-proprietary' architecture. The reference model for Open Systems Interconnection, known simply as the OSI model, was developed as an open architecture. It is structured into seven layers representing the logical sequence of functions carried out when messages are constructed for transmission and sent, and dismantled on reception. The last function to be performed by this hierarchy is the actual physical transmission of the message. The OSI reference model is illustrated in Figure 4.4. At reception, the first function to be performed is the conversion of the transmitted message into the original digital form (Etheridge and Simon, 1992). Each layer in the vertical protocol stack performs a well-defined function. The functions are:

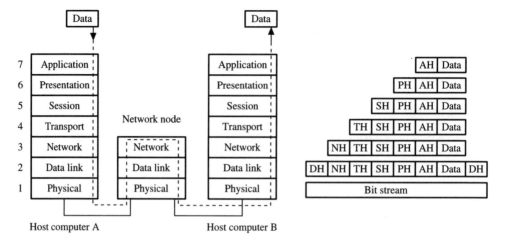

Figure 4.4 The OSI reference model.

- **Layer 7** – Application layer: provides the user application programming interface to application-oriented network services (e.g. file transfer, electronic mail, etc.).
- **Layer 6** – Presentation layer: responsible for the conversion between the (universal) syntax used for data transfer and that used in the application process in the end systems.
- **Layer 5** – Session layer: provides the control of the establishment, management and termination of a logical connection (session) between two co-operating user application programs.
- **Layer 4** – Transport layer: provides a reliable communication service for higher layers.
- **Layer 3** – Network layer: provides upper layers with independence from the technology of the network; responsible for routing and connection.
- **Layer 2** – Data link layer: provides for the reliable transfer of blocks (frames) of data across each physical link in the network.
- **Layer 1** – Physical layer: concerned with the transmission of a bit stream across physical links in the network.

Each layer is said to provide a service to the layers above it. The *service* defines what operations the layer performs, and the *protocol* is the implementation of that service. Within the framework of the OSI reference model, a number of standards have developed to specify the services and protocols of the OSI architecture. The standards have been developed by bodies such as the ITU-T and the IEEE and have been published by the ISO, so that computer manufacturers and software suppliers can develop hardware and software products which conform to OSI. Example standards are:

- ITU-T X.25 packet switching, described in Chapter 6.
- IEEE 802 LAN standards, described in Chapter 5.
- ITU-T ISDN standards, described in Section 4.2.
- ANSI FDDI standard, described in Chapter 5.
- ITU-T X.500 directory services. This standard is described in Chapter 8.

The OSI model has become the standard reference point for positioning various OSI and non-OSI standards, giving a good indication of the functionality offered by a particular networking product.

Standards exist which cover each of the seven layers of the OSI reference model, the lower layers of which are more mature (and more widely used). The ITU-T's X.25 standard for (public) packet switched networks is the basis of the OSI standard for WANs and embraces the lowest three layers of the OSI reference model. Most of the major computer manufacturers (including those with proprietary architectures) support the X.25 interface standard, so that multivendor X.25 networks can be implemented. The IEEE's LAN standards have been adopted by the ISO and embrace the lowest two layers of the OSI reference model.

Because of the maturity of LAN and WAN standards, it is useful to draw a distinction between the lower layers (layers 1–3) of the OSI reference model and the higher layers (layers 5–7). Layer 4, the transport layer, acts as a bridge between higher and lower layers (it is commonly positioned as a lower layer standard). Lower layers deal with the functionality of the network; higher layers deal with application functionality.

4.1.4 Types of backbone networks

Backbone networks carry traffic between access networks separated by large distances and which span public highways. Each access network may be located in different districts within a city, or in different cities or countries. Two classes of backbone networks are defined:

1. **Wide area networks** (WANs), which provide inter-city, national and international coverage.
2. **Metropolitan area networks** (MANs), which provide coverage over a large town or city.

Wide area networks have a long history going back to the 1960s, as they were the first type of computer network in widespread use. The majority of data-carrying WANs have, for many years, used packet switching protocols, either using proprietary protocols (e.g. IBM's systems network architecture (SNA)) or based on the international standard ITU-T X.25 packet switching protocol. A distinguishing feature of WANs is that the circuits are normally owned by a network carrier company and rented or leased to other organizations or residential users. A WAN is formed from use of one or more of the following basic communication options combined with either circuit switching or packet switching protocols:

- Private leased circuits, provided by a public telephone operator (PTO), for example BT in the UK. These services can offer either analogue or digital circuits.
- Public switched telephone networks (PSTN), designed for telephone services but used extensively for data transmissions also.
- Public data networks, usually based on packet-switching, for exclusive support of data transmissions.

In the 1990s a number of additional communication technologies and services have emerged:

- Integrated services digital network (ISDN)
- Frame relay
- ATM
- Mobile communications.

4.2 INTEGRATED SERVICES DIGITAL NETWORK (ISDN)

The integrated services digital network (ISDN) is a set of standards developed by ITU-T to implement public **end-to-end digital transmission** services able to support a wide range of services, including voice, data, text, facsimile and video through a defined set of user-to-network (UNI) interfaces. These interfaces are available in predefined packages incorporating both connection-oriented and connectionless services.

4.2.1 Frame relay

Since the 1970s there have been three main methods of transporting data across a wide geographical area: a public analogue switched telephone network, a public X.25 packet switching network, or the use of analogue (and more recently digital) leased lines to provide a private point-to-point or packet switching networks. As more digital leased line services came into operation the quality and speed of transmission improved significantly. X.25 is sometimes known as the **paranoid protocol** because of the extensive error control applied both at level two and level three. X.25 was designed for noisy analogue communication lines. Today the extensive use of fibre optic cabling has made nearly error-free bandwidth widely available. This has led to the need to eliminate the now excessive error control procedures inherent in X.25. Instead, it is more appropriate to assume that no errors occur during transmission over digital links.

Frame relay is a packet switching interface standard that adopts a minimalist approach to error correction since the underlying transmission medium is assumed to be very reliable with low error rates. It merely provides a mechanism for error detection and notifies the end system that errors have occurred during transmission. It is the end system's responsibility to provide error correction usually by requesting re-transmission. This results in significant improvements in packet throughput (achieving around four times the throughput of X.25) and delay (and delay variance) making it much more suitable for high bandwidth 'broadband' networks.

The ITU-T originally developed frame relay as part of the ISDN set of standards for digital wide area networks which exhibit very low error rates. All error correction and X.25 level 3 functions are handled by a user endpoint (e.g. a LAN router) rather than by the frame relay switches. Frame relay defines how frames are assembled and routed (at layer 2 of the OSI reference model) using **virtual circuits**. Consequently, frame relay switches can switch packets much faster compared with X.25 switches. A connection between end-points is made by setting up a *permanent virtual circuit* (PVC) using a similar mechanism to the X.25 standard. Frame relay can accommodate speeds of tens of megabits per second.

The delay characteristics (delay jitter in particular), although significantly reduced in comparison with X.25, cannot be guaranteed to be within the tolerances required for frame relay to be a suitable technology for the transmission of voice and video in addition to high-speed data transmission. The main reason for this is that it supports variable length transmissions with a maximum frame size of 8191 bytes. Frame relay is ideal for applications exhibiting intermittent high-speed bursts of data, for example:

- LAN to LAN interconnections;
- some static image and graphics applications;
- distributed databases.

Frame relay is an OSI layer 2 protocol, consequently it can be integrated easily with existing high-level protocols such as TCP/IP.

4.2.2 Narrowband and wideband ISDN

A distinctive feature of the ISDN standard is the *separation of control and management dialogues* (known as signalling) from user-defined messages, unlike public analogue telephone networks where call set-up and other signals flow down the same channel as subsequent voice conversations. A separate **signalling channel** (known as the delta or **'D' channel**) means that control and management messages can be generated or received by users in real time while user dialogues are transmitted down separate Bearer or **'B' channels**. The D channel can also be used to support user dialogues, particularly telemetry and low-speed packet switching. The frame relay standard was derived from a protocol called link access protocol for the D-channel (LAP-D) defined as an efficient packet switching protocol operating over an ISDN D channel.

Initial implementations of ISDN offer two types of interface: the *narrowband ISDN interface* which consists of the basic rate UNI, and the *wideband ISDN interface* which consists of the primary rate UNI. The basic rate UNI–known as 2B+D—allows the user to have two full-duplex 64 kbit/s B channels and a 16 kbit/s D channel which carries signalling messages (e.g. telephone number, call set-up and call clear down messages) as illustrated in Figure 4.5.

A B channel can be used to transmit digitized voice (encoded at 64 kbit/s or less) or non-voice transmission. A basic rate UNI provides two B channels allowing parallel transmission of voice and non-voice (e.g. to support videoconferencing). This interface is designed primarily for small businesses and residential users. Non-ISDN devices can still interface to an ISDN line using a special device called an **ISDN terminal adapter**.

The primary rate UNI is designed for a larger business owning one or more digital telephone switches (commonly known as a private branch exchange or PBX) with private network trunk links. There are differences in the configuration of primary rate UNI due to differing underlying network infrastructures in various countries. In Europe, CEPT (Conference of European Telecommunication Authorities) standards are based on a network infrastructure that multiplexes 32 channels at 64 kbit/s each giving an aggregate transmission

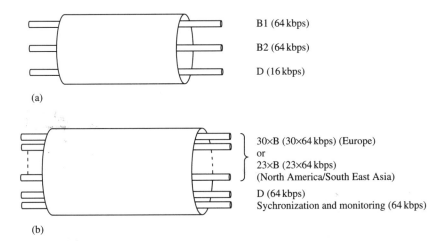

Figure 4.5 ISDN configurations: (a) narrow band; (b) wide band.

rate of 2 Mbit/s. In North America and South-east Asia, existing digital network infrastructures use a multiplexing technique based on the DS1 standard which combines 24 channels at 64 kbit/s and additional control information resulting in an aggregate 1.544 Mbit/s. Thus, in Europe the primary rate standard is 30 B channels and a 64 kbit/s D channel whereas in North America and South-east Asia it is 23 B channels and a 64 kbit/s D channel. Within a campus or building, primary rate ISDN is supported by a PBX designed to deliver ISDN services to the desktop — known as an integrated services PBX (ISPBX). The ISPBX provides basic rate and n x 64 kbit/s services to desktop devices.

4.2.3 Broadband ISDN

The ITU-T envisaged the need for much higher speed service called **broadband ISDN** (B-ISDN) to cope with future demands for bandwidth. It offers two types of channel structure:

1. **Synchronous channel structure** which consists of a number of **constant bit-rate** component channels. The transmission rate of a component channel is constant but may vary from one component channel to another. A component channel may be a B channel, D channel or an additional channel type – an H channel – designed to support transmission rates in excess of 64 kbit/s.
2. **Asynchronous channel structure** which consists of **variable bit-rate** component channels dynamically created by an application in support of its transmission needs. This is useful in many data applications where only a fraction of the capacity of a constant bit-rate component channel would be used. This is true particularly for applications which exhibit significant idle periods or widely varying transmission rates (i.e. bursty traffic). A virtual component channel can have a constant or variable bit-rate depending on the rate of information generation by an application. This approach is generally termed 'bandwidth-on-demand'. Obviously the flexibility of this service is constrained by the flexibility offered by the underlying physical network over which this channel structure is implemented.

In 1988 the ITU-T adopted **asynchronous transfer mode** (ATM) as the underlying physical network technology to support B-ISDN services (although B-ISDN can also use other underlying physical network technologies). The B-ISDN model is illustrated in Figure 4.6. An ATM-based physical network supports on-demand transmissions of hundreds of megabits per second. A B-ISDN component channel maps to a logically connected stream of ATM cells (an ATM virtual channel connection). ATM is covered in detail in Section 4.3 and in Figure 4.7.

B-ISDN relies on an ATM-based network to enable asynchronous and synchronous services to be offered to end-users. The broadband access UNI is designed to support the transmission of voice, video, videoconferencing and other high-bandwidth, delay-sensitive applications.

4.3 ASYNCHRONOUS TRANSFER MODE (ATM)

Fast packet switching (a colloquial term covering a range of techniques) seeks to provide a technology that minimizes overheads, similar to frame relay, but also supports the transmission requirements of voice, video and other information requiring low delays and delay variance. It combines the benefits of packet switching with the benefits of circuit switching (high

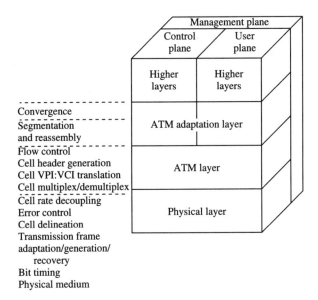

Convergence
Segmentation
and reassembly
Flow control
Cell header generation
Cell VPI:VCI translation
Cell multiplex/demultiplex
Cell rate decoupling
Error control
Cell delineation
Transmission frame
adaptation/generation/
    recovery
Bit timing
Physical medium

Figure 4.6 The broadband ISDN reference model.

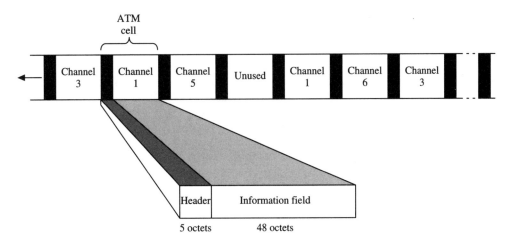

Figure 4.7 ATM cell format.

throughput and low delays). The main differences compared with frame relay is in the use of short, fixed length units called cells, and a high-speed switching technique which can easily be implemented in hardware.

Asynchronous transfer mode (ATM) was originally developed as a fast packet switching technique in 1980 by AT&T to provide the ability to inter-mix voice and data transmissions over a single physical network. In 1988 at an ITU-T meeting, a recommendation was made to use ATM as the underlying technology for Broadband ISDN. The ATM protocol standard is a fast packet switching technique that allows for the dynamic allocation of bandwidth to an application at call set-up.

Message format

In ATM, data, text, voice, static image or video, all forms of information are transferred in a sequence of fixed-length data units called cells. Each cell has a 5-octet header and an information field that can carry 48 octets (384 bits) of user data as illustrated in Figure 4.7. Hence, ATM is also known as 'cell relay'. An ATM network topology is basically a *distributed star topology*. A user device or LAN segment (via a router) is connected directly to an ATM switch. The physical link can be viewed as supporting a conveyor belt of empty and full containers (slots) each capable of carrying 48 octets of user data.

ATM is a connection-oriented service using switched and permanent virtual connections. In ATM, a **virtual channel** (VC) is a logical connection between two ATM switches or between a user endpoint and an ATM switch. The route that cells follow consists of a sequence of VCs between two user endpoints. The sequence of VCs that form a route associated with a virtual call is known as a virtual channel connection (VCC), which is similar in concept to X.25 virtual circuits.

Each virtual channel belongs to a virtual path (VP) between switches. A virtual path is a grouping (across a single physical link) of several VCs into a single logical entity as illustrated in Figure 4.8. While virtual paths are persistent, virtual channels are set up when a connection is initiated and associated with a virtual path. The header contains information required to switch the cell from the input port of the ATM switch to a destination port according to information in the switch's routing table. There are a number of fields in the header of an ATM cell. There is also a slight difference in header structure used at the user–network interface (UNI) compared with the network–network (switch to switch) interface (NNI) as illustrated in Figure 4.9. The fields are:

- *Generic flow control field (GFC);* used for flow control purposes. This field exists for the UNI interface only. It is not used in the NNI interface.
- *Virtual channel identifier* (VCI): identifies the logical connection to which this cell belongs.
- *Virtual path identifier* (VPI): used to multiplex several different virtual channels into a virtual path that is transmitted and switched as a single unit.

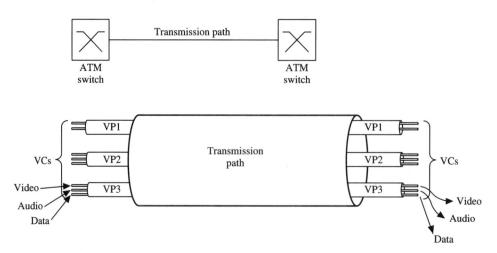

Figure 4.8 Virtual channel (VC) versus Virtual path (VP).

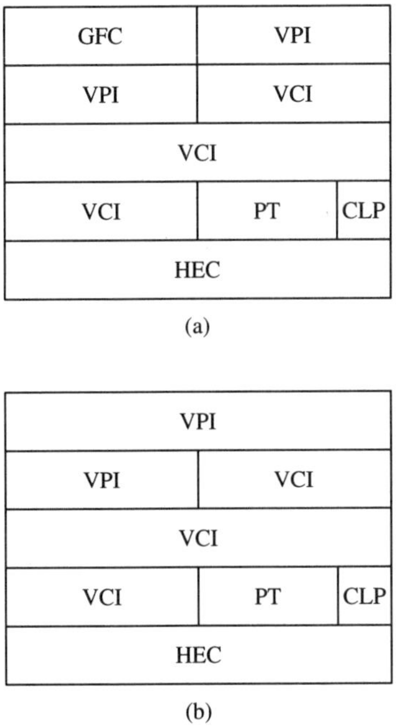

GFC	VPI	
VPI	VCI	
VCI		
VCI	PT	CLP
HEC		

(a)

VPI		
VPI	VCI	
VCI		
VCI	PT	CLP
HEC		

(b)

Figure 4.9 Cell header format: (a) UNI cell format; (b) NNI cell format. CLP, cell loss priority; GFC, generic flow control; HEC, header error control; NNI, network-node interface; PT, payload type; VCI, virtual channel identifier; VPI, virtual path identifier; UNI, user-network interface.

- *Payload type* (PT): identifies a cell as either user information or supervisory (management) information. It also contains a special field – the ATM–layer–user to ATM–layer–user (AUU) field which is used by the ATM adaptation layer.
- *Cell loss priority*: a single bit which is set to one if this cell may be discarded by the ATM network when congestion occurs.
- *Header error check* field (HEC): provides for error correction of single bit errors or the detection of multiple-bit errors in the header (not including the GFC field). User data is not subject to error control since ATM relies on digital circuits which are relatively error-free. Any errors in the user data must be detected by higher-layer protocols,
- The remaining bits in the header are reserved for future uses such as a priority scheme.

A **VPI:VCI** value combination is the cell address meaningful only to the ATM switch that is to receive the cell. A VP:VC switch is a type of ATM switch which switches at the virtual channel level. A VP:VC switch holds a VPI:VCI value in its routing table for each possible incoming cell. The routing table identifies the new VPI:VCI value of the outgoing cell and the outgoing port through which the cell will be sent. A VP switch is only interested in the VPI value in a cell because it switches the whole virtual path rather than individual channels within a path. So the VCI values are not stored in the routing table. Logically, an ATM network infrastructure is structured in two levels as illustrated in Figure 4.10:

1. A virtual channel network of VP:VC switches, each connected to the virtual path network via one or more direct connections local VP switches. VP:VC switches are used by user endpoints to set up virtual channels to other user endpoints and to implement other VC

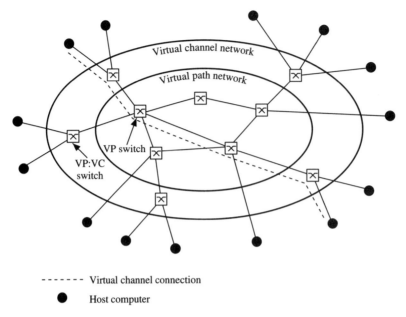

- - - - - - - Virtual channel connection

● Host computer

Figure 4.10 ATM network architecture.

related functions. Each endpoint utilizes one or more virtual channels each identified by a VCI:VPI value unique to the VP:VC switch to which it is attached (and assigned only for the duration of the virtual call). The new VPI:VCI is inserted into the cell header before transmission. Non-ATM devices can access the virtual channel network via a special user device called an **ATM terminal adapter** (similar in concept to an ISDN terminal adapter). The terminal adapter prepares a user endpoint data stream for transfer across the ATM network, and sets up a virtual channel connection to the destination endpoint.

2. A virtual path network of interconnected VP switches which supports VP related functions such as virtual path switching and multiplexing/demultiplexing VPs over the same transmission path. In a VP switch all VCs in a virtual path are switched together. Thus all cells with the same VPI value are switched to the same outgoing physical port and a new VPI value inserted in the cell header prior to transmission. The VCI value remains unchanged.

User endpoints can request either a virtual channel connection or a virtual path connection on a semi-permanent or on-demand basis. A virtual path connection allows the user to set up multiple channels (e.g. three separate channels for voice, video and data transmissions to support videoconferencing) giving flexibility to allocate VCI values, or to set up a single VP pipe typically to support LAN to LAN connections.

The rate at which cells are generated at a user endpoint is determined by the bandwidth demands of the end-user application. Cells are transferred across each physical path at the fixed transmission rate associated with the link. In the absence of any user traffic, unassigned or idle cell streams are present on the link.

The following example illustrates how ATM works. Suppose a device requests a 64 kbps connection. The corresponding cell rate is 64 000/(48 x 8) = 167 cell/s (ignoring higher-level protocol overheads). If the trunk links between ATM switches have a data rate of 353 kcells/s, a cell belonging to this service would be transferred across a trunk link on average once in every 2114 cells of the cell stream. The other cells are used to multiplex other virtual channels across the same trunk link. A digitized voice transmission is derived by sampling a voice analogue signal at the rate of 8000 samples/s each sample encoded in 8 bits giving a band-width requirement of 64 kbps. Each ATM cell can hold a maximum of 48 octets worth of voice samples, which corresponds to (48 x 8)/64 000 seconds or 6 ms of speech. A critical factor in digitized voice transmission is the delay between cells in a voice cell stream. Excessive delay will result in slurred or appreciable distortion of the voice output at the desti-nation. At an ATM switch the cell switching delay is typically around 25 µs. This means that the total end-to-end one-way delay for voice transmissions should be well within the 250 ms suggested in Section 4.2 (ITU-T recommends a maximum delay of 400 ms), and delay jitter limits.

A potential problem with an underlying ATM network is the possibility of queuing delays when cell streams over physical trunk lines become over-utilized as the capacity of a network component is exceeded or, at worst, data is lost due to the unpredictable aggregate bandwidth demand at any instant. Congestion control protocols are required to ensure that these situa-tions are avoided.

4.3.1 Access control method

Essentially ATM is a connection-oriented, multiplexing standard which, because of the use of short fixed-length cells, is able to support the transmission of a wide variety of traffic types. In order to set up a virtual channel connection between two user endpoints (e.g. between a PC and a remote server), a route from source endpoint to destination endpoint must be established con-sisting of a series of virtual channels between ATM switches. ATM is a connection-oriented net-work therefore a virtual call set-up procedure must be completed before user-data transmissions can take place (mainly to identify the route through the network that all data carrying cells must follow and updating the routing tables of all ATM switches in the route).

To facilitate call set-up, an endpoint first sends a request (a single cell message) over a well-known, persistent virtual channel called the **metasignalling virtual channel** (MSVC) in order to ask the ATM network to set up its own signalling channel known as a **signalling virtual** chan-nel (SVCI) for use in making and receiving virtual calls. The MSVC is a permanent virtual channel with a VCI value of one. The network allocates the endpoint's SVC by assigning a SVC identifier (SVCI) and communicating this value to the endpoint. All subsequent signalling takes place over the SVC. The user endpoint now makes a virtual call attempt by generating a SET-UP message using an ATM unique access protocol (ITU-T Recommendation Q.2931; a modi-fied version of ISDN's ITU-T Q.931 signalling standard) specifying the address of the destination endpoint and the type of service to be supported. The address format used to identify a remote endpoint conforms to ITU-T recommendation E.164 which is an ISDN standard.

The ATM switch to which the source endpoint is attached has to find a suitable route to the destination endpoint which satisfies the sender's bandwidth and quality-of-service require-ments. Predefined SVCs between connected ATM switches are used to carry signalling mes-sages between switches. Each switch that receives the set-up request decides on the next ATM switch to receive the request. This is difficult since ordinary ATM switches cannot read ITU-T E.164 compliant addresses and therefore have no idea where to route it next. One way to resolve this is to implement a higher layer **routing service** to which the first ATM switch sends the SET-UP signalling message. The routing service returns a chosen route to the switch enabling it to choose a suitable outgoing port and assign a new VPI:VCI value. Note

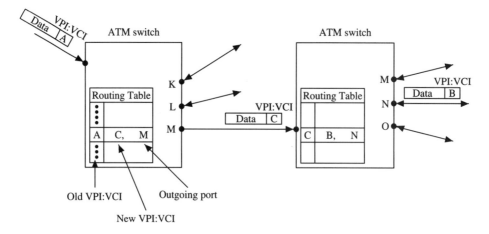

Figure 4.11 ATM cell set-up and cell routing.

that routing tables are not updated until the destination endpoint accepts the call set-up request. This is illustrated in Figure 4.11.

Once the called party has answered and accepted the call, an ANSWER signalling message is sent back along the route causing each switch to update its routing table thereby making a connection. Call set-up is now complete and any user data generated by the endpoints will be switched automatically and speedily through the ATM network. When the call is completed, a CLEAR DOWN signalling message is sent causing each ATM switch to clear its associated routing table entry.

4.3.2 The ATM adaptation layer

To maximize the potential of ATM and to provide services customized for various application domains, a higher protocol layer known as the **ATM adaptation layer** (AAL) provides functions for encoding many different types of data into a standard ATM cell. AAL is a 'user' process (i.e. it is resident in user nodes rather than in ATM switches) which forms the highest layer of the ATM part of the B-ISDN model. This provides an easier interface for user processes to access the basic ATM service. In particular, it can offer support for segmenting variable-length packets into fixed-length cells, managing the reassembly of cells at the other end. The AAL is divided into two sublayers, as shown in Figure 4.12:

1. The **convergence sublayer** (CS) which is responsible for providing AAL functions to the higher layer in the B-ISDN model. Its main function is to make visible an AAL service to a higher layer process and to prepare user data for segmentation into ATM cells and reassembly.

2. The **segmentation and reassembly** (SAR) sublayer, responsible for segmenting higher layer data into segments suitable to hold in cells and reassembling segments into higher layer data. The SAR sublayer defines additional fields (e.g. SAR header and trailer fields) which store sequence numbering, error checking and field length data for each segment. For some applications it may not be necessary to utilize CS and SAR services.

To support the wide range of traffic streams which may flow over an ATM network, the AAL layer supports several connection types which determine the format of messages.

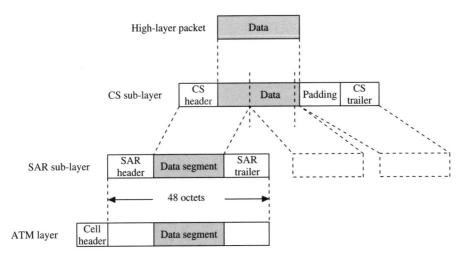

Figure 4.12 CS and SAR sublayers of the ATM adaptation layer (AAL).

AAL 1 – constant bit rate (CBR)

CBR is used for for constant-rate isochronous traffic such as E1 or 64 kbit/s digital voice streams. This allows an ATM network to support traditional circuit-switching links.

AAL 2 – variable bit rate (VBR)

VBR is used for variable-rate (bursty) data transmission requirements which need transfer of timing between endpoints. A typical example is packetized video, allowing the direct connection of a video codec into the ATM switch.

AAL 3/4 – VBR data transfers

AAL 3 and 4 have now converged and can be regarded as a single AAL type. It is defined to support bursty, relatively time-insensitive data transfers between two users over a connection-oriented ATM service. A typical application is large batch file transfers.

AAL 5 – simple and efficient adaptation layer (SEAL)

SEAL is a more efficient version of AAL 3/4. Error recovery is assumed to be provided by the higher layers. The AUU field in the cell header is used instead of a distinct SAR header and trailer fields, in order to conserve bytes in the information field. This results in all 48 bytes of the cell information being used for data, resulting in increased efficiency and data throughput. This service however imposes the restriction that only one message is active across the UNI at any time, hence other data must be queued for transmission. In other words, AAL 5 does not support a multiplexing function. AAL 5 supports both connection-oriented and connection-less operations. This type has become a popular option for supporting Class C services but is not well suited to support Class D services. The main anticipated uses are for frame relay over ATM, data applications and for signalling purposes.

Some example AAL formats are shown in Figure 4.13. It is evident that the AAL type determines how much user data can be carried in a single cell. As more applications for ATM

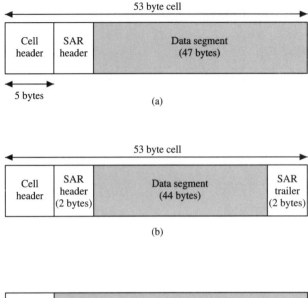

(a)

(b)

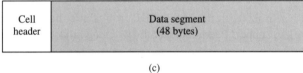

(c)

Figure 4.13 ATM AAL types. Cell format for (a) AAL type 1; (b) AAL type 3/4; (c) AAL type 5.

emerge, other AAL formats will be defined. Currently, the ATM Forum is discussing an AAL 6 format to provide specific support for MPEG-coded video.

To support a specific level of service for a particular connection, ATM traffic and congestion control mechanisms support the specification of a set of quality-of-service (QoS) classes. The ATM QoS layer is defined by a set of parameters summarized below:

- Peak arrival rate of cells   The maximum resources required by a connection at peak load.
- Peak duration   The average duration of the maximum load.
- Average cell arrival rate   The amount of network resources requested by the source. This is calculated as (the number of cells measured during the duration of the connection)/(the connection duration).
- Burstiness   The ratio between the peak cell rate and the average cell rate.
- Cell loss ratio (CLR)   The ratio of the number of lost cells to transmitted cells. This type of error normally occurs due to congestion in ATM switches.
- Cell insertion ratio (CIR)   The number of misinserted cells per connection. Cell misinsertion occurs when the address field in the cell header is corrupted to another valid address.
- Bit error rate (BER)   The number of bits in error divided by the number of bits delivered. Error bits are normally caused by the transmission system.

4.3.3 Transmission media

As mentioned earlier, ATM can operate over any type of transmission line. However, specific physical layer interfaces are being defined to provide very high-speed transmissions. Across the world PTTs are busy replacing old copper wire, coaxial cable and microwave transmission media with fibre optic cable. The main benefits are very low error rates, high noise immunity and the potential to support very high speed (Gbit/s) transmission speeds. As always, standards play a key role in ensuring that high-speed transmission services will be available across the world.

A significant development in this area was the **synchronous optical network** (SONET) standard developed by Bell Communications Research (Bellcore) a US company funded by the seven regional Bell companies. SONET specifies how synchronous digital signals can be carried over fibre optic networks. The ITU-T developed a similar standard called **synchronous digital hierarchy** (SDH) which formed the international standard (ITU-T recommendations G707-709). SONET uses a frame structure to perform basic synchronization, and has a basic rate of 51.84 Mbit/s. The SDH optical transmission hierarchy is based on a basic rate of 155.520 Mbit/s. Its standardized parameters means that global networks can be built from multi-vendor components. High-speed interfaces are created simply by multiplexing (using byte interleaving) lower-speed channels. This simplifies the process of creating the range of transmission speeds offered by a particular service. Some common interface speeds currently recognized by SONET/SDH are given in Table 4.2.

Table 4.2 SONET and SDH interface speeds

SONET Optical carrier (OC) level	SDH STM level	Line rate (Mbit/s)
OC-1		51.840
OC-3	STM-1	155.520
OC-12	STM-4	622.080
OC-24	STM-8	1244.160
OC-48	STM-16	2488.320

A maximum 2.4 Gbit/s link implied by the table above is not the highest rate achievable by SONET/SDH, it simply represents the highest rate considered practical for standard product development today. The SONET/SDH transmission speed hierarchy extends indefinitely, limited only by advances in technology to support higher-speed transmission. The ITU-T SDH standard concentrates on transmission speeds of 155 Mbps and above.

When used within a campus as the backbone LAN, the ATM switch supports categories 3 and 5 UTP cable and fibre optic cable. High-speed ATM-to-ATM switch connections can be supported by fibre optic links able to support speeds of 155 Mbps or more. Client workstations can either be connected directly to an ATM switch or via a shared medium LAN such as Ethernet. Category 5 cabling is able to support speeds of around 100 Mbps whilst Category 3 will support up to 50–60 Mbps. The ATM forum has defined standard specifications for 25 or 51 Mbps over Category 3 or 5 cable.

4.3.4 Support for high-bandwidth and delay-sensitive applications

It is clear that ATM has been designed from the outset to support the transmission of a wide range of types of traffic and can operate much faster than conventional packet switching techniques by avoiding error and flow control during transmission, and by using fixed length cells. An ATM switch is able to keep the switching delay to around 25 ms. With the addition of on-demand bandwidth negotiation with guaranteed quality of service, ATM-based networks are highly suited to support high-bandwidth and low-latency applications for the foreseeable future.

ATM is often referred to as the ideal network technology to create a seamless corporate network encompassing both access and backbone network components. However, ATM is an inefficient technique for supporting low-bandwidth, bursty applications using links of less than around 2 Mbit/s. To illustrate the problem consider a 9600 bps connection to an ATM switch. This channel would require a cell rate of about 23 cells per second to cope with a continuous stream of data transmitted at 1200 bytes per second. The efficiency of usage of these cells is likely to be low, however, because very few low-end applications can guarantee to continuously fill the cells. If the ATM cell is not filled, the ATM network can either transport half-empty cells (thus wasting bandwidth) or wait until it is filled possibly creating synchronization problems.

An ATM network is not a cost-effective solution if it supports a significant number of low-speed links used by low-end applications. An alternative technology (e.g. frame relay) may be better equipped to send low-speed, variable length frames to match the requirements of the application. It is much more likely that high-end workstations and, more typically, LAN hubs and routers, PBXs and servers will connect directly to an ATM switch.

4.4 MOBILE COMMUNICATIONS

Mobile communications is a relative newcomer as a mainstream option for access and backbone network services but may bring about fundamental changes in the use of telecommunications services. During the 1980s the geographic coverage and take-up of **mobile telephony** was rapid, due mainly to a rapid fall in the cost of equipment. A business person is now unlikely to be without a mobile phone: despite the fact that call charges are relatively expensive, it is no longer regarded as a luxury item. Extending both voice and non-voice services to a person rather than to equipment at a fixed location, gives the individual the freedom to communicate at home, at work or on the move.

In mobile communication systems information is carried from sender to recipient by electromagnetic waves through air-space. Electromagnetic waves are generated by a rapidly changing electric field in a transmitting antenna (a wire). These waves can be detected by another antenna (a receiver) because the latter induces another rapidly changing electrical field. If a station both sends and receives then it requires both a transmitting and receiving antenna. A receiving antenna needs to tune in to a transmitter in order to receive any information being carried. Information is in fact carried by using the well-known technique of varying one or more characteristics of the carrier signal, e.g. the amplitude of the signal or its frequency.

The spectrum of electromagnetic waves is potentially infinite and is measured in terms of wave cycles per second (frequency) or the length between waves (wavelength). Wave frequency is measured in hertz which is defined as one wave cycle per second. It includes visible light, radio waves, microwaves, X-rays, infra-red and ultra-violet waves. One important characteristic of electromagnetic waves in the context of computer communications is that at a given power level, the lower the frequency the further it propagates and disperses. Also, lower-frequency waves are less affected by natural obstacles such as mountains, buildings and walls. The higher the frequency, however, the greater the potential bandwidth for carrying data which translates to higher throughput and faster speeds of transmission. High-frequency waves such as microwaves are used for high-speed, short distance transmissions (unless multiple transmitters are employed to extend the signal over long distances).

Mobile non-voice services are less well supported by mobile technology and remain the poor relation due to inherent transmission and reception problems (such as loss of signal and greatly varying signal-to-noise ratio) which whilst not causing too much difficulty with voice traffic, can have a profound effect on data transmissions. Dramatic improvements in transmission speeds and reliability have been realized as high-speed, digital technologies are widely deployed. There are a number of types of communication service options available, each designed to meet the needs of particular applications:

- **Radio paging systems.** This type of system supports the transmission of short 'page' messages on a single simplex (one-way only) channel which is received by multiple receivers. Only one receiver however is triggered (e.g. by setting off an audible alarm and displaying the message) and is identified by a coded signal.
- Radio systems which use a limited number of channels, with exclusive access to a channel on a demand basis. This improves utilization of the radio spectrum but anything other than localized coverage is difficult due to the cost and complexity of automatic retuning to different frequencies as the user travels through different areas nationally and internationally.
- **Community radio stations** which support the sharing of a common channel amongst users. An example of an application is a local taxi radio service. However, factors such as security and restrictions imposed on the type of user dialogue it can support (simplex or half-duplex via a system operator) renders this option less suitable as a general wide area service.
- Large service organizations, such as major vehicle rescue businesses and emergency services, may justify development of a **private mobile radio** (PMR) system capable of full-duplex voice and (low data rate) data transmission because of the nature of the business (i.e. the need to provide first-class customer service). However, the limited frequency bands normally reserved by countries to support PMR users are usually congested leaving little room for a public wide-area service.
- **Cellular radio systems** offer automated, shared access to full-duplex (primarily voice) channels on a demand basis with sole use of a channel for the duration of a call. The area of coverage is divided into hexagonal cells, each with its own transmitter/receiver (transceiver) as shown in Figure 4.14. In addition, national and international coverage is possible with automatic (transparent) channel switching as users progress from the domain of one cell transmitter to another (this is known as hand-off). International coverage is facilitated by allowing users to 'roam' from one national cellular service to another automatically as national borders are crossed. Cellular radio systems provide mobile phone connections to other public switched networks and into an organization's private PBX via a private leased circuit (bypassing the PSTN). It is this technology which forms the basis of public wide-area mobile communications services.

The foundation for commercial cellular radio systems can be traced back to work by AT&T in the US when in the 1940s at its Bell Laboratories the concepts of cellular radio emerged. The development of key building blocks such as integrated circuits and low-cost microprocessors paved the way for the development of modern mobile technology. In 1974,

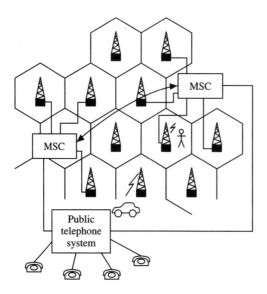

Figure 4.14 A cellular communications network. MSC, mobile switching centre; base station.

the US Federal Communications Commission (FCC) allocated 40 MHz of spectrum in the 800 MHz frequency band for cellular radio services. AT&T held the first US licence to operate a cellular service in 1974 and subsequently created a subsidiary—Advanced Mobile Phone Service (AMPS)—to conduct field trials and to prove the technology. AMPS was adopted as the base technology for cellular radio systems in many other countries.

In 1979 at a meeting of the World Administrative Radio Council (WARC) it was agreed to reserve a part of the radio spectrum (862–960 MHz) for use by future mobile radio systems. By the early 1980s the UK government released 30 MHz at around 900 MHz frequency for exclusive support of a national cellular radio system. An AMPS-based system called Total Access Communications System (TACS) operating at 900 MHz was launched in 1985. Licences were issued to Cellnet (a collaboration between BT and Securicor) and Vodafone (a collaboration between Racal and a US company called Millicom). The 30 MHz spectrum is divided into 1000 full-duplex channels over which telephone calls are established using cellular technology. Cellnet and Vodafone were allocated 300 channels each for analogue channels and each has achieved coverage to around 95 per cent of the UK population. The other channels were reserved for a future pan-European system.

Cellnet, Vodaphone and other operators are licensed to operate cellular networks but are not licensed to deal directly with end-users. To encourage competition, cellular service provider organizations provide the interface between end-users and licensed operators such as Cellnet and Vodaphone. This market structure has caused the market to mushroom and licensed operators are now finding it difficult to maintain the quality of service demanded by users due to congestion problems.

4.4.1 European and international harmonization

The European Community has pioneered the development of **digital mobile communications**. First steps to European harmonization were taken when a study was conducted by

CEPT (Conference of European Telecommunication Authorities) in the early 1980s. This resulted in the following subsequent decisions and objectives endorsed by 18 member countries of CEPT:

- A harmonized pan-European cellular mobile network was seen as a very important development in the European context, to replace incompatible analogue national systems. A wide range of new services was envisaged such as call barring, call forwarding, three-party calling, call waiting and charging advice.
- The network should offer voice and non-voice services with access to other services (such as ISDN) and with a high degree of security and privacy (using encryption techniques).
- Two 25 MHz frequency bands at 890–915 MHz and 935–960 MHz were to be reserved primarily for cellular mobile services.
- A special group was formed called the **Groupe Special Mobile** (GSM) to co-ordinate and produce standards for the pan-European network.

This standard, known simply as GSM, is oriented towards high-powered vehicular rather than pedestrian equipment. Speech is encoded at 13 kbit/s and processed in 20 ms blocks (i.e. 260 bits at a time). Forward error correction is used to recover from the effects of interference making it suitable both for voice and data transmissions.

In North America a dual-mode digital cellular standard will operate at 800 MHz frequency band. In Japan, there are plans for a digital cellular system at 800 MHz and 1.5 GHz. Across the world, several digital cellular radio network standards are implemented which are incompatible with GSM. It remains to be seen whether GSM will become a global standard. Already, GSM-based networks are being implemented but with differences in frequency band allocation and other features.

4.4.2 Personal communications network (PCN)

While GSM is designed primarily to meet the needs of the business community, there is a demand for mobile services for the mass market (including businesses) which provides for low-power, lightweight and inexpensive **pocket (handheld) mobile devices** designed for carrying on the person rather than in a vehicle. Combined with the use of personal numbering (everyone having their own personal and permanent identification number) and number portability across national and international networks, a PCN will deliver a high degree of flexibility and mobility – but with significant social implications. Important social implications include safety (in Europe it is planned to use the 1.8 GHz frequency band) and privacy protection. At gigahertz frequencies with millions of users, the biological effects of radio frequency radiation is a major consideration.

GSM forms the base technology for European PCN systems, and a variant called digital cellular system (DCS1800) operating in the 1800 MHz frequency band providing a range of between 500 m and 6 km is the basis of a pan-European standard.

4.5 METROPOLITAN AREA NETWORKS

The widespread use of LAN technology has created a need to interconnect these networks reliably and efficiently. Interconnection technology must satisfy requirements in terms of high speed, distance, cost, and adherence to standards. Developments in wide area networks, such as ATM and broadband ISDN, will ultimately provide the required technology and services. In the meantime, intermediate technologies are available. A metropolitan area network (MAN) is designed to interconnect LANs over a public area such as a large town or city. The technology can also be used to implement a private network over a large campus but is primarily designed to be installed and implemented by a public carrier. Three technologies are designed to implement MANs.

1. Broadband cable networks.
2. IEEE 802.6 Distributed queue, dual-bus (DQDB).
3. Fibre Distributed Data Interface (FDDI) systems.

FDDI is examined in Chapter 5.

4.5.1 The broadband cable network

For most countries, the copper wires used to connect subscribers to the local telephone exchange represents a vast investment on the part of the principal national public telephone operator. The bandwidth sustainable is limited by the quality of the copper wiring in place. In practice, this type of connection will not be able to support the bandwidth requirements in the future.

As noted earlier, the high competition for bandwidth in the radio spectrum means that broadcast technologies such as television and cellular radio will not be able to support the bandwidth demands of public and private communication services to which local users require access. Limited bandwidth will be a feature of these technologies for the foreseeable future.

Broadband cable television was originally introduced in the US in the late 1940s. At that time the population density was low and outside large city areas towns were typically very small communities making it cost-prohibitive to install television transmitters so that every household could receive a strong signal. It was under these circumstances that **community antenna television** (CATV) evolved in its basic form consisting of a large aerial directly connecting many homes in an area using open copper wire transmission lines. With the increasing number of television channels in the US, the system was improved by adding amplifiers, replacing open wire lines with coaxial cable and developing technology for tapping signals from the main signal flowing along a main trunk cable. CATV cable, amplifiers and taps have been standardized.

CATV systems have been designed to carry multiple broadcast channels by using frequency division multiplexing to create a number of sub-channels. Consequently, television channels, interactive systems, LANs and other systems can operate simultaneously over a single broadband cable simply by ensuring that each is allocated unique sub-channels on the cable. A broadband cable system has a usable frequency spectrum ranging from about 5–440 MHz (a bandwidth of 400 MHz). In a standard CATV system, the television signal is fed into the system at the headend. The headend then distributes the signal to subscribers by broadcasting each TV channel on a forward channel (forward channels are allocated in the frequency range 40–440 MHz).

Interactive services are implemented by splitting the bandwidth into **forward channels** and **reverse channels** so that, for example, subscribers could participate in 'pay-as-you-view' services (so that whenever you tuned into a chargeable channel, a signal would automatically be generated down the reverse channel to the billing computer!). Reverse channels are also used to deliver local services by sending the local signal to the headend which would then be broadcast on a previously reserved forward channel. In a dual-cable CATV system the forward and reverse channels are on separate physical cables thus allowing the allocation of a greater number of channels.

Fibre optic cable is being used to provide long point-to-point links in these types of networks. However, fibre optic cable cannot yet be used extensively as a complete replacement for coaxial cable because it is still difficult and not cost-effective to tap the cable frequently as would be required in a residential network.

Broadband cable systems (based on the CATV approach) are of good quality, making efficient use of bandwidth and offering the potential to support high-bandwidth systems. Digital signals can be carried by these systems by using modems that modulate a digital signal to radio frequencies suitable for transmission over a broadband cable network. Thus broadband cable can be utilized to provide a wide-bandwidth connection point to a range of information services. The bandwidth requirements of typical digital transmission requirements are illustrated in Table 4.3.

Table 4.3 Broadband bandwidth requirements

Transmission requirement	Data rate	Typical bandwidth required
Low speed data	< 19.2 kbps	30 kHz
Medium speed data or voice	64 kbps	300 kHz
High speed data	2 Mbps	6 MHz
Compressed Video	2–10 Mbps	6–8 MHz

An IEEE 802.3 (CSMA/CD) LAN is an example of a *baseband* LAN, that is, one in which digital signals are transmitted across the cable using the full frequency spectrum supported by the cable. Baseband LANs can normally be installed and maintained without the services of highly skilled in-house engineers. Broadband cable technology, which uses analogue signals and frequency division multiplexing to create multiple channels, is much more difficult to install and maintain (requiring skilled engineers) and too elaborate and expensive to be utilized as an office LAN. However, it has been used successfully as the main campus backbone in, for example, hospitals, universities and in manufacturing organizations.

The broadband LAN infrastructure is used to carry simultaneously analogue services (such as video and voice) and digital services (such as multiple LAN segments). Its principal advantages are very wide geographic coverage (tens of kilometres), high capacity, the ability to support multiple services simultaneously and reliability based on the use of mature CATV technology.

Broadband cable systems are also highly suited to providing a public and private regional or metropolitan area backbone network for business and residential services. These systems are being used to deliver telephony services (e.g. basic rate ISDN), broadcast television and information services to business and residential communities.

4.5.2 IEEE 802.6 – DQDB

In 1982 the IEEE 802 project set up a working group to define a MAN standard (eventually to be known as IEEE 802.6). The group focused initially on broadband cable television technology as a basis for a standard. However, at the time, the cable television industry was highly focused on providing entertainment services resulting in little interest and participation in developing a MAN standard for data communications. Work on broadband cable based solutions were replaced by fibre optic based proposals. Further proposals were considered (including FDDI-based proposal), and eventually in late 1987 the distributed queue, dual-bus (DQDB) proposal was selected. DQDB was developed originally at the University of Australia by some postgraduate students as an adaptation of a MAN proposal by Bell Laboratories in 1983. The IEEE 802.6 standard has been developed from the outset to be compatible in operation with ATM and B-ISDN public networks.

Message format

The access control method relies on the generation of a continuous stream of small fixed length units called slots. MAN nodes generate data (referred to as segments) for transmission by slots. Thus slots can be viewed as a conveyor belt of empty and full containers each capable of carrying a 44-byte segment of call data. IEEE 802.6 is designed to carry both asynchronous and synchronous segment streams. Each slot is 53 bytes long (although, like ATM the slot header is 5 bytes long, the header fields are based on an early version of the ATM cell header format) for compatibility with broadband ISDN wide area networks.

Topology

Each node in an IEEE 802.6 MAN is connected to a pair of bus segments. A slot generator device is positioned at the head of each bus and generates a continuous stream of empty slots. Slot streams flow in opposite directions on the buses thus forming a dual, contra-directional bus topology (the two ends remain unconnected). Each bus is implemented as a series of point-to-point segments thus facilitating the use of fibre optic cable. Two types of configuration result depending on the location of the terminating points of each bus as illustrated in Figure 4.15. The looped bus configuration is the more resilient since in the event of a link

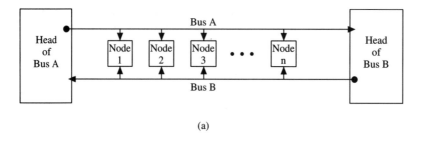

(a)

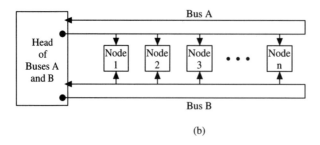

(b)

Figure 4.15 DQDB topology: (a) open bus; (b) looped bus.

failure it can reconfigure to preserve full connectivity whereas the open bus configuration will partition if the link between two nodes fail. A single IEEE 802.6 subnetwork can span up to 50 km in diameter and with an operating speed of up to 155 Mbps.

Access control method

Access control is based on the distributed queue, dual bus architecture. It recognizes the need to support efficiently and effectively both isochronous and non-isochronous streams. Isochronous traffic have pre-allocated (pre-arbitrated) bandwidths. Pre-arbitrated slots are specially marked with a particular VCI value in the slot header to signify that these cells are reserved to carry isochronous streams.

Non-isochronous streams contend for bandwidth using a distributed queuing algorithm and queue-arbitrated slots. Each station wishing to send data requests the use of empty slots and maintains a counter (a queue-position counter) which determines its position in the distributed queue. The queue-position counter is decremented each time an empty queue-arbitrated slot passes by on the bus. When the queue-position counter reaches zero, the station is authorized to use the next empty slot. Pre-arbitrated and queue-arbitrated slots are distinguished by setting particular values in the content type field of the slot header.

Transmission media

As noted earlier, DQDB is based on the bus topology implemented as a series of point-to-point connections between nodes. IEEE 802.6 is in fact defined independently of the underlying physical layer network.

Switched multi-megabit data services (SMDS)

The switched multi-megabit data service (SMDS) is a higher-layer connection interface designed by Bell Communication Research, Inc. (Bellcore) as a high-speed, reliable, connectionless data transport standard. It is based on IEEE 802.6 although it can also be used as a connection interface specification to other types of physical networks. For example, SMDS is classified as a Class D connectionless service with respect to the ATM AAL layer and is also generally regarded as a common connectionless service, for access both to IEEE 802.6 and ATM networks. SMDS offers a range of access speeds up to about 34 Mbit/s and defines a number of facilities including sender authentication, closed user groups and group addressing.

An SMDS service transports variable length user data up to a maximum of 9188 bytes. This is far greater than the maximum transmission unit of any access network technology. Many SMDS-based public networks are designed primarily to provide an affordable way to interconnect LAN-based access networks. The **connectionless broadband data service** (CBDS) is the European version of SMDS with only minor differences between the protocols. It defined a connectionless (CL) layer sited above the ATM AAL layer, and uses the AAL type 3/4 format. Two protocols are defined: connectionless network access protocol (CLNAP) which applies to the UNI, and connectionless network interface protocol (CLNIP) which applies to NNI. Source and destination addresses adhere to the standard ISDN E.164 addressing format. The address can be an individual or group address (the datagram is copied inside the network and delivered to the group members). Datagram is transferred in a 'best efforts' manner and any lost or corrupted data is not automatically retransmitted. An example SMDS/CBDS protocol stack is shown in Figure 4.16.

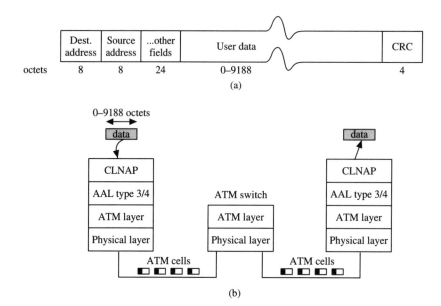

Figure 4.16 SMDS/CBDS protocol format and stack. (a) CLNAP format; (b) SMDS/CBDS protocol stack.

4.6 SUMMARY

Backbone networks support information exchange across a wide geographic area nationally and internationally. Backbone network technologies are based on mature network components which have been used since the 1970s when time-sharing computers were prevalent. Newer technologies have emerged to interconnect access networks and to support high-bandwidth, delay-sensitive traffic types. Broadband ISDN services are designed to provide the key backbone network services, relying on an underlying physical network based on ATM techniques. ATM is positioned as the key technology for building wide area and metropolitan area networks to support all traffic types in the long term. Intermediate technologies such as metropolitan area networks (MANs) are designed to interconnect access networks across a large town or city. Example MAN technologies include broadband cable and the IEEE 802.6 standard.

4.7 REVIEW EXERCISES

1. Describe the advantages and disadvantages of five types of media used to implement a communications channel?
2. Why is optical fibre not currently used throughout a network?
3. Why is it useful to arrange network software into a hierarchy of layers? Describe the ISO OSI reference model. Are there circumstances where less than seven layers is appropriate?
4. List some national or international standards that shape some of the artefacts in your home. Reflect on what would result if these standards did not exist. Discuss the advantages and disadvantages of having international standards in the communications industry.

5. What types of errors occur when you use the telephone system to make a call to a friend? Find out the costs of using the telephone system for data communications and compare it with the cost of using a leased line connection. What is the break-even point (in terms of the duration of the call) when it becomes cheaper to use a leased line? Assume communication occurs between 14.00 and 17.00 hours.

6. List four main types of network topology used to implement wide area networks.

7. Discuss the differences between broadcast, circuit switched and packet switched networks. Give examples of the types of traffic most suitable for each type of network.

8. Explain what is understood by the following terms in relation to packet switched networks: i. datagram; ii. virtual circuit.

9. Discuss the motivations for the development of the frame relay standard. Describe the differences between frame relay and the X.25 standard.

10. Explain why ISDN is a suitable wide area network service for carrying multimedia data streams. Compare the costs of using an ISDN service with a analogue public switched telephone network.

11. What are the differences between narrowband, wideband and broadband ISDN services?

12. ATM has been described as the network technology likely to replace all existing network technologies. Describe a typical ATM network. Comment on whether ATM will be pervasive in the future.

13. Provision of service for mobile users is an increasingly important factor when designing a network infrastructure. Describe the current options available for connecting a laptop or handheld computer being used by a person, for example at a service station on a road highway to the branch office computer.

14. Discuss the differences between WAN and MAN technologies. Is MAN technology likely to be distinct from WAN technology in the long term?

4.8 FURTHER READING

Halsall (1992) and Stallings (1994) are good general texts on backbone (and access) networks. Helgert (1991) details the ISDN architecture and protocols (focusing mainly on the narrowband standards). Handel *et al.* (1994), give a very detailed coverage of ATM networks and protocols. Metropolitan area networks are covered in Stallings (1993). Partridge (1994) provides an in-depth coverage of high-speed network architectures. Hehmann *et al.* (1990) consider the high-speed network requirements to support multimedia applications. As an example of a high-speed network supporting multimedia applications, Martin (1994) and Pusztaszeri *et al.* (1994) present the BETEL ATM network and a teletutoring application, respectively.

5

NETWORK TECHNOLOGIES – ACCESS NETWORKS

5.1 INTRODUCTION

An access network supports information exchange within a site and provides a gateway to remote resources and information services not available at the site. It is largely met by local area network (LAN) technologies such as Ethernet, token-ring and FDDI and supporting software optimized for moderate geographic coverage such as encompassing a single office building or a building complex or campus. The network is usually owned, administered and used by a single organization. In this chapter we will describe network technologies which can be used to implement an access network.

5.2 STRUCTURED CABLING INFRASTRUCTURE

An important strategic consideration when implementing an access network at a site is physical cabling. Organizations are dynamic entities continually changing in response to changes in the business environment. This gives rise to occasional (or frequent) restructuring and attendant staff moves. Cabling a building or building complex as part of implementing an access network can represent a major long-term investment and where short-term expediencies can lead to significant long-term costs. Structured cabling is an approach to cabling building complexes widely recognized as the best method of providing communications services within a building to support the business needs of an organization. The following benefits can be realized:

1. The ability to relocate staff cost-effectively and quickly thus saving costs in the long term.
2. Reduced cable maintenance costs.

3. The ability to add additional users and upgrade to incorporate new technologies incrementally, quickly and easily.
4. Improved reliability.

Structured cabling is not applicable to all building complexes. For freehold or long leasehold properties the return on investment will be realized. However, structured cabling may not be economic in short-term occupancy situations. The characteristics of the building may also render it unsuitable for structured cabling.

A cable infrastructure could have a useful life of up to 15 years (a major building refurbishment typically occurs every 10 to 15 years) although some investments will give benefits for the life of the building. Most structured wiring schemes are based on:

- The use of a star wired topology using saturation wiring from a communications closet to the wall outlet. This provides optimum versatility because:
  1. the building can be cabled independent of actual LAN topologies,
  2. it can accommodate the inter-mixing of LAN types,
  3. changes to the topology are much easier to configure,
  4. star topologies are easier to manage.
- The use of four-pair 100 Ω UTP cabling in the horizontal work area on each floor. A variety of grades of UTP cable can be bought. Cable types have been specified by the Electrical Industries Association (EIA). The relevant standards are EIA/TIA building wiring standard Category 3 to 5. Category 3 UTP cable is designed to carry voice and low/medium speed data. Category 5 cable is able to support data rates up to around 100 Mbit/s.
- The UTP cable run from user-device to the closet should not exceed 100 m (and 90 m from the room socket outlet to the closet).
- The use of fibre optic cables as backbone cabling which are housed in building risers and take the wiring to each floor.

An example structured cabling configuration is shown in Figure 5.1. Access network technologies should complement any structured cabling scheme adopted by an organization.

Traditional LAN technologies are designed to carry data messages efficiently. Voice and video transmissions generated by multimedia applications pose major problems to these networks. Many LAN technologies are being enhanced to cater for the increased demand for bandwidth.

The Institute of Electrical and Electronics Engineers (IEEE) has been the major influence in developing standards for LANs. In 1985 it established the **IEEE 802** LAN standards (IEEE, 1985a, b) by initially defining four standard LAN types and defining a common addressing scheme. The IEEE 802 reference model is illustrated in Figure 5.2. The 802.2 Logical Link Control (LLC) layer provides a common interface for higher layer protocols. A higher layer can make use of LLC services which are independent of the underlying LAN technology implemented. Differences in frame formats and protocols are embodied in the medium access control (MAC) header formats defined uniquely for each LAN type. Fundamentally, each MAC frame format identifies the destination and source node address fields, the information field and fields used for error detection and access control. IEEE 802 standards are continually being extended technology advances. This chapter focuses on the design and implementation of the following access networks:

- CSMA/CD LANs.
- Token-ring LANs.

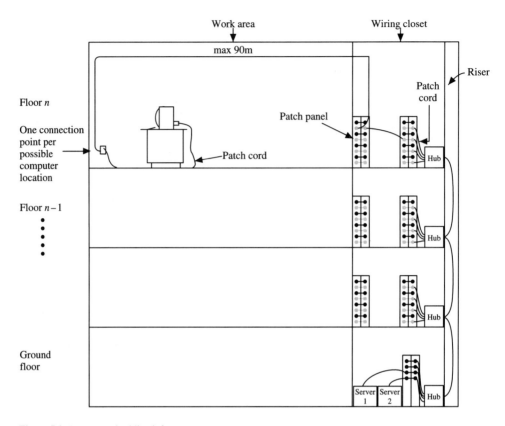

Figure 5.1 A structured cabling infrastructure.

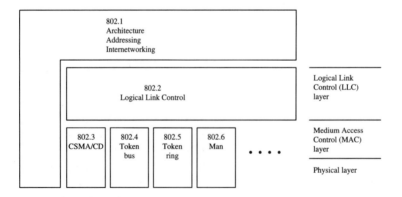

Figure 5.2 The IEEE 802 model.

- FDDI LANs.
- ATM LANs.
- Wireless LANS.

Each is examined in terms of five main characteristics: message format, network topology options, physical cabling options, access control technique and typical operating speeds.

5.3 CSMA/CD LANs

CSMA/CD (commonly known as Ethernet) LANs are currently the most popular access network technology to support data exchanges. The original **Ethernet** system was developed at the Palo Alto Research Centre of Xerox from 1973 (Metcalfe and Boggs, 1976). The first commercial implementation (known as the DIX 1.0 specification, developed by Digital, Intel and Xerox) was published in 1980 (DIX, 1980). Version 2 of the Ethernet specification, known as **Ethernet II**, was used (almost unaltered) for the widely used international standard CSMA/CD LAN known as **IEEE 802.3** (IEEE, 1985c). A variant of IEEE 802.3 called Ethernet sub-network access protocol (SNAP) was developed to enable higher-layer protocols such as TCP/IP to be used on networks which do not use the standard Ethernet II frame format. The term 'CSMA/CD' will be used as a generic term to refer to all of the above specifications unless otherwise stated.

5.3.1 Message format

As discussed above, a CSMA/CD LAN is available in several flavours. Figure 5.3 illustrates the message format of Ethernet II, IEEE 802.3, IEEE 802.2 and Ethernet SNAP. The main difference of note is that IEEE 802.3 redefined the Ethernet II Type field as a Length field. The contents of the Ethernet II Type field is passed to higher-layer protocols to identify the type of packet encapsulated in the Data field. The possible values in the Type field are well defined (maintained by the IEEE), a selection of which is shown in Table 5.1.

Table 5.1 A selection of TYPE field values

TYPE *value*	*Meaning*
0800	IP packet
0805	X.25 level 3
0806	TCP/IP address resolution protocol (ARP)
8137–8138	Novell Netware protocols
6003	DECnet
0600	XNS packet

Instead of a Type field, an IEEE 802.3 frame uses either the IEEE 802.2 LLC header or the SNAP header can be used to identify the higher layer protocol. The destination and source service access point fields (DSAP and SSAP, respectively) of LLC and the organization code and EtherType fields of the SNAP header are used for this purpose.

Because of these and other differences, CSMA/CD hosts must know whether Ethernet II or IEEE 802.3 specifications are to be used. Although the frame lengths and most other fields are the same, the network interface card software driver in the sending host has to insert the appropriate value into the type/length field, and the corresponding driver in the destination host has to interpret it correctly. If a software driver assumes an 802.3 frame format, the value represents a length and should be in the range 0 to 0x05DC (0–1500 decimal). If a driver assumes an Ethernet II frame, the value indicates which higher layer protocol is to receive the frame and the value should correspond to a valid TYPE value as defined by the IEEE (values are normally greater than 0x0600, i.e.1536 decimal).

Mixing Ethernet II and IEEE 802.3 frames on the same network could lead to a lot of

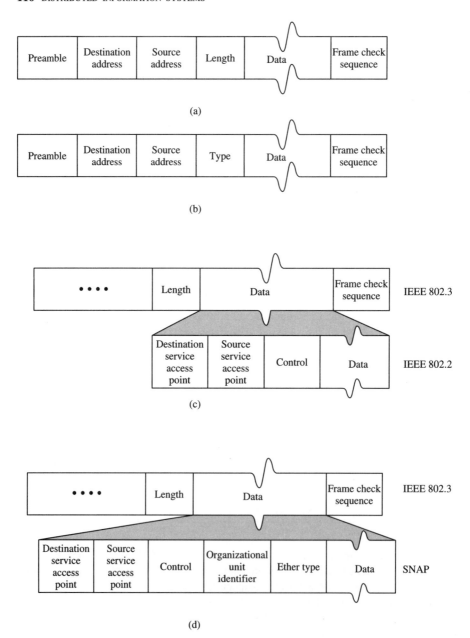

Figure 5.3 CSMA/CD frame formats: (a) IEEE 802.3; (b) Ethernet II; (c) IEEE 802.2; (d) Ethernet SNAP.

turmoil unless carefully managed! Drivers can in fact distinguish between an Ethernet II and an IEEE 802.3 frame by observing that if the TYPE field contains a value 1536 or greater then it is an Ethernet II frame otherwise it is an IEEE 802.3 frame.

The preamble field (a series of seven bytes each containing 10101010) allows the receiver to synchronize before receiving actual data. The frame check sequence field uses cyclic redundancy checking (CRC) to detect transmission errors in the destination address, source address, length, and data fields. Higher-layer protocols (e.g. the LLC layer) are responsible for error correction since the receiving CSMA/CD station simply discards frames with incorrect checksums.

5.3.2 Topology

CSMA/CD LANs are based around the bus topology that can be extended to a branching, non-rooted topology by the use of special devices known as repeaters, bridges, and routers (see Chapter 6). This is illustrated in Figure 5.4. A recent addition to IEEE 802.3 is the hybrid star-bus topology known as *10BaseT*, as illustrated in Figure 5.5. In this arrangement, the bus segment is logically collapsed into a concentrator (also known as a hub) and all network stations are wired directly (point-to-point) to the hub in a star-like topology. Thus, outwardly, the topology resembles a star topology but behaves as a bus topology. This affords a more manageable approach to constructing large multi-segment CSMA/CD LANs. Structured cabling generally rely on the use of multiple, interconnected IEEE 802.3 10BaseT LANs. The IEEE 802.3 10BaseT standard has been designed to complement structured cabling schemes since it is based on a logical star topology with UTP cable lengths of up to 100 m.

5.3.3 Transmission media

IEEE 802.3 supports a wide range of transmission media. There are four major cable types which reflects the fact that each cable type has particular strengths and weaknesses:

1. 10Base5 (thin Ethernet): thin coaxial cable with access unit interface (AUI) connectors and a (shielded twisted pair) drop cable connecting the network station to the bus segment (via a transceiver);

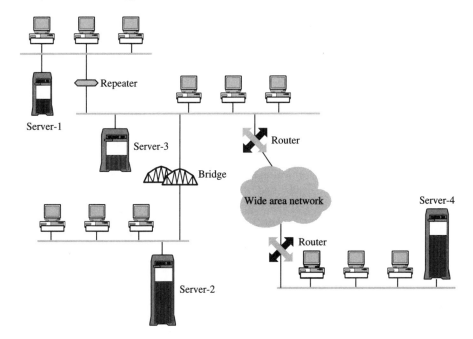

Figure 5.4 An example CSMA/CD configuration.

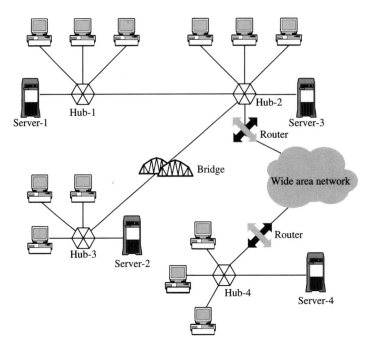

Figure 5.5 A 10baseT configuration.

2. 10Base2 (thick Ethernet): thick coaxial cable with BNC connectors;
3. 10BaseT: unshielded twisted pair (UTP) cable;
4. 10BaseF: fibre optic cable.

Thick Ethernet was the first Ethernet cabling option and is therefore more commonly found in older installations as the cabling infrastructure for local minicomputer and mainframe links. The coaxial cable is quite rigid due to its thickness (about 1 cm in diameter) but allows a maximum segment length of 500 m (and a minimum of 2.5 m between cable connection points). Earlier wiring strategies used 10Base5 as a backbone joining a number of Ethernet segments.

Thin Ethernet coaxial cable is much cheaper, thinner and the minimum distance between connection points is reduced to 0.5 m making it suitable for cabling a work area on a particular floor. The functionality of the transceiver is built into the network interface card (NIC). To add stations, the cable must be cut and fitted with special BNC connectors which can be attached directly to the NIC forming a daisy chain of network stations (avoiding the need for a drop cable). The drawbacks are that a 10Base2 segment has a maximum segment length of around 200 m and reliability is reduced due to use of BNC connections (which can be disconnected easily).

Although coaxial cable has been the mainstay of Ethernet networks for many years, twisted pair cabling, particularly the unshielded variety, is a very attractive alternative as it is well understood, easily installed, economical and light. It used to be regarded as the poor relation to coaxial cable because of its low immunity to electromagnetic interference and inability to carry Ethernet traffic over relatively long distances. However, standards have been defined for higher quality grades of UTP cable that are better suited to support high bandwidth transmissions. Modern structured building cabling schemes favour the use of twisted pair to cable the work area on each floor, thus 10baseT is a popular option compatible with these schemes.

Fibre optic cable has become an affordable option for some parts of an Ethernet LAN. It is rapidly replacing coaxial cable backbones and long segments. Fibre optic cable is so thin that several fibre optic strands can pass through the eye of a needle. Data is carried by an optical (light) signal which travels by internal reflection from source to destination and offers a much higher capacity (of the order of Gbit/s), lower signal attenuation (reducing the requirement for repeaters) and lower error rates than is typical of coaxial cable. This makes it ideal for high-bandwidth applications. Because the signal is not electrical and the light is reflected internally, the signal is very difficult to tap thus providing a very secure medium against physical tampering. The main drawback is the cost of cabling and installation, although this is reducing.

5.3.4 Access control method

The carrier sense multiple access/collision detection (CSMA/CD) technique is used to control access to the shared medium by multiple network stations. A data frame is between 64 and 1518 bytes (excluding the preamble field). Before transmitting, a CSMA/CD station must first determine that no-one else is transmitting by sensing whether a (carrier) signal is present on the cable – this is known as carrier sensing. If no data is being transmitted then any station is free to begin transmission by *broadcasting* the data on the cable making it accessible to all stations. Any station examines the destination address field of any transmission to determine whether it is for them.

One situation that can arise is the case when several stations, with data to transmit, carrier sense simultaneously and all conclude that the cable is not in use. If, subsequently, two or more stations transmit at this time then signals will collide and data will be corrupted. This is known as a **collision** and collision detection is done by monitoring voltages at the same time as data is being transmitted to detect if the voltage level of the signal surges beyond predefined limits (the minimum frame length of 64 bytes ensures that collisions can be detected by all stations). When a collision is detected a predefined backoff recovery procedure is triggered which is designed to ensure that a collision involving the same stations is avoided in future attempts. As part of the recovery procedure, every station involved in the collision first terminates data transmission and sends a 'jam' sequence to ensure that all active stations are made aware of the collision. Secondly, retransmission is scheduled by each colliding station after waiting for a random time period which is calculated using a random number generator (based on the unique Ethernet address associated with each network interface card) to ensure that the backoff time will be different for each card. Thus there is a low probability that two cards attempt retransmission simultaneously.

5.3.5 Support for high-bandwidth and delay-sensitive applications

With light–medium data workloads, CSMA/CD is an efficient shared medium LAN able to handle most data applications. Careful design is required to ensure that data flows are localized (using bridges and routers) to single segments to avoid unnecessary traffic flows occurring. Heavy workloads result in excessive collisions and a low throughput of messages. In practice, most CSMA/CD LANs supporting data applications are lightly loaded with hardly any collisions as there are many more system bottlenecks that constrain the demand for bandwidth.

There are several features of a CSMA/CD network that make it less-suited to support delay-sensitive applications on a large scale. Response times are non-deterministic, that is, transmission of a message within a defined time period cannot be guaranteed. Therefore end-to-end delay and delay jitter guarantees cannot be made. CSMA/CD is a contention protocol with no priority scheme. Another factor is that a shared medium LAN with a standard operating speed of 10 Mbps does not have the capacity to support high-bandwidth applications (e.g. multimedia applications) under normal workloads consisting of a mixture of stream and bursty traffic. Finally, scalability of CSMA/CD LANs is very limited since few options are available to enhance the operating speed and capacity of the network. Nevertheless, on a very lightly loaded network a small number (approximately 5–10) of isochronous streams (e.g. videoconferencing traffic) can be carried with reasonable results. Two variants of CSMA/CD LANs have emerged to provide a migration path to support applications with high-bandwidth and delay-sensitive requirements: IEEE 802.3 100BaseT and switched Ethernet (Figure 5.6).

5.3.6 IEEE 802.3 100BaseT

This variant was voted into the IEEE 802.3 sub-group in July 1994. The original proposal came from a consortium of major manufacturers of CSMA/CD products. 100BaseT involves

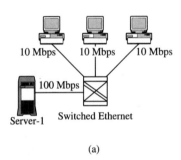

(a)

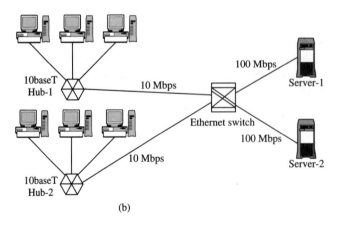

(b)

Figure 5.6 Example of switched Ethernet configuration. (a) fast Ethernet server link eliminates server bottleneck, (b) client workstations connected to servers via 10BaseT hubs and switched Ethernet.

a minor change to the physical layer concerning the encoding of the digital signal and shortens the maximum cable segment length to ensure that 100 Mbps transmissions over high-quality UTP cable would not exceed electromagnetic emission limits imposed by government regulatory bodies. There are no changes to the MAC layer in terms of frame format and access control technique (CSMA/CD). This is an important consideration as implementing a network implies a number of costs including cabling, network interface cards (per client workstation and server computer) and concentrators or hubs in the wiring closet. Thus a standard 10BaseT CSMA/CD LAN can be upgraded to 100BaseT by purchasing new network interface cards (for all client and server computers) and 100BaseT hubs (assuming that high-quality UTP cable has been installed).

To support true multimedia communications, a LAN must be able to carry video and audio signals which demand low latency as well as high-speed transmission. This can only be achieved if asynchronous, synchronous and isochronous traffic can be prioritized or the speed and latency requirements can be guaranteed without resorting to priority mechanisms. The CSMA/CD access control method does not facilitate priority access. Thus, 100BaseT is suited to high-speed data applications such as client/server databases, document imaging, CAD/CAM and medical imaging but may struggle to support all traffic types including isochronous unless additional higher-layer protocols are implemented to handle bandwidth allocation and other functions.

5.3.7 Switched Ethernet

This technology essentially adopts a point-to-point circuit-switching mechanism giving each workstation or CSMA/CD segment a dedicated, point-to-point link with an operating speed of 10 or 100 Mbps depending on whether 10BaseT or 100BaseT is in use. Thus the switch is used either to provide point-to-point connections between workstations or to act as a bridge between individual CSMA/CD segments. The switching is carried out by a central switch matrix in the switched Ethernet hub and is analogous to the function of a PBX in a telephone system. The channelling of traffic takes place within the switching matrix and each workstation or Ethernet segment is connected to a dedicated port so that the data, voice or video transmission will not conflict with other workstation or segment transmissions and the full 10 Mbps bandwidth is available.

To transfer a frame from an input port to the destination port with minimum delay, each switch must be able to support simultaneously all of its connections at full bandwidth (known as non-blocking operation). For example, a 16-port switch must have a 160 Mbps switching speed if it is to support sixteen 10 Mbps connections without blocking. A parallel bus-based switching architecture is commonly used to achieve non-blocking operation because of inherent support of full-bandwidth multicast and broadcast. The key to Ethernet switching is to examine the destination address in the standard CSMA/CD frame and to set up an internal 10 Mbps virtual circuit with the destination port to which the destination device or segment is attached.

Standard CSMA/CD network cabling and interface cards are used avoiding replacement costs, but the switching mechanism completely replaces the CSMA/CD access control mechanism. The switches typically use a high-performance processor to monitor all the packet addresses and send them on their way. Filtering and forwarding rates are high enough to guarantee 10 Mbps throughput unimpeded. A further development of this technology takes advantage of the four pair cables of a 10BaseT installation (or two-wire fibre optic cabling) to provide simultaneous send and receive (i.e. full-duplex) Ethernet operation. In this configuration, the two wire pairs reserved for carrier sensing are used together with the two data wire pairs to form separate send and receive channels (carrier sensing is redundant since in this case there is no possibility of collisions occurring). Thus an aggregate 20 Mbps bandwidth is available for point-to-point connection between devices.

An example use of Ethernet switching is to dedicate each network segment containing client workstations to a port. Server computers are directly attached to a port ensuring a dedicated 10 Mbps (or 20 Mbps) channel accessible by all client segments. While this improves the amount of bandwidth available to each client or server, in this configuration Ethernet switching still suffers from the same limitations inherent in CSMA/CD LANs with respect to support for delay-sensitive applications. Example switched Ethernet configurations are shown in Figure 5.6.

5.4 IEEE 802.5 TOKEN RING

Research on token ring LANs can be traced back as early as the late 1960s (Farmer and Newhall, 1969). However, it was not exploited for widespread commercial use until the early 1980s when IBM proposed a specification that later formed the IEEE 802.5 standard (IEEE, 1985d).

The token ring standard is based on the definition of a special bit pattern called a token to determine who has permission to access the shared medium (the ring) at any given time. This token circulates around the ring and any station wishing to transmit must first wait to receive a 'free' token which has the effect of giving it the authority to transmit. It transmits by first setting the 'free' token to 'busy' and sends the data frame. The transmitting station then restores the free token. So no two or more stations can transmit simultaneously.

5.4.1 Message format

The message format of a data frame and a token are illustrated in Figure 5.7. Unique signal encoding is used to identify the start and end points of the frame (the start delimiter (SD) and end delimiter (ED) fields) to ensure that they can never appear in other encapsulated fields (data transparency). The data frame has the usual addressing, data and CRC fields. Figure 5.7 identifies these fields and several other fields illustrating that a token ring frame is much more complex than IEEE 802.3. The access control (AC) field contains bits used by the token-passing protocol. The token bit (T) is set to zero in a token frame and to one in a data frame. The priority mode and priority reservation bits are used to implement a priority access mechanism as part of the token-passing protocol. This provides eight levels of priority in accessing the shared ring. When a token ring station becomes active, one station assumes the role of the *active monitor* (all stations are capable of assuming the role of monitor station), responsible for the general welfare of the ring which includes placing the token on the ring to initiate the token-passing mechanism. The monitor count (MC) bit is used by the active monitor to prevent a data frame from continually circulating around the ring (e.g. due to failure at the source station).

The frame control (FC) field is used to distinguish between a data frame and a MAC frame (MAC frames provide network management and other functions). The destination and

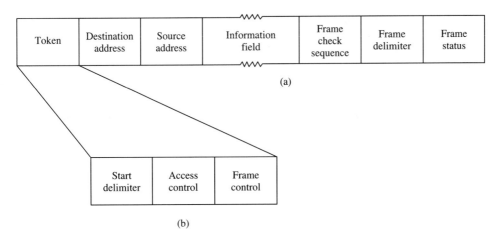

Figure 5.7 IEEE 802.5 token (b) and data frame (a) formats.

source address fields are either two or six bytes long and support individual, multicast and broadcast addressing. An optional routing information (RI) sub-field is used to describe a path from source to destination that traverses one or more (source routing) bridges.

The data field length is limited only by the maximum transmission time allowed for each station when the token is held. This can be set by an installation and typically results in a maximum length of 4–5000 bytes. The 32-bit CRC frame check sequence (FCS) is used to detect errors occurring in the FC, DA, SA, DATA, and FCS fields. Finally, the frame status (FS) field contains the address-recognized (A) and frame-copied (C) bits that are used to enable the receiver to indicate to the sending station that it recognized the data frame and it copied the frame. Thus token passing has a full acknowledgement scheme that enables the sending station to determine whether the receiver is inactive or non-existent, or is active but did not copy the frame, or is active and copied the frame.

The token frame simply consists of the starting delimiter, access control and end delimiter fields. The access control field contains the token bit which receiving stations use to immediately identify frame as a token (when set to zero).

5.4.2 Topology

One inherent weakness in the basic ring topology is the possibility of network failure due to ring cable or node failure. To overcome this weakness the star-ring hybrid topology is used which is illustrated in Figure 5.8. Network stations are cabled directly to a wiring concentrator thus resembling a star topology. However, each drop cable consists of two twisted wire pairs, one for transmit, the other for receive. These are used to join the ring electronics internal to the wiring concentrator. When a station is inserted into the wiring concentrator it triggers an electronic relay which joins it onto the ring. If the node or drop cable malfunctions, the wiring concentrator immediately isolates it by bypassing the drop cable connection point, thus removing it from the ring. It is possible to inter-mix several cable types as this is determined by the connection points offered by the wiring concentrator. The wiring concentrators can be joined together by point-to-point links to extend the network. Bridges and routers can also be used to form an internetwork of token-ring LANs. This topology complements structured cabling schemes.

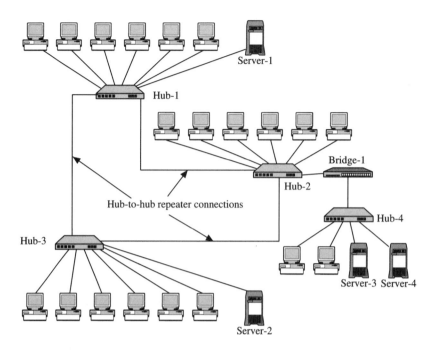

Figure 5.8 IEEE 802.5: an example topology.

5.4.3 Transmission media

In the IBM specification several cable types are defined. The more common cable types are detailed in Table 5.2. The types of cable which are utilized depends on the precise configuration adopted, which in turn depends on the number and location of concentrators and whether a particular structured cabling scheme is being adopted.

Table 5.2 Common token-ring cable types

Cable type	Typical use
Type 1	Double screened twisted pair (STP): used to implement large token-ring systems adhering to a structured cabling scheme.
Type 2	STP for data and UTP for voice: used to support a face plate with two sockets, one for a network station the other for a telephone.
Type 3	UTP cable for installing a small moveable configuration using cheaper wiring than type 1.
Type 5	Two (multimode) fibre optic cables: used for interwiring closet connections.
Type 6	UTP cable: known as 'patch' cable and is used to connect rack-mounted concentrators together, or to connect stations to a concentrator in small configurations.

The performance and configuration constraints of cable types 1, 2, 3 and 6 are difficult to calculate as they depend on the precise configuration adopted. Typical figures are summarized in Table 5.3.

Table 5.3 Token-ring distance limits

	Type 1	Type 2	Type 3	Type 6
Maximum distance between concentrator and station (m)	375	100	100	45
Tested data rate (Mbit/s)	16	4	4	4
Concentrator to concentrator (m)	200	120	120	45
Maximum number of devices per ring	260	72	96	96
Maximum number of concentrators in a configuration	33	12	12	12

A typical token-ring network employs STP cabling, possibly with a fibre optic backbone. The STP cable is specific to IEEE 802.5 (and IBM's own structured cabling scheme) and is not a feature of most other structured cabling schemes. The UTP specification in IEEE 802.5 is designed for small token-ring configurations rather than for structured cabling.

5.4.4 Access control protocol

The access control protocol is called token passing and can be used with a ring topology (as in the IEEE 802.5 standard) and the bus topology (as in the IEEE 802.4 standard as detailed in IEEE (1985c)). If we assume that initially a token frame is being passed from station to station, a station wishing to send data must wait to receive the token frame. When it receives a frame, it checks the token bit to see if it is a token frame. If it is a token then, if the priority of the token is less than or equal to that of the waiting data unit to be sent, it sets the token bit to one and inserts the frame control, source address, destination address, routing information (optional) and data fields (using the appropriate message format). It also computes the CRC and sets the FCS field, and has the option of setting the priority reservation (PR) bits to request that the next token be issued at the requested priority. The data frame is transmitted from station to station until it arrives at the destination station. The destination station copies the data and sets the address-recognized and frame-copied bits appropriately. When the data frame returns to the sending station, the data frame is removed and a new token frame generated (assuming that the maximum transmission time allowed is likely to be exceeded if a further transmission takes place).

5.4.5 Support for high-bandwidth and delay-sensitive applications

Performance studies (Stuck and Arthurs, 1985) have shown that with light–medium data workloads a token-ring network is less efficient than a CSMA/CD network particularly when a large number of active stations are connected to a single ring. As with Ethernet, careful design is required to maximize performance by ensuring that data flows are localized (using bridges and routers) by forming a topology consisting of an interconnection of multiple rings (with one token per ring). Client stations and associated servers should be on the same ring thus ensuring that data transmission is largely destined for stations on the same ring, avoiding unnecessary traffic flows. Performance studies have also shown that heavy workloads are much better handled by token-ring networks. In particular, token-ring networks continue to perform well in the face of overload conditions whereas CSMA/CD-based networks become very unstable.

One major advantage of token-ring networks over CSMA/CD is that response times are deterministic, that is, there is an upper limit on the message transmission time. Furthermore, the token passing protocol offers a priority scheme to support video and voice traffic. However, a token-ring network is a shared medium LAN with a limited range of operating speeds of (4 or 16 Mbps) which means that it has limited capacity and scalability to support high-bandwidth and delay-sensitive applications under normal workloads. Furthermore, although network response time is deterministic in that a worst case response time can be calculated, this time cannot be controlled easily to meet a latency demanded by a particular application (e.g. a video transmission). The operating speeds of IEEE 802.5 mean that only about 10 isochronous streams can be supported. Therefore it is not a technology to support multimedia applications on a large scale. Bandwidth improvements and a more sophisticated priority access scheme are featured in a similar approach known as FDDI which is examined in the next section.

5.5 FIBRE DISTRIBUTED DATA INTERFACE (FDDI)

The fibre distributed data interface (FDDI) LAN is an ISO standard for a LAN (ISO 9314). FDDI-based LANs use optical fibre cabling instead of copper wires. The primary advantages are a high data rate (100 Mbit/s), greater geographic coverage (up to 100 km), immunity to electromagnetic interferences (attractive in terms of improved security). FDDI is based on the IEEE 802.5 exhibiting much of the characteristics of token-ring systems and as such can be viewed as an enhanced version of it. The speed and geographic coverage of FDDI positions it as a technology able to support LAN and MAN requirements.

5.5.1 Message format

The message format is similar to the IEEE 802.5 standard for token ring LANs to facilitate the internetworking of high and low-speed ring networks (Stallings, 1990). Note that an access control field present in an IEEE 802.5 is not defined in the FDDI standard. This is because FDDI does not use the IEEE 802.5 priority scheme to control the allocation of bandwidth.

5.5.2 Topology

The topology of FDDI is based on a set of dual, counter-rotating rings which provides a high degree of reliability, as shown in Figure 5.9. In normal operation only one of these rings (the primary ring) carries data. The secondary ring provides a backup to the primary and is used for automatic recovery in case of a single point of failure on the primary ring. When a network fault occurs, the two FDDI stations at the ends of the broken link automatically detect the break and bypass the fault by switching their transmission to the secondary ring, which then carries the data in the opposite direction to the data flow on the primary ring. Stations attached to both rings (thus having four fibre attachments) are known as 'dual attach stations (DAS)'. FDDI also specifies an alternative approach which allows 'single attach station (SAS)' devices to connect directly to FDDI concentrators which in turn attach to the rings. Thus an FDDI LAN may consist of a ring of star-wired SAS devices which are typically FDDI client workstations, host computers, Ethernet and token-ring bridges and other devices.

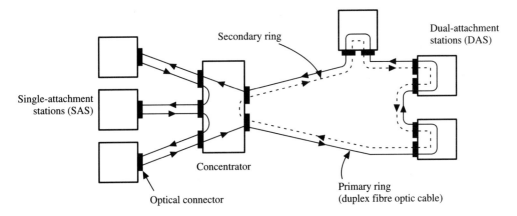

Figure 5.9 A FDDI topology.

The ring topology was chosen because, in conjunction with a token passing protocol, it has the potential to support both synchronous and asynchronous traffic and exhibit a high level of fault tolerance.

5.5.3 Transmission media

FDDI, as the name suggests, uses fibre optic cable throughout the building. An end-to-end fibre optic cable between user-device and communications closet obviously renders it more expensive (and more difficult to implement) than the other options we have considered. An alternative option, known as copper distributed data interface (CDDI) or alternatively as TP-PMD, utilizes the FDDI protocol and data rate but using copper (UTP and STP) instead of fibre optic cable. This is particularly attractive as the basis for cabling SAS devices on a floor area as copper cable is much easier to install as well as being significantly cheaper.

In the interests of safety (laser light can damage the retina), minimizing costs and the complexity of the network interface cards, FDDI uses light-emitting diodes (LEDs) in the transmitters, photo diodes in the receivers and the 4B/5B encoding scheme. The nominal operating wavelength is 1300 nm. Fibre optic cables have a core/cladding diameter of either 62.5/125 or 85/125 μm.

5.5.4 Access control method

The access control method is very similar to IEEE 802.5. There are two major differences; the token release mechanism and the bandwidth allocation mechanism. With IEEE 802.5 (the 4 Mbps variety), the transmitting station restores a free token only after the leading edge of its transmitted frame returns. If FDDI adopted this scheme the increased bandwidth could not be fully utilized. Instead, FDDI allows the free token to be emitted immediately following the data frame.

IEEE 802.5 uses a priority and reservation scheme to control bandwidth allocation. Typically, IEEE 802.5 does not make use of the scheme and thus provides equal, fair access to all stations. FDDI provides a more sophisticated scheme that is used in the IEEE 802.4 (token bus) standard and aims to provide better support for mixed asynchronous and synchronous traffic typical of multimedia environments.

5.5.5 Support for high-bandwidth and delay-sensitive applications

FDDI is inherently a shared medium LAN with only one operating speed defined (100 Mbps). Although bandwidth and priority scheme are improved relative to IEEE 802.5, the demands of multimedia applications would still overwhelm an FDDI LAN in some circumstances. A second approach, known as FDDI-II splits the usable bandwidth into two streams: stream one supports asynchronous traffic using the standard FDDI protocols described earlier, the second stream is dedicated to supporting synchronous traffic by providing a number of synchronous pipes to support voice and video traffic. Currently very few FDDI products offer FDDI-II. It is likely that this technology will be superseded by ATM-based solutions in the future.

5.6 ASYNCHRONOUS TRANSFER MODE (ATM)

The asynchronous transfer mode (ATM) switching technique has its roots in the provision of high-speed or 'broadband' wide area networks as discussed in detail in Chapter 4. However, the technique is also being applied to LANs providing the potential for a simple interconnection of local and wide area networks.

ATM has been designed from the outset to support the transmission of all types of traffic (synchronous and asynchronous) and can operate much faster than conventional packet switching techniques by avoiding error and flow control during transmission. An ATM switch is able to keep the switching delay to around 25 µs which when used as the basis of a local area network provides very fast switching. The speed of an ATM network is limited only by the capacity and quality of cabling, the switching speed of ATM switches and the speed of the ATM network interface cards. A wide range of speeds can potentially be offered making it a highly scalable technology. On-demand bandwidth negotiation with guaranteed quality of service means that ATM-based networks are highly suited to support high-band-width and low-latency applications for the foreseeable future.

A simple ATM LAN consists of a single ATM hub (VP:VC switch) to which ATM workstations and servers are attached thus forming a star topology. Each link between a user device and an ATM hub provides dedicated bandwidth. However, ATM will more usually be introduced initially as an alternative campus backbone technology interconnecting LAN segments. Some workstations, servers and other devices (e.g. a PBX or video-based equipment) will be directly connected to the ATM switch where bandwidth and latency requirements dictate. The ATM Forum has specified a low-cost ATM interface (running at 25 and 51 Mbit/s) for workstations which is also better suited to the category 3 cabling prevalent in many existing cabling infrastructures. The ATM backbone is also used to make direct connections to a private or public ATM WAN. An example configuration is shown in Figure 5.10. This configuration using ATM technology is attractive because of its ability to provide:

- scalable speed and throughput. Throughput requirements are met by matching the cell rate for a connection to the bandwidth requirements;
- very low switching delay. This enables an ATM solution to support delay-sensitive applications such as digitized voice;
- it is evolving as an international standard;
- easy internetworking with future broadband WAN services.

Currently, the cost of implementing an ATM is relatively high, but costs are reducing.

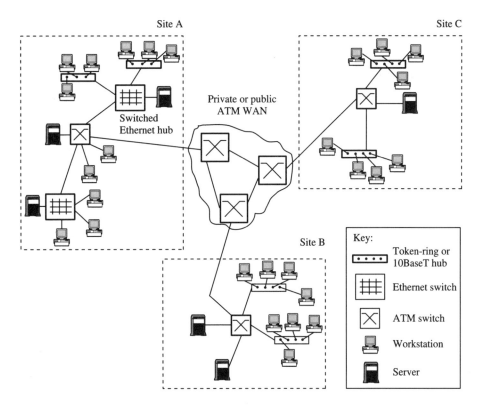

Figure 5.10 An example ATM configuration.

5.7 WIRELESS LANs

During the 1980s mobile telephony services have evolved to the extent that the mobile phone is now a standard facility both for businesses and home users. The conventional approach to providing the data access network is to pre-cable each user location, anticipating future user requirements and enabling the mobility of personnel through use of a structured cabling scheme. The introduction of portable computers and the increasing frequency of organizational changes and the need to offer customer-oriented services has led to the need for people to be able to wander freely around customer premises or to use a portable computer while at a motorway service area, whilst having continual access to corporate and workgroup applications and data. Another requirement may be to respond quickly to a need to set up a temporary 'casual workgroup' with minimal effort and and with a relatively small investment in technology.

Wireless LANs are seen as a solution to the need for installation flexibility and mobility when locating and configuring IT resources in a variety of circumstances. The benefit is that no cabling has to be installed. Due to their relatively high costs, wireless LANs have initially been used in environments where cable is either impossible to install, disruptive or prohibitively expensive. There are three basic techniques to enable interconnection of computers without physical cabling: spread spectrum technology; narrowband, high frequency radio; and infra-red technology.

The technologies differ in geographic scope, bandwidth and configuration options which make them suitable for different applications.

5.7.1 Spread spectrum technology (SST)

Radio communication is normally the most appropriate medium for wireless networks. Radio frequency bands range from several hundred MHz to around 60 GHz. However, the demand for radio bandwidth allocation is high causing the radio spectrum to be regarded as a precious, limited resource and usually operates under a strict regulatory framework. This means that in practice a wireless network is normally required to operate within a very limited bandwidth that has to be used as efficiently as possible. The radio frequency band allocation and channel access technique employed are important factors. Higher radio frequency bands are less able to penetrate dense structures used in buildings – an important consideration for wireless LANs.

The two most common channel access schemes are frequency division multiplexed access (FDMA) and time division multiplexed access (TDMA). FDMA is ideal for voice circuit switched networks whereas TDMA is the basic access technique used in packet switched data networks and shared medium LANs due to the typically bursty nature of data transmissions.

A third channel access scheme, known as code division multiplexed access (CDMA) has its origins in military communications systems and is therefore inherently efficient and secure, and very low power transmission is possible. In a CDMA-based system the total available bandwidth is allocated to a single channel. Multiplexed access is achieved by combining each individual signal to be transmitted with a unique high bit-rate bit stream or 'code' known as a pseudo-random bit sequence (PRBS). The modulated signal is spread over the entire frequency spectrum which is why it is often referred to as spread spectrum technology (SST). The original signal is derived by subtracting the correct PRBS code from the transmitted signal. By using a unique PRBS code for each network, it is possible to use multiple SST networks in the same area or region. To control units that receive transmissions from different SST networks, the data transmissions appear as noise. Each network normally competes for the same frequency spectrum, at worst, causing performance degradation. Of course, multiple networks are possible on different frequency spectrums without interference. SST is the most widely used technology for wireless LANs as it provides inherent security and reliable communications.

Frequency bands in the range 2.4 to 5.8 GHz have been made available in several countries to facilitate (without requiring a licence) SST systems within buildings. Additional bands are also available dependant on the country operating the network (e.g. 902–928 MHz in the USA). Typical SST wireless LANs operate at around 2 Mbit/s at up to 200 m (depending on the power transmission limits imposed by regulators). Distance limits are inversely proportional to band frequency due to propagation losses.

5.7.2 High performance, high frequency radio

An alternative approach to the implementation of a wireless LAN is to use a low power but high frequency band as its transmission medium. Frequency bands of 5 GHz, 17–18 GHz and 60 GHz have been associated with these systems. The operating speeds of these systems are typically around 15–20 Mbit/s but with a significantly lower distance limit of about 10–50 m due to the low transmission power and high frequency. Thus wireless LANs in this category are appropriate for higher speed, very short range systems. Unlike SST networks, a separate security mechanism needs to be implemented to prevent unauthorized access to the transmitted signal. There is no standard approach to security available. A number of systems attach a network i.d. to each network which is used to encrypt the data before it is transmitted.

5.7.3 Infra-red

Use of infra-red technology is commonplace in the home where it is the basis for remote control units in televisions, hi-fis and video recorders. Infra-red is light operating at a frequency around 1000 GHz which is slightly lower than the lowest frequency the human eye can detect. Distance limitations are due primarily to the fact that infra-red generally only operates between devices that are in line-of-sight, effectively limiting point-to-point connections to about 30 m (depending on transmission power).

There are no licensing problems since the use of infra-red frequencies is not controlled by any regulatory body as there is little interference between infra-red signals. Although there are no impositions on the use of bandwidth and a potentially large amount of bandwidth is possible, the majority of systems provide data rates of about 1 Mbit/s or less. Like high performance, high frequency radio systems, a separate security mechanism needs to be implemented.

5.7.4 Wireless LAN topologies

There are two main topologies which are used to implement wireless LANs: hub-based and peer-to-peer.

Hub-based

A centralized hub unit is used to control access. Peripheral nodes wishing to transmit or receive data must first communicate with the hub. Thus this approach resembles the star topology typical of hub-based architectures such as IEEE 802.3 10BaseT. The hub can also be connected to an existing cabled LAN segment such as a token-ring or Ethernet segment to provide access to corporate applications and data. As with other hub-based architectures, this topology provides a coherent, manageable approach to implementing wireless LANs.

Peer-to-Peer

Here, each station communicates with other stations directly. This is less expensive than the hub-based alternative but suffers from a transmission problem known as the 'near-far' problem. If a number of stations wish to communicate with a particular station at the same time, the nearest stations have good signal strength which may drown the signals of far stations. The net effect is an imposed priority scheme according to the relative distance of stations from the destination station.

5.7.5 Future possibilities

The key factors that will determine future applications for this technology are the availability of adequate bandwidth, secure transmission and bit-error rates comparative to standard cabled

LAN technology. Most of the current wireless LAN products exhibit low performance while cabled LANs are improving performance by a factor of ten or more (e.g. 100 Mbit/s Ethernet). However, newer technologies (e.g. digital cellular systems) may lead to significant improvements in data rates and error rates in the future. SST technology offers an inherent security mechanism while other technologies require a separate (non-standardized) mechanism.

Wireless LANs are thus suitable for specialized applications requiring location flexibility or mobility but with low bandwidth requirements. For the foreseeable future, wireless LANs are complementary to cabled LANs (the mainstay of general office environments) rather than a replacement option. For new or refurbished office buildings, structured cabling will remain the most cost-effective solution to many requirements. Examples of application requirements that may justify the extra cost of deploying a wireless LAN are:

- retail point of sale (PoS) systems where reorganization of the floor layout, including many cash registers, are frequent;
- in disaster recovery situations where a makeshift network is required in temporary accommodation;
- a temporary network (e.g. for demonstration purposes) in an area not intended for general office use. Examples are, recreation areas, storage areas and restaurant and refreshment areas;
- problem areas (e.g. listed buildings) where perhaps cabling is difficult, expensive or impossible to install;
- outbuildings or outside areas such as car parks, garages and under-canvas exhibitions;
- a backup network in the event of failure of the cabled LAN.

5.8 SUMMARY

Access networks enable information exchange within a site. An access network connects to one or more backbone networks to provide gateways to remote resources and information services. Shared-medium local area networks such as Ethernet and token-ring have been the mainstay of access networks. Multimedia developments have given rise to the need to enhance LAN technology to cope with the demands of mixed-media transmissions. ATM promises to deliver a highly functional and scalable solution both for access and backbone networks. Wireless LANs provide a complementary technology for specialist applications requiring location flexibility or mobility but with low bandwidth requirements.

5.9 REVIEW EXERCISES

1. Describe three communications media commonly used to cable a building. Explain the term structured cabling and describe a typical approach.
2. What are the primary LAN topologies?
3. Discuss the influence of the IEEE on international LAN standards. Describe the IEEE 802.3 and 802.5 standards. What steps do each take to ensure that multiple users can share the same communications channel?
4. Can traffic be prioritized in IEEE 802.3 and 802.5?
5. Suppose you wanted to run a videoconferencing system over a LAN. Currently a 10 Mbps

Ethernet LAN is installed. Will it run? If you were able to install a new LAN, which type of LAN would you choose?

6. Describe the differences between the IEEE 802.5 and FDDI standards. Which standard better supports multimedia traffic streams?

7. Under what circumstances might an FDDI LAN be the most suitable option?

8. Describe how the ATM standard can be used to implement a LAN. Comment on the assertion that ATM will eventually replace all current LAN technologies.

9. Under what circumstances would a wireless LAN be the most suitable option? Give an example of a wireless LAN configuration.

10. A company needs to cable and link three buildings together using suitable cabling and network technologies. All three buildings are four storeys high and are on the same building complex. Each floor houses a single department except for building 3 where the lower three floors are occupied by manufacturing (the ground floor houses the manufacturing equipment). Many departments access outside information services using the Internet wide area network. Departments also access a mainframe which is located at headquarters 200 km from the building complex. Almost all staff have a PC on their desk. Each department has a local server which, together with all PCs, are directly wired to a stack of IEEE 10baseT hubs which are positioned in a small closet.

   Outline possible configurations and propose a network design to enable any PC to access any server (subject to security constraints). Applications such as electronic mail, computer conferencing should be facilitated.

5.10 FURTHER READING

Stallings (1990) gives a full treatment on shared-medium LAN architectures and protocols. A useful discussion on practical design considerations when implementing LAN technologies is found in Hodson (1992) and Smythe (1995). Standards, technology and user experiences in the ATM-LAN area are only just emerging at the time of writing. For more detail on wireless LAN technologies see IEE (1992).

6

INTERNETWORKING

6.1 INTRODUCTION

An internetwork (often abbreviated to **internet**) is formed from the interconnection of separate networks (each referred to as a sub-network or 'subnet'). A typical internet consists of a LAN–WAN–LAN interconnection or a campus LAN consisting of multiple LAN segments (each segment constitutes a subnet) connected to a backbone LAN. A **subnet** is regarded as a self-contained network where traffic flows mostly between devices in the same subnet. The complexity of a subnet configuration range from a single LAN segment (or ring) through to a complex campus LAN configuration. We distinguish between the terms **internetworking**: the interconnection of multiple sub-networks, and **interoperability**: the integration of networked data and applications. Interoperability issues are discussed in Chapters 7 and 8.

It is desirable to use the internetwork approach as a basis for enterprise network design for the following reasons.

- Subnets generally fail independently. When a fault occurs, the interconnecting device can offer dynamic re-routing facilities using alternative routes to ensure that the effect of subnet failure on an internet is minimized. This leads to improved reliability since only a subset of users and services are compromised.
- Normally, the performance of a shared-medium LAN declines as the number of users increases. However, a network, carefully partitioned into subnets so that traffic flows largely between devices on the same subnet, leads to improved performance. For example, all client computers and servers to which most client requests are directed should be located on the same subnet, although there are circumstances where this is not possible. An internet designed in this way consists of a large number of small, interconnected

subnets each supporting a small community of users (i.e. a workgroup or department) which generally share the same resources.

- The device interconnecting two subnets can augment security by acting as a **firewall** against unauthorized access to subnet resources (see Section 13.2.3)
- Partitioning a network into subnets can extend the geographic scope of a network configuration since only each subnet is limited to the constraints imposed by the technology used to implement the subnet. An interconnection device can be used to connect two or more subnets which are widely separated.

The main issue to be addressed when creating internets is the differing network characteristics of subnets in areas such as the following.

- The maximum frame/packet size that can be transmitted or received. For one subnet the maximum transmission unit (MTU) could be 4000 bytes. If a 4000 byte packet needs to span a subnet which has an MTU of 1500 bytes then the subnet will not accept the packet. The interconnecting device will need to segment the packet into three small segments and subsequently reassemble the packet.
- Some subnets are connection-oriented (e.g. X.25 and ATM WANs) while most LANs are connectionless,
- Addressing scheme. There must be some means of identifying a device in an internet uniquely. Each subnet will implement its own addressing scheme. For example, IEEE 802 LANs use a 48-bit MAC address whereas an X.25 public network uses a 12-digit decimal address (encoded as four bits per decimal digit resulting in a 48-bit address).
- Message format. The message formats and the order in which the actual bits appear in a packet may differ. For example, one difference between Ethernet and token-ring LANs is that whilst one puts its most significant bit first, the other puts it last.
- Error control protocols. As a packet traverses many subnets, it may be subject to widely ranging error control techniques from no error detection through to those with sophisticated error detection and correction techniques. End-to-end error control for this packet is related to the subnet with the least comprehensive error control procedure unless higher protocol layers implement end-to-end error control.
- Different acknowledgement scheme and time-outs. In one subnet protocol the message format may require the setting of acknowledgement bits whereas in another subnet no acknowledgement bits exist. Inappropriate setting of acknowledgement flags can lead to problems such as premature time-outs.
- When a frame has to traverse a number of subnets the time-out settings in the sending computer has to be adjusted to avoid a time-out occurring before a frame has reached its destination.
- Differing priority schemes.

If two subnets with differing characteristics are to be connected then some device has to connect to both subnets and resolve these differences whenever a packet is required to be transferred from one subnet to another. Interworking units (IWUs) are devices designed to achieve this. The two subnets to be connected must be close enough to each other to support direct coupling via an IWU. The basic issues to be addressed by an IWU can be summarized as:

- naming and addressing
- routing
- segmentation and reassembly of packets to resolve maximum transmission unit problems

- congestion control
- error control and recovery.

There are three types of IWU devices commonly used to create internetworks: repeaters, bridges and routers. A repeater operates at the physical layer (OSI Layer 1) and simply receives a digital signal from one network segment, amplifies it and re-transmits the signal on to the other network. The net effect is that the two network segments to which the repeater is attached behave as if they were seamlessly joined together. Repeaters are commonly used simply to extend the length of a CSMA/CD LAN segment. Whilst in circumstances where segment length limits are constraining a network design a repeater can be useful, bridges and routers are much more effective IWUs not least because they enable subnet traffic to be isolated. Repeaters cannot achieve this because they do not recognize frame formats.

6.2 BRIDGES

A bridge is an IWU used to connect subnets of the same type, e.g. CSMA/CD LANs. They work at Layer 2 of OSI which means they can recognize the format of a frame and, in particular, source and destination addresses. The format of addresses in IEEE 802 LANs have been standardized and are known as media access control (MAC) addresses. All bridges make routing decisions based on MAC addresses which are guaranteed to identify a device in a network uniquely. Bridges are commonly used to:

- improve the performance of a LAN by isolating network traffic to particular network segments. The use of multiple LAN subnets reduces the number of users per subnet which in turn means that every user gets a larger share of the available bandwidth;
- extend the geographic scope of the network. The constraints in terms of geographic coverage imposed by a LAN technology can be overcome by joining separate LAN subnets;
- extend the maximum number of users a network can support. The constraints on the maximum number of users imposed by a single LAN technology is extended by joining separate LAN subnets.

There are two types of bridge technologies in widespread use: transparent and spanning tree bridges, and source routing bridges.

6.2.1 Transparent and spanning tree bridges

These are in widespread use for connecting CSMA/CD LAN segments. The basic operation of a transparent bridge is illustrated in Figure 6.1. The bridge ensures that traffic flows between nodes A and B remain on Segment X by simply not copying any frames with destination address equal to a node on Segment X. However, if node A wishes to transmit to node C, the bridge automatically transmits the frame onto Segment Y so that node C can receive it. To do this, the bridge must be aware of the MAC address of all nodes on each network segment. The bridge keeps a routing table which has an entry for every node on the segments to which it is connected and identifies which LAN segment each node is connected to. The routing table can be created as a static list by a network administrator, and re-configured when the network topology changes. This approach is suited to small internets which, in configuration terms, are relatively stable. However, large internets, which are typically characterized by frequent re-configuration, are more easily managed if bridges change (or learn) dynamically in response to topology changes.

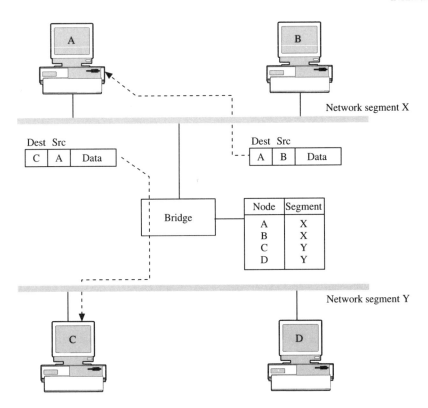

Figure 6.1 Joining networks with bridges.

Learning transparent bridges acquire routing table information automatically by observing the source address of every frame transmit on all networks to which it is attached. The bridge gradually populates the routing table, maintaining a list of source addresses and corresponding network segment. When it receives a frame, it looks at the destination address and looks for an associated entry in its routing table to see whether it should forward the frame or ignore it (because the destination node is on the same segment). In some cases there will be no entry in the routing table corresponding to the destination address in which case it forwards the frame by default. After a fixed period of inactivity, the bridge re-configures itself by resetting (emptying) the routing table and re-learning the network configuration.

A more complex configuration involves the use of multiple bridges where two or more bridges are connected to the same two network segments for increased reliability. This results in the availability of alternative routes which form a closed loop. This can lead to looping frames because when a frame is transmitted by a node, all bridges connected to the segment will receive it and act independently according to the current routing table information. Some bridges may choose to forward the frame leading to multiple transmission of the same frame onto the same LAN segment. To eliminate this problem a complex configuration protocol among all bridges is implemented using an IEEE 802.1 **spanning tree** routing algorithm to ensure that only one of the bridges connecting two segments is active. The algorithm checks for circular routes and ensures that bridges block certain routes to give a single route between any source and destination on the network. If the active bridge fails or topology changes occur, a new spanning tree is derived automatically. The IEEE 802.1 specification was not sufficiently tightly defined to ensure interoperability between different vendor products. It is usually the case that the same vendor product is used in a single network.

A transparent bridge is so named because nodes on a segment are completely unaware of the existence of the bridge. A node sees the network of subnets interconnected by bridges as a single 'logical' network where all devices are accessible and bridges are invisible.

6.2.2 Source routing bridges

These bridges are primarily used to interconnect IEEE 802.5 token-ring LANs. It was developed by the IEEE 802.5 committee specifically for token-ring LANs. The message format of an IEEE 802.5 frame has been augmented to include an extra field called the routing information (RI) field which supports the source routing approach. The RI field consists of the routing control field followed by up to eight route designation fields. Thus the RI field is of variable length.

Unlike transparent bridges, source routing bridges are visible to sending nodes and it is the sending node which determines the route that the frame will follow. Routing information is not stored in the bridge but in the RI field of the frame being transmitted. Thus, routing information is carried with the frame as it traverses subnets. Each LAN and bridge is numbered and the routing information consists of up to eight route designators each of the format {LAN(a), Bridge(x), LAN(b)} where LAN (a) is the LAN from which the frame arrived, Bridge (x) is this bridge and LAN (b) is another LAN to which Bridge (x) is attached. Routes are determined and stored in routing tables maintained by host nodes (rather than bridges). This is done by implementing a dynamic route discovery procedure whenever a node needs to learn a route. An 'all-routes' request is initiated by sending out a special discovery frame to the destination node. Routing information is recorded as discovery frames traverse the internet. The destination sends back each discovery frame it receives thus allowing the sending station to choose one of a number of possible routes in a multiple alternative bridge configuration.

Both types of bridges operate at Layer 2 of the OSI reference model using frame level addresses (e.g. MAC addresses in IEEE 802 LANs) as the key value in routing tables. The use of bridges are an appropriate solution to some requirements because they:

1. exhibit attractive price/performance ratios,
2. adapt quickly to changes in the network,
3. require relatively low maintenance and are easy to set up. Transparent (learning) bridges are 'plug and play' devices, whereas source routing bridges do require significantly more set-up and maintenance effort.

However, they are less suitable as the basic IWU device in large, multi-subnet internets because some subnets are likely to use different network technology, and frames that need to pass through multiple bridges can introduce delays that affect higher-level software significantly. These problems manifest themselves as time-outs, software lockouts and so on. Bridges have their place in the development of enterprise networks, but larger networks incorporating a variety of subnets and network types require the use of more sophisticated IWU devices.

6.3 ROUTERS

A router IWU is used to interconnect subnets which may be of different types. Routers operate at Layer 3 of OSI incorporating a special protocol designed to route packets from subnet-to-subnet, based on an OSI Layer 3 **global addressing scheme** and **routing strategy**. Router IWUs are also known as:

- *Gateways*; a term used mainly by TCP/IP.
- *Intermediate Systems (IS)*; a term used mainly by ISO.

We prefer the term router since it better describes the IWU's operation. Formally, a **gateway** is a device for connecting two systems that use different communications architectures (i.e. it is a protocol converter). A router connects two systems which may or may not be similar. In general, router protocols impose a global addressing scheme at OSI Layer 3 to facilitate routing, and specify in detail the various message formats and routing algorithms to be used.

Any computer can be turned into a router by installing one or more additional network interface cards and software which implements the routing protocol. However, it is more usual to purchase dedicated router devices mainly for performance reasons. To illustrate the use of router technology and protocols we examine two standards:

1. The ITU-T X.25 connection-oriented protocol.
2. The TCP/IP connectionless protocol since it is the most widely used. A similar standard; ISO 8473 connectionless network protocol (CLNP) is founded on the TCP/IP standard.

6.3.1 Connection-oriented routing – ITU-T X.25

The basic operation of an X.25 network was detailed in Section 4.1.1. X.25 specifies the interface between a host computer (known as data terminating equipment or 'DTE') and its local router (known as a packet switching exchange or 'PSE'). Local routers are connected to a mesh topology of PSEs. Before data flows between two hosts, a connection must first be established. When data exchanges are complete, the connection must be cleared.

The term **virtual circuit** (also known as 'virtual call') is used to indicate a logical connection between two hosts. A host will connect with another host through a **logical channel**. A host can maintain simultaneous connections to multiple hosts by establishing multiple logical channels. A logical channel is assigned a unique logical channel identifier which has two parts: a logical channel group number (4 bits) and a logical channel number (8 bits).

In order to set up a connection, the calling host constructs a **call request** packet and transmits it to the PSE to which it is connected. Information in the call request packet identifies the calling host, the called host and the logical channel identifier that is to be used by the calling host for this connection. The local PSE forwards this request through the network until it reaches the PSE to which the called host is connected. The call-request packet threads its way through the network of PSEs, setting up an appropriate route for the connection (all subsequent data packets will follow this same route). The way routing is carried out is not part of the X.25 specification, it is at the discretion of the network provider so long as X.25 conformant packets entering the network also leaves it in the correct format. In other words, X.25 does not specify a routing protocol! A commonly used approach is where the network provider sets up the routing table in each PSE, which consists of a set of choices for outgoing links based on proprietary route calculations. When a call request packet arrives at a PSE, a link selection algorithm is invoked to determine the specific outgoing link and local logical channel identifier to be used for a given host destination. Thus possible routes are set up by the network provider but the final routing decision is made locally at the PSE at call set-up. If no route is available at a PSE, the call is cleared back to the previous PSE and an alternative route is tried.

Each PSE maintains a table of active virtual circuits. An entry in the table records the incoming line number and logical channel identifier, and the corresponding outgoing line number and logical channel identifier (assigned by the PSE). The destination host eventually receives an **incoming call** packet from its local PSE (the local PSE assigns a new logical channel identifier for use by the destination host). A **call accepted** packet is sent back if the destination host accepts the call. Finally the end of the call set-up phase is signalled to the calling host on receipt of a **call connected** packet from its local PSE.

Once the route is set up, all data packets follow the same route and therefore normally arrive at the destination host in the same order they were sent and without loss or duplication. Both hosts can send data packets independently of each other (i.e. a full-duplex connection). Each packet carries a sequence number used for flow control using a sliding window protocol. X.25 also supports fragmentation and reassembly, end-to-end acknowledgements and the ability to negotiate quality of service parameters at call set-up time.

The call can be cleared down at any time by a host or by the network when it detects a problem (e.g. if a link along the route goes down). This is achieved by issuing a **clear request** packet.

A **permanent virtual circuit** (PVC) eliminates the call set-up and clear down phases since on subscription the network provider decides on the fixed route for all packets associated with a particular PVC between two hosts, and permanently updates each relevant PSE routing table to reflect the chosen route.

6.3.2 Connectionless routing – TCP/IP

TCP/IP is an acronym for a pair of internetworking protocols, the **transmission control protocol** (TCP) and **internet protocol** (IP). These protocols are part of a set of standards known as the Internet suite of protocols which evolved from the Internet project, a US research project initiated in the mid-1970s by the US Department of Defense (DoD). Today it is a well-established, world-wide internetwork connecting thousands of subnets and host computers in the research, academic and commercial domains. The TCP/IP protocols took shape around 1979. The US DoD ensured the widespread use of TCP/IP by:

1. demanding (from 1983 onwards) that all computers connected to its ARPANET networks use TCP/IP;
2. agreeing to include TCP/IP with UNIX distributions released into the public domain, resulting in the widespread use of TCP/IP within the academic community and other organizations;
3. encouraging the addition of remote processing facilities (e.g. rcp, rsh and rlogin) under UNIX for ease-of-use of underlying TCP/IP facilities. Thus TCP/IP became well supported by the UNIX operating system.

TCP/IP has been readily embraced by commercial organizations as a *de facto* standard for connectionless routing because of the maturity and non-proprietary nature of these protocols. Today, the technical body that oversees the development of TCP/IP-based protocols is the **Internet activities board** (IAB). The process of evolving Internet protocols can be regarded as 'open' since it is achieved by a combination of the submission of technical reports (called **Request For Comments** (RFC)) and reviews of RFCs proposals carried out by Internet task forces (steered by members of the IAB). Some RFCs are never used or implemented. A library of RFCs are made available across the Internet by the Internet Network Information Centre (NIC) and is the definitive source of technical documentation on Internet standards and proposals.

TCP/IP is used by organizations either to connect to the Internet network or to implement a private internet. To avoid confusing these two distinct uses of TCP/IP, we use 'Internet' to refer to the international network created by the US DoD Internet project and 'internet' to refer to the use of TCP/IP protocols to implement a heterogeneous network which may or may not be connected to the Internet.

The emphasis of the Internet protocols is internetworking of diverse WAN and LAN technologies the architecture of which may not be known by an organization but which implements TCP/IP simply to provide a means of routing data to the intended recipient. This is made possible by introducing a global addressing scheme – the IP address – which represents the original source and final destination computer involved in data exchange. The final destination computer can potentially be anywhere in the world and multiple subnets may be involved in transporting the data to it.

To understand how a router is used to form an internet, consider its relation to a world-wide postal system (Figures 6.2 to 6.4). A postal system routes letters from originating person to recipient person. The recipient is identified by the postal address on the envelope. The user's view of the postal system is represented by walking to the nearest post-box and submitting the letter to the postal system. The letter is then delivered to the recipient's home. Without the envelope address, the postal system could not deliver the letter. The user doesn't care how it gets there as long as it arrives eventually (delivery time is dependent on the recipient's location, the efficiency of the postal system and the class of service paid for).

The postal network infrastructure in fact consists of an interconnection of sorting offices as shown in Figure 6.2. Each office routes letters to the next sorting office depending on the envelope address. A sorting office is only concerned with which sorting office to send a letter to next. If an envelope address indicates that it is a house within the sorting office's district (or 'domain') then it is delivered directly to the recipient's home. Thus a 'store-and-forward'

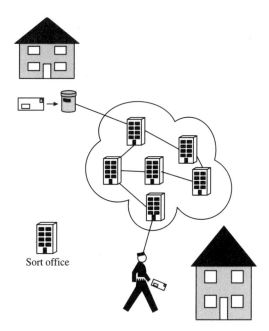

Sort office

Figure 6.2 The postal internetwork.

mechanism is used to route our letters between sorting offices until it is delivered to the home by the local sorting office.

In a computer internetwork, a router device acts as the 'sorting office' and is used to interconnect subnets which may be of different network types. The user view of a TCP/IP router is represented by the creation of a datagram addressed to the recipient host. The datagram is then posted to the local router as shown in Figure 6.3. The local router decides whether to deliver it (if the destination is in its district) or to send it on to another router depending on the destination address. The physical view of a TCP/IP network is illustrated in Figure 6.4.

6.4 TCP/IP PROTOCOLS

The Internet protocols are based on a layered set of protocols as illustrated in Figure 6.5:

1. Application services which provide users with access to services across a TCP/IP internet. These are primarily:
   - **File transfer protocol** (FTP); a file transfer application protocol. This is described in detail in Section 8.5.1.
   - **Simple mail transfer protocol** (SMTP); a simple electronic mail application proto col. This is described in detail in Section 8.13.1.
   - **TELNET**; which provides virtual terminal (remote login) access to host computers.
2. A connection-oriented transport service, provided by the TCP which establishes, controls and terminates connections processes (applications) that reside on the source and destination host computers. This protocol provides a reliable data transport service, guaranteeing data delivery uncorrupted, in the right order and without loss or duplication.
3. A connectionless transport service, provided by the user datagram protocol (UDP) which provides an unreliable (best-efforts) data delivery between processes on source and destination host computers. Thus it cannot guarantee delivery and does not implement other

nic.ddn.mil

Figure 6.3 User view of TCP/IP network.

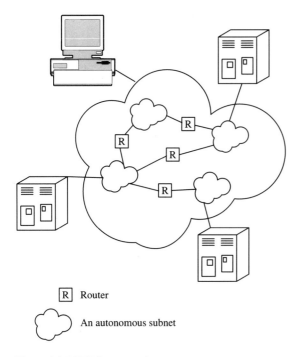

Figure 6.4 TCP/IP internetwork.

OSI layer	TCP/IP layer

OSI layer					
7	FTP	TELNET		SNMP	
6			SMTP		TFTP
5					
4	TCP			UDP	
3	IP layer				
2	Network-specific protocols				
1	(e.g. Ethernet, Token-ring, X.25)				

Figure 6.5 TCP/IP protocol family.

mechanisms that are a feature of TCP (for example, flow control, segmentation and reassembly). The main advantage of the UDP service is performance and faster through-put of data. Also, if an application chooses to introduce its own error control, flow control and other protocols, it would provide these by enhancing the basic UDP facilities rather than using TCP.
4. A **connectionless network protocol** called the Internet protocol (IP) that supports com-munication between network devices and provides routing facilities based on the imple-mentation of a global addressing scheme. IP also relies on another protocol called the **Internet control message protocol** (ICMP) to report errors, and allows tests to be carried out and other control functions.

An important feature of the TCP/IP layered structure is that it does not specify protocol stan-dards for the underlying network technology. Thus TCP/IP can be implemented over any type

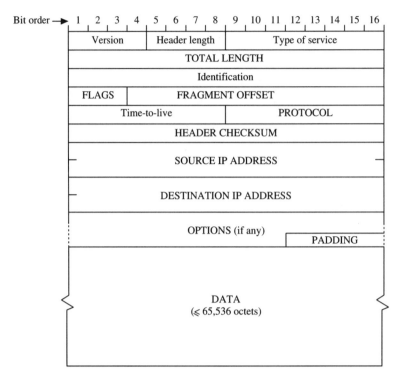

Figure 6.6 IP datagram format.

of network enabling a heterogeneous internetwork to be created. The format of an **IP data-gram** is shown in Figure 6.6 and consists of the following fields.

Version field (V): contains the current version of the IP protocol.

The length field (HLEN): gives the length of the IP datagram header (measured in 32-bit word units). The normal value is 5, representing 20 octets. However, there is a variable length field called IP OPTIONS and corresponding PADDING fields that extend the size of the IP header.

The type-of-service field (SERVICE TYPE): this field indicates how the IP datagram should be handled. Settings in this field give a hint to routers as to the type and priority of data being sent (e.g. the IP datagram may desire a low delay, high throughput, or highly reliable transport link). Routers can then choose the most appropriate path if a number of alternative paths are available.

The TOTAL LENGTH field: contains the total length (header and data) of the IP datagram measured in octets. As this field is 16 bits long, the maximum length of an IP datagram is 65 535 octets. This becomes a significant limitation when multimedia traffic is being carried over broadband networks based, for example, on ATM.

The Identification field (IDENT): when an IP datagram cannot fit into a frame in the underlying physical network it needs to be divided temporarily into smaller units called *fragments*, the size of which does not exceed the maximum transmission unit of the subnet to which it is being sent. For example, an IP datagram of size 10 000 bytes will need to be fragmented so that the fragment size does not exceed 1500 bytes if it is to be sent over an Ethernet-based subnet. Each fragment has exactly the same format (header plus data) as a non-fragmented IP datagram. This field acts as the sequence number field for IP datagram fragments to permit the receiving host to reassemble the original IP datagram by knowing which arriving fragments belong to which original IP datagram.

The **FLAGS** field: signifies whether fragmentation is allowed. If fragmentation is allowed then this field also indicates the type (middle or end) of IP datagram fragment is being received. Receipt of an 'end' fragment signifies to the receiver that this is the end fragment of the original IP datagram.

The **FRAGMENT OFFSET** field: used to enable sender and receiver to keep track of where the data contained in this IP datagram fragment fits relative to the rest of the data sent. This is a 13-bit field, thus values range from 0–8191 units where a 'unit' is 8 octets. To illustrate the use of this field, suppose a router receives an IP datagram of around 6400 octets and needs to send it to a subnet whose maximum transmission unit is 1600 octets. The router splits the datagram into four fragments of size 1600 bytes. The fragment offset field for the four fragments are set to 0, 200, 400, and 600 respectively (recall that these values are in units of 8 octets). The FLAGS field is set to 'more fragments' for the first three fragments, and is set to 'end-fragment' for the fourth.

The **time-to-live field** (**TTL**): an 8-bit field giving how long in seconds the datagram is allowed to remain in an internet. The TTL value is decremented by routers and hosts as time passes. If the TTL value reaches zero, the router discards the IP datagram and an error message is sent back to the originating host. The TTL mechanism thus guarantees that IP datagrams do not circulate around an internet forever.

The **PROTOCOL** field: identifies the higher-layer protocol used to create the IP datagram. The DATA field of the IP datagram will be structured according to the higher-level protocol. Three common higher-layer protocols are TCP, UDP and ICMP.

The **HEADER CHECKSUM** field: is used for error detection of the header part of the IP datagram. Error detection for the DATA field must be carried out by higher-layer protocols (e.g. TCP).

The **SOURCE and DESTINATION IP ADDRESS** fields: contain the 32-bit IP address of the sender and destination nodes.

The **IP OPTIONS** field: is a variable length field containing various options primarily for network management purposes.

The **PADDING** field: contains zeros required to ensure the datagram header is an exact multiple of 32 bits.

The DATA field: contains the data created by the higher-layer protocol.

Setting up a TCP/IP-based network is influenced by whether a connection to the Internet is required. If a connection is required then an organization must apply to the Internet Network Information Centre (NIC) for a unique network identifier. An organization's network administrator then assigns a unique host identifier value to each host computer attached to the network. The combination {network identifier, host identifier} is known as the **IP address** and functions as a globally unique identifier of each host computer in an organization. If a host computer moves to another network (which will have a different network identifier) then it must be assigned a new IP address.

6.4.1 IP address formats

An IP address is in fact a 32-bit address divided into the network identifier part and host identifier part. The addressing format is designed to ensure that IP addresses are unique and to facilitate flexible and efficient routing of IP traffic. An important advantage of this approach is that routing tables are considerably smaller since a router makes routing decision based on the network identifier thus requiring one routing table entry per network identifier rather than per IP address. IP address formats are written as four decimal values (each representing the value of a byte) separated by periods (e.g. 134.220.1.10). The split between network identifier and host identifier is determined by use of a 32-bit network mask also written in the same format as an IP address. For example, a network mask of value 255.255.0.0 indicates that the two left-most bytes are used for the network identifier. There are four defined network masks as illustrated in Figure 6.7:

1. **Class A addresses**: identified uniquely by observing that bit 1 is always zero. The remaining 7 bits in the first byte represent the network identifier and the remaining three the host identifier. Thus the network id ranges from 1 to 127 with support for many host identifiers. Class A addresses were intended for networks with a large number of hosts. An example of a class A IP address is 118.6.20.250.
2. **Class B addresses**: identified uniquely by observing that the two left-most bits of the first byte have the value '10'. The first and second bytes (excluding two bits from the first byte) form the network identifier and the remaining two bytes the host identifier. Most organizations have a preference for class B addresses because they provide for flexible address allocations. A typical class B address (with network ids ranging from 128 to 191) is 134.220.1.5 which represents a network id of 134.220 and host id of 1.5.
3. **Class C addresses**: identified uniquely by observing that the three left-most bits of the first byte have the value '110'. This format supports many networks with few hosts. Only one byte is reserved for the host id Class C addresses range from 192.0.1.0 to 223.255.255.0.
4. **Multicast addresses**: Multicast addresses (see Section 3.5.1) are identified uniquely by observing that the four left-most bits of the first byte have the value '1110'. The other 28 bits represent the multicast address. Multicast addresses provide a limited form of broadcast in which a subset of host computers on a network respond to a multicast address. Thus a single transmission with a multicast address results in simultaneous reception by the multicast group of host computers. If the bits in the host id portion of the address are all of value 255, the address is intended for all hosts on that network.

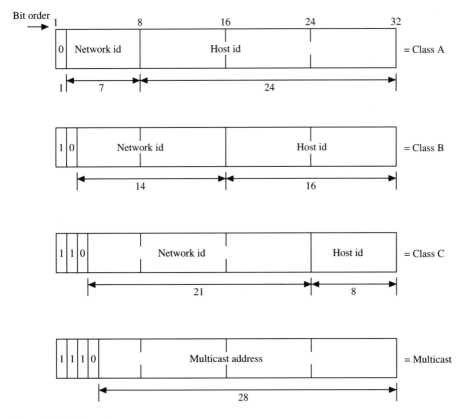

Figure 6.7 IP address formats.

An internet address of 255.255.255.255 is the broadcast address. Any host receiving an IP datagram with this address automatically copies the datagram. If the host id is all zeros (e.g. 134.220.0.0 for a class B address) then this represents the address of that network segment not any of the hosts connected to it.

6.4.2 Subnet masks

The network infrastructure within a large organization typically consists of multiple, logically separate physical networks each typically serving a department or workgroup. For example, at the University of Wolverhampton there is generally one physical network (an Ethernet segment) supporting each teaching laboratory. Further physical networks support academic staff and systems, administrative systems and research staff. Most networks consist of a single Ethernet segment to which PCs and a single server computer are attached. The intention of the IP addressing scheme is that each physical network is assigned a unique network identifier and thus treated as an autonomous subnet interconnected by routers that effectively isolate the traffic on each subnet unless access is required to a device not on the subnet.

However, one consequence of the popularity of the Internet is the unanticipated large number of small PC and other networks connected to it. There was a reluctance on the part of NIC to allocate a new network identifier to each small subnet for fear that they would run out of unique values. A new mechanism was required to minimize the number of new network identifiers required to be allocated to organizations, without loss of the functionality of the original IP addressing scheme. The preferred solution is to share one network identifier among multiple physical networks usually within a single organization but still allow an organization to partition its physical network into multiple subnets each treated as an autonomous network with appropriate traffic isolation. The technique to achieve this is known as **subnet routing**.

Suppose an organization has an enterprise network consisting of two separate CSMA/CD LANs. In the original scheme the organization would apply for two separate network identifiers, for example class B addresses 134.220 and 134.221. Subnet routing simply uses a single network identifier, say 134.220 and uses the third byte of the IP address as a **subnet address** field leaving only the fourth byte as the host identifier field. Thus the resulting subnet address format is `net.net.subnet.host`. For example, the physical networks in the previous example can be assigned subnet addresses 1 and 2 by the network administrator, resulting in IP addresses 134.220.1.0 and 134.220.2.0. This is illustrated in Figure 6.8. The rest of the Internet thinks that there is a single subnet with network identifier 134.220 (they view the subnet id as part of the host id). Only local routers (known as **interior routers**) can distinguish between the host id and the subnet id The network administrator must specify, using a subnet mask, which portion of the IP address is the host id. In class B networks the subnet portion is usually the third byte (although it can be on a bit boundary within the host id

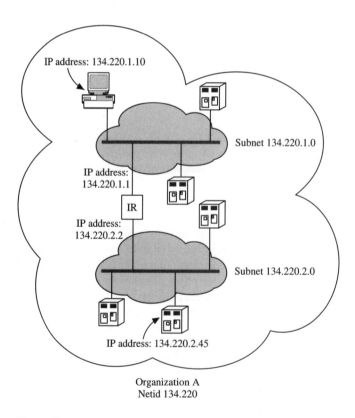

Organization A
Netid 134.220

Figure 6.8 Creating a subnet.

portion) and the subnet mask is therefore 255.255.255.0. In our example, once an IP datagram reaches the local router, it must determine the correct physical network of the destination host by examining the subnet id.

6.4.3 IP routing algorithm

The routing algorithm in TCP/IP networks relies on the sub-division of an internet into multiple autonomous systems, each with its own interior routers and management authority. An internet is therefore viewed as an interconnection of separate autonomous systems where an autonomous system is a collection of subnets interconnected by homogeneous (interior) routers under control of a single organization or entity. An autonomous system is connected to the Internet via an **exterior router** which connects to the core backbone network. Thus Internet internetworking is achieved through co-operation between three components.

1. *Host computers,* which maintain sufficient routing information to enable them to forward IP datagrams to other hosts on the same network, or to an interior router attached to the same network.
2. *Interior routers*, which maintain sufficient routing information to forward IP datagrams to hosts or to another interior gateway within the same autonomous system.
3. *Exterior routers,* which provide a link between two or more autonomous systems. An exterior router maintains sufficient routing information to forward IP datagrams either to an interior gateway if it is intended for a host in the same autonomous system, or to another exterior gateway if it is not. On the Internet, exterior routers are interconnected via a core backbone network.

To illustrate the co-operative relationship between hosts, interior and exterior routers, suppose an exterior router is connected to two IP class B networks 134.220 (a LAN network connection) and 129.60 (a WAN connection onto the Internet) each on subnet 1. On each network a router has, by convention, a host identifier starting at 1, resulting in IP addresses 134.220.1.1 and 129.60.1.1 for the exterior routers. Note that a router has a unique IP address *for each connection* to a subnet. Suppose an interior router is connected to subnets 1 and 2 with IP addresses 134.220.1.2 and 134.220.2.1 respectively. If a host with IP address 134.220.1.10 wishes to send data to host 134.220.1.20 (i.e. both hosts are on subnet 1), the sending host simply needs to obtain the layer two (Ethernet) address of the destination host before it can deliver it via the data link protocol (CSMA/CD). An IEEE 802 LAN, for example, only recognizes MAC addresses using the appropriate frame format and access control technique. An **address resolution protocol** (ARP) program is responsible for converting an IP address to a corresponding layer two address (e.g. a MAC address). A special mechanism is also defined for keeping a cache of {IP address, datalink address} pairs.

Data from host 134.220.1.10 wishing to access a remote host (e.g. host 192.112.36.10) somewhere on the Internet is encapsulated in an IP datagram with destination address set to 192.112.36.10. The IP datagram is then sent to the interior router attached to its subnet which, in turn, based on its routing table, sends it to the exterior router (134.220.1.1). The exterior router's routing table enables it to decide where to send the IP datagram next so that eventually it will reach the recipient identified by the destination IP address.

A host generally keeps the IP address of its local interior router attached to the same subnet. It is the contents of the routing table and the destination IP address, which enables a router to decide where to send an IP datagram to next. Each interior routing has two types of routing table.

1. A local routing table containing entries identifying IP address and associated data link layer address (e.g. an Ethernet address) for known hosts and routers on the same network segment. This is known as the address pair {IP address, data link layer address}and enables the router to forward any IP datagrams directly to hosts on the same network using the underlying data-link layer protocol (e.g. CSMA/CD).
2. A remote routing table with an entry for each router of the format:

    `{Destination subnet i.d., Routing Metric, IP address of next router}`

    where the destination subnet id is the value pair {network identifier, subnet identifier} of a subnet and the next router field the IP address of another interior router to which all IP datagrams destined for that subnet is sent. A routing metric is also stored (e.g. transmission delay) to decide on the optimum route for the IP datagram in the case where alternative routes are available. An exterior router's local router table has exactly the same format as an interior router's remote routing table. An exterior router knows every network id and corresponding interior router IP address. An exterior router's remote routing table has reachability information which enables it to communicate with other exterior routers in an internet, exchanging routing information of the following format:

    `{Network Id, Routing Metric, Route from the reporting exterior router}`

    This information is then used by an exterior router to select the best exterior router to which the IP datagram is forwarded in order to route it to the autonomous system identified by the network identifier.

First-generation routers perform static routing using fixed routing tables created by the network administrator. The table is updated whenever new networks are added or new routing information is known. This is acceptable if there are few changes to the network, indeed, many organizations adopt this approach to configure interior routers. However, some networks need the routing flexibility and reduced maintenance offered by dynamic routers. A standard dynamic routing protocol is also required for exterior routers.

There are two types of router protocols: interior gateway protocols (IGPs) which involve routing information exchanges between interior routers, and exterior gateway protocols (EGPs) which involve routing information exchanges between exterior routers. Examples of dynamic routing algorithms which dynamically update routing tables are the routing information protocol (RIP), the proprietary interior gateway routing protocol (IGRP) and the open shortest path first (OSPF).

The RIP protocol has been widely used because it is readily available (for example, bundled with the BSD version of UNIX). RIP-based routers send routing information updates to neighbouring routers periodically (about every minute). When routing datagrams, the interior router is able to compare all the remote routing tables it has received and then choose the route which requires the minimum number of hops (network traversals). If a router does not receive updates from a particular interior router within a specified time it will not use it subsequently. If no response is received after about eight minutes typically, that router is removed from its routing table.

The hop-count is used as a routing metric to decide the best route through an internet. However, RIP is unsuitable for large, complex networks since the hop-count mechanism is too simplistic and large internets may exceed the 15 hop limit imposed by RIP. Also, routing loops can occur due to the time it takes for routing tables to be updated. IGRP, a protocol developed by Cisco, a major manufacturer of router products, is also a hop-count protocol but takes account of the link speed of the slowest link, propagation delay (important for satellite links), and the reliability of the network link. IGRP can also make use of multiple (parallel) routes to improve throughput. IGRP-based routers therefore make much more intelligent routing decisions.

OSPF was developed by the IETF as a routing protocol more suited to large, complex networks and serves as a combined IGP and EGP protocol. Based on a distributed database, OSPF ensures that every router has a database of every other routers' connections. Information is exchanged on a need to know basis only for updating routing tables and so conserves important bandwidth.

6.4.4 Domain names

In the above discussion we have used IP addresses as an extremely efficient way for TCP/IP services to identify hosts and routers on an internet. Almost all TCP/IP services require that users or applications provide IP addresses of host computers and routers. However, the use of human-friendly, meaningful names is preferable because they are more easily predicted, remembered and understood by human users. For example, instead of referring to a computer as 121.34.25.1, the name *compserver* is far easier to remember. When an object has a name there is said to be a *binding* between the name and the object. The object named is described by defined attributes such as an IP address. Thus, a host computer named *compserver* has an attribute, an IP address, whose current value is 121.34.25.1. A **name service** stores all names and corresponding object attributes. The collection of all valid names recognized by a name service is referred to as the **name space**. A name service maintains a namespace which can be viewed as a database of all known bindings between names and the attributes of an object associated with each name. Naming service operations enable clients to create new bindings, delete bindings, list bound names and resolve name queries. A valid name is one that satisfies the syntax the namespace uses. A valid name which is not bound to an object is said to be *unbounded*.

There are two types of namespace structures: a *flat* or *hierarchical* namespace. Early systems used a flat namespace which is a simple name to object attribute mapping. A hierarchical namespace sub-divides the total namespace into a tree-like hierarchy or levels of sub-namespaces. An object is named by a concatenation of name values. For example the **absolute name** (also known as a *fully-qualified* name) name pc.admin.companyx refers to an object called pc in the sub-namespace 'admin' which, in turn, is defined in the sub-namespace 'companyx'. The use of hierarchical namespaces introduces the concept of **relative names**. A relative name is the absolute name minus the parent name of the current position (or 'context') in the naming tree. For example if the current context is companyx, the relative name admin.pc is valid. It is, however, invalid in a different context. Obviously absolute names must be used when passing binding information outside of a given context.

One of the most attractive reasons for defining hierarchical name spaces is to facilitate local administration of namespaces. This is desirable in a large internet because it becomes impossible for a central administration to control namespace maintenance and provide the naming flexibility demanded by autonomous organizations. A useful concept is the notion of **administrative domain**. An administrative domain is a set of objects managed by the same organization. A namespace can be defined as an administrative domain. A hierarchical namespace provides a mechanism for co-ordinating the management of a global namespace whilst retaining local autonomy by defining multiple administrative domains.

To illustrate the concept of administrative domains, the **domain name system** (DNS), an Internet project which defined a name service based on a hierarchical namespace, is examined to see how it supports the naming of Internet hosts and routers as an alternative to the explicit use of IP addresses and provides local autonomy in the naming of hosts and routers. The earliest Internet naming service consisted of a single static file called HOSTS.TXT, maintained by the Network Information Centre (NIC), listing all known host, network and router names with corresponding IP addresses using a flat namespace. The file was distributed to all hosts via file transfer. As the Internet grew, the size, centralized maintenance and distribution of HOSTS.TXT became impractical. Internet DNS was introduced with the following objectives:

- To replace centralized maintenance with distributed control of name creation and maintenance. Administrative domains should be responsible for the naming of their hosts and routers. This mechanism can be viewed as a distributed database of names and associated addresses where each database is maintained by a separate administration.
- Names assigned by administrative domains should be globally unique. This is achieved by adopting a hierarchical naming structure.
- An organization's name list must be accessible to all users of the Internet.

Similar in concept to the hierarchical numbering of a typical telephone system where the number consists of a country code, an area code, an exchange code and a line number, a DNS name contains a reference to a host or router name which is part of an individual organization which, in turn, is a part of a group of related organizations in a particular country. Distributed naming control is achieved by establishing a naming tree and ensuring that an organization gets authority over a section of the tree. The organization is then free to add to or change portions of the tree below that section. This is illustrated in Figure 6.9. For example, the host computer at the University of Wolverhampton, which is part of the academic community in the UK, is known as ccub.wlv.ac.uk which signifies that host name *ccub* is defined in the domain wlv.ac.uk. The domain wlv.ac.uk is that section of the DNS name space allocated to the University of Wolverhampton. The University therefore has the authority to define hosts,

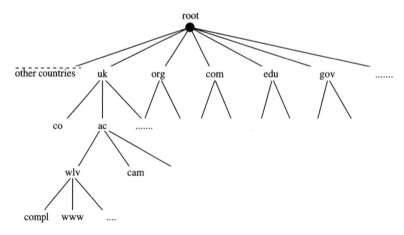

Figure 6.9 The DNS name space hierarchy.

routers and other object names and associated addresses in the domain `wlv.ac.uk`. The absolute name of any domain is a list of its label together with the label of all its ancestors, all the way back to the root of the tree. The top-level domain in this case is uk, followed by domain ac (the academic community) and finally domain `wlv`.

A DNS database is structured as a series of **resource records**. Each resource record is of a predefined record type some of which are given in Table 6.1. Resource records contain information about name and address translations, mail servers, alias host computer names, etc. A DNS database fragment is shown in Table 6.2.

One important advantage of using names is that they can remain unchanged even when the host or router moves location (i.e. they are **location independent**), whereas IP addresses are location dependent names. If a host moves from one network segment to another, its IP address changes. However, it can still retain its DNS name. An organization's name list is simply updated by the local administrator to reflect the new name and IP address mapping.

An organization's name list is made available to the Internet through the implementation of **name servers** and **resolvers**. DNS name servers hold the name list for an organization and make it available to the Internet by supporting DNS query requests. DNS name servers can be replicated and distributed throughout the Internet. Each DNS server holds at least a map of the domain name sub-tree below its domain. DNS servers use caching extensively to avoid frequent accesses to other DNS servers to obtain information about domain names not contained in its table. Each host computer must know the IP address of the local DNS name server as a starting point for handling requests.

Because the nearest DNS name server typically knows only a small portion of the total DNS name space, a special program called a *resolver* is defined in DNS to take a user request and

Table 6.1 Example DNS record types

Record type (meaning)	Use
A (address)	IP address of a particular host computer
NS (name server)	Delegates a sub-tree to the name server
SOA (start of address)	Holds details of sub-tree zone delegated
MX (mail exchange)	Name of the host computer that processes incoming mail for the designated targets
CNAME	An alias for the real name of the Host
PTR	Used to facilitate the mapping of IP addresses to host names

Table 6.2 A DNS database fragment. SC1.FIRM.CO.UK is defined as the main name server, mail server and world-wide web server. BACK.UP.CO.UK also acts as a name server

firm.co.uk.	IN	NS	sc1.firm.co.uk.
firm.co.uk.	IN	NS	back.up.co.uk.
sc1.firm.co.uk.	IN	A	221.23.34.67
back.up.co.uk.	IN	A	6.7.8.9
*.firm.co.uk	IN	MX	sc1.firm.co.uk
www.firm.co.uk	IN	CNAME	sc1.firm.co.uk

seek out the proper DNS name server to answer the request using a *name resolution protocol*. For example, when a user invokes a program specifying a domain name (e.g. TELNET nic.ddn.mil) the program uses a resolver to handle the mapping of the domain name (e.g. nic.ddn.mil) to the associated IP address. This may involve sending a request to the DNS name server for that domain or, in the case where a popular domain is specified, the name and IP address has been cached to eliminate the need to send the request to the distant name server.

An example name resolution protocol is shown in Figure 6.10. Here the client sends to its local DNS name server a request for resolution of the host name nic.ddn.mil. The local server cannot resolve the query, so it sends it to the name server maintaining the namespace for domain mil. That server returns the name and IP address of the DNS name server for the domain ddn.mil. The request is sent the name server for ddn.mil. The name server resolves the request by returning the IP address for the requested host name nic.ddn.mil (i.e. IP address 192.112.36.5). Fortunately, this process is normally completely hidden from the user who invoked the ftp request by use of the resolver program!

The DNS name service can be used to define a name and store information associated with that name. This means that a name can be associated with a variety of types of data in addition to IP addresses. Each name defined in a domain is stored in a set of resource records which may be either empty, or it may hold an IP address, mail information, etc.

6.4.5 The TCP transport service

IP does not provide guaranteed delivery of data. The transport control protocol (TCP) provides reliable virtual circuit connections to user processes, with no data duplication, no lost data, no data corruption or data segments delivered out of order. TCP is necessarily a complex protocol and a full description is beyond the scope of this book. The reader is referred to texts which describe TCP/IP in detail, for example Comer (1995).

The unit of data transfer in TCP is the TCP *segment*. The ordering of TCP segments is maintained by TCP sequence numbers in every segment. Sequence numbers are also used to eliminate data duplication. Tracking lost or corrupted data is achieved by the use of an acknowledgement number which indicates the sequence number of the last sequential byte

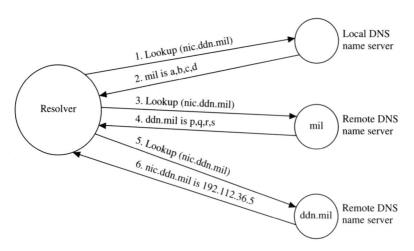

Figure 6.10 DNS name resolution.

successfully received. A *positive acknowledgement with re-transmission* is used for error detection and correction.

TCP is a connection-oriented protocol. It establishes an end-to-end connection between the two communicating processes. Before data is sent, control information exchange, called a *handshake,* is carried out to establish the connection. The control function associated with a TCP segment is indicated by a special bit in the `Flags` field in the TCP header, as illustrated in Figure 6.11 which details the UDP and TCP message formats. TCP conducts a three-way handshake illustrated in Figure 6.12. First the client TCP module initiates a connection request by sending the server TCP module a segment with the 'synchronize sequence

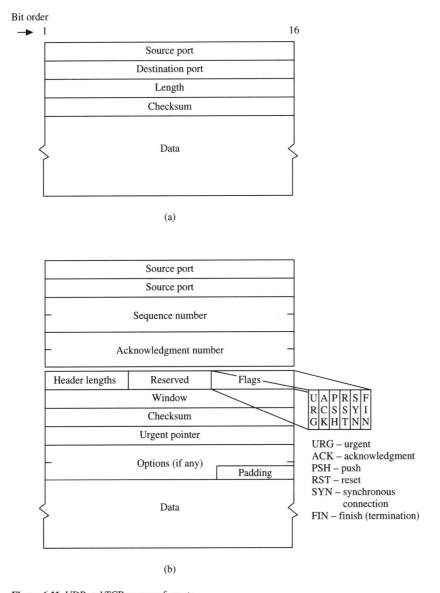

Bit order

(a)

(b)

Figure 6.11 UDP and TCP message formats.

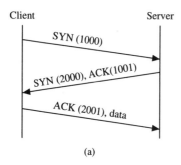

(a)

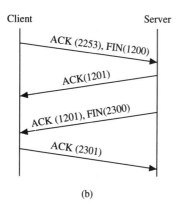

(b)

Figure 6.12 TCP handshakes: (a) three-way connection handshake; (b) termination handshake.

numbers' (SYN) bit set in the Flags field of the TCP header. The sequence number field contains the sequence number to be used as a starting number for client segments. The server responds with a segment that has the 'acknowledgement' (ACK) and SYN bits set. The sequence number field contains the sequence number the server will start with. This segment thus acknowledges receipt of the initial client segment and establishes the initial sequence number value. The third and final step in the handshake is when the client sends a segment that acknowledges receipt of the server's segment and transfers the first data segment (with the correct sequence number setting). The connection is established and data is freely exchanged because the connection is full-duplex.

When data exchange has been completed, a termination handshake is initiated by the client sending a segment with the 'no more data to send' (FIN) bit set. The server finally acknowledges receipt of the FIN segment and the connection is terminated at both ends.

The above description is an oversimplified view. In practice, data is not necessarily sent as soon as the client application sends it to TCP. It is usually buffered to optimize the efficiency of data transfer. If the data is required immediately by the server process, the user can request that TCP *push* the data through the connection to the server (by setting the push flag in the TCP header). Also data is acknowledged using a *sliding window* mechanism which avoids having to send an acknowledgement for every data segment sent and provides an efficient flow control mechanism.

6.4.6 TCP/IP ports

Once an IP datagram is routed successfully to the destination node associated with the destination IP address the data contained in the DATA field of the IP datagram is sent to the higher-layer protocol software module indicated in the `PROTOCOL` field. Normally a user process initiates the data message to be sent across the network to another user process running on the destination node. How are the sending and destination user processes identified? This issue was considered in Section 3.7. One technique, known as *indirect communication* is adopted by TCP/IP. Well-known port numbers are established to create a semi-permanent association between a destination process and a port number. A server process is almost always associated with the same port number no matter which computer it is running on. This is analogous to the use of PO Box numbers when sending letters to some individual or organization. Source and destination port numbers are used by the UDP and TCP protocols when sending messages. UDP provides few enhancements to the basic IP protocol. Its main function is to enable IP datagrams to be routed to the correct application processes by use of source and destination port numbers in the UDP header (see Figure 6.11).

Table 6.3 details the well-known port numbers for a selection of common TCP and UDP user processes. For example, if a TELNET client wishes to connect to a remote computer it needs to send a **TCP connection request** message to the TELNET server process on the remote process by sending the message to port number 23. Any data sent to port 23 will be received by the TELNET server program.

6.5 EXAMPLE: TELNET SESSION

To illustrate a typical sequence of events required to set up a connection to a remote host computer, below are the main steps to establish a remote login (TELNET) session between my computer (called mycomputer) and a remote computer called nic.ddn.mil as illustrated in Figure 6.13.

1. The user invokes the TELNET client program specifying the domain name of the destination host, by typing: `telnet nic.ddn.mil`.
2. The TELNET program running on `mycomputer` (host id `134.220.1.10`) uses an ARP program to broadcast an ARP query (an ICMP message) to identify the MAC address of the DNS server whose IP address is `134.220.1.10`.
3. The name server responds with its MAC address `08002006F324H`. Host mycomputer can now generate an IEEE 802.3 (Ethernet) frame with the correct destination address for the DNS name server. The frame contains a DNS query message for the IP address of a host with the domain name `nic.ddn.mil` to which the user wishes to login.
4. The DNS name server receives the query and generates a response indicating that `nic.ddn.mil` is located at IP address `192.112.36.5`.
5. Since nic.ddn.mil is on a different subnet, mycomputer must contact the local interior router asking it to locate destination host computer with IP address `192.112.36.5`. Host `mycomputer` broadcasts an ARP request looking for the local router whose address is `134.220.1.2`. The router responds with its MAC address `08002006B432H`.
6. The TELNET program creates an initiate connection TCP data segment (by setting certain TCP header flags) with destination port number set to 23 (the well-known port number for

Table 6.3 A selection of well-known port number mappings

Port number	Process	Description	TCP or UDP?
0	Reserved		
7	ECHO	echo (used by ping)	TCP/UDP
11	USERS	Active users	TCP/UDP
13	DAYTIME	Day time	TCP/UDP
17	QUOTE	Quote of the day	TCP/UDP
20	FTP-DATA	ftp data channel	TCP
21	FTP	ftp server	TCP
23	TELNET	TELNET server process	TCP
25	SMTP	Mail server	TCP
37	TIME	Time service	TCP/UDP
42	NAMESERVER	Host name server	TCP/UDP
53	DOMAIN	DNS name server	TCP/UDP
67	BOOTPS	Bootstrap protocol server	UDP
68	BOOTPC	Bootstrap protocol client	UDP
69	TFTP	Trivial file transfer	UDP
70	GOPHER	Gopher service	TCP
79	FINGER	finger	TCP
80	HTTP	World Wide Web service	TCP
88	Kerberos	Kerberos authentication	UDP
103	X400	X-400 mail service	TCP
104	X400-SND	X-400 mail sending	TCP
109	POP-2	Mail	TCP
110	POP-3	Mail	TCP
111	SUNRPC	SUN remote procedure call	TCP/UDP
113	AUTH	Authentication service	TCP
119	NNTP	USENET News Transfer	TCP
123	NTP	Network Time Protocol	UDP
139	NETBIOS-SSN	NETBIOS Session Service	TCP
160–223	Reserved (TCP)		TCP
161	SNMP	SNMP network monitor	UDP
162	SNMP-TRAP	SNMP traps	UDP
513	WHO		UDP
514	SYSLOG	System log	UDP
525	TIMED	Time daemon	UDP
6667	IRC	Internet relay chat	TCP

a TELNET server program). The TCP data segment is encapsulated in an IP datagram with source IP address 134.220.1.10 (mycomputer) and destination IP address 192.112.36.5 (nic.ddn.mil). This is sent encapsulated within an Ethernet frame with the destination MAC address of the local router: 08002006B432H.

7. Interior router 134.220.1.2 receives the IP datagram and determines that the IP address is for a host in another autonomous system, so it sends it to exterior router 134.220.1.1 via the data link layer (using ARP if necessary to find the exterior router's ethernet address).

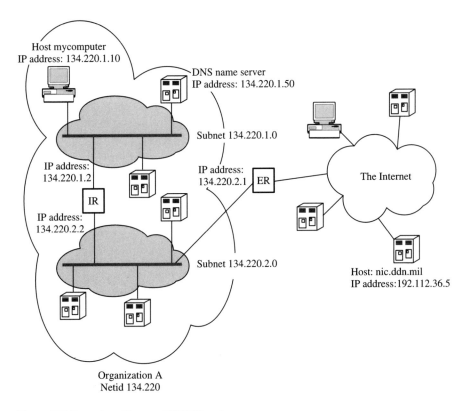

Figure 6.13 Example: setting up a TELNET session.

8. The exterior router `134.220.1.1` receives the IP datagram and uses the network identifier of the destination host (i.e. the class C network address `192.112.36`) as the lookup
   value in the routing table to determine the IP address of the next exterior router to which
   the IP datagram is forwarded. The datagram is sent to the next exterior router. This
   process is repeated until the datagram is delivered to the destination exterior router associated with the autonomous system to which host nic.ddn.mil belongs. Interior routers
   within `nic.ddn.mil` use their local routing tables to deliver the IP datagram to the
   host `nic.ddn.mil`.
9. Host `nic.ddn.mil` has a TELNET server program running and associated with the
   well-known port number 23. It receives the connection request encapsulated within the IP
   datagram and generates an appropriate response (i.e. a prompt for the user's login name)
   after negotiating parameters such as the terminal type.
10. The user can now type in a login name and password and use the remote computer's
    facilities.

Steps 2–9 are totally transparent to the TELNET user. The example above demonstrates
how co-operation between TCP/IP client/server applications, hosts, interior and exterior
routers, DNS servers and ARP are used to create the illusion of a single network of diverse
host computers, each located by name and offering useful applications for inter-personal communications, file transfer and remote login.

6.6 CONNECTION-ORIENTED VERSUS CONNECTIONLESS OPERATION

Is one type of routing better suited to an organization's needs than the other? To answer this we must make the distinction between a service as perceived by users of the network and the inherent operation of the network. A user may be offered both connection-oriented (virtual circuit) and connectionless (datagram) services over the same physical network. Some X.25-based physical networks offer both services to users. The physical network will adopt one approach although a hybrid protocol could also be implemented. In practice it is sometimes difficult to make a distinction between the two types of network operations. In general, the following may be argued.

1. Connection-oriented services are well suited to applications where the order of packet receipt is critical, and lost packets cannot be tolerated. Connection-oriented services take the burden of dealing with these issues away from the application. However, when network problems which affect a connection occur, the network typically clears down the call with potential loss of packets.
2. Connectionless services are well suited to applications which can tolerate occasional lost packets. Example applications include multimedia applications involving the transmission of voice or video packets. If a voice packet is lost, it can result in gaps in the voice output. If a video packet is lost, it can result in the slight freezing of frames since only changed pixels are normally transmitted. The extent of distortion depends on the size and rate of lost packets.
3. Connection-oriented network operation enables faster routing of packets during the data transfer phase. The bulk of routing delay is establishing the route during call set-up.
4. Connection-oriented network operation is more able to guarantee bandwidth and other end-to-end quality of service requirements negotiated on a per connection basis. In a connection-oriented service, a call set-up request is refused if the end-to-end quality of service requirements cannot be met. In connectionless operation, each packet is routed independently making it much more difficult to commit to end-to-end guarantees.

It is likely that future high-speed networks (e.g. ATM) will operate on a connection-oriented basis for faster routing and to support on-demand bandwidth and other negotiated quality of service requirements. There will still be a need for both connection-oriented and connectionless services delivered to users. Thus SMDS and TCP/IP services will operate over ATM and other high-speed connection-oriented physical networks in the future in addition to traditional connectionless router-based networks.

6.7 MULTIPLE NETWORK PROTOCOL SUPPORT

Client and server computers may need to support multiple network protocols over a single network connection. A client may, for example, need to access simultaneously multiple servers each based on different network protocols, or a server may need to support multiple client platforms each utilizing a different network protocol. In a typical organization, file and print services may be provided by Novell Netware's IPX/SPX proprietary protocols whereas access to Internet information services may require an implementation of the TCP/IP protocol. A feature of client and server computers for the foreseeable future is the need to support multiple network protocols since it is unlikely that existing protocols will converge to a single open network standard.

Network communication software such as TCP/IP do not normally interface directly to a network interface card (NIC). Instead, the NIC is supplied with a software driver which provides a defined interface to higher-layer protocols and interacts directly with the NIC itself. Since the driver typically works at layer 2 of OSI it is often referred to as the link-layer (or MAC-layer in LAN environments) driver. Drivers in widespread use are aligned either to a popular protocol suite (e.g. TCP/IP) or to proprietary networked system suppliers. To facilitate multi-protocol support over a single connection, the driver must make possible the concurrent use of a range higher-layer protocols. It must therefore examine the packet type of every packet received and pass it to the appropriate higher-layer protocol without blocking access to the card by other protocols. Several driver specifications have emerged which provide this capability, for example:

- Packet driver specification widely used in TCP/IP networks.
- Microsoft's network driver interface specification (NDIS).
- Novell's open data-link interface (ODI).

To illustrate the general architecture Novell's open data-link interface (ODI) is shown in Figure 6.14. The ODI link support layer (LSL) provides a common interface for all protocol stacks and routes received packets to the correct protocol stack. LSL provides the means of binding a NIC to one or more specific protocol stacks. The possible combinations of protocol stacks and specific NICs is not restricted. The LSL is normally supplied with the network operating system whereas the multiple link interface driver (MLID) driver controls a product-specific NIC and is usually supplied by the NIC manufacturer. This two-level driver definition allows multiple NICs (which implies multiple MLIDs) to be installed in a client or server computer underneath a common LSL layer.

This type of multi-protocol architecture will be required for the foreseeable future since it is unlikely that existing protocols will converge to a single open network protocol. The above

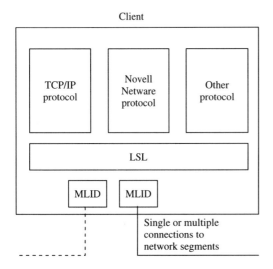

Figure 6.14 Multi-protocol support using Novell Open Data-link Interface (ODI).

approach enables existing and future protocols to co-exist which results in a high level of flexibility.

6.8 SUMMARY

Internetworks are separate networks (subnets) linked together by bridges and routers. Routers are more widely used as interworking units because they are able to link subnets which may or may not be of the same type. Bridges are simpler devices which are less costly and faster when compared with routers. However, bridges can link only subnets of the same type.

In order to successfully route user data successfully across a multi-subnet internet, an internet protocol is required which imposes a global addressing scheme and routing protocol. Two types of internet protocols could be implemented: a connection-oriented protocol (e.g. ITU-T X.25) or a connectionless protocol (e.g. TCP/IP). The TCP/IP protocol suite is in widespread use in world-wide networks. TCP/IP provides a basic connectionless routing protocol and connectionless and connection-oriented transport interfaces to application-level processes. TCP/IP also provides application-level protocols for electronic mail, file transfer and remote login. The Internet domain name service (DNS) supports the naming of resources in the Internet so that users can avoid the explicit use of IP addresses.

6.9 REVIEW EXERCISES

1. Explain the differences in functionality between a repeater and a bridge. Describe circumstances where a repeater might be a more suitable option.
2. Explain the differences between a transparent bridge and a source routing bridge.
3. Explain the differences in functionality between a bridge and a router.
4. Compare and contrast connection-oriented and connectionless routing. Describe how the X.25 service routes packets through a network.
5. In the context of the ISO OSI reference model, briefly describe the protocols which form the TCP/IP protocol suite. Explain which protocols define and use the following: (i) Port numbers; (ii) IP address interpretation.
6. Suppose TCP/IP is implemented over an IEEE 802.3 LAN. In the context of the ISO OSI reference model, sketch the relative position of protocols used from OSI Layer 1 to Layer 7.
7. When would TCP be used rather than the UDP transport service? Given the characteristics of the UDP service, why do many applications choose to use it?
8. What is the function of the Domain Name Service (DNS)? Describe how DNS is used when a user invokes FTP specifying a domain name.
9. Why is an address resolution protocol (ARP) required?
10. Describe how a router and IP addressing are used to route IP datagrams through a nework.
11. Explain the term subnet. Discuss how the use of interior and exterior routers enables the implementation of multiple separate networks with traffic isolation.
12. What problems arise when TCP/IP is implemented over an ATM network?

6.10 FURTHER READING

Repeater, hub, bridge and router technologies are examined in detail in Smythe (1995). It also gives useful practical guidance on internetwork design. The TCP/IP protocol suite is described in detail in Comer (1991). Network planning and design issues are discussed in Etheridge and Simon (1992) and Smythe (1995).

PART THREE

Design and implementation

7

BUILDING DISTRIBUTED SERVICES

7.1 INTRODUCTION

A distributed IT infrastructure makes available numerous resources that may be required by users. A resource may be a reusable hardware component (e.g. a *physical* resource such as a disk drive) or a software component (e.g. a *logical* resource such as a database) of a computer system that may be useful to users or processes in an information system. Resources may be continually requested, used and released by multiple users or processes. When all the resources required by a DIS are available on the computer on which the DIS executes (a centralized configuration), the computer's native operating system is responsible for allocating resources and ensuring that non-shareable resources are used appropriately. When the computer is connected to a network, however, the native operating system does not control all resources and may not be able to allocate remote resources and devices to applications except through co-operation with remote resource managers (i.e. servers). In addition to a basic inter-process communication facility, complex protocols are required to achieve flexible but efficient resource allocation, synchronization and sharing. This is particularly the case when handling multiple real-time data streams when some data streams carry voice and video media types.

In this chapter we examine the general design principles and functions required to develop scalable, responsive and dependable services to users.

7.2 OPERATING SYSTEM SUPPORT FOR DISTRIBUTION

An operating system which supports the allocation and management of distributed resources can be categorized into network operating systems and distributed operating systems.

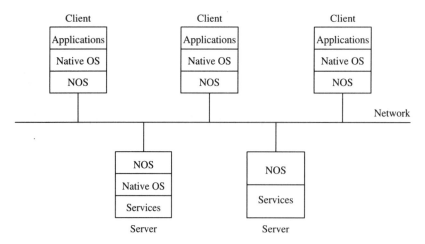

Figure 7.1 Network operating system (NOS).

7.2.1 Network operating systems

In the case where the native operating system has little support for network access to distributed resources or where in a heterogeneous environment there needs to be a compatible access protocol, additional software is used to provide the function required. The collection of software for this purpose is known as the **network operating system** (NOS) and is illustrated in Figure 7.1. NOS software attempts to extend the native OS to enable applications and users to access remote resources and to implement a degree of distribution transparency.

NOS software reside on both client and server platforms. In some cases the server has a native operating system and the NOS runs alongside it. In other cases the NOS becomes the native operating software on the server for improved performance and reliability rather than co-existing with a native operating system. Examples of commercial NOS software include Novell Netware and Microsoft WindowsNT. Network operating systems offer many application support functions that are inherently distributed using the client/server model and provide distribution transparency to application processes running on the client. A word processor running on a client, for example, is unaware that files and printing facilities are remote as it accesses them in the same way as for local resources because it simply refers to files and printers using the normal DOS naming conventions.

7.2.2 Distributed operating system

In this case a single native operating system is resident in all hosts in the network thus forming a homogeneous network. The native operating system is known as a distributed operating system (DOS) if it inherently supports and manages network access to remote resources in a globally coherent manner as illustrated in Figure 7.2. Basic functions include communication functions such as asynchronous and synchronous message passing, remote procedure calls, broadcasting and multicasting, and fault tolerance functions such as support for replication, backup and distributed control. Examples of DOSs include Amoeba (Mullender *et al.*, 1990), Locus (Popek and Walker, 1985) and Mach (Rashid, 1986a, b). Manufacturer-specific versions of the UNIX operating system have been augmented to function as DOSs with a single

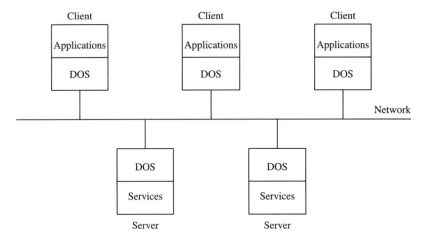

Figure 7.2 Distributed operating system (DOS).

version of UNIX running both on client and server computers. Examples in this category include Sun Microsystems' Solaris and IBM's AIX operating systems. For an excellent description of major distributed operating systems, the reader is referred to Tanenbaum (1995) and Coulouris *et al.* (1994).

In practice, many commercial network operating systems are gradually incorporating distributed operating system functionality pioneered by the systems mentioned in the previous paragraph. In the future, we are likely to see less of a distinction between a NOS and a DOS. For simplicity we shall use the term NOS to encompass both NOS and DOS approaches, making the distinction when necessary.

7.3 DEFINITION OF A SERVICE

In order to implement distribution transparency, rather than a client explicitly handling the dialogue with the server, it is more usual that a **user agent** process acts on its behalf, interacting directly with the appropriate servers and giving a client the illusion that the resource is local. The main function of the user agent is to accept a user request, establish whether it is local or remote and use the appropriate mechanisms to service the request. For example, when an Internet user invokes the FTP program and specifies the DNS name of a remote computer, a user agent process called a resolver creates a DNS query and sends it to the local DNS name server in order to obtain the IP address associated with the specified host name.

A service may utilize other services offered by different servers. In this case a server becomes a surrogate client as illustrated in Figure 7.3 where a user agent issues a print request to a print server. The print server issues a request to the file service to create a print spool file. Thus, a distributed IT infrastructure may offer a wide range of basic services which are utilized to deliver higher-level services using a multilevel client/server architecture.

7.3.1 Maintaining state data

State data must be maintained by each service, recording the current usage of each resource a

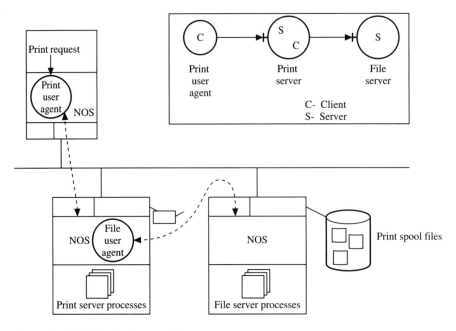

Figure 7.3 Multilevel client/server architecture.

server manages and for each client being serviced. The state of a resource determines its behaviour. A server can be described as *stateless* if it maintains no specific state data about active clients, or *stateful* if it does. In the case of stateless servers, clients hold information about the state of any session with a server. The advantage of this approach is that a system can maintain consistent state information in the presence of client, server or network failure or message loss. All relevant state information is sent with client requests and server replies. Thus if a server fails temporarily, a client can often survive by resending the request since no client-specific state information was lost. The disadvantage of stateless servers is that it is much more difficult to implement concurrency control (using locking mechanisms), security control and other control mechanisms that require an overview of state information across all active clients.

7.3.2 Quality of service

A client process desires that any request can always be serviced within a user-defined quality of service (QoS). QoS parameters typically include response time, throughput, reliability and availability. The key design considerations pertinent to the quality of services offered are scalability, performance, reliability, availability and fault tolerance. Each of these factors are examined below.

7.4 SCALABILITY

The path between the user and the services of interest may involve use of many elements of the IT infrastructure as illustrated in Figure 7.4. Each component has a finite capacity.

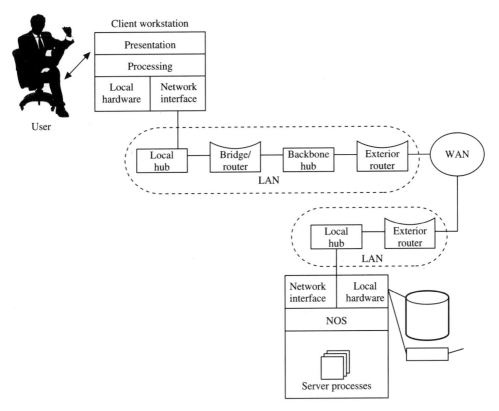

Figure 7.4 Multi-component path between user and services.

Designing for scalability involves calculating the capacity of each of these elements and the extent to which the capacity can be increased. For example, an Ethernet network is a shared-medium LAN which should never exceed around 50 per cent utilization and capacity is not easily increased. 10 Mbps is the most common data rate, although this can be upgraded to 100 Mbps. The cost of upgrade is significant since network interface cards, hubs and possibly cabling may need to be replaced. Good DIS design minimizes utilization of components which are not scalable. Also, the element which is weakest in terms of available capacity (and the extent to which that capacity can be easily increased) should be of prime consideration in terms of design. There are four principal components to be considered when designing for scalability: client workstation, LAN, servers and the WAN.

7.4.1 Scaling client workstations

Workstations are scalable due to the wide range of processor, main memory, disk and other sub-component options available at a reasonable cost. The other attraction is that it is usually a dedicated (non-shareable) resource. However, when scaling workstations, a proper balance between CPU speed, RAM, disk capacity, disk I/O rate and network interface (measured by packets transferred per second) is required to maintain adequate performance as new applications are added.

7.4.2 Scaling the LAN

As noted earlier, traditional shared-medium LANs do not offer a wide range of speeds within a particular network type (e.g. Ethernet). This is not too much of a problem in a small client/server configuration typical of a small workgroup of say 10–30 users. For example, on an Ethernet LAN with 20 client PCs, with each user generating 10 packets per second (each packet of size 300 bytes on average), then this equates to about 17 per cent utilization of the Ethernet capacity (an Ethernet LAN will become congested if more than 1200 300-byte packets per second are sent). However, if the number of clients increases to 120, then the LAN will saturate.

Exceeding LAN capacity can be avoided if peak traffic loads can be reduced or smoothed out by rescheduling some application workloads outside of peak times (e.g. large data transfers). One candidate is the transfer of graphics and other image data that result in the transmission of large numbers of maximum-size packets (1500 bytes in the case of Ethernet). At 1500 bytes per packet, it takes only 375 packets per second to saturate the Ethernet LAN. Another situation that should be avoided is the case where client application repeatedly poll (send requests to) servers – for example to determine the server's status. This is acceptable when the number of clients is small, but does not scale well since if 100 clients are repeatedly sending requests to a server, the network is easily saturated. Finally, the network infrastructure should be carefully designed to localize traffic, that is, avoid unnecessary traffic flowing over the backbone network. This is achieved through intelligent use of bridges and routers, and careful placement of servers (taking account of client-to-server access profiles).

ATM is an attractive LAN option as it is a non-shared medium, scalable network technology (see Section 4.6). If the IT infrastructure is based on ATM then the network can be regarded as scalable provided that the ATM switching and port speed options are flexible.

7.4.3 Scaling the server

A server is by definition a shared resource. Therefore there is always a risk of exhausting the capacity of the server. The critical measures of capacity for a server depends on what services are being offered. Usually processing power is a critical component (measured crudely in terms of MIPS consumed per client request type). Another component may be disk I/O rate (measured in I/Os per second) and disk capacity (megabytes per client or client request). Dependent on the design of the server, either the server will reach the capacity limit and a fault will result blocking all future client requests or queues will build up as client requests contend for access to server resources. Calculating the results on response times of increasing client requests is not simply a linear projection, the effects of queuing delays must be estimated. However, linear projection can be used as a rough guide to the effects of increasing the number of clients.

A number of techniques can be employed to improve scalability. A scalable server design will minimize and impose a limit on the amount of work done on behalf of a client. In practice this can be implemented by delivering partial results and allowing the client to subsequently request more data. The amount of work done by a server on behalf of a client can be scaled down by moving some work back onto clients since this is a dedicated resource. This is the first course of action. The frequency of requests to the client can perhaps be reduced by moving some data on to the client (e.g. using caching) for local processing. However, server-based processing may be more appropriate if significant network traffic would result from the movement of data to a user workstation in order for processing to take place locally. In this case a server-based 'stored procedure' may be a better option since the server is typically more scalable than a shared-medium network.

Scalability can also be enhanced by ensuring that the server controls the dialogue between itself and its clients. When a client issues a request, the server which is in control can choose to service it immediately, queue it for servicing later, or reject it because perhaps it is too busy. If a client request is rejected it could continually re-send the request until the server responds. This is not a scalable solution since many rejected clients would further delay the server (while it rejects the new requests) and increases network load. A more scalable approach is to ensure that when a server rejects a client request, it indicates in the reply when the client can re-issue the request. Clients should not re-issue a request until that time has expired. This has the effect of maintaining the service at the expense of higher response times. In the longer-term, if the average number of client request rejections per unit time or the average blocking time (measured as the time between the first request and receipt of the required reply data) is unacceptably high, additional servers should be added or the existing server upgraded.

7.4.4 Scaling the WAN

Network capacity for WANs is at least an order of magnitude less than LANs and WANs are much more error prone. This translates to a much reduced maximum packet rate. Thus, the rule-of-thumb is to minimize the amount of data that needs to be sent over a WAN. A rough guide is that a WAN is ten times slower than a LAN. With the introduction of broadband WANs, the differences between WAN and LAN speeds and error rates are reducing rapidly. Separate design rules for WANs and LANs will no longer be required since each will exhibit similar performance and reliability.

7.5 PERFORMANCE

There are two common measures of performance for distributed interactive systems:

1. Response time: defined as the average elapsed time from the moment the user is ready to transmit (i.e. the 'enter' key or mouse station is depressed) and the entire response is received. The response received depends on the nature of the user interaction.
2. Throughput: the number of requests handled per unit time.

Satisfactory performance as perceived by users is dependent on the nature of the task being performed. As mentioned earlier, the components in the path between user and application all have performance characteristics that will determine overall performance as perceived by the user. Servers will queue client requests until the necessary resources become available. For example the sample values in Figure 7.5 indicate that the maximum throughput is 25 client requests per second and the main bottleneck is server disk I/O. In order to calculate performance in terms of response time the utilization of each component needs to be established and the effects of queuing calculated. A full analysis may reveal a throughput of less than 25 client requests per second due to other components which are overutilized. Client request response time reduction is achieved by partitioning the workload across multiple instances of server resources. This has the effect of reducing the workload to each server thus reducing queue lengths and the mean response time per server. Each instance services a portion of the overall

1 Client request/second = 6 packets per second network traffic
2 disk I/Os per second on a server

Component	Client processing (CPU)	Client network interface	Workgroup LAN	Bridge/ router	Backbone LAN	Exterior router	WAN	Exterior router	Server LAN	Server network interface	Server processing (CPU)	Server disk I/O
Maximum Throughput	100 client requests per second	2400 packets per second	1200 packets per second	3000 packets per second	10 000 packets per second	5000 packets per second	500 packets per second	5000 packets per second	1200 packets per second	2400 packets per second	300 client requests per second	50 I/Os per second

Estimated maximum throughput = 25 client requests/second
Estimated main bottleneck = Server disk I/O

Figure 7.5 Estimating throughput and bottlenecks.

workload. To illustrate this approach and the problems which result from partitioning, we examine the case where a workload is partitioned across multiple CPUs and memory.

An alternate approach to improving CPU performance is to implement multi-processor or multi-computer configurations where each CPU handles a portion of the total workload. Effectively, the total workload is handled by a service which is partitioned across a multiple CPU server group. In a multi-processor server configuration, for example, a client request is sent to the multi-processor server and scheduled for execution using one of the processors, whereas in a multiple single-CPU server group in which each server handles a specific workload, a client request must be directed to the appropriate server. This is dependent on which part of the overall service is offered by each server in the server group.

Thus when a workload is partitioned across multiple servers, a *resolution protocol* is required to find the server which is able to satisfy the client request. For example the Internet DNS naming service partitions the namespace amongst multiple dispersed DNS name servers. A client must utilize a name resolution protocol to locate a name server which is able to satisfy a particular DNS query.

Performance improvements can be made in a distributed systems environment by migrating much of the processing on to a user's client workstation. This reduces the processing on the server per client request which leads to faster and more predictable response times overall, provided the client workstation has the required capacity. As noted previously, this approach also increases server scalability in terms of the number of client requests services per server unit resource.

Data intensive applications can improve performance by avoiding I/O operations to read from disk storage. Reading from buffer areas in memory is much faster. Applications invoking remote operations offered by remote servers can improve performance by avoiding the need to access a remote server to satisfy a request. A caching system reduces the performance cost of I/O and remote operations by storing the results of a recently executed I/O or remote operation in local memory and reusing the results whenever the same operation is re-invoked and when it can be ascertained that the results data is still valid. Whenever an I/O or remote operation is requested, the local cache is searched first. For example, in the Internet DNS name service the resolver looks in the local cache first. Any entry which may satisfy the request is known as an unauthoritive response.

The main problem with caching is maintaining consistency between multiple caches and the server which holds the authoritive state data. Cache consistency techniques range from restricting cached data to state data that does not change (read only) through to the maintenance of cached client lists by servers holding authoritive state data so that they can be informed when data is changed. When state data is updated all cached copies become invalid and each must be refreshed. Extensively cached data should be relatively stable (not very volatile) so as to minimize cache consistency problems.

7.6 RELIABILITY AND AVAILABILITY

Reliability is defined as the probability that a system will continue to function within a given timescale, whereas *availability* is defined as the extent to which the system is operable when a system user requires it. The design objective is to maximize reliability and availability.

In a distributed IT infrastructure reliability and availability are usually key service-level requirements. Many underlying IT infrastructure components operate with a high probability that the component will not fail when the client wishes to use it. However, the IT infrastructure must be designed to provide the desired resilience to component failure. This increases the cost of implementation due to the need to configure components in addition to those required to meet throughput and response time requirements. The aim is to use redundant common components to guarantee system performance in the event of component failure. The mode of operation of the additional components could be parallel, load sharing, hot standby, etc. Typical reliability and availability measures are (Etheridge and Simon, 1992):

- mean time between failures (MTBF) – the average period of time that a component will operate before failing; usually quoted in hours;
- mean time to repair (MTTR) – the average amount of time required for a failed component to be back in service.

7.6.1 Reliability

Reliability measures the stability of the network and the error profile of IT infrastructure components. The terms 'error', 'fault' and 'failure' are often confused or used in an ambiguous way in this context. Cristian (1991) suggests that a *fault* is a condition that causes a device, element or component to fail to perform in the required manner. A *failure* occurs when the system is made unavailable either temporarily or permanently due to a fault. An error is an item of information which, when processed by the normal algorithms of the system, will produce a failure. The MTBF is a direct measure of reliability, but some faults do not cause outright failure of a component (e.g. a user may experience slow response times due to excessive errors on the communication link which are eventually recovered using error detection and correction techniques). A failed component can cause down time and reduced availability unless alternative components are used to provide a backup facility. The reliability of a component normally reduces over time and can therefore be modelled using the following probability density function which expresses the probability that a component will not fail within time interval (t) (Nickel, 1978):

$$R(t) = e^{-at} \quad \text{where } a = 1/\text{MTBF}$$

Thus for a MTBF of 2500 hours then over the week (assuming an 8-hour day) from installation the reliability is $e^{-(1/2500)(40)} = 0.984$ (i.e. 98.4 per cent reliability).

The total system reliability is calculated as the product of the reliability of each of its components. This has the effect of reducing overall reliability. Distributed IT infrastructures introduce more components between the user and the service being accessed than an equivalent centralized infrastructure. Thus, for example, if each of the seven components of the link between a user and the host processor have a reliability of 0.95, then the total reliability is $0.95^7 = 0.698$. It is therefore important that the distributed IT infrastructure is designed to maximize reliability. Reliability can be improved by installing backup components, particularly at points where the component reliability is lowest or where a component is shared by many clients. Communication links are a frequent candidate for backup links. Also, servers are good candidates since they are a very critical component. The following formula is used to calculate the effect on the reliability of a component of adding a backup component (Nickel, 1978):

$$R_{\text{backup}} = 1 - (1 - R_{\text{nobackup}})^2$$

In general, if there are (*n*) backup components each with reliability (*R*) the overall reliability is given as:

$$R_{overall} = 1 - (1 - R)^n$$

and in the case where there are (*n*) backup components, and component (*i*) has reliability R_i:

$$R_{overall} = 1 - (1 - R_1)(1 - R_2)...(1 - R_n)$$

Thus if a component has a reliability of 0.95 then adding a single backup component of equivalent reliability would increase the reliability to $(1 - (1 - 0.95)^2) = 0.9975$, and utilizing five backup components would yield an overall reliability of $(1 - (1 - 0.95)^5) = 0.999999687$. which represents a significant increase in reliability (there is a small probability that both components fail at the same time).

7.6.2 Availability

The availability (*A*) of a component (*n*) is usually calculated using the following formula:

$$A = \frac{MTBF}{MTBF + MTTR}$$

For example, a component has a MTBF of 2500 hours and a MTTR of 0.5 hours. The availability is therefore $2500/2500 + 5$, i.e. 0.9998. Thus on average we would expect the component to be unavailable two times in every 10 000 tries. Nickel has shown that for a specific time interval (*t*), availability can be defined as:

$$A(t) = \frac{b}{a + b} + \frac{ae^{-(a+b)t}}{a + b}$$

where $a = 1/MTBF$ and $b = 1/MTTR$. Thus for the example above, the availability for an 8 hour day is ($a = 0.0004$ and $b = 2$):

$$A(8) = \frac{2}{2 + 0.0004} + \frac{0.004e^{-(2+0.0004)8}}{2 + 0.0004}$$

$$= \frac{2}{2.0004} + \frac{0.0004 \times 0.000\,000\,112\,2}{2.0004}$$

$$= 0.9998 + 2.2 \times 10^{-11}$$

$$= 0.9998$$

The link between a user and a service of interest consists of multiple components as illustrated previously in Figure 7.5. All components must be available to make the system available to the user. System availability is calculated by obtaining the product of the availability of the individual components. Thus if the processing path consists of 8 components each with an availability of 0.991, then the system availability seen by the user is $0.991^8 = 0.93$. In general if there are (*n*) components with component (*i*) exhibiting availability A_i:

$$A_{overall} = 1 - (1 - A_1)(1 - A_2)...(1 - A_n)$$

7.7 FAULT-TOLERANT SERVICES

Although reliability and availability are factors, distributed systems must be **dependable** systems. Dependability is the trustworthiness of a computer system. It is very difficult to predict the behaviour of information systems under real workloads. Unpredictable fluctuations in workload levels, IT infrastructure component utilizations, software bugs and malfunctioning hardware can result in unusual circumstances which trigger a major system failure. A DIS can consist of a complex web of interconnected (hardware and software) sub-systems which can easily result in implementation of a very fragile system.

The designer of a DIS should recognize that services may fail in a variety of ways and seek to minimize the risk of failure due to hardware or software faults by assuming that unlikely events that cause failure *will* occur at the worst possible times. A distributed IT infrastructure is subject to three main types of component failures which can result in failed client requests:

- client-end failures: client software or hardware fails;
- server-end failures: server software or hardware fails;
- network failures: either the client request or the server reply is lost.

A network failure can fragment the network into isolated subnetworks called **network partitions**. If a client is in one partition and the server in another, client requests will never get through to the server or reply never get back to the client. A further complication is that a network can appear partitioned when it is not. For example if slow responses are experienced, network failure time-outs could be triggered, but after a period of time network responses become acceptable. These are very difficult problems to handle when attempting to implement a fault-tolerant service.

Birman (1989) suggests the following design approach for building dependable distributed systems which exhibit a high level of stability and fault tolerance.

- *Interconnect for good reasons.* A complex web of interconnected sub-systems should be avoided. The more complex the web, the more fragile is the overall system. Interconnect only when defined objectives are met by doing so.
- *Support only necessary services.* When implementing services, it is tempting to implement a full range of services which a client may wish to use. Many services are implemented by default whether needed or not (perhaps because these services were built into the network operating system). For security reasons and in order to minimize maintenance, services should be supported only if there is an identifiable need. Other services should be disabled. An enabled system may represent an unwanted sub-system which may compromise the robustness of the overall system.
- *Include self-diagnosis and authentication mechanisms.* A DIS should attempt to monitor itself, identify any inconsistencies and gracefully shut down any faulty components and restart or switch to a replica. Client requests should be authenticated for origin and legality to avoid malicious or erroneous failures.
- *Design for fault tolerance.* The assumption that failures will occur leads to the goal of trying to design systems which are tolerant of some classes of failures. A fault-tolerant system is one which continues to operate as required in the presence of faults from either hardware or software components. The level of fault tolerance required is system dependent.
- *Design for scale.* DIS designs can result in major performance problems or become

extremely difficult to manage when the number of users grows beyond a small number. In a large-scale DIS, scale is a design parameter rather than a capacity planning exercise after the system has been developed.

- *Avoid mechanisms that can cascade failures.* In systems under heavy workloads or when some failures occur, failures can cascade as recovery and other mechanisms are activated.
- *Avoid using 'magic' mechanisms.* Use simple, well-understood mechanisms rather than elaborate but poorly understood ones.
- *Robustness is expensive.* Achieving a desired level of robustness inevitably involves compromise in terms of cost, performance, functionality and other often conflicting objectives from a design point of view.

Building a fault-tolerant service involves recognizing the different types of failures that can occur (**failure classification**), the different ways in which a particular service may fail (**failure semantics**), and designing mechanisms for hiding (masking) failure from the users of a service (**failure masking**) or converting it to a recognizable fault. Failure masking is a well-used technique in computer science, used extensively in the design of robust operating systems and networks. For example, layered architectures in networks, such as the OSI reference model, are designed so that lower-layer failures can be masked by higher layers. When a data frame is lost at Layer 2 in the OSI reference model, Layer 4 transport layer protocols can implement additional recovery mechanisms to mask frame losses from Layers 5–7 by detecting the frame loss and asking for retransmission.

A failure classification scheme devised by Cristian (1991) is summarized in Table 7.1. An omission failure occurs when a server does not respond to a client request. A timing failure occurs when a server responds correctly but in an untimely manner. The time interval is either

Table 7.1 Classification of server failures

Class of failure	Subclass	Description
Omission failure		A server does not respond to a request
Response failure		The server response is incorrect
	Value failure	A wrong value is returned from a server
	State transition failure	The response is not consistent with the current state of the client/server dialogue
Timing failure		Response was not available within a reasonable period of time
	Performance failure	The response is too late
	Flow control failure	The response is too early
Crash failure		A repeated omission failure (i.e. a server repeatedly fails to respond to a request until it is restarted
	Amnesia crash	A server starts in its initial state as if the crash never occurred
	Pause crash	A server starts in the state before the crash
	Halting crash	The server never restarts
Byzantine failure		A service that exhibits all of the above failure semantics. This represents the worst possible semantics of a server

too early or too late. These can also be classified as performance failures. A response failure occurs when a server responds incorrectly. Either the value of the server output is incorrect (a value failure) or the state of the server changes incorrectly (a state transition failure). A crash failure occurs when a server repeatedly fails to respond to client requests until restarted. More formally, Cristian defines a crash failure as a repeated omission failure. Sometimes server crash failure may not be detectable by clients and other servers. Clients try to detect this type of failure by using a time-out mechanism. However, when a client experiences a time-out it cannot determine whether the failure is due to a communications failure, server failure or a timing failure (e.g. the server is responding very slowly). The normal course of action is to retransmit the request and after n retries terminate the communication session. The service is resumed by restarting the server and can potentially restart at different states. Cristian defines four types of crash failure distinguished by their state at restart:

- Amnesia crash – the server restarts at its state when it was initially started. Operations carried out prior to the crash are not reflected in the restarted state. This type of crash failure restart is adequate for some services, particularly those where all service operations are idempotent or for stateless server configurations.
- Partial-amnesia crash – this occurs when the server state is recovered incompletely and some prior state changes are lost.
- Pause crash – the server restarts in the state just before the crash failure occurred. The crash is thus manifested as a pause in the service. It is important that stateful servers are designed with recovery mechanisms to ensure that amnesia crash behaviour is avoided and the state prior to the crash failure is restored.
- Halting crash – the server never restarts. The server is not in a state that permits clients and other servers to confirm that it has failed.
- Fail stop crash – the server fails by halting the service. Once halted the server remains in the halted state. The halted server state is detectable by other clients and servers. A fail stop server never exhibits value, omission or timing failures. Other servers can perform operations safely on behalf of the failed server.

Servers can exhibit a range of the failure classes defined above. The worst possible scenario is when a server exhibits all failure classes: omission, response, timing and crash failure semantics. Servers of this type are said to exhibit *arbitrary or Byzantine* failure behaviour (Lamport *et al.*, 1982). The term 'Byzantine' is derived from the Byzantine Generals problem studied by Lamport *et al.* The scenario is based on several divisions of the Byzantine army posted outside an enemy camp. Each division, headed by a general, tries to decide whether or not to attack the enemy camp. The problem is that some of the generals are traitors and will try to prevent the honest generals from reaching agreement. Communication between generals is by messenger only (conflicting or forged messages can be sent by traitors). How can agreement be reached? Lamport *et al.* showed that in the absence of an authentication procedure, 'Byzantine' agreement can be achieved if there are at least $3n + 1$ generals where n is the number of traitors. When applied to the case of servers which can exhibit Byzantine failure behaviour, at least $3n + 1$ server replicas are required to achieve Byzantine agreement despite n servers failing.

If a treacherous general cannot masquerade as an honest general (e.g. by forging signatures) then this simplifies the Byzantine Generals problem. Thus if servers implement an authentication technique to guarantee that messages and signatures are not corrupted or are erroneous, this reduces the number of server replicas required for fault tolerance despite n

replica failures. If it can be assumed that messages are not corrupted and a sender-authentication protocol is used, the majority output is sufficient to guarantee correct output and at least $2n+1$ replicas are required to tolerate n failed servers. Authentication and other security issues are examined in detail in Chapter 13.

The Byzantine Generals problem assumes that all generals can communicate with each other via messengers. Additional problems arise if communication failures occur which partition a communications network to the extent that certain nodes cannot communicate with each other (i.e. messengers cannot get through to some generals. Communication paths can be represented by a connectivity or 'topology' graph. The connectivity of a graph is defined as the minimum number of nodes whose removal causes the graph to partition. Fischer, Lynch and Merritt (1986) showed that Byzantine agreement is possible if the connectivity graph has connectivity greater than $2n+1$ where n is the number of traitors. Applied to the case of replicated servers, if removing half of the server replicas can partition the remaining replicas then Byzantine agreement will not be possible.

At the other extreme is fail-stop failure behaviour which assumes that servers crash cleanly, never perform erroneously and fail in such a manner that others can detect the failure. Building fault tolerant servers can be simplified greatly if it can be assumed that servers exhibit fail-stop failure behaviour. If a fail-stop server fails, then fault tolerance is achieved by ensuring that at least one replica is available. Client requests can be redirected by selecting one of the replicas. Thus fail-stop agreement is achieved if at least $t + 1$ server replicas are available since only one additional replica is required to maintain the service if t servers fail.

A system designed to tolerate Byzantine failure behaviour can tolerate anything – but at what cost? Such an assumption can be cost-justified only for highly mission-critical or safety-critical systems (e.g. aircraft control systems). For most systems we will probably need to assume failure semantics which fall somewhere between fail-stop and Byzantine behaviour in order to achieve the appropriate balance between robustness, cost, performance and functionality.

Masking failures

A service is normally provided by one or more servers. Each server is constructed from a number of hardware and software components. Each hardware or software component may be further divided into sub-components. For example, a file server has a number of disk components attached to it. Each disk component has one or more disk controller and hard disk sub-components. A server may fail due to a hardware or software malfunction. A server may also fail because another server on which it depends fails. We can thus construct a hierarchy of relationships of components and 'lower-level' components on which it depends. A level of fault tolerance can be achieved by ensuring that lower-level component failures can be masked from higher-level components. This is known as *hierarchical failure masking*. Exception handling is typically used to propagate information about low-level component failures to higher-level components. If the higher-level component can recover and continue to provide a service it is said to be *masking* the failure of a lower-level component. A typical masking mechanism is to replicate lower-level components and build logic to automatically switch to a replica automatically when the primary replica malfunctions and reports the fault to the higher-level component. This technique requires that all replicas are kept in the same state as the primary at all times. If a fault cannot be masked then at the very least it should be detected and reported to the next layer in the hierarchy.

Another masking technique is to replicate a server forming a *server group*. The server group co-operate in a manner which ensures that if the primary server fails, other servers in the group continue to provide the service, the failure being transparent to clients. This is known as *group failure masking*. The appropriate group failure masking technique is dependent on the failure semantics exhibited by servers in the group. For example if we assume fail-stop failure semantics, then any single replica can be used to replace the failed primary. However, if servers can exhibit value failure semantics (i.e. we cannot rely on the output of servers) then a 'majority vote' mechanism must be used which assumes that the majority response among servers is the correct one.

It is useful to measure the level of fault tolerance in terms of the level of failure a system can withstand before the system becomes fault intolerant. A system with a set of components is *t-fault tolerant* if it performs as required provided that no more than t of those components become faulty at the same time within a defined time interval. We have already observed that when servers exhibit Byzantine failure semantics, a *t-fault tolerant* service must have at least $3t + 1$ replicas (in the absence of authentication) and a connectivity greater than $2n + 1$, whereas servers that can be assumed to exhibit fail-stop semantics are t-fault tolerant if there are at least $t + 1$ replicas since only one additional replica is required to maintain the service if all t servers fail. This assumes that all replicas receive and process the same requests and in the same order as the primary server.

Hardware failure masking

A technique widely used for hardware failure masking is known as triple-modular redundancy (TMR). A hardware unit has two replicas, each receiving the same data in the same order. Output from all units is compared and the majority output is assumed to be the correct one. This approach only accounts for component faults not design faults that result in value failure semantics. Hierarchical failure masking is also widely used. For example, disk controllers employ parity checking techniques to mask certain read/write value and other failure semantics exhibited by disk drives. Bit errors during frame transmission across a communications link are masked by modems or LAN network interface cards by utilizing appropriate communication protocols and techniques.

An alternative approach is to design a system using modular components that can be replaced easily when a fault occurs. Units could be a single component type (e.g. a CPU, disk controller or disk drive) or a multi-component unit such as an arrangement consisting of a CPU, memory boards, bus and I/O controller. *Field replaceable units* require a field engineer to be called in to replace the faulty unit, whereas a *customer replaceable unit* is straightforward and therefore replacement can be carried out by suitably trained customer personnel. If units that are replaceable are duplicated, when a fault occurs the system switches to the backup. The faulty unit is then replaced, thus regaining fault tolerance. An example of this approach is the commercially successful single-fault tolerant TANDEM architecture (Cristian, 1991; and Borg *et al.*, 1989), which duplicates all components (including software). When a fault occurs, control is immediately passed to the backup. The faulty unit is replaced quickly to regain single-fault tolerance.

Software failure masking

A technique similar to TMR, known as N-version programming, can be employed by software components. In a three-version method, three different versions of the same program are developed independently by three different project teams. When the program is executed in a production environment the correctness of processing is tested and the correct output chosen either by majority output or by validating the various outputs against a defined acceptance test.

However, the main approach is to employ transaction processing and recovery mechanisms. These are discussed in detail in Section 9.3. Many software systems employ hierarchical failure masking and replicate software components. Servers are replicated to form a server group. Group failure masking techniques are employed to ensure that one or more server failures are tolerated.

Example: redundant arrays of inexpensive disks (RAID)

A file server implements a remote file service. The disk component is therefore a critical component of the server. Three common techniques for improving fault tolerance are disk mirroring, disk duplexing and server mirroring, as illustrated in Figure 7.6. Disk mirroring duplicates a disk drive, both attached to a single disk controller and using the same power supply. Disk duplexing is more reliable since the disk controller and power supply are also duplicated. Fault tolerance is further improved by employing server mirroring as illustrated in

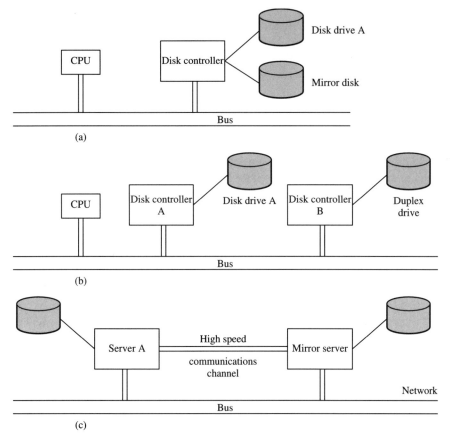

Figure 7.6 Disk mirroring (a) and duplexing (b), and server mirroring (c).

Figure 7.6. Server failure is masked by duplicating all actions on a separate mirror server. A disk sub-system called redundant arrays of inexpensive disks (RAID) is designed to exhibit fault tolerance and to improve performance by utilizing multiple hard disk drives in such a way that the sub-system appears as one large disk to the operating system (Patterson *et al.*, 1988). Data is written across the drives using a technique called striping. RAID masks the failure of a disk drive by employing a separate disk to hold parity data (in conjunction with striping) which enables data on a failed disk to be restored from existing data stored on other disk drives. Eight RAID levels are defined each giving a level of fault tolerance, performance and cost.

RAID 0 – No redundancy. Striping is used, therefore there is a performance benefit at a high price and with no fault tolerance.

RAID 1 – Disk mirroring. Data is striped to an array of drives and each drive is mirrored to a backup drive. This achieves redundancy (fault tolerance).

RAID 2 – Data is striped at the bit level across all drives with variable parity drive. Hardware components are checked. Whilst this is an improvement on RAID 1, this is not a popular option because it is functionally equivalent to RAID 3 but requires more redundancy and therefore is more costly to implement.

RAID 3 – Striping at the bit or byte level and a single parity drive. This level performs well for large read/writes but is slow for small read/writes.

RAID 4 – Striping with a larger sector size for improved small read/write performance but at the expense of massive overheads or parity checks before writes.

RAID 5 – As with level 4 but with parity data spiralled across drives for improved performance (at the expense of multitasking performance).

RAID 6 – I/O traffic for data and parity separated by having separate bus and cache for each.

RAID 7 – All drives operate asynchronously thus allowing multiple concurrent I/O for improved performance. Connectivity for up to 12 computers and up to 48 disk drives of any capacity and speed. Complete fault tolerance is achieved by full redundancy and transparent recovery on disk failure.

The file server operating system failure semantics is dependent on the RAID level implemented. In general, a component which is dependent on a sub-component which exhibits Byzantine failure semantics will also exhibit Byzantine failure semantics. The key to fault tolerance is ensuring that low-level components exhibit strong failure semantics. It is the responsibility of the systems designer to define the required failure semantics of a service. The failure semantics of a nuclear power station is likely to be much different to that of a payroll system. The system designer must make appropriate assumptions about the failure semantics of a service and decide which failure masking techniques must be employed. In practice, the fault tolerance of a service cannot be guaranteed due to the existence of components that exhibit Byzantine failure semantics. However, it is important to understand and estimate the risk involved when various failure behaviour is exhibited and, where possible, mask failures for improved fault tolerance.

7.8 GENERAL DESIGN PRINCIPLES FOR DISTRIBUTION

From the various systems and techniques examined so far, we can identify three principal techniques used to implement scalable, dependable services: replication, partitioning and caching.

7.8.1 Replication

A service is replicated when multiple identical instances (known as replicas) of the service appear on different nodes (servers) in a distributed IT infrastructure. Shared state consistency among replicas ensures that client requests to access shared resource or information are handled in a completely consistent manner. Each replica holds an instance of the shared system state. Replicas that hold the most recently written state data are said to hold **authoritative data**. Ideally, a client request can be directed to any replica and all replicas have consistency of state (i.e. hold authoritative data). When multiple servers handle client requests, this improves availability and performance (by reducing the load per replicated server). The number of servers required is determined by the level of performance and fault-tolerance required and the size of the client request workload. The placement of replicas is another important issue and depends on whether replication is primarily to improve performance or to improve availability. Placing replicas in different parts of the network improves availability when the network fails by ensuring that replicas can be found in areas where client requests are concentrated and in network partitions. For improved performance, however, one or more replicas should be placed nearest to the client workstations which contribute most server utilization in order to reduce network overhead.

Replica control mechanisms are required to ensure that replicas continue to hold authoritative data when a request is sent to one or more replicas with the effect of changing/updating state data. **Strict** or **strong consistency** techniques ensure that all replicas hold the same authoritative state data at any given time. This is achieved if: (1) all replicas receive every shared state data update request; and (2) all replicas process received requests in the same (correct) sequence.

Thus both the correct reception of update requests and the order of processing by replicas are important. Correct sequence implies the order in which they were issued by a single client. Note that it cannot be guaranteed that updates will be *received* in the correct sequence due to varying network delays. Correct processing can be achieved by assigning unique sequence identifiers to update requests. Note, however, that one update request may precede or follow another, or two update requests may be unrelated. For example, if client X sends update request A to server·S, causing update request B also to be sent by client Y to server S, then request A should be processed before request B by the replicas of server S. The two requests A and B are said to be *causally* related. If, however, the relationship between requests A and B is *commutative*, that is, processing the requests in the order request A followed by request B, has exactly the same effect as processing in the reverse order, then the order of processing is not important.

Because of the difficulties of achieving the above requirements, strict consistency techniques do not generally scale well. The number of replicas are therefore kept to a minimum (e.g. two to three replicas). Three main strict consistency techniques are examined: the active replication method, the primary-copy method and the quorum-consensus method.

The active replication method

This is a strict consistency technique where a client request can update any replica but the update must also be sent to all other replicas and updates processed in the correct order. Client requests are blocked until the update has been propagated successfully to all replicas. Client read requests can be directed to any replica since every replica has the same view of state data. The main difficulties are two-fold. Firstly, the need for synchronous update can impose a large processing and communication overhead and is not generally a scalable approach. Secondly, maintaining replica consistency is difficult when not all of the replicas are operational. If any replica is unavailable at the time an update is propagated, it will be inconsistent with all other replicas. In this case, replica consistency cannot be guaranteed. The use of additional protocols is required, for example maintaining a directory of replica state (Bernstein *et al.*, 1987), to provide a mechanism for managing replica updates by providing a recovery mechanism when non-operational replicas become operational.

The main advantage of this method is that client requests can be directed to any replica (usually the local one) which improves read performance and provides for high availability except in the case of network partition failures. When a network partition's, client requests will not be propagated to all replicas and will therefore abort.

Primary backup and primary copy methods

In both the primary backup and primary copy methods, all client update requests are directed to a primary replica. The primary replica is responsible for forwarding updates to all other replicas. Updates may be forwarded individually, or the whole data base may by downloaded to replicas. In the **primary backup** method, client read requests can be directed only to the primary replica because backup replicas cannot guarantee that state data is authoritative. In the **primary copy** method, read requests can be directed to any replica because the update protocol guarantees that the other replicas are up-to-date. The main advantage of the primary copy method is that reads and updates are handled more efficiently and recovery is faster in the event that the primary fails.

In both methods, an **election** protocol is required to designate one of the replicas as the new primary replica if the primary fails or becomes inaccessible due to network partitioning. There are two main types of election algorithms: the *ring algorithm* (Tanenbaum, 1995) and the *bully election algorithm* (Garcia-Molina, 1982). In both algorithms each replica is given a unique number. In general, if the primary fails, the replica with the highest unique number becomes the new primary. In the ring algorithm, each replica knows which replica succeeds it in priority order (i.e. the next highest unique number). When a replica notices that the primary has failed, it constructs an 'election' message inserting its unique number and sends the message to its successor. If the successor is down, it is sent to the next in line. When a successor receives an election message it simply adds its unique number to the message and passes it on. Eventually the original sender receives the message. A co-ordinator message is then sent informing everyone who the new primary replica is (i.e. the replica with the highest unique number in the election message). The bully election algorithm, as the name suggests, is much more contentious. A replica will assume the role of the new primary if two conditions are met:

1. It sent an election message to all replicas with higher unique numbers.
2. No one responded.

If a successor received the election message, it simply responds with OK (meaning 'I'm alive and well') and the replica relinquishes control to it. The successor also needs to meet the above conditions. Eventually, the replica with the highest unique number will meet the conditions. Election algorithms are used frequently in distributed systems whenever any process amongst a group of peer processes needs to assume a co-ordinating role.

7.9 CASE STUDY: SUN NETWORK INFORMATION SERVICE

An example of the implementation of a replicated service using the primary-copy method is Sun Microsystems's Network Information Service (NIS) which was developed primarily to simplify system administration of a large network of Sun UNIX workstations. Simplification is achieved by centralizing key system configuration files such as:

```
/etc/hosts       - records the mapping between host name and IP address
/etc/passwd      - records the mapping between userid and password
/etc/services    - records the mapping between TCP/IP port numbers and
                   servers
/etc/aliases     - records the mapping between system-wide mail alias names
                   and constituents.
```

The NIS master server holds the authoritative data. An NIS slave server holds a read-only replica of the master. An NIS domain is a group of workstations and servers that share common configuration and are under the same administrative authority. There is one master server (and potentially many slave servers) per domain. Each system configuration being maintained is stored as a simple indexed database called a *map* and is structured as two text fields: a key field and an associated data field. A map (say, mymap) is represented by two files: mymap.pag which holds the data, and mymap.dir which is a (hashed) index file. For example, the /etc/host file is converted into two maps: hosts.byaddr and hosts.byname. The hosts.byaddr map has a key value which is an IP address and an associated data value corresponding to the host name. Conversely, the hosts.byname map has a key value of a host name and an associated data value corresponding to the IP address. Another example of this structure is the /etc/passwd file which is converted into two maps: passwd.byname and passwd.byuid (which uses the numeric userid as the key value). To enable client processes to access these maps, *resolver* functions are provided with associated command line utilities. The command line utility ypcat is used to display the contents of a map, and ypmatch is used to interrrogate the map by performing a look-up of a map using the supplied key values. Example resolver functions are:

```
gethostbyname( )  - takes an Internet domain name as argument and returns the
                    corresponding IP address value from the hosts.byname
                    map.
gethostbyaddr( )  - takes an IP address as argument and returns the corre-
                    sponding domain name value from the hosts.byaddr map.
getpwnam( )       - takes a UID value as argument and returns a structure
                    containing (amongst other values) the corresponding user
                    name value from the passwd.byuid map.
```

NIS is designed to handle efficiently system configuration files that are frequently read but infrequently updated. When a map needs to be updated, NIS allows only the master server held maps to be updated. Updated maps are then propagated to slave servers. Resolver and command line functions that do not update maps can be directed at any server (master or slave). Updating maps is an inefficient process that involves regeneration of the entire map. An exception is the passwd map. In reality the passwd maps are often changed frequently as new users are added and removed and passwords are changed. To improve the efficiency of user initiated password changing, a special command called yppasswd co-operates with a server process yppasswdd running on the NIS master server.

7.10 REPLICATION: THE QUORUM CONSENSUS METHOD

Consensus methods avoid strict consistency and yet ensure that clients receive authoritative data by allowing a client request to proceed to completion if it obtains sufficient positive responses from a group of servers. In general the types of client requests are classified as either reads or writes. A quorum group is defined as a group of servers which allows a request (i.e. read or write) to complete successfully only if it obtains a positive response from all servers in the group. Read operations can be handled concurrently, but write operations must be mutually exclusive. Mutual exclusion of writes is ensured by imposing the restriction that write quorum groups must have a common member (i.e. intersections are non-empty).

To ensure that read requests will always receive at least one response containing authoritative data, a read quorum group must intersect with any write quorum group. Suppose that we have N replicas. If the number of replicas in a particular read and write quorum are R and W respectively, choice of replicas must be subject to the following additional constraint (Gifford, 1979):

$$R + W > N$$

The extreme case is when $W = N$ and $R = 1$. In this case an update operation using the W write quorum, simply updates all replicas. Data can be read from any replica. The other extreme is when $R = N$ and $W = 1$. In this case, a write operation is to any replica since any read operation reads data from every replica. How does the client know which replica value is the most recent? The only way of knowing this is to return an indication of the currency of the data as well as the data itself.

To illustrate this, consider a group of six server replicas. Each replica stores the bank balance in a data field called 'balance'. The current value of balance for customer X is $5000. Each replica stores the number of times the balance has been updated in a variable called 'bc'. When the balance is to be updated, a write quorum group is chosen (for example, write quorum group {B, C, E, F}) and the write request directed to all replicas in the group as shown in Figure 7.7. A subsequent read on quorum group {A, C, E} is guaranteed to result in the receipt of the new balance. The authoritative data is detected by choosing the server reply with the highest bc value. Alternatively a timestamp could have been used to detect the reply with the authoritative balance data. The main disadvantage of quorum consensus methods is the performance overhead of multiple read requests required to ensure that authoritative data is used as the reply to a client request.

7.11 REPLICATION WITH LOOSE CONSISTENCY

In many distributed systems the need for strict consistency can be relaxed since the semantics of operations on data items are such that data inconsistency can be tolerated. This is known as *loose* (or *weak*) consistency. Loose consistency techniques guarantee that non-faulty replicas will eventually be consistent but may introduce a significant delay in propagating state

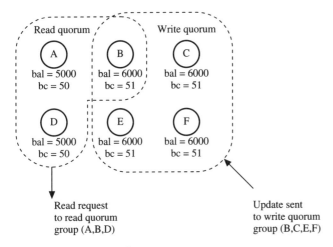

Read quorum

Write quorum

A
bal = 5000
bc = 50

B
bal = 6000
bc = 51

C
bal = 6000
bc = 51

D
bal = 5000
bc = 50

E
bal = 6000
bc = 51

F
bal = 6000
bc = 51

Read request
to read quorum
group (A,B,D)

Update sent
to write quorum
group (B,C,E,F)

Figure 7.7 Example use of quorum consensus.

changes to replicas, and consequently cannot guarantee that client requests receive the most recently written state data. If a client request is directed to a replica which has not been updated, incorrect data is returned. This may not be a problem for some applications, particularly when the receipt of incorrect state data can be detected by the client.

Loose consistency techniques support a larger replica group (thus greatly improving availability) simply because the cost of propagating updates is greatly reduced due to the use of simpler, more scalable algorithms. This may be an acceptable approach for some services (e.g. name services) especially when the client can ascertain the correctness of data returned by a service. As an illustration, when the new telephone directory book is delivered to a home it is out-of-date immediately. However, this is not normally a problem since we can always call directory enquiries and make a local amendment until the new telephone directory is delivered.

Choice of consistency technique is inevitably a trade-off between the need to maximize availability, the need to ensure that client requests are serviced using the most recently written state data and the need to minimize client response times. Loose consistency approaches are based on exploiting prior knowledge of the semantics of client operations, such as:

1. Client requests are idempotent. These requests can be directed to any replica providing replicas are 'fail-stop' thereby guaranteeing that replies are not incorrect (so long as they remain operational). Although not incorrect, a reply may not reflect the most recently written value.
2. A commutative relationship exists between requests. In this case the order of processing is relaxed since the replica responses are the same irrespective of the order of processing.
3. The correctness of replica values can be determined by the client. In this case it may be that corrective action can be taken by the client when the most recently written value is not received.

Example loose consistency replication control protocols applied to the distribution of data are examined in detail in Chapter 9. Recursive and multicasting resolution protocols are shown in Figures 7.8 and 7.9.

7.12 PARTITIONING

A service is partitioned when the resources maintained by the service are partitioned across multiple servers. Thus each server implements only a part of the total service. Partitioning can improve performance by reducing the load per server, and facilitates the creation of multiple (decentralized) administration domains. In a large-scale distributed service with a massive database, partitioning may be the only means of implementing the service because a single centralized server could not be implemented with an acceptable quality of service. Partitioning reduces the size of the database and reduces the number of client requests per server.

An administration domain is given the authority to maintain the information (i.e. keeping it up-to-date) or resources which represent that part of the service relevant to it. Information or resources are stored in servers, and servers are placed near the users that will most frequently access it for improved performance, administration and management. The main difficulty is finding a server with the requested information or resource. Each partitioned service must define a **resolution protocol** to resolve client requests by finding the appropriate server. There are three classes of resolution protocols: recursive (or chaining), multicasting and referral protocols.

In a *recursive* or *chaining* resolution protocol a user agent sends the request to the local server, as shown in Figure 7.8. If the local server cannot satisfy the request it is migrated from server to server until the authoritative server is found. The reply is migrated back to the local server taking the reverse path. The reply is delivered to the user agent by the local server. As far as the user agent is concerned, it is the local server that is responsible for completing the operation and sending a response.

In a *multicasting* resolution protocol the local server multicasts the request to selected servers, as shown in Figure 7.9. In a *parallel multicasting* protocol multicasted servers

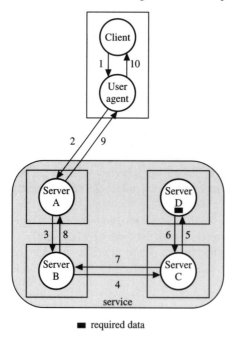

Figure 7.8 Recursive resolution protocols.

receive a request at the same time. In a *sequential multicasting* protocol the request is sent to each server in turn and a reply received before passing the request to the next server. Each server tries to service the request locally. The local server subsequently sends an appropriate reply message dependent on the replies from multicasted servers.

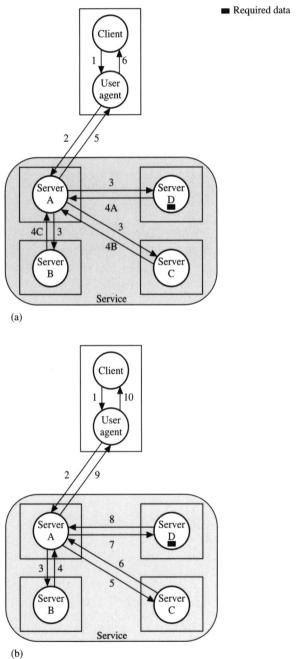

(a)

(b)

Figure 7.9 Multicasting resolution protocols (a) parallel multicasting; (b) sequential multicasting.

In an *iterative* resolution protocol the user agent is responsible for managing the resolution process. In this case, servers do not call each other directly. Instead, the user agent sends a request to each server, as illustrated in Figure 7.10. Requests are sent either one at a time (*sequential iteration*) or simultaneously (*parallel iteration*) using a multicasting facility. Each

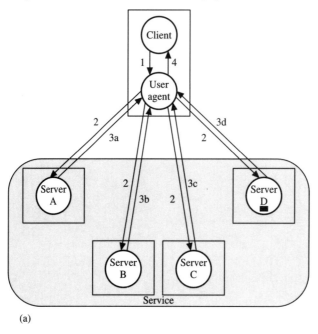

(a)

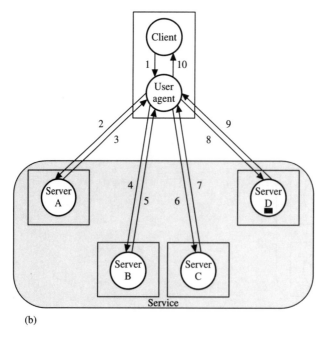

(b)

Figure 7.10 Iterative resolution protocols: (a) parallel; (b) sequential.

server tries to service the request locally. The user agent selects the appropriate server reply. In a *referral* resolution protocol, client requests are redirected to another server based on the reply from a previous server. This is illustrated in Figure 7.11. The reply from a server is either state data, a referral to another server, or an error (or 'nothing known') message. Referral processing

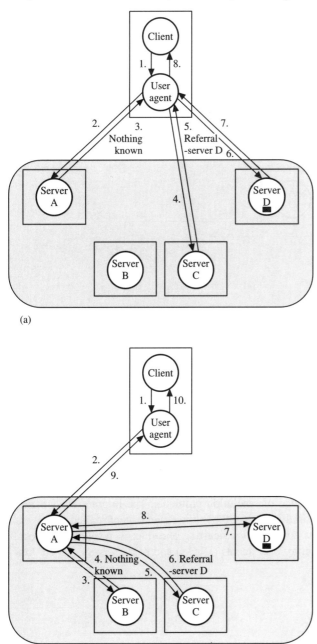

(a)

(b)

Figure 7.11 Referral resolution protocols: (a) agent based; (b) server based.

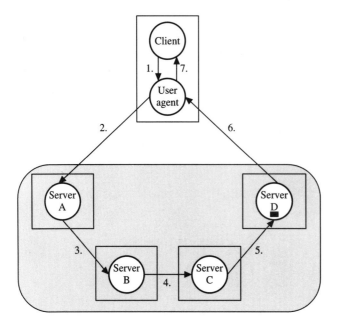

Figure 7.12 Transitive resolution protocols.

can be carried out either by the user agent (an *agent-based referral* resolution protocol) or by the local server (a *server-based referral* resolution protocol).

In a *transitive* resolution protocol a user agent passes responsibility for resolution to the local server. If the local server cannot resolve the request it passes it and responsibility for operation completion and reply generation to another server. Thus the client request and responsibility is migrated from server to server until the authoritative server completes the operation and generates the reply to the user agent. This scheme is shown in Figure 7.12.

Choice of resolution protocol should be based on the nature of the service being provided, the capability of the underlying communication protocols (e.g. the availability of a multicast facility) and the relative processing capacity of clients and servers. An iterative resolution protocol requires more processing capacity at the client since a user agent has to do a lot more work, but the reward is perhaps a more intelligent resolution protocol. Ideally, a partitioned service should offer a range of resolution protocols. The Internet DNS naming service implements a recursive resolution protocol involving client agents called 'resolvers'. The ITU-T X.500 standard defines chaining, multicasting and referral resolution protocols involving client agents called directory user agents (DUAs) and name servers (called directory system agents (DSAs)).

7.13 CACHING

Caching is an important technique for building responsive, scalable distributed systems. A cache is an area of storage for holding data temporarily. Data is written to a cache when it is first read from a remote server. Improvement in performance is gained on subsequent reads by searching for data in a local cache first rather than sending a request for data to a remote server. Caching works well when the same data is frequently read and is never updated by the client. Two important design issues must be specified by the system designer: the placement of caches and techniques for maintaining cache consistency when clients wish to update data that may be held in the local cache.

A cache can be maintained either by the client, or the server or by both. Each configuration is shown in Figure 7.13. Caching at the client is an effective way of pushing the processing workload from the server out to client devices if a client has the capacity. If results data is likely to be reused by multiple clients or if client devices do not have the capacity then caching at the local server is more effective. Caches can be maintained at multiple levels. For

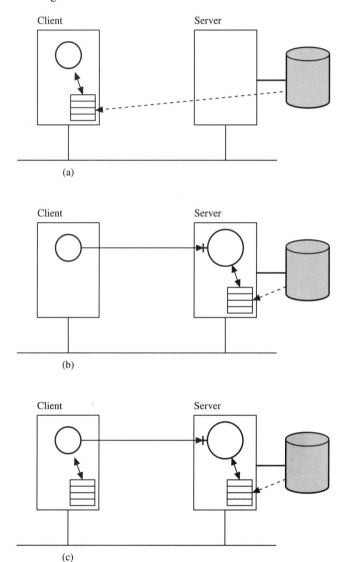

Figure 7.13 Caching: (a) client-based cache; (b) server-based cache; (c) multi-level caching.

example, caches can be maintained at all clients and all servers. Use of a cache at one level reduces the number of requests handled at the levels below.

When a client wishes to update data, data inconsistencies can occur because multiple clients may have a copy of the data in their local cache. How can a client update data and still maintain data consistency? There are four main approaches to handle possible cache inconsistency.

- Simply inform clients of the possibility of cache consistency but do nothing. Users are required to evaluate the currency of any data retrieved from the cache.
- Employ a time-out mechanism. A 'time-to-live (TTL)' value is attached to each cache entry which is an estimate of the length of time the state data is valid. When the TTL expires, the cached entry must no longer be used. For example in the Internet DNS system a TTL value is assigned to a name binding by the administrator for the zone where the data originates. A short TTL can be used to minimize caching if it is known that a name changes frequently. A zero TTL value prohibits the use of cached values. If a binding change can be anticipated, the TTL can be reduced prior to the change to minimize inconsistency during the change and then increased back to its former value following the change.
- If it is possible to detect when invalid data is being used, cached data can be allowed to be inconsistent. The client can detect invalid data at the time it is used without any special mechanisms being employed. If the cached data is found to be invalid, the client must obtain data from the server that originally provided the data. For example, it is straightforward to detect when an invalid name and address translation is being used; the named object is simply not found! Thus in a naming service the cached value is always used first and if the object cannot be found then the appropriate name server must be contacted.
- Update data in the local cache and send an update request to the authoritative server. This is known as the **write-through-cache** mechanism (Figure 7.14). Cache consistency is not guaranteed, however, as some clients may still have old data in their local cache.
- The server containing the state data maintains a record of all caching client sites. If the data is updated (e.g. through a write-through-cache mechanism), a message is sent to all client cache sites notifying of the need to refresh their copy. Alternatively, a copy of the updated data could be sent to each client. This unsolicited notification is facilitated by a **call-back mechanism** (Figure 7.15) which initiates a call-back process on each client. The call-back process then takes appropriate action.

The effectiveness of caching is dependent on the read/write profile of client requests and the size, location of the cache and the basic cache unit (e.g. record, block or whole files). The cache design parameters are the ratio of reads to writes, the amount of data typically accessed

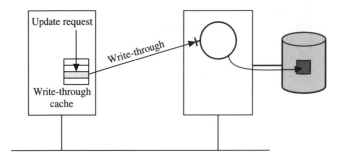

Figure 7.14 Maintaining cache consistency: write-through caching.

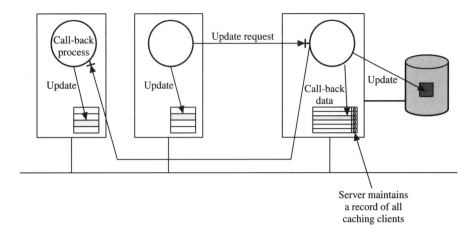

Figure 7.15 Maintaining cache consistency: using a call-back mechanism.

together, the level of concurrent access, the volatility of data and the typical unit of access (e.g. by record, record set, block or whole files typically read sequentially). These parameters should be evaluated for each application to determine whether caching is an attractive option for improving performance and scalability.

7.14 PLATFORM ARCHITECTURES

DISs place stringent demands on an distributed IT infrastructure. In Chapters 4 to 6 we detailed the network technologies which are likely to provide satisfactory solutions to the ever-increasing demand for network bandwidth available across a world-wide internet. Equal demands are placed on client and server resources.

7.14.1 Server platform architecture

Clearly a server architecture must implement efficient mechanisms for multi-tasking (or multi-threading), multi-processing and must exhibit some fault tolerant features. Multimedia information systems create the requirement to store and process large volumes of data quickly. Choice of architecture is dependent on the nature and scale of service to be provided. Servers should be based on scalable architectures with processing speeds typically ranging from 50 MIPS to tens of thousands of MIPS (using massively parallel processing (MPP) architectures). Disk storage capacities and input/output rates should be commensurate with the type of services being offered. We will continue to see dramatic increases in server capacity and scalability in terms of CPU, disk storage, memory and other resources. The range of application and information services available to clients will also continue to increase.

7.14.2 Client platform architecture

Client workstations are required to handle the execution of multiple applications, access to multiple services and the presentation of information all under the control of the user using a graphical user interface (GUI). The client platform must therefore provide all the basic facilities to support a graphical user interface (GUI), access to local resources, network access to remote resources and the concurrent execution of GUI-based applications. Emerging technologies to support multimedia increases significantly the demand for CPU, disk storage and memory resources. Clearly, the platform must support multi-tasking of application and user agent processes, preferably using multi-threading for enhanced performance. User agent processes include file service redirectors, naming agents and other application support layer functions that facilitate distribution transparency.

By the new century client workstations will typically have processing power perhaps in the range 50 to 1000 MIPS, with masses of memory and disk storage, connected to a network with dedicated bandwidth of 100 Mbps or more and supporting sophisticated DISs. Servers of various capacities offering a very wide range of services over a world-wide broadband internet will be accessible from the client workstation which may be located at a business site, home, at a customer site or in an aircraft half-way over the Atlantic ocean.

7.15 SUMMARY

There are many issues to consider when developing distributed services. Many of the distributed services are built on the general design principles discussed in this chapter. Principally, replication for improved availability and performance, partitioning for scalability and performance and caching for improved performance. As old problems are solved, however, new problems arise, such as state data inconsistencies which must be handled by complex mechanisms such as replica control methods and cache consistency techniques. Distributed systems design must ensure that whilst taking advantage of the benefits of replication, partitioning and caching, dependability is not compromised by the introduction of fragile algorithms for coping with the new problems that arise.

7.16 REVIEW EXERCISES

1. Explain the differences between network and distributed operating systems.
2. What quality-of-service factors are particularly important when implementing a distributed service?
3. Discuss the scalability of local area network technologies.
4. What measures can be taken to improve the scalability of a server?
5. What general measures can be taken to improve the performance of a distributed service?
6. Explain, with the aid of examples, the difference between reliability and availability. What measures can be taken to improve both?
7. Classify the types of failures that may occur in a distributed system.
8. What is the difference between fail-stop and Byzantine failure?
9. Suppose a service is to be implemented using replication to tolerate up to n replica failures. How many replicas are required: (i) If replicas exhibit fail-stop behaviour; (ii) If replicas exhibit Byzantine behaviour?
10. What are the three fundamental design principles used to implement scalable, responsive and dependable services?
11. Predict the nature of client and server architectures that may be prevalent in ten years time.

7.17 FURTHER READING

Coulouris *et al.* (1994) and Tanenbaum (1995) provide excellent coverage of distributed operating systems. They cover distributed operating system features, distributed services (e.g. file, name, time, co-ordination and security) and example systems (e.g. Amoeba, Chorus, Mach and Clouds). Novell Netware 4 is covered in detail in Bierer (1995). Microsoft Windows NT Server is detailed in Minassi *et al.* (1994). Fault tolerance issues are discussed in detail in Cristian (1991). Some interesting papers on aspects of fault tolerance, performance, distributed services and distributed systems design issues are found in Casavant and Singhal (1994). Mullender (1993) contains papers from researchers at the leading edge of distributed systems research.

8

GENERIC SERVICES

8.1 INTRODUCTION

In the client/server model for structuring distributed systems, a client process requests service from one or more servers. Two distinct layers of services can be identified:

1. **Generic services**: distribution services that higher-level functions can combine and use to achieve interoperability, portability, resilience and scalability. These are low-level services which are normally invisible to users and generally regarded as an integral part of a distributed IT infrastructure.
2. **Corporate application and information support services**: which are support services that combine and use generic services to provide a wide range of higher-level services to a DIS. For example, corporate customer database implemented using an underlying remote data access service. The customer database is used by many DISs to handle customer-related queries.

When a DIS is developed, it exploits **reusability** by making use of corporate application and information services and generic services to deliver services which are unique to a project.

In this chapter a range of generic services are described. Technologies for implementing application and information services are also examined. In general, users are not generally interested in how a service is implemented, but, more importantly, what services are available which are relevant to the tasks for which they are responsible. This leads to the requirement for transparent access. Access and location transparency are implemented through user agents which act on a user's behalf, and in conjunction with server wrappers and generic services to provide **middleware** functions such as name-to-address resolution, dynamic server process invocation, locating particular servers, load balancing, security, failure recovery, message routing, reliable message delivery, and so on. Middleware is the key to delivering resilient, secure and transparent services to users. Middleware is essentially a layer of software running between client and server processes. It shields the client (and application developers) from the complexity of underlying communications protocols, network operating systems functions and hardware configurations. A common set of application programming interfaces (APIs) is provided to application developers to enable rapid development of DISs and flexible access to distributed resources. Several types of middleware services have evolved:

- **Remote data access** (RDA). This middleware implements a RDA protocol for sending data manipulation language statements to an appropriate database server for processing and transporting the result set back to the invoking process. Example RDA middleware functions and standards are covered in Sections 9.4.7 to 9.4.9.
- **Remote procedure calls** (RPCs). These are the oldest and most mature type of middleware solution and are used to implement most network operating system services. RPC middleware work best for tightly coupled client/server processes. Many mature standards exist for this type of middleware.
- **Message-oriented middleware** (MOM). These are essentially indirect message passing mechanisms using store-and-forward message queuing. Client and server processes are perceived to exchange messages. This form of middleware is ideal for supporting loosely coupled client/server processes which tend to communicate asynchronously. Another positive feature is its ability to recover from a wide range of errors, due to the store-and-forward nature of communication. A MOM API is normally much simpler to use than RPC-based middleware. Some MOM-based middleware do allow synchronous, multicast and broadcast communication. One of the current problems in this area is lack of a standard API for application developers.
- **Object request brokers** (ORBs). This is relatively new technology and are closely linked to the distributed object model for structuring distributed systems. ORB-based middleware facilitate the invocation of a remote object by allowing a source object to send a message to it which is routed to the destination object. The *de facto* standard for ORB implementation is the CORBA standard. CORBA allows both synchronous and asynchronous communications and the API is well defined.
- **Distributed transaction processing** (DTP). This type of middleware implements client/server interaction with transactional (i.e. all or nothing) execution semantics. Transaction processing techniques have been the mainstay of centralized mainframe systems, and are equally appropriate for building many types of client/server systems. Transaction processing is covered in detail in Sections 9.3, 9.5 and 10.7.

A general architecture for service delivery is summarized in Figure 8.1.

8.2 DIRECTORY SERVICES

One of the major problems in a distributed systems environment is that its configuration is constantly subject to change. These changes are typically as a result of:

- systems, users, processes, objects, peripheral hardware, etc., being continually added, moved and removed;
- parts of the communication path between users being changed by introducing or reconfiguring (or removing) network components;

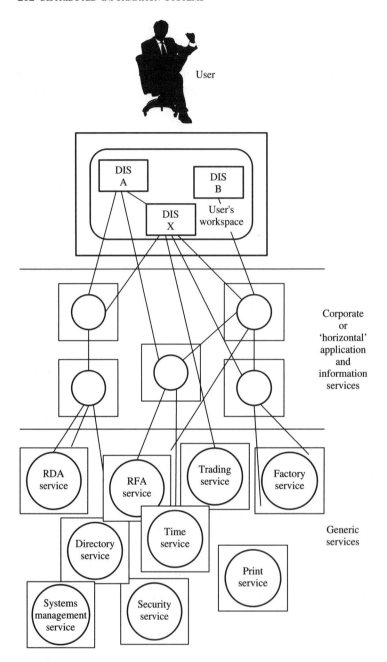

Figure 8.1 An architecture for service delivery.

- changing characteristics (e.g. addresses, attributes, and so on) of users, systems and IT infrastructure components.

These changes are often occurring with little or no warning to other systems or users of the IT infrastructure. However, although the overall rate of change may be high, the change rate of a particular component is usually relatively low compared with the number of times it is referenced by other components.

A **directory service** maintains a database of name-to-name mappings and provides a well-defined interface through which clients can request information in real time. The term *name* refers to a human-readable (and meaningful) identifier which refers to an entity, whereas an *address* tells where that entity is located. In some circumstances it is useful to give an entity a location dependent name, but in general location independent names are preferable to achieve location transparency.

A directory service is a critical generic service, binding host computer names to addresses, services to clients, and so on. Directory services differ in the range of entities about which they hold information. A **name service** specifically holds name-to-address mappings, whereas a **trading service** generally holds information to assist in matching client requests to servers which are able to service the request type. In general, a directory service seeks to:

- isolate IT components from change by placing a level of 'indirection' between reference to a component (referred to by name) which we seek to access and its *address* (e.g. an Internet IP address) which identifies the location of a component. Other name-to-name mappings (e.g. user name to electronic mail identifier) are also stored. A hierarchical naming structure is typically used to implement meaningful, globally unique object names about which information is stored;
- provide a more user-friendly view of the distributed IT infrastructure. This is achieved by the definition of meaningful names that increases the chances that names are predicted, remembered and understood by human users. The following services aid in matching names to resources;
  - a **look-up** facility which enables a user or application to supply the name of the service or resource to be accessed, together with an attribute type. The directory returns any value(s) corresponding to that attribute type. For example, interprocess communication when a process wishes to bind to another process it needs to find the address of the server and port through which the process can receive requests. A look-up facility, given the name of the process, returns the address of the server and the port number. When the directory service contains data on individuals, an electronic mail address can be supplied by doing a lookup specifying the name of the recipient.
  - a **browsing (white pages)** facility in the case when it is not possible to quote a name but the user will 'know it when he sees it'. Browsing would allow a human user or application to interrogate the directory looking for the appropriate entries (e.g. a lecturer with surname = 'Simon', employed at some university located in Wolverhampton, England, UK).
  - a **yellow pages (look-up by category)** facility which allows users or applications to find out the capabilities of a service or resource. The user specifies selection criteria using a series of {attribute type, value} associations. The directory returns a list of those entries which satisfy the selection criteria.

The directory service can vary in sophistication from a simple local 'address book' on a small-scale unsophisticated system, to a global service overseeing a large distributed IT infrastructure spanning many countries. A global directory is necessarily more sophisticated because maintaining up-to-date information on all resources can be a major management task involving millions of name-to-name mappings (constantly undergoing change), therefore a scalable architecture is required based on partitioning the name space into *domains*, each of which is maintained by a separate administrative authority.

The major issues with respect to the implementation of a directory service are the potential size of the directory store, the frequency of client requests, and fault tolerance. Three techniques are usually employed to implement a scalable, fault-tolerant directory service.

1. Partition the service over multiple directory servers. Different parts of the directory's namespace are assigned to different servers. The namespace is usually hierarchical which allows different parts of the hierarchical tree to be assigned to different autonomous organizations, each responsible for maintaining that part of the tree. Because the namespace is partitioned, each directory query and update request may be handled faster than the case of a large single flat namespace. A name resolution protocol is required to determine which server is able to handle the lookup request. For example, the Internet DNS system uses a recursive resolution protocol.
2. Replicate directory servers for improved availability and performance. When a replicated directory service is unavailable, the name resolution protocol must locate a replica. The main difficulty with replication is maintaining consistency across all replicas of directory server.
3. Cache the results of directory queries to improve performance and reduce network and directory server utilization. The process of resolving names can be complex. If a name is resolved once, it will often need to be resolved again either by the same client or by a different client wanting to access the same entity. A cache in this context is a temporary database of previously resolved names. Cache consistency problems are normally handled by observing that when the cached entry is incorrect the client agent can detect this since the object will not be found. Thus the cached entry can always be used first, and an authoritative server used if it is found that the cached entry is incorrect. The Internet DNS system uses this approach in conjunction with a recursive resolution protocol. Time-to-live values can be attached to cached entries to ensure that entries are refreshed after a period of time.

The ITU-T X.500 standard and the Internet DNS system (described in detail in Chapter 6) are examples of directory services which employ a hierarchical namespace and utilize the above techniques to implement a scalable, robust service.

8.2.1 ITU-T X.500 directory services

In the management of a world-wide electronic mail infrastructure, the ITU-T envisaged the need for a global (in scope), widely distributed but logically centralized database concerning objects in the real world. The ITU-T X.500 standard (ISO 9594) was developed. An X.500 directory consists of a set of distributed databases and associated software functions known as directory system agents (DSAs). A user (human user or application process) accesses the directory by means of another software component called a directory user agent (DUA), which may or may not co-exist with a DSA on the same IT component, more typically, it is executing on the same IT component as the application process. DUAs access the directory information on behalf of users, and may also perform local functions (e.g. storage and processing). The information contained in the directory is (collectively) known as the directory information base (DIB). The DIB is composed of entries, each containing information about a single 'object' in some 'world'.

X.500 uses the term 'object' to represent some concrete or abstract entity in the real world.

Two types of entries are defined: object entries and alias entries. One object entry (and zero or more alias entries) describes a particular object in the real world, such as a person, application service or device. Alias entries simply 'point' to an object entry. Every entry holds a set of attributes each of which describes some aspect of the object. An attribute has a type and one or more values. X.500 defines the concept of 'object class' which is a collection of objects of the same sort, e.g. people, groups, application-types, distribution lists, etc. Every entry belongs to an object class. X.500 defined a number of object classes, some of which are detailed in Table 8.1. Object-oriented concepts such as inheritance are used to define hierarchical relationships between X.500 defined object classes, as illustrated in Figure 8.2.

Entries in the DIB form a hierarchical naming structure based on the natural hierarchies among the objects. This structure is known as the directory information tree (DIT) an example of which is shown in Figure 8.3. The DIB entries (corresponding to nodes in the DIT) are distributed among the DSAs in the directory to form a distributed database which is logically viewed as a single global database via the DIT (each DSA holds a fragment of the DIB). There is a master copy of each entry which resides in exactly one DSA. Entries may be replicated for improved availability and performance.

X.500 currently defines three types of access from a DUA to a DSA:

Table 8.1 X.500 object classes and example attributes

Object classes	Example attribute types	
	Attribute category	Attribute type
TOP (or Root)	Explanatory	Description
County		Search guide
Locality		Business category
Organization	Geographical	Country name
Organization unit		locality
Person		State of province
Organizational person		Street address
Organizational role	Labelling	Common name
Group of names		Surname
Alias		Serial number
Residential person	Organizational	Organization
Application process		Organization unit
Application entity	Postal	Physical delivery office
DSA		Postal address
Device		Postal code
Strong authentication user		Post office box
Certification authority	Relational	Owner
		Member
		Role occupant
	Security	User password
		User certificate
	System	Object class
		Aliased object name
	Telecommunications	Telephone number
		Telex number
		Fax telephone number
		X.121 address
		International ISDN
		Number

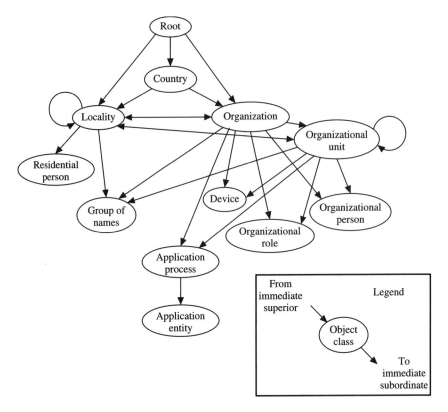

Figure 8.2 Relationships between X.500 object classes.

1. **Read** ports, for reading information from a named DIB entry.
2. **Search** ports, for searching the DIB.
3. **Modify** ports, for modifying, adding and removing DIB entries.

The name resolution protocols associated with the above operations are collectively known as the directory access protocol (DAP). When a DSA receives a request to perform an operation, it may take one of three actions:

1. perform the operation itself;
2. engage the assistance of other DSAs in order to perform the operation. A special name resolution protocol called the directory system protocol (DSP) defines the co-operative DSA–DSA interactions;
3. refer the requesting DUA to one or more other DSAs that it is not readily able to access but have the ability to perform the operation

The relationship between DUAs and DSAs is illustrated in Figure 8.4. In this illustration, each regional directory holds information on the region's users, organizational units and resources. Each region is responsible for keeping the DIB up-to-date. The backbone directory holds company-wide information on major users and organizations outside of the regional structure (e.g. centralized support services). Not all enquiries are routed through the backbone directory. Each regional directory contains enough information about the other peer local directories to enable it to route most enquiries directly to the relevant local directory.

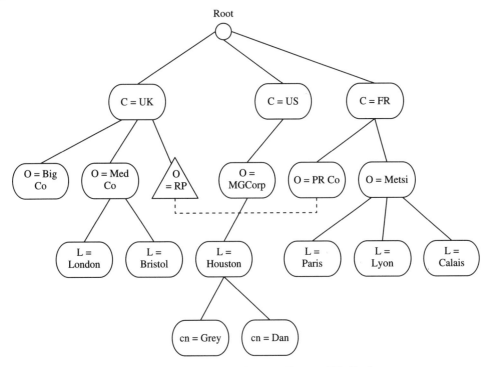

Example distinguished name: { C= US, O = MGCorp, L = Houston, CN = Dan}

Figure 8.3 An example directory information tree (DIT).

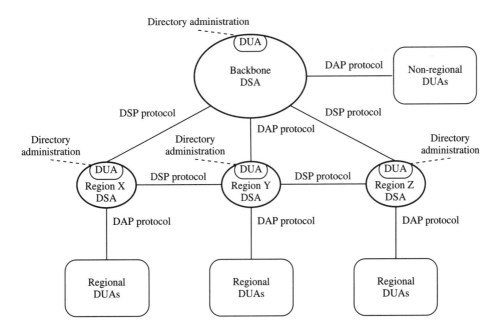

Figure 8.4 An example of the DUA–DSA relationship for supporting a global directory service.

An example of the use of X.500 concepts to implement a global directory service is Novell Netware's Netware Directory Service (NDS) which is described at the end of the chapter.

8.2.2 Trading services

An essential generic service in a distributed systems environment is one which helps clients to dynamically locate a server which offers a particular service and supply a reference which enables a client to bind to the server. Services may be replicated or partitioned (i.e. offering only a portion of the overall service) and may be active or inactive. Clients must therefore be able to determine which services are active at the time it wishes to connect one. An enhanced directory service can support the registering of available application services (known as **offering** a service) and allow a client process to find an available service dynamically which satisfy a specified service requirement. The process of determining appropriate server objects which match a particular client's service requirements is known as **trading** (ANSA, 1992) which is a form of 'yellow pages' directory service. A trading service consists of one or more trading servers or **traders**. A trading service promotes access and location transparency by permitting a client to dynamically bind to a server without reference to its location and in much the same way as invoking a local object. While the basic information a client supplies to a trader is the service type (the type of the server object), additional information (properties) may be specified which may affect the choice of a particular server where two or more servers of the same service type are available. Properties should be used so that the trader is directed to a small number of candidate servers from which one is selected or all server references are returned to the client for selection.

It is common for several traders to exist, each supporting different user communities. To promote co-operation between different traders, additional information known as the *context* is used to define federated trading (ANSA, 1992). A service offer is registered into a particular context which is part of a hierarchically structured *context space* as illustrated in Figure 8.5. Federation allows queries on one trader to translate to queries on another trader's context space. Thus an object registering an offer to the trader must therefore supply the following request data:

1. the service type;
2. the context name in which the offer is to be placed.
3. the names and values of properties to be associated with this offer;
4. the object reference for the instance.

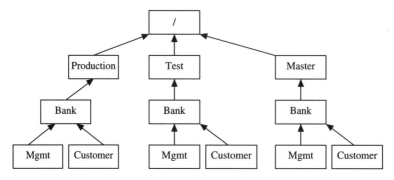

Figure 8.5 An example context space.

When a client wishes to bind to a server, it must provide the following information:

1. the service type;
2. the context name in which the search is to be initiated;
3. An expression in terms of property names and values which further constrains the search.

The trader tries to find offers matching the service type and property values in the context sub-tree rooted at the specified context name. The trading process is illustrated in Figure 8.6, identifying the following steps:

1. The server **exports** its offer to the trader.
2. The client **imports** its request to the trader.
3. The trader matches the client request to service offers and returns the object reference of a matching server.
4. The client can now use the object reference to invoke operations on the server.

The trader may make a nested call to another trader to find a server offer matching the client's request. This can be facilitated by effectively grafting a portion of one trader's context space on to another's by embedding a reference to it. When a context sub-tree is searched in the trader with the embedded reference, it causes another trader's sub-tree to be searched automatically.

In the trading mechanism described previously, the trader is passive. An extension of the trading concept is the ability of traders to proactively monitor the network, seeking out (perhaps using a user-defined rule-base) services which may be of interest to its community of users (Herbert, 1995).

8.2.3 Factory services

In a distributed system, client and server objects are being continually instantiated, migrated, copied and destroyed. When a client makes a request (say, to a trading service) for a service that is not running, the client request will normally fail. To avoid client failures in this environment, services must be active at all times. It is desirable, however, to relax the requirement that

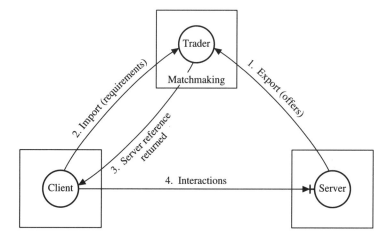

Figure 8.6 Finding a server using a trading service.

a service must be active, and implement a mechanism for dynamic object instantiation. Ideally, a client object can instantiate, migrate, copy or destroy a remote object whilst maintaining consistency of state in respect of its relationship other instantiated objects. A **factory** service (ANSA, 1993) defines operations to allow objects to be dynamically instantiated, migrated, copied or destroyed. A factory server is a location at which objects are 'manufactured'. The resources necessary to carry out these operations are assem-bled by the factory using the set of resources available to it. The factory service is provided by factory servers. Each server provides a factory service in respect of the resources (CPU, processor, disk, etc.) it controls.

If an object wishes to create another object at a specified remote location, it must locate the factory controlling resources at that location. Clients therefore require a trading service for locating factories according to some defined search criteria. In addition, another service must maintain service offers on behalf of deactivated services and ask a factory service to activate a new service in response to a client request for service (forwarded by the trading service). The service responsible for handling service requests (sometimes known as *proxy offers*) on behalf of deactivated services is known as a **node manager** (ANSA, 1992). The term *node* is used to refer to a single client workstation or server but may also include other environments where services are activated. The whole process is summarized in Figure 8.7, identifying the following steps:

1. the node manager exports (registers) a proxy offer with the trader;
2. the client performs an import specifying service requirements;
3. the trader recognizes that the offer is federated (indirect), and forwards the import to the node manager;
4. the node manager asks the Factory to create a new server instantiation;
5. the factory instantiates a new server object;
6. the node manager returns the object reference to the trader;
7. the trader returns the object reference to the original client;
8. the client can now use the object reference to invoke operations on the server.

Factory and node manager type services are a feature of a number of distributed object technologies, for example, the ANSA dynamic object instantiation mechanism described

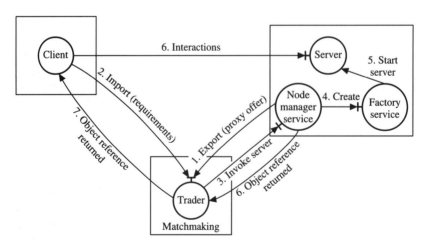

Figure 8.7 Dynamic server invocation using node manager and factory services.

above (ANSA, 1992) and CORBA (OMG, 1992). CORBA defines a *dynamic invocation interface* that allows dynamic construction of object invocations without the need for a client stub which is specific to each operation invocation. Through a special call, a client program may specify the object to be invoked, the operation to be performed and the operation parameters. This, however, is a programming language dependent, complex mechanism which is likely to be more error-prone than stub-based (static) invocations. It is therefore used primarily as an interface for implementing browser-type functionality rather. For example, a client program using a dynamic invocation interface does not have the benefit of compile time error checking.

8.3 TIME SERVICES

In a centralized system it is straightforward to collect all information and store it in a single repository and run an algorithm which makes a decision based on the data accumulated. Moreover, if synchronization between processes is required, a common clock is available to timestamp events uniquely, or shared memory can be used in conjunction with mutual exclusion techniques such as semaphores. In a distributed system, a centralized approach is normally unacceptable if a single point of failure is to be avoided, therefore relevant data is distributed, requiring distributed algorithms and distributed co-ordination. For distributed services where the order of events must be determined, some mechanism for event ordering must be implemented. An example of a distributed service which relies on a timestamp is a security service where it is used to help detect replaying of messages by an intruder. To detect replay, all clocks must be synchronized since the server checks if the time the message was received differs from that stored in encrypted form inserted in a field of the message by the originator. If not, the message has been replayed. We will examine two event ordering mechanisms: timestamping using globally synchronized **physical clocks**, and the use of **logical clocks**.

8.3.1 Physical clock synchronization

The purpose of a time service is to synchronize the clock of a local computer with the clocks of other computers on a network and to ensure that all clocks agree with some real-world clock. One approach to implementing a time service is to designate a number of servers as 'reference servers' which are assumed to provide an accurate, stable time source to clients and other servers in the network. Each reference server uses time synchronization algorithms without adjusting its own clock, because it is assumed it has a more reliable clock. All clients and non-reference servers adjust their clocks to agree with the time reported by a reference server. Reference servers must, however, synchronize amongst themselves by reaching a consensus about the time they provide.

There are a number of problems to be overcome by global time synchronization services.

- Although the local clocks are usually reasonably stable, clocks drift which can, for example, cause drifts of say one part in one million, can lead to differences in local clock times of tens of milliseconds amongst computers in a network. This can lead to serious problems if a distributed system relies on the use of globally accurate timestamps for event ordering. Lamport (1978) suggests that *absolute* clock synchronization based on real time is not required for event ordering in distributed systems. Instead, it is agreement on the ordering of events that is important. If, for example, the granularity of event generation is so that the time between events is never less than 30 ms, it is acceptable for clocks to be synchronized to within 5 ms (an arbitrary limit well within the inter-event delay). Furthermore, if processes on two computers never interact, they do not need to be synchronized!

- Network delays are normally unbounded. When a message is sent from one computer to another, the transmission delay is normally unbounded. When a server sends a message to a reference server the reference server returns a reference to time. The time reference is made inaccurate by the variable time it takes to send the time reference over the network. Therefore the accuracy of time synchronization is limited by unbounded network delays. In practice, reference servers must estimate the likely delay caused by network communication in order to attain reasonable accuracy.
- Client and server processing delays are unpredictable. The time taken to process a message received is unpredictable. For example, a reference server may service multiple clients, which introduces unpredictable delays due to interrupt handling and other events that take priority.

Many algorithms have been proposed for physical clock synchronization (see Ramanathan *et al.*, (1990) for a useful survey). Cristian (1989) proposed an algorithm which uses a time server which is synchronized to co-ordinated universal time (UTC) – the time system on which most modern time-keeping is based. A client wishing to synchronize on the UTC-based time server first measures the round-trip network delay of a message sent and received from the server. Suppose the send time is s and receive time, r. If the time returned by the time server is t, then the time to which the client's clock should be set is estimated at $t + (s + r)/2$. To improve accuracy, the Cristian algorithm makes several measurements of round-trip delay and ignores values above a defined threshold due perhaps to network congestion. The average or minimum delay can be chosen as the representative value. Note that any computer could potentially act as a passive time server. Since many critical services, such as security services, rely on it, a system must be careful to implement appropriate authentication to ensure that an intruder cannot set up a computer to masquerade as a time server.

An alternative approach, known as the Berkeley algorithm (Gusella and Zatti, 1989) is based on a computer elected as a master time server that actively polls other computers. The master time server first sends a message to all clients asking for the current time. Based on the responses and observing the round-trip times, it computes the average time and sends a message back telling each machine to set its clock to the new time or slow the clock down until the specified reduction has been achieved. Client responses with spurious values or with a clock value outside of a threshold are ignored when computing the average time. If for some reason, the master time server fails, an election protocol is used to choose a new master. Internet-based computers can use the network time protocol (Mills, 1991) to synchronize clocks to UTC. Because of the widely varying network delay which is a feature of the Internet, NTP uses a statistical approach to estimating the adjustments required. Also, because of the vulnerability of Internet computers to malicious attacks, an authentication protocol is included. NTP defines a hierarchy of *primary* and *secondary* time servers, with root-level servers being the most accurate time sources. Primary servers frequently synchronize with each other. Secondary servers synchronize frequently with a peer secondary and a few primary servers. NTP achieves clock synchronization to within 30 ms most of the time. Bounded clock synchronization cannot be guaranteed, however, because messages can be lost due to use of the 'best-efforts' UDP transport service.

8.3.2 Event ordering using logical clocks

Event ordering can be achieved without the use of real-time clocks. In some services, a real-world time value must be the basis for timestamping and event ordering (e.g. authentication in security services, or to establish expiration dates). If real-world time values are not required, a simple clock mechanism can be devised for event ordering purposes (Lamport, 1978). Lamport devised a synchronization mechanism based on the **happened-before** relation which is summarized as:

- When two events a and b occur in the same process, and a occurs before b then event a happened-before event b.
- When a message is sent from one process to another, the 'message sent' event happenedbefore the 'message received' event.
- When all processes agree that event a happened before event b then we express this using the 'happened-before' relation written as $a \rightarrow b$. This relation is also known as *causal* ordering.

Ordering of events at a process can be achieved by defining a *logical clock* mechanism Each process maintains a local variable *LC* called its *logical clock* that maps each event occurrence to a unique positive value. Thus if event e_i occurs then it is assigned the current logical clock value which is denoted $LC(e_i)$. This value can be considered the timestamp on event e_i. If this event causes a message to be sent to another process then it is used to timestamp the message. Before the initial event, all processes must initialize their logical clocks to zero. When an internal event (or a 'send message' event) e_i occurs, the process increments the logical clock and, if a message is to be sent, timestamps the message. When a 'message received' event e_q occurs, the logical clock is updated to be one greater than the maximum of the current logical clock value and the timestamp of the incoming message. The effect of this is to synchronize the local logical clock of a process with the remote process that sent the message. The effect on logical clock values of three processes communicating by sending messages to each other is illustrated in Figure 8.8. Notice that for each process, the logical clock values are always increasing according to the 'happened-before' (causal) precedence relationship between events (i.e. message sends and corresponding message receipt). This algorithm can easily be extended to provide total ordering of events in a distributed system by

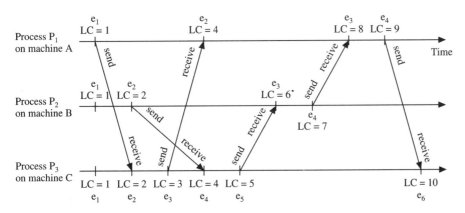

Figure 8.8 An example of the use of logical clocks.

appending to each logical clock the identifier of the process at which the event occurred. This converts the logical clock into a globally unique timestamp.

8.4 NOTIFICATION SERVICES

In Chapter 3 we outlined several techniques that may be employed to synchronize processes in the case where co-operating processes are confined to the same computer. The use of shared memory techniques such as semaphores, eventcounts and sequencers may be used to synchronize processes within a single client or server. Distributed services often require the synchronization of local processes with remote. Message passing and RPC mechanisms provide a simple synchronization mechanism by blocking a process until the response from a request is received (see Section 3.6.3). Non-blocking versions of message passing and RPC are also available. However, a more complex mechanism is required in some circumstances. For example, an application-sharing DIS consists of multiple processes each running on a participating member's workstation. Each editor process needs to be notified when particular events occur, for example when a participant signals that he wishes to take control of the application to illustrate a problem. An efficient mechanism to deliver this functionality is an event-driven notification service. In this approach, each participant process would register interest in being notified if particular events occur. The service is informed when registered events occur and informs all processes which have registered an interest in the event. Another scenario is the implementation of a mutual exclusion mechanism amongst remote processes to prevent more than one process executing a critical section of program code. There are three main solutions to the mutual exclusion problem in distributed systems, illustrated in Figure 8.9.

1. Provide a (centralized) co-ordination service. Before entering a critical section, a process must send a `Wait(critical_section)` message to the co-ordination server which ensures that no other process is currently in the `critical_section`, using a semaphore-like mechanism. If another process has entered, the process is suspended. On exit from the critical section, the process sends a `Signal(critical_section)` message to the co-ordination server. Like most centralized algorithms, this is the most efficient method, but the main problem is recovery when a co-ordination server fails.

2. A token-passing algorithm. Processes with the same critical section are ordered into a logical ring. No process can enter the critical section of code unless it receives a special message called a 'token' that all processes regard as signalling permission to enter. On exit from the critical section, the process sends the token message to the next process in the logical ring. The main problem arises when the token is lost in transit. Like all tokenpassing algorithms, the solution is to regenerate the token. The problem in this case is that a process can hold the token for an indeterminable amount of time, making it difficult to decide whether a token is lost or is being held legitimately by another process.

3. A distributed algorithm using message broadcasts or multicasts. Decision-making is distributed by asking each process to send an 'I want to enter the critical section' message to all other processes before entering. Timestamping or distributed semaphore (Andrews, 1991) mechanisms can be used to enable a process to decide how to respond to the message in order to ensure that the rules for entering the critical section are maintained. The main disadvantage of this approach is that broadcast and some multicast mechanisms do

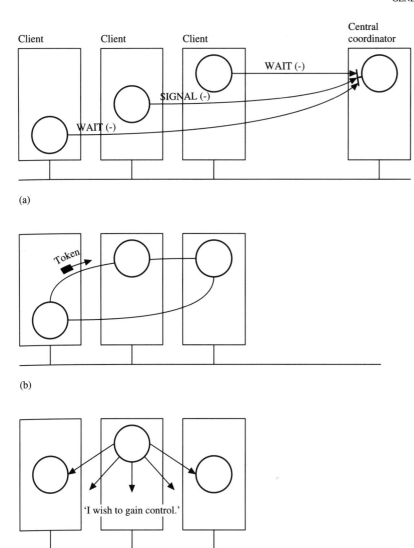

Figure 8.9 Co-ordination: (a) centralized; (b) token-passing; (c) distributed co-ordination algorithm using message broadcasts.

not scale well. Also, distributed mutual exclusion algorithms tend to be very complex, less robust and very expensive to implement.

None of the above approaches are particularly suitable in an environment where system crashes or network problems are relatively frequent. In a reliable system, a centralized co-ordinator appears to offer the best compromise. In general, a **notification service** provides generic support for events to enable synchronization or decoupling of communication between distributed objects, for example:

- **Register(event)**; an object registers interest in a particular event described by the event object `event`.
- **Notify(event)**; the notification server notifies an object that the specified event has been signalled. It should be possible to specify a call-back procedure that is called by the server when it notifies the client.
- **Signal(event)**; an object signals that an event has occurred.
- **Register(event, source)**; an object registers interest in a particular event described by the event object `event`, signalled by the specified source object.
- **Pull(event)**; an object requests event data from all supplier objects. This supports the asynchronous communication of event data between supplier and consumer objects, controlled by consumer objects.

The Opera project (Bacon and Moody, 1995), defines an approach to specifying event objects, and composite events in an event management system.

A notification service provides the basic mechanism for implementing distributed, event-driven information systems. For example, an electronic mail system can be enhanced so that it notifies the user immediately when an urgent message is received. Support for group working can benefit from a notification service. For example, a synchronous computer conferencing system with a whiteboard facility can utilize the notification service to inform a manager object when a user joins a conference, when a user attempts to add to the whiteboard, and so on. This is illustrated in Figure 8.10. A notification could be catering for a large number of events. Scalability is accommodated by defining domain-specific or application-specific notification servers.

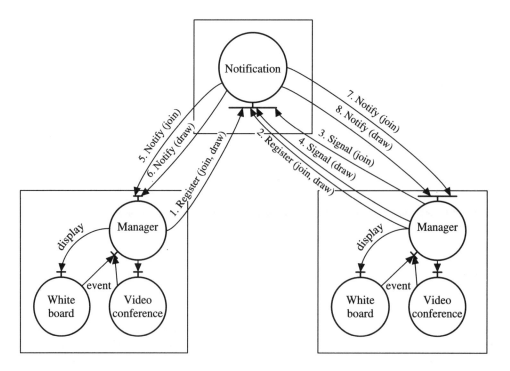

Figure 8.10 Example use of a notification service.

8.5 REMOTE FILE ACCESS SERVICES

Files are a fundamental resource in distributed systems. Although in most systems users are able to create and maintain files on the client computer using native operating system functions, it is desirable to also provide a distributed file service to facilitate file sharing and for improved availability, reliability, data administration and control. A remote file server (RFS) implements a shared file service to remote clients and is one of the most frequently used services in a distributed system. A RFS accepts client requests such as create, read, write, modify or delete files and returns the results back to the client.

8.5.1 Internet FTP

A simple example of a remote file access service is the Internet file transfer protocol (FTP). FTP is primarily a file *transfer* service rather than a file *access* service but nevertheless illustrates some of the basic RFS principles. The main issues that need to be addressed when implementing a RFS are user authorization, and file naming across heterogeneous operating systems and file systems. FTP offers authentication control and supports heterogeneous file systems.

The components of an FTP-based RFS are illustrated in Figure 8.11. FTP uses a set of commands and responses to control the file transfer process. While FTP commands are sent

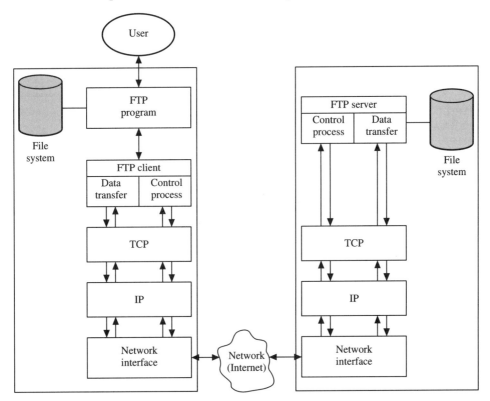

Figure 8.11 FTP-based remote file access.

over one TCP connection (port 21), actual data is transferred over a separate connection (port 20). In a typical FTP transaction:

1. The user invokes the FTP program and requests the transfer of a file from a remote server. For example:

   ```
   ftp domain_name
   ```

   The remote computer is identified by its Internet domain name.
2. The FTP program sends a request to its FTP client, which establishes a TCP connection to port 21 on the remote server, the FTP server process. The FTP client and server negotiate the parameters of the transfer, then the server establishes a TCP connection to port 20 on the FTP client's computer, which will be used for the subsequent file transfer.
3. The FTP client sends a USER command which identifies the user requesting the file transfer. The FTP server responds with a 331 User OK message.
4. The FTP server then sends a PASS command containing the user's password. If the password is correct, the FTP server sends 230 User Logged In as a response and the user is authenticated. Access control is governed by the access control restrictions defined for that user by the remote operating system.
5. The user is now free to use a range of commands for moving around the directory structure of the remote file system, initiating a file transfer, such as:

   ```
   type  - specify the type of data stored in the file (e.g. ASCII or Binary)
   cd    - change directory
   get   - transfer a file from the remote computer to the local computer
   put   - transfer the named files from the local computer to the remote
           computer
   ```

   These cause specific FTP commands to be invoked, such as:

   ```
   TYPE  - specifies the data type (ASCII, EBCDIC or BINARY)
   MODE  - specifies the transmission mode (Stream, block or compressed
           transmissions)
   STRU  - specifies the file type (file or record)
   STOR  - specifies the name of the file to be transferred from the client to
           the server
   ```

While the authentication protocol in FTP makes it secure, it prohibits people from accessing a file until they obtain a user identifier and password for the computer on which the file resides. **Anonymous FTP** access removes the need to apply for a user account, instead the user identifier anonymous can be used on most remote computers but restricts access to publicly available file archives only.

8.5.2 Sun NFS

An important characteristic of an RFS is that it should implement a degree of distribution transparency. For example, a user accessing a file on the file server uses exactly the same commands and parameters as the case when the file is on a client's local disk. An example RFS implementation which implements a level of distribution transparency is the network file system (NFS) originally designed and implemented by Sun Microsystems (Sandberg *et al.*, 1985), and in widespread use particularly on UNIX-based systems. NFS provides support for

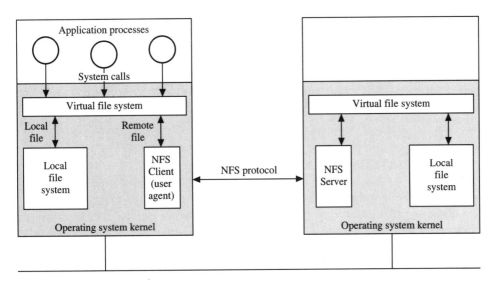

Figure 8.12 NFS remote file access architecture.

transparent access to files located in remote file systems. NFS client software is available for most client native operating systems. The Sun NFS architecture is based on the client/server model and is illustrated in Figure 8.12. The system layer handles client commands such as `open`, `read`, `write`, and `close`. The system call layer passes each valid request to the virtual file system (VFS) layer which maintains a table with an entry for every open file. Each entry indicates whether a file is local or remote and stores sufficient information for the file to be located and accessed. The remote procedure call is used to enable communication between client and file server.

Before a remote file system is accessible by client programs it is first *exported* by the file server and *mounted* by clients. Mounting file systems is a normal UNIX procedure since in a UNIX environment, both local and remote devices are mounted. The network administrator issues a mount command specifying that it is a NFS mount of a remote file system. The mount command also specifies the mount point in the local name space (this is completely determined by the client). The mount program then contacts the named machine and obtains a file handle for the named directory. References to this file handle are stored in both the internal tables of NFS and in the UNIX kernel.

Local transparency is achieved by grafting the remote file system on to the local name space at mount time. Once the mount is complete, the UNIX system acts as if the remote file system was a locally mounted partition. Access transparency is achieved by emulating the syntax and semantics of local UNIX file system commands, and ensuring that the NFS client software is integrated with the UNIX kernel rather than as an adjunct set of library functions.

The Andrew project at Carnegie Mellon University developed the Andrew File System (AFS) which is intended for large-scale networks of personal computers (Howard *et al.*, 1988). AFS clients use their disks for *whole file* or *file block* caching of recently referenced files which minimizes client load on servers and networks. The basic unit of replication is a *volume*. A volume supports a sub-tree of the overall naming tree and is normally dedicated to a particular user. A *volume location database* manager dynamically maps volumes to AFS servers to balance server and disk space utilization. AFS supports the replication of read-only volumes to provide higher availability for system executables and other low-volatile files.

The CODA system (Satyanarayanan, 1990, 1993; Satyanarayanan *et al.*, 1990) is a descendent of the Andrew File System designed to support replication and disconnected operation. Disconnected operation allows a client (e.g. a mobile user) with cached files to continue to work with files while disconnected from the server. This improves availability particularly when network partitions occur when network links are down.

8.6 REMOTE DATABASE ACCESS SERVICES

A data manipulation language such as SQL is used to allow a process to query a local or centralized database. In a client/server environment, the database system (i.e. the database management system (DBMS) and database tables) can reside on multiple servers. A remote database access (RDA) service provides transparent access to a remote database by transparently transporting a client-generated SQL query to a specified server and returning the results (a record set). The current SQL standard does not address the issue of transporting SQL statements between client and server processes. An additional protocol is required to address issues such as initiating a connection to a database server, returning status codes and a result set. At the client, an RDA user agent implements transparency by giving a local process the illusion that the database to which an SQL query is directed is local to the process as illustrated in Figure 8.13. The issue of distributed databases, implementing distribution transparency and protocol extensions to SQL are discussed in detail in Chapter 9.

8.7 PRINT SERVICES

Printer devices can vary in quality and cost from slow dot-matrix through high-speed, colour laser printers. In a typical office environment there is a need to share some printers amongst user workstations. This functionality is provided by a print utility service. A print server process receives printing requests from client workstations and executes the request by

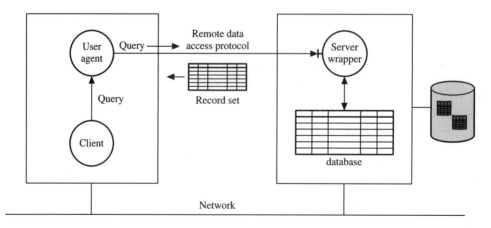

Figure 8.13 Remote data access service.

printing to an attached printer (and possibly a printer attached to another computer). The general architecture of a printer server mechanism was shown in Figure 7.3 in Chapter 7.

The printer server accepts print requests from users and uses a well-known technique called spooling to redirect the print output to a disk file and the print request is recorded in a print queue. The printer server then prints spooled prints according to the position of print requests in the queue (usually operated on a first-in, first-out basis). Thus, the printer server can handle multiple, simultaneous printing to a single printer.

Access transparency is achieved by allowing users to print directly to a printer port. A print program automatically captures all the output directed to a printer port and spools it the appropriate print queue associated with a printer server. Any user application will think it is printing directly to a local printer.

This is one case where location transparency may not be desirable since a user may wish to know the location of the printer to which his print will be directed! Normally a special procedure is used to map a local printer port to a printer server's print queue. It is also useful for users to be able to manage print jobs and queues

8.8 COMPUTE SERVICES

In compute-intensive applications the client hardware platform may not have the capacity to execute an application or particular parts of an application. A processor pool utility service offers CPU capacity for use by client processes and other utility services. To utilize a process pool server, a client application must locate a server with sufficient spare capacity to run the application process. Processor allocation in a pool is typically based on a least-loaded processor algorithm that meets the minimum capacity requirement. When one is found the application process is scheduled for execution on that server. For example, an application may consist of five key tasks which can be executed in parallel. The application may schedule each to run on five different process servers thus improving dramatically overall response time.

As processor speeds offered on client and server platforms continue to improve dramatically, the need for compute services diminishes except for relatively rare application requirements.

8.9 SECURITY SERVICES

The need to employ more sophisticated security technology is paramount because many organizations have become highly dependent on networked information systems. Security mechanisms protect an information system from unauthorized usage or from unauthorized access. Because messages on a network are open to forgery, replay and other breaches, the network must be regarded as completely insecure. Equally, client and server processes can also be subject to tampering and malicious attacks. Thus, an information system with little or no security is open to a number of threats which may compromise confidentiality, integrity, accountability and availability. Some threats are immediately obvious, but most malicious threats are difficult to detect until the damage caused by them are visible. Security mechanisms include authentication of communicating entities to verify their identity, authorization which determines the rights of entities when an object is being accessed, and guarantees of integrity and privacy, particularly when messages are being sent across a network.

Cryptography is the fundamental technique underlying most security technology. Security issues are explored in detail in Chapter 13.

8.10 MANAGEMENT SERVICES

The complexity of distributed IT infrastructures is in danger of becoming the main barrier to progress and to the effective utilization of information technology. Whereas, in a centralized system consists of effective end-to-end centralized management involving a manageable number of components, a distributed system requires distributed systems management involving many more components (likely to be procured from multiple vendors). End-to-end systems management requires interoperability between individually managed components. Distribution transparency hides this complexity from users, but it is the systems management team that has to cope with the complexity of organizing, monitoring and controlling the environment. Distributed systems management mechanisms and standards are discussed in Chapter 11.

8.11 APPLICATION SERVICES

A DIS can be made available to multiple users using a variety of approaches, namely:

1. A copy of the system resides on each client workstation local file system from where it is loaded and executed. This may be costly if the number of users is large and incurs a large administrative overhead.
2. A single copy of the system resides on a file server. Whenever a client computer wishes to use the system, a copy of the system's files is transferred from the file server, loaded into the client computer's main memory and executed. This reduces systems administration overhead but performance may be compromised.
3. A single copy of the system resides on a server (known as an application server), and when a user wishes to use a system it sends a request for execution to the server. The system receives the request, executes the associated operation and sends a reply back to the client. The client processes the reply. Note that the operation executes on the application server. The balance of processing between client and server processes is determined by the system designer. A common split between client and server processing is where the presentation component resides on the client and all other processing on the server.
4. A single copy of the system resides on a computer. To access the system the user must perform a remote login to the computer and invoke the system. The system runs wholly on the remote computer, no processing occurs on the client (apart from handling terminal emulation processing). This is typical of centralized mainframe and other remote multi-user computer configurations. This provides the best configuration for systems management of systems with simple (character-based) user interfaces, but is impractical for a DIS which involves a sophisticated graphical user interface. Dedicated clientside processing is required to support a DIS.

Applications personal to a user or which do not lend themselves to distributed system service configuration can reside wholly on the client as in option 1, or shared via a distributed file service as in option 2. The most suitable DIS and IPC configuration depends on a number of factors such as the following.

- Hardware and software facilities available at each client and server. When a DIS involves a large number of existing client workstations, the specification of each workstation may limit the amount of client processing in the case when it is cost-prohibitive to upgrade all relevant client workstations.
- The level of co-ordination of processing required. If tight co-ordination between DIS components is required then a reliable message passing, RPC or process group mechanism must be used. Otherwise, loose co-ordination can be implemented, for example, using a message queuing mechanism.
- The level of concurrent access to the server portion of the system. Typically if a large number of clients access the system server simultaneously, then scalability is enhanced if the amount of server processing per client request is minimized and if the service can be partitioned and replicated to reduce the workload per server.

A system designer may be required to develop the client, server or both ends of the system. Development productivity is increased significantly when in developing a DIS, existing corporate application and generic services are reused. The system development effort is focused on how existing functionality can be packaged together to deliver a custom application to the user, client-end processing and presentation aspects.

8.12 WIDE AREA INFORMATION SERVICES

A DIS is designed to offer a highly functional multimedia user interface giving access to a wide range of application and information services. Until recently, information services have traditionally been offered by internal service providers (e.g. the computer services department) using database management systems (DBMSs) holding largely internal data; few external services were accessed by the average user. The main technical challenges for internal information provision is how to control the distribution of data when users are demanding local access to locally owned data. This issue is discussed in Chapter 9.

A feature of information service provision in the 1990s is an increasing number of *external* information providers who are providing an extensive range of useful services to users, accessible over the Internet and other global networks. It is also surprisingly straightforward for any organization to become an information provider, supplying multimedia information to potential customers around the world – a massive, global marketplace of consumers.

Whilst traditional data stores such as file systems and relational database systems will continue to hold vast amounts of data, an information service places emphasis on *access* and *distribution* of information that is stored in repositories to a global market. For example, traditional suppliers of national telecommunications infrastructures now offer a wide range of value-added information services to consumers. Another example is the availability of marketing on higher education courses and services being advertised. Many universities are now offering distance learning (i.e. a knowledge transmission service) over the Internet using multimedia systems such as videoconferencing. There is now a proliferation of information providers selling commercial information services.

8.12.1 Technical challenges

The technical challenges to information providers when implementing information services in a distributed systems environment are:

- users should be able to access the information services easily anywhere and at any time;
- the service should be resilient and responsive. Distributed service design techniques such as partitioning, replication and caching should be employed to achieve quality of service requirements in terms of availability, reliability, dependability, and configurability;
- the user interface and infrastructure should support multimedia interactions. In particular, the quality of service offered addresses the time-critical nature of interactive multimedia;
- user interaction and business transactions should take place in a secure environment;
- implementation of appropriate remuneration schemes.

To meet the above challenges, an information service will need to make use of generic services outlined in this chapter, such as directory and trading services, to provide the flexibility, robustness, security and ease of use being demanded by users. A widely used technology for delivering information services is the World Wide Web (abbreviated to the Web, or WWW or W3) initially developed at CERN, the European Particle Physics Laboratory in Switzerland (Berners-Lee, 1992a, b). The Web has become the *de-facto* standard for implementing an information service over the Internet, and is examined in detail in the next section.

8.12.2 World Wide Web based information services

The Internet can be viewed as a global information space served by thousands of information servers maintained by a multitude of information providers. Information is generally available from:

- software and data archives – which can be retrieved using FTP;
- bulletin boards and group conferences (e.g. the USENET conferencing facility);
- mailing lists through which users are kept informed concerning particular items.

A significant problem with the Internet was the lack of tools for storing information and making it easily available to users who may be interested in it. Initially, publishing on the Internet entailed the use of the following basic TCP/IP facilities:

- *SMTP mail,* for low-cost global electronic mail;
- *FTP* for uploading and downloading files;
- *TELNET* for terminal access to a remote computer.

To facilitate searching the Internet, a number of useful additional software tools for information management became available.

- *Archie* which provides keyword searching of file archives. Once found, Archie can download the file(s) using FTP. Archie servers provide search indexes to large archives of files.
- *Gopher* which provides a hierarchical, menu-driven interface to resources (Anklesaria *et al.*, 1993). Selection at the lowest level of the menu causes textual or graphical information to be retrieved and displayed. A number of Gopher servers are used each of which structures data collections for use by Gopher client software. The collection of world-wide Gopher servers is known as 'Gopherspace'.
- *Wide Area Information Server (WAIS)* which provides keyword searching for words which may occur in textual documents (Kahle and Medlar, 1991). A sophisticated indexing system is used to find (and rank based on frequency of occurrence) all documents in a collection of WAIS-indexed documents. Each WAIS server handles a collection of WAISindexed documents (known as a 'source'). A directory of servers lists hundreds of

sources and can be used to find out which sources contain information relevant to a particular subject area.

- *Usenet (also known as News or Network News (NN))* which provides a distributed bulletin board service through which users can exchange views and information. Articles are organized by topic into news groups of which there are over 2000. Users must subscribe to a news group in order to receive articles. Articles (or items) can be written and then transmitted ('posted') to the relevant news group which is automatically transmitted (broadcasted) between computers in the network so that all subscribers eventually receive it. A Usenet news group can be thought of as an electronic magazine or journal that you can use to search for information or discuss topics.

- *World Wide Web (WWW)* which provides hypermedia links to information and services available across the Internet. Gopher, FTP archives and other sources can also be accessed through a hypertext link. The main difference between the Web and Gopher is that the Web has links embedded within a Web document (i.e. the documents are the menus), whereas Gopher menus are a list of links to documents (i.e. links are outside of Gopher documents).

The Web is a large-scale distributed *hypermedia* system used to navigate the variety of information available and can be used as a multimedia front-end to all other services provided over the Internet. A hypermedia system allows a user to embed within a document cross-reference information which can be navigated usually by means of a graphical 'point and click' user interface. The document can contain multiple media types (whereas a *hypertext* system cross-references textual information). The innovative aspects of Web technology are the use of Internet-wide cross-reference links called *universal resource locators* (URLs), client/server based on a protocol known as *HTTP* (hyper text transfer protocol) and a language known as HTML (hypertext markup language) to define graphical user interface structures for hypermedia documents.

A typical Web configuration is illustrated in Figure 8.14. The program on the client side (known as a *browser*) is a presentation object which interprets an initial HTML document (called the *home page*) and creates the corresponding user interface. The home page may contain references to many other HTML documents and files containing media types such as sound, static images and so on. Cross-references (known as hypermedia links or *hyperlinks*) are specified as URLs which take the general form:

```
resource-type://Internet host name:port number/path/filename
```

Many resource types are available, such as:

> `http` – a HTML document residing on a Web server;
> `FTP` – a file residing in an FTP server;
> `gopher` – reference to a gopher index;
> `wais` – reference to a WAIS database
> `telnet` – a terminal session with a remote host;
> `news` – a link to a USENET news group.

URLs differ depending on the native operating environment of the server and, for example, naming conventions for pathnames. Particular media types are not handled directly by the browser, instead an appropriate *viewer* program is called to handle the media type. User interactions are handled by the browser. In particular, when the user clicks on a hypertext link, the browser sends a message to the Web server named in the URL using the HTTP protocol which is

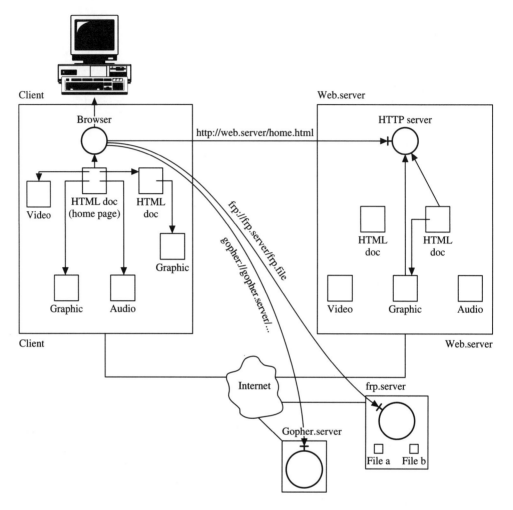

Figure 8.14 World wide web functionality.

essentially an RPC mechanism. The Web server retrieves the HTML document also named in the URL and sends its contents to the browser. The data stream which returns server data to a browser can consist of multiple media types. Media types are identified in the data stream using MIME headers (Borenstein and Freed, 1992) which are created by the Web server. The MIME message representation protocol is used extensively in the Web (see Chapter 2). This mechanism provides an effective technology for (one-way) information retrieval services.

Another aspect of Web technology is support for user interaction with an information service using traditional data repositories such as data files and databases. An HTTP server cannot interface directly with other data sources such as ASCII data files and data stored in databases. This is restrictive as an organization holds most of its computer-based data in files and databases. Moreover, a service provider may wish to allow a user to search for information or carry out a business transaction having supplied relevant information. This functionality is provided by the Web through a mechanism known as the *common gateway interface* (CGI) and

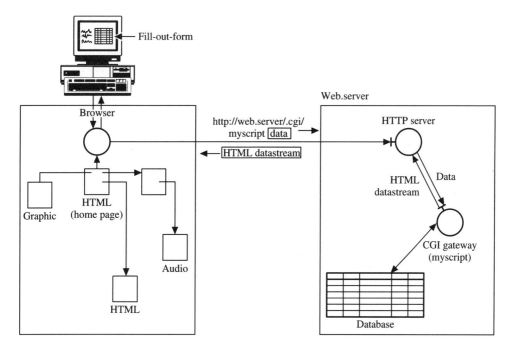

Figure 8.15 Extending web services through the CGI gateway.

a feature of HTML known as *forms*. CGI allows information to be accessible even if it is not in a form readable by the HTTP server or browser. Server programs known as *gateways* are executable programs or scripts that are executed when referenced in a URL. An example configuration is shown in Figure 8.15. Gateways can be written in any language so long as the Web server environment can execute it. Coupled with CGI gateways are forms which are areas on the client screen in which a user can input data. The data entered is passed to the CGI gateway via the HTTP server. The HTTP protocol defines two form operations (known as 'methods'): POST and GET which can be specified when the form is developed using HTML form statements. For example, the HTML statement:

```
<FORM METHOD="post" ACTION="http://www.wlv.ac.uk/cgi/myscript">
```

identifies a CGI script called myscript at Web server www.wlv.ac.uk to which the form data is posted. When a HTML form is executed by a browser and the user enters data, the data is appended to the end of the URL given in the ACTION attribute of the FORM tag (i.e. http://www.wlv.ac.uk/cgi/myscript). The data is then passed to the script myscript when it is invoked. CGI gateways get data input mainly from environment variables and the standard input (when using the POST method). Searching criteria is input into a script acting as a search engine using the same mechanism. Scripts return output to the browser by first returning the output to the HTTP server as a data stream (for example, using the 'pipe' mechanism in UNIX systems). The HTTP server is responsible for 'packaging' the data stream according to HTTP protocol rules. This involves adding MIME conformant headers for each media type indicating the media type and encoding used.

Although the Web has developed a popular and novel approach to information service access and delivery, it suffers from a number of significant problems:

- Response times are unpredictable and often excessive causing time-outs and other problems.
- It is not possible to enquire about the nature of a HTML document pointed to by a particular URL without fetching the document. The solution is to store meta-information which describes the HTML document pointed to by a URL. A user can send an enquiry which returns the meta-information. This improves resource utilization and response times.
- Often multiple users use a single (overloaded) web server to access information when in fact the information is replicated across multiple 'mirror' sites. There is no mechanism, however, to make users aware of mirror sites. If mirror site information is stored as meta-information, a degree of load balancing can be achieved by enabling users to choose the local mirror site. This improves scalability by implementing a replication control and load balancing mechanism.
- The current naming model is protocol and underlying file system dependent which makes it difficult to use because of differing conventions. A better naming model is required.
- Matching user requirements to information service provision is currently totally user driven. A trading service is required to enable easy discovery of particular information services based on user-defined topics of interest.
- The HTTP server to external gateway interface exhibits basic functionality which can be enhanced significantly to provide tighter integration between Web and non-Web services. Distributed object technology such as OMG/CORBA and OSF/DCE can be used as the basis for tighter integration, offering users and information providers a seamless interface to Web and non-Web services.
- Security services are primitive. This is primarily due to the fact that the Internet was not designed for commercial use. Enhancements such as the HTTP secure sockets layer (SSL) provide enhanced security over the Internet.

Future work which addresses the above issues is taking place energetically under the auspices of the World Wide Web (W3) Consortium based at the Massachusetts Institute of Technology (MIT) and Internet Engineering Task Force (IETF) working groups. Web-based technology is seen as being appropriate not only to deliver external information services but also for internal information services, acting as a multimedia front-end incorporating data from a variety of internal and external sources.

8.13 MESSAGING AND OTHER GROUP SERVICES

The implementation of electronic mail (email) services to a workgroup, department or across an organization can lead to substantial benefits. Firstly, there is a considerable reduction in the amount of paper used for short memos which typically have very limited life (but cost a signficant amount in terms of paper and internal postage processing). Secondly, messages are transmittedly quickly and received by the recipient in a time frame which is appropriate to the recipients work pattern. For example, if the source user was located in London, England and the recipient was located in New York, USA, the message would probably be waiting for him when he arrives in his office. Email systems assign an electronic **mailbox** to each user in which other users can place messages (read and unread) and attached documents. A user simply reads messages stored in his or her mailbox. A single message can be sent to a single or multiple mailboxes as indicated by a distribution list. Each user is responsible for mailbox management which mainly involves periodically deleting messages so that the mailbox does not run out of space. Another messaging requirement is to support *email-enabled applications* which implement inter-application communication by sending email messages to each other via a standard email facility.

Two main standards are widely used to implement messaging services: the Internet simple mail transfer protocol (SMTP) and the ITU-T X.400 protocol.

8.13.1 Internet SMTP

In Chapter 6, the TCP/IP protocol was described and included application layer processes. One application layer process which was defined is the simple mail transfer protocol (SMTP) which delivers electronic mail services. SMTP is implemented as a client/server system where clients support message creation and the transfer of the message and distribution list to the SMTP server process. The server process delivers the message to its intended recipients. A set of commands and responses are defined in plain 7-bit ASCII text, consequently they are human readable. Each command consists of a four character command followed, in some cases, by data. Each response is three ASCII digits optionally followed by a description. Example commands and responses are detailed in Table 8.2.

Table 8.2 SMTP commands and responses

Command/response	Description/operands
Commands:	
DATA	user data
EXPN	expand the list mail distribution list by adding address information
HELO	specifies the sender address. It is an abbreviation for HELLO
HELP	request for information about the mail server
MAIL	specifies that mail is to be sent, and identifiers the sender's mail
QUIT	request that the SMTP connection be closed
RCPT	specifies who is to receive the mail message
RSET	requests abrupt termination of sending
<CR><LF>.<CR><LF>	indicates the end of the mail message. This means that SMTP forbids a mail message to have a period on a line by itself
Responses	
211	System status
220	Service ready
221	Closing connection
250	OK, normal completion
251	Non-local user, will forward
354	Start mail input
421	Service not available, closing connection
500	Syntax error
501	Path too long
502	Command not implemented
550	Mailbox not found
551	Not a local user, cannot forward

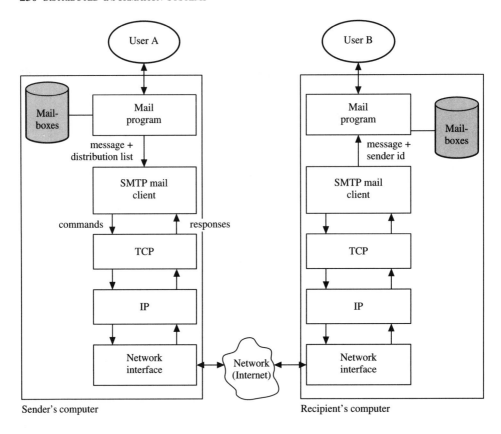

Figure 8.16 The TCP/IP SMTP components.

The components of an SMTP-based mail service are illustrated in Figure 8.16. An important aspect of any electronic mail system is to uniquely identify the recipients of a mail message. In the situation in which all users are local and registered with the same SMTP mail server, each user is given a unique user name. Mail is simply stored under the user's name in the appropriate mailbox (usually a file under the user's directory in a file system). This is known as **single system electronic mail** and is typical of an isolated email system servicing a workgroup or department.

In practice, users often wish to send email messages to users in other organizations, possibly in different countries. There is a need, therefore, for messages to be routed through multiple, interconnected mail servers until the message arrives at the mail server to which a recipient user is registered. This is achieved only if the format and syntax of message headers and email addresses are standardized. Within the Internet, the standard electronic mail address format is:

```
local_user_name @ domain_name
```

The `local_user_name` is the user name as registered to the local mail system. The `domain_name` is the Internet DNS name of the SMTP mail service. For example, the author's electronic mail address is:

```
e.simon@wlv.ac.uk
```

Thus the mail message is routed to the specified mail server at the specified domain (e.g. `wlv.ac.uk`) and stored in the local mailbox of the user defined in the local domain (e.g. `e.simon`).

Suppose `e.simon@wlv.ac.uk` wishes to send a message to `h.smith@uppl.ac.uk`. A typical SMTP email transaction is:

1. The mail program is invoked by the user `e.simon` and supports the creation of a message and distribution list (in this case `h.smith@uppl.ac.uk`).
2. The mail program requests that the SMTP mail client establish a reliable TCP stream connection to the SMTP mail server at `uppl.ac.uk` and sends the message. The SMTP client establishes the connection and waits for the `uppl.ac.uk` SMTP mail server to send a `220 Server Ready` response.
3. Upon receipt of the 220 response, the SMTP mail client sends the command:

   HELO wlv.ac.uk

   The mail server responds by identifying itself (i.e. `250 uppl.ac.uk`).
4. The SMTP mail client initiates the mail message transfer, identifying the sending user by sending the command:

   MAIL FROM:<e.simon@wlv.ac.uk>

   The mail server responds with `250 OK`.
5. The SMTP mail client then specifies the recipients of the mail message by sending the command:

   RCPT TO:<h.smith@uppl.ac.uk>

   The mail server responds with 250 OK. The maximum number of recipients is one hundred.
6. The SMTP mail client indicates that it is about to send the actual message by sending the command:

   DATA

   The mail server responds with `354 Start mail` input. The maximum length of a line of text, including the terminating <CR><LF>, is 1000 characters. The format of an SMTP message is a message header, followed by a blank line, followed by the message body. The header consists of lines which begin with a keyword, such as FROM:, TO:, SUB-JECT:, DATE: and CC: and is not used by the mail client and server but is simply there for use by the recipient.
7. The SMTP mail client sends the mail message and terminates the transmission by sending the termination sequence <CR><LF>.<CR><LF>. The mail server responds with `250 OK`.
8. Finally, the SMTP mail client sends a `QUIT` command which requests that the SMTP connection be closed. The mail server responds with `221 Closing connection`.

Clearly, SMTP was designed for the exchange of text messages. The basic SMTP protocol has been extended to support the ability to include multimedia body parts using the MIME protocol which was detailed in Section 2.4.

8.13.2 ITU-T X.400

A comprehensive electronic mail application layer protocol was developed by the ITU. The standard, known as ITU-T X.400, defines a range of services and protocols needed for message handling and electronic mail. These have been adopted by ISO as part of the OSI standard (known as ISO 10021). An X.400 message consists of an *envelope*, a *header*, and a *body*. An X.400 body consists of one or more *body parts*. Each body part may contain ASCII text or any bit pattern, such as digital audio, digital video, static images and graphics, an animated sequence, or binary data. The X.400 envelope contains information to enable a message to be routed to recipients (e.g. a message identifier, class of message, and priority). An X.400 user is identified by a hierarchical addressing structure which identifies to which country and organization, and organizational unit the recipient belongs, and the user's local name. An example X.400 address is:

```
     COU = gb
    ADMD = ptt400mail
    PRMD = ac
     ORG = wlv
 ORGUNIT = scit
 ORGUNIT = staff
  S.NAME = simon
  G.NAME = errol
```

ADMD is the *administrative domain*, which is normally a licensed network provider in a particular country. The PRMD is the *private management domain*, which is typically a grouping of organizations which have some common network which can be used to route X.400 messages. An example of a PRMD is the academic community in a particular country which share a common network, or a private organization with a number of autonomous subsidiaries. There are some problems with the definition and specification of ADMDs and PRMDs. For example, in a multinational company with a private international network, a single PRMD name describes the whole network and the ADMD is in fact redundant. Another problem is where a PRMD connects to multiple ADMDs in a single country, which complicates message routing. X.400 user address information should be contained in a distributed database with query facilities for easy identification of the X.400 address of a particular user. The ITU-T X.500 directory service was designed for this purpose.

The components which are used to create an X.400 mail service is illustrated in Figure 8.17. The components are described in Table 8.3. To send a message, a user submits a message to the local user agent (UA). The UA sends the message to the local message transfer agent (MTA) that is associated with the local UA. The message is then routed through the message transfer system (a network of MTAs) until it reaches the MTA associated with the recipient's local UA. Message routing is based on the X.400 address structure and envelope information.

The X.400 standard is often used as a **mail gateway protocol** to build a global mail system by using gateways to provide mail-to-mail translation. For example, each email system has its own X.400 gateway component so that the X.400 protocol is used as the backbone email service and each gateway carries out the local mail protocol-to-X.400 mail translation.

Table 8.3 X.400 components

Component	Description
User	A person or application program that creates and originates a message or receives a delivered message. Strictly, a user is not a component of an X.400 service but is simply a user of the service.
User agent (UA)	A software component that interacts with the user, acting as an interface to the message transfer system.
Message transfer agent (MTA)	A software component responsible for routing messages across a network to recipient UAs. This involves interacting with UAs and other MTAs.
Message transfer system (MTS)	The set of all interconnected MTAs and network links.
Message handling system (MHS	The set of all X.400 components used to create an X.400 service.
Message store (MS)	A software component which handles the storage of messages until a disconnected UA is reconnected.
Access unit (AU)	A software component that acts as a gateway between the MTS and non-X.400 messaging systems.

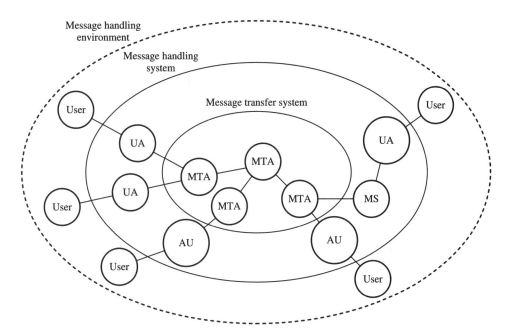

Figure 8.17 X.400 components.

8.13.3 Other group services

Other services which provide common functions to groups of users need to be made available. Examples of such services are:

- **calendar** and **meeting scheduling services**, which provide support for scheduling meetings and appointments for group members;

- **workflow management services**, which provide support for the flow of routine processes within a workgroup, department or across the whole organization. The execution and control of workflows accounts for a high proportion of a manager's time. Automation of workflows can reduce this time making more time available for more productive tasks;

- **computer conferencing**, which consists of various electronic groups, known as *conferences*, each conference comprising a set of members and some sequence of messages related to the area of interest. Group conferences can differ in terms of their size, duration, objectives and formalization. A good example of a computer conferencing facility is the Internet Usenet system;

- **live video conferencing**, which consists of person-to-person or group video conferencing sessions in real time. The group service facilitates the binding of participants in the video conferencing session. This may simply function as a reflector service by taking an input audio/video stream and broadcasting it to all participants. More complex functions involve data and application sharing services.

Many of the above group services rely on an underlying messaging service. Group services are examined in detail in Chapter 11.

8.14 CASE STUDIES

8.14.1 OMG/CORBA object services

OMA define three categories of objects that can interact as illustrated in Figure 8.18:

1. Object services: these provide basic infrastructure services for initiating and maintaining objects. Example object services adopted or in progress are:

    — name services (naming and addressing scheme);
    — synchronization and concurrency control;

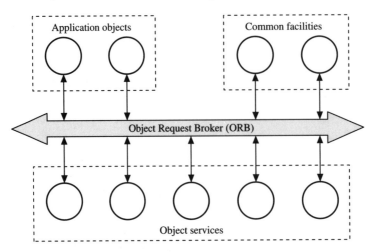

Figure 8.18 Object management architecture.

- notification (event) services;
- activation and passivation of services (factory services);
- exception handling;
- security services;
- object persistence services;
- transaction services;
- licensing services;
- query services (remote data access);
- time services;
- trading services;
- change management.

2. Common facilities: objects implementing common infrastructure services (i.e. corporate application services) useful to any DIS (e.g. compound document support).
3. Application objects: objects developed for a particular DIS.

The OMG plan to extend the functionality of CORBA by continually extending the range of object service specifications.

Distributed information systems involving voice and video streams place stringent demands on the IT infrastructure and application support services. A synchronous videoconference may involve controlling and synchronizing multiple voice, video and data streams as a whole. Thus the binding of the various objects with stream interfaces in this scenario requires complex binding mechanisms. The need for an application interface which provides fine-grained control of distributed multiple streams and the resources required to support them was established in Chapter 2. In terms of the CORBA standard, this translates to the need for (Herbert, 1994):

- naming and binding ORB services for objects with stream (e.g. voice and video) interfaces;
- alternative transfer syntax support and mechanisms for user-defined media encoding/decoding;
- fine-grained control over resources and scheduling;
- the ability for an ORB to offer alternative network protocols and services to objects, with application control over protocol selection at bind time;
- more flexible factory services;
- transaction, replication and security mechanisms.

Thus significant enhancements to the current CORBA standard are required to provide full support for DIS implementation. This is equally the case for other current object management systems such as Microsoft's OLE system.

8.14.2 OSF/distributed computing environment

The OSF/DCE RPC standard was detailed in Section 3.9.4. DCE is in fact an architectural framework and the definition of some fundamental services required to develop distributed systems. The DCE architecture is illustrated in Figure 8.19. Several key services are defined which are detailed below.

- DCE relies on a **threads** facility (known as DCE threads), modelled on the P1003.4a IEEE POSIX specification, to implement services and distributed applications that can utilize computational parallelism through multi-threading. If the target operating has a threads

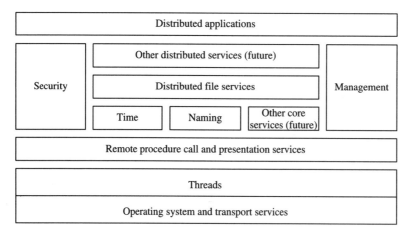

Figure 8.19 Distributed computing environment (DCE).

facility, DCE can be set up to utilize it. DCE provides thread synchronization mechanisms. Threads provide an efficient way to partition tasks, service multiple client requests, and for clients to interact with multiple servers in parallel.

- RPC for remote IPC. DCE RPC was described in Section 3.9.4. At most once, at least once and one-way execution semantics are offered.
- Distributed time services, known as DCE DTS, to keep local physical clocks synchronized. A novel feature of DTS is that it records time as a lower and upper bound interval which indicates how accurate time has been recorded rather than as an absolute value.
- Directory services. The DCE directory service is partitioned into naming and management domains called *cells*, each of which are managed by a cell directory service (CDS). A global directory service (GDS) implements a global (inter-cell) naming service using the ITU-T X.500 standard. Although the GDS is based on the ITU-T X.500 standard, DCE also provides support for the Internet DNS standard through a special user agent, known as the global directory agent (GDA), which runs on a CDS server and allows a CDS to query both a GDS and a DNS name server to resolve a name. An example configuration is given in Figure 8.20.
- Distributed file services, known as DCE DFS, is an enhanced version of the Andrew File System (Howard *et al.*, 1988). DCE can interoperate seamlessly with other common remote file systems such as NFS.
- Security services, known as DCE Security Service, is described in Section 13.3.3.
- Management services.

In addition, DCE defines a Catalogue server, derived from a DCE CDS, giving the ability to replicate the CDS. To aid administration and management, and to promote local autonomy, DCE-compliant computers are grouped into management domains called cells. Every DCE-compliant computer must, as a minimum, run DCE threads, DCE RPC and the client components of the other six services. Every DCE cell must run at least the CDS, security and DTS services. An application running on a client machine searches a CDS server (using DCE RPC) to find out where a service can be located. Implementations of DCE are available on several platforms including PCs and many UNIX platforms.

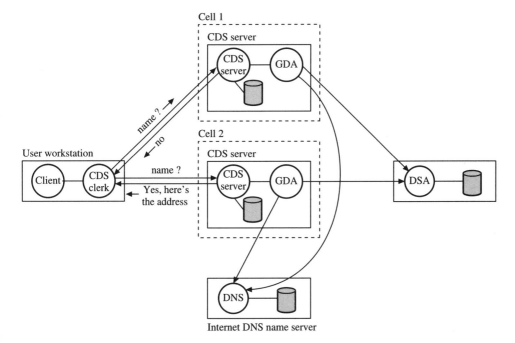

Figure 8.20 DCE directory services.

8.14.3 Novell Netware

The Novell Netware software product has traditionally been positioned as a network operating system offering file and print services in a PC LAN environment. A wide range of 'value-added' third-party products offer additional services such as remote data access, application services, etc. Recently, Novell launched a significantly upgraded version of Netware (version 4) with some interesting new features for supporting large-scale networked applications. Netware 4.x provides:

- Netware directory service (NDS), a directory service based on the ITU-T X.500 standard;
- time services, which provide physical clock synchronization services;
- file and print service, which is a mature service offered by Netware since the early 1980s;
- software to perform routing services based on its own protocol (IPX/SPX) and TCP/IP;
- administration and management services, which provide facilities for configuration management, network management and server management;
- security services, such as authentication (based on public-key cryptography), authorization (based on access control lists), auditing, archiving and backup. These services are described in Chapter 13.

The NDS is used as a repository of information about all Netware resources, including users, user groups, servers, printers, print queues, etc. Integrated into the NDS system is an authentication protocol which is described in detail in Chapter 13. One obvious function which is missing from NDS is its use as a trading service to dynamically bind clients to relevant servers (despite holding much of the information required for trading). Instead, a broadcast protocol, known as **service advertising protocol** (SAP) is used to facilitate dynamic binding. Each server type is allocated a unique advertising number. Some of the important advertising numbers are given in Table 8.4.

Table 8.4 Important Netware server types and advertising numbers

Server type	Advertising number (in hex)
File server	4
Print server	7
Archive server	9
Remote router server	24
Router server	26
TCP/IP gateway	27
Portable Netware server	9E

A special packet, known as SAP packet, is broadcast to allow Netware servers to advertise their services to other servers. Users can search the network for a particular service by broadcasting a request, for example:

- a request for information on all servers of a particular type;
- a request for the name and address of the nearest server of a particular type;
- a request for information regarding all services available on the network.

Each Netware server maintains a SAP information table, recording for each server the server name, type, and address. SAP information tables are updated by default every minute by requiring each server to generate SAP packets. On a large network with a large number of server types, the level of SAP traffic is significant. Thus, this approach is not scalable. A replicated, federated trading service would provide a scalable alternative design.

8.14.4 Microsoft WindowsNT

Microsoft WindowsNT is an operating system which can be configured to run as network operating systems (NOS) supporting client workstations running Microsoft Windows 3.11, Windows9x, OS/2, or Apple Macintoshes. It can also be configured to be run both on client workstations and servers. As a NOS, WindowsNT compares favourably with others, such as Unix and Novell Netware, offering file and print servers, and as an application server. Because users are generally very familiar with Microsoft Windows' software architecture and user interface, WindowNT's similar architecture and interface enables easier administration and management.

The WindowNT Registry holds data for server configuration management purposes, such as the server hardware configuration, applications installed and user profiles. User administration facilities are very similar to other NOSs such as Novell Netware. One important difference is the lack of global directory service. Although WindowsNT offers some support for administering multiple server configurations, it is not as elegant as Novell Netware's NDS. A global directory service is planned for the next major release of WindowsNT.

WindowsNT provides inherent support for disk mirroring and RAID disk subsystems configurations. Security is based on access control lists for authorization, and authentication based on user id and password (but with no other authentication mechanism such as secret key or public key authentication).

A significant strength of WindowsNT is that the same tools which are familiar to PC-based application developers can easily be tailored to produce server-side business logic because the environment is similar. Obviously, application server code must be built for efficient multi-tasking (multi-threading) with low processing-per-client for scalability and performance. Application code can easily be developed and tested on the client side and migrated to the server. WindowsNT is also backed by Microsoft who are keen to see it succeed in this role. These factors are likely to position WindowsNT as a strong contender for the low-to medium-sized application server NOS of choice.

8.15 SUMMARY

In this chapter, we have reviewed a range of distributed services which implement the functionalities required by a wide range of DISs. These services are accessed in a distribution transparent way by means of a middleware software layer, user agents and server wrapper software. A distributed IT infrastructure provides the potential for building scalable, fault-tolerant and responsive services which can be extended to meet future DIS requirements. The combination of replication, partitioning and caching provide the mechanisms for delivering the desired quality-of-service for each service implemented.

8.16 REVIEW EXERCISES

1. Describe the role of a directory service.
2. Explain the differences between a name service and a trading service.
3. Under what circumstances is a factory service required?
4. What problems can arise when using timestamps in a distributed system?
5. Explain the role of a time service. What is the difference between a physical and logical clock?
6. Describe how a logical clock can be used to achieve total ordering of events in a distributed system.
7. Discuss possible approaches to implementing co-ordination amongst distributed processes.
8. Discuss what services might be offered by a notification service.
9. Describe in detail the differences between a remote file access and a remote data access service. Discuss how each is implemented.
10. Describe in detail how the World Wide Web can be used for electronic publishing.
11. What is the purpose of the common gateway interface (CGI) in the World Wide Web?
12. Identify any shortcomings in World Wide Web technology.
13. Compare and contrast the services offered by OSF/DCE, OMG/CORBA Novell Netware and Microsoft Windows NT Server.

8.17 FURTHER READING

Coulouris *et al.* (1994) provides excellent coverage of some generic distributed services (e.g. file, name, time, coordination and security services). OSF/DCE is covered in OSF (1992),

Bever (1993), Shirley (1992) and Tanenbaum (1995). Novell Netware 4 is covered in detail in Bierer (1995). Microsoft Windows NT Server is detailed in Minassi *et al.* (1994). Some useful papers on distributed services are found in Casavant and Singhal (1994) and Mullender (1993).

9

DISTRIBUTING DATA

9.1 INTRODUCTION

An important design consideration when developing a DIS is where to place data objects. A data component may consist of multiple data objects possibly of different media types. Three principal data handling systems are required to support the variety of data objects which may be created and used by a DIS:

- A *database management system* (DBMS); comprises a collection of programs for structuring, storing, updating, and retrieving data. A database system consists of a DBMS and one or more databases that it manages. Client access to remote database systems is facilitated by a remote data access (RDA) service.
- Data files captured and stored in a *file system*. For example, text, graphics, audio, video files may be managed by a local or remote file system. Compound document files (such as hypermedia document files) in which multiple media types are stored, also reside in a file system. A remote file access (RFA) service supports client access to remote files.
- Real-time, continuous *stream handling systems*. Multimedia data objects such as audio and video are time-based, continuous streams of information that must be delivered at a constant rate with bounded delay between source and target users in order to meet a user's real-time interaction demands. In a real-time video conference, for example, realtime compression, transportation, decompression and presentation on the target user's presentation devices (e.g. video image and sound) imposes stringent demands on the IT infrastructure. In particular, the client and server workstation environment and network require continuous stream handling capabilities to provide real-time control and synchronization of audio and video streams that together can act as a single unit.

Each of the above systems address a subset of the data objects which may be used by a DIS. Multimedia data objects pose significant technological challenges in terms of data storage and management such as the requirement for isochronous presentation and storage sizes measured in megabytes rather than kilobytes. A digitized movie, for example, occupies approximately 1 gigabyte of storage space. This chapter examines the key concepts and techniques which underpin the development of technology that addresses the need for controlled distribution of data in an organization. It is assumed that the reader has a rudimentary knowledge of relational databases and the SQL relational data manipulation language. Relational databases and SQL are described fully, for example, in Carter (1992) and Korth and Silberschatz (1991).

9.2 DATABASE MANAGEMENT SYSTEMS

The objective of a database management system (DBMS) is to provide mechanisms for managing a large, integrated, shared data repository, and to make the data easily accessible to multiple users (while maintiaining data integrity, availability and security). Repository data model entities in the real world such as customers, products, and so on. The way in which real-world entities are modelled depends on how the DBMS structures the data which represent it. A *data model* is a collection of well-defined concepts to reason about data and relationships between data which model real-world entities and entity relationships. A *schema* defines the static properties (entities, attributes, relationships and constraints) of a database, and *operations* define the dynamic properties.

A useful framework for describing various database management concepts and architectures is the ANSI/SPARC three-level architecture illustrated in Figure 9.1. The three levels are defined as internal, conceptual and external. The *internal* level is the one closest to the physical storage of data on storage media such as hard disk drives, that is, it is mostly concerned with how data is actually stored and retrieved from physical storage (e.g. using indexes and special storage structures). The *external* level is the one closest to the users of the database system and is concerned with the way data is viewed by individual users. The *conceptual* level sits between internal and external levels and provides the 'community user' view of the data because it represents the abstract view of the data in its entirety. The three levels of abstraction of data are described by an internal schema, a conceptual schema and one or more external schema. Users normally access and manipulate some portion of the database (described by an external schema) through a special-purpose *data manipulation language*.

In this section we describe how database systems have evolved and the extent to which the technology supports the need to distribute data to different parts of an organization. DBMSs can be classified according to the way in which data is characterized in the conceptual schema (referred to as a data model). There are three common classes of DBMS: hierarchical, network, and relational.

The characteristics of each of these classes is described in the next section which presents a brief historical perspective on the evolution of DBMSs.

9.2.1 Historical perspective

The ideas of storing data records in files as part of a simple file system and of linking data records to represent more complex data structures evolved in the late 1950s and early 1960s. The notion of master and detail data records, a common technique for file processing, formed

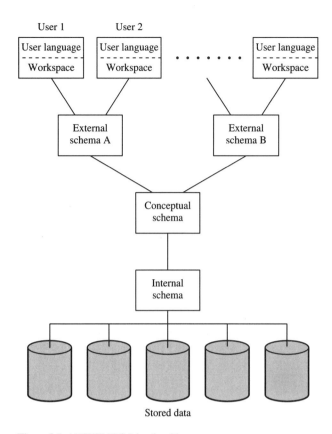

User 1   User 2

Figure 9.1 ANSI/SPARC 3-level architecture.

the basis for the hierarchically structured links between data records and later the *hierarchical data model*, data manipulation language and DBMS which emerged in the 1960s. In 1959, the Conference on Data Systems Languages (CODASYL) established two committees, one which developed the COBOL business programming language, the other to investigate database concepts (later named the CODASYL Database Task Group (DBTG)). In 1969, the DBTG published its specification of the *network data model*, data manipulation language and DBMS (CODASYL, 1971).

In the late 1960s, Ted Codd of IBM developed a programming language which became the basis for the *relational data model*, relational data languages and DBMS (Codd, 1970) and the basis of much of relational database theory and technology which have grown in popularity.

Thus three classes of DBMS evolved: hierarchical, network and relational data models. In the hierarchical model, data is organized hierarchically as a collection of data records connected to one another according to parent–child (one-to-one) relationships forming a tree-like structure. A hierarchical database is therefore an ordered set of trees with the use of pointers between records in order to traverse a tree starting at the root/parent node. In addition to defining the data, the navigational paths to data need to be defined (as pointers) and embedded in the database. Access to data is directed by the user using data manipulation language commands which guide the DBMS in locating relevant data. The use of pointers improves performance but reduces access flexibility. Another drawback is the need to duplicate data in order to model some complex relationships, for example, if data records belong to more than one tree (i.e. a child data record has multiple parents). This may result in unnecessary waste of storage space and potential data inconsistency when updating takes place.

The network data model is an extension of the hierarchical model in that each data record type can be associated with one or more different record types using a system of pointers which form an arbitrary graph rather than a tree-like relationship structure. Parent-to-children (one-to-one and one-to-many) relationships between record types are modelled as separate structures called sets. A set identifies links between one parent and one or more record types. A child record type can have more than one parent. In this way more complex relationships can be modelled more flexibly involving less data redundancy than hierarchical data models. Access paths are also pre-defined using pointers and are traversed using data manipulation language commands.

In the relational data model all data are represented by only one data structure: two-dimensional tables. Often the most natural way to represent data is with a two-dimensional table. A table consists of a row of column headings and zero or more rows of data values (the ordering of rows and columns is not significant). The intersection of a row and column identifies a single value (multiple values per intersection is not allowed). All columnar data is of the same kind (e.g. module name is an alphanumeric string). A *primary key* is specified for the table and is used to identify each row in the table uniquely. For primary key columns, duplicate values are forbidden and no part of the primary key may be a null value. Relations such as illustrated in Table 9.1 are normally written in the following form, with the primary key underlined:

EMPLOYEE(<u>Empl-No</u>, Name, Dept, Title)

Table 9.1 An example relation called Employee

Emp-No.	Name	Dept	Title
4678	Clarke	05	Technician
3786	Brown	09	Programmer
3587	Davis	13	Dept Head
6849	Lucas	24	Secretary

Relationships between tables are established by *normalizing* initial table structures to identify primary keys and remove data redundancy. A *foreign key* is an attribute (or set of attributes) common to two or more tables and which is a primary key in an associated table. The values of the foreign key is constrained to a subset of the values of the associated primary key. It should not be possible to insert a row with a foreign key value for a non-existent primary key value (i.e. a primary key value for whom there is no corresponding row in the associated table). Foreign keys are identified during the normalization process and represent links (or relationships) between relations. For example, consider the following database consisting of four normalized relations:

```
ORDERS(Orderid, Salesid, Commision-plan, Clientid, Shipdate, Ordertotal)
LINEITEMS(Orderid, itemno, Productid, Unitprice, Qty, Itemtot)
CLIENT(Clientid, Name, Address, City, County, Postcode, Country, Phone,
       Creditlimit)
PRODUCT(Productid, Proddesc, Stdprice, QtyinStock)
```

The attribute `clientid` is a foreign key of relation ORDERS and the primary key of relation CLIENT. Similarly, attribute `Productid` is a foreign key in the relation LINEIT-EMS and the primary key of relation PRODUCT.

This orthogonal approach, in which pointers are not explicit but are represented by primary and foreign keys, gains in terms of flexibility of data access since access paths are not pre-defined, data needs are defined by a relational data manipulation language which is founded on set theory; a mature 'provable' mathematical concept. A relational data manipulation language defines *what* data is needed by a user or application but does not specify *how* to perform the operation. The relational DBMS determines the best means of supplying the requested data by using cost-based or rule-based optimization techniques (this process is known as **query optimization**). The main drawback is that relational databases whilst offering flexible data manipulation, perform less well than hierarchical and network databases for pre-defined user operations which are supported by 'hard-wired' access paths through the use of pointers.

Whatever the data model employed, the fundamental goals of a DBMS are:

1. Changes to the underlying physical storage of data and access mechanisms should not affect any programs that access the data. Conversely, an application program can be changed without affecting other programs. This is known as the *data independence* property.
2. A database should not contain (unnecessary) duplicate or redundant data. This is the *data integration* property.
3. The business view of data should be separated from the physical representation of data on some storage device. A logical data model represents data as the user wishes to see it whereas a physical data model represents the structure of the data as it is stored on a storage device.
4. No inconsistencies or inaccuracies should arise as a result of changes to the data. This is the *data integrity* property.
5. Data access should be subject to security restrictions and concurrency of access controlled (whilst maximizing the potential for data sharing).

Knowledge about the meaning of data (data semantics) also needs to be incorporated in a database. This 'metadata' (i.e. data about data) is normally stored separately in a **data dictionary**. The data dictionary is used for ensuring the semantic integrity of a database. The remainder of this section concentrates on the relational data model as it has become the most popular option for implementing database systems.

9.2.2 Relational DBMSs

There are three major aspects of relational DBMSs: tables (data structure rules), representation of relationships through primary and foreign keys (data integrity rules), and use of a relational data manipulation language (data manipulation rules). A relational data language operates on one or more whole tables and typically results in the retrieval of one or more records (rows) forming a new table. Codd's initial work (1970) resulted in the definition of a relation data language called SQUARE and later SEQUEL. In 1982 IBM produced its first commercial relational DBMS SQL/DS which used a relational data language called structured query language or SQL (often pronounced SEQUEL). SQL has become the *de facto* standard language for accessing both relational and non-relational DBMSs.

A distinctive characteristic of SQL is its non-procedural *set oriented* nature compared with the 'one-record-at-a-time' approach used by most 3GL programming languages. Many problems are in fact naturally expressed in terms of sets, for example:

```
List all Orders for Client X
Find all products shipped to Client X in the last 6 months
```

SQL allows complex data retrieval operations to be carried out in a relatively easy to interpret language. Each operator in a relational language takes either one or two relations as input and produces a new table as output. There are eight operators defined as shown in Figure 9.2 and summarized in Table 9.2.

Several operators may need to be executed against relevant data to achieve a desired result set. This is equivalent to navigating pre-defined pointers to the desired result set. Most versions of SQL allow nesting of SQL statements up to many levels. SQL commands can be executed interactively or in a procedural 3GL program using **embedded SQL** statements. One issue with embedded SQL is the inability of procedural languages to cope with set processing. Special additional mechanisms (e.g. the use of *cursors*) are used to enable one-record-at-a-time processing of the results of executing an embedded SQL statement.

In 1982 ANSI and ISO began work on standardizing SQL. ANSI SQL was produced in 1986 (known as ANSI-86 or SQL-86). ISO produced the ISO 9075 standard which was similar (but not equivalent) to ANSI-86. ANSI-89 standard followed and later SQL-2. ANSI defined three categories of SQL commands:

Table 9.2 Eight relational language operators

Operators	Description
Special relational operations:	
SELECT	Extracts specific rows from a specified table.
PROJECT	Extracts specific columns from a specified table.
JOIN	(Natural) Builds a table from two specified tables consisting of all possible concatenated pairs of rows, one from each of the two specified tables, such that in each pair the two rows satisfy some specific condition.
DIVIDE	Takes two tables, one of two columns (binary) and one of one column (unary) and builds a table consisting of all values of one column of the binary table, that matches all values in the unary table (in the other column).
Traditional set operations:	
UNION	Builds a table consisting of all rows appearing in either or both of two specified tables.
INTERSECTION	Builds a table consisting of all rows appearing in BOTH of the two specified tables.
DIFFERENCE	Builds a table consisting of all rows appearing in the first but not in the second of the two specified tables.
CARTESIAN PRODUCT	Builds a table from two specified tables, consisting of all possible concatenated pairs of rows, one from each of the two specified tables.

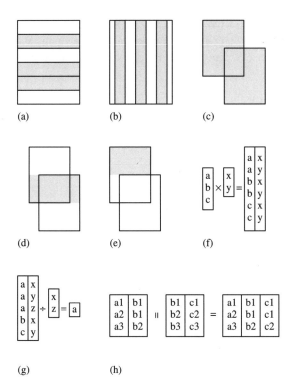

Figure 9.2 Relational operators: (a) select; (b) project; (c) union; (d) intersection; (e) difference; (f) product; (g) divide; (h) natural (join).

1. *Data definition language (DDL) operations*   These are operations for creating, altering and deleting tables. DDL operations are normally restricted to a database administrator or application developer to ensure data integrity and security. The SQL CREATE command performs the main DDL operation to set up a data structure. Other commands are ALTER (change data structure) and DROP (remove data structure).

2. *Data control language (DCL) operations*   These provide data security operations. Operations include the definition of VIEWS to restrict an application's window on a particular table by specifying which columns and rows can be seen by the application. Access to tables can be restricted further by use of GRANT and REVOKE facilities which impose access limitations on specific users. Protection from partial failure of SQL operations is implemented via COMMIT and ROLLBACK processing which allows applications to ignore the effects of other applications that may be accessing shared data concurrently and provides a recovery mechanism after application or system failures.

3. *Data manipulation language (DML) operations*   These are operations for querying, inserting, deleting and modifying data values on the database. Data manipulation is by means of four fundamental operations each of which returns a 'virtual' table (called a *result set*) holding the results of the operation: selection, projection, join and concatenation. A selection operation returns a result set which, based on a specified selection criteria, returns a subset of table rows. A projection operation selects a subset of the columns (attributes) defined for a table. A join operation joins two or more tables together based on a specified row selection criteria. Concatenation operations combine two tables according to criteria based on the set operators: union, difference, intersection and divide.

Details of the SQL language and operators are beyond the scope of this book. The reader is referred to some excellent introductory texts detailed in the further reading section at the end of the chapter. In summary, there are three requirements for a product claiming to be a relational DBMS:

1. The DBMS supports a relational data structure at the conceptual and external levels, whereby:
   - all data is maintained in the database in the form of a set of tables (or relations);
   - each item (field) is a single value;
   - each table has a fixed number of columns (called attributes);
   - all values in a column are of the same type;
   - each column can hold only a defined range of values (called a domain);
   - columns are named but without ordering;
   - each table has a variable number of rows (called tuples);
   - each row (record) is unique with no implicit ordering;
   - one attribute or group of attributes is designated as the primary key which uniquely identifies each row in the table;
   - all physical implementation details are hidden from the user.
   At the internal levels there are no restrictions.
2. The DBMS supports a relational data language through which all database operations are performed. Although there are alternatives, the SQL language is the industry standard.
3. The DBMS has relational integrity rules to ensure data security, integrity and consistency when supporting concurrency. A DBMS should support three types of integrity rules: domain, referential and application-specific. Domain integrity rules ensure that data items in a table column are valid (i.e. within a range of valid values). Referential integrity rules ensure that relationships between data are maintained. For example, if a module is withdrawn then dependent data such as student enrolment records must also be deleted. Alternatively, a module record may not be allowed to be deleted if students have enrolled. Application-specific rules ensure that integrity rules specific to an application are applied.

A DBMS can generally be described as *minimally relational* if it supports a database with a relational data structure at conceptual and external levels and implements the select, projection and (natural) join relational language features. A DBMS is relationally complete if it also supports the full range of relational data language features and integrity rules.

9.2.3 SQL extensions

Many relational DBMS products have extended features and associated SQL language to incorporate some shortcomings and to offer added value to customers. The effect of this is the existence of many incompatible versions of SQL. Examples of extensions are:

- *Indexing*   Options for improving data access performance.
- *Complex data type handling*   Traditional DBMSs have been tuned to store and process simple data types efficiently, such as character strings, numbers and date types. The increasing trend towards multimedia has given rise to the need to store more complex data types such as text, graphics, digitized sound and video. Many DBMSs allow any large binary object to be stored in a single 'attribute' for later retrieval.
- *Stored procedures*   A stored procedure is a set of SQL statements (with supplier-specific

extensions) embedded in a procedural program that is stored as a single unit in the database catalogue. Stored procedures can be executed directly by clients using appropriate SQL commands. Stored procedures provide a convenient mechanism for enabling pre-written, complex SQL processing (business logic) to be initiated by users. Stored procedures will have been properly tested to ensure that application-specific integrity constraints are met. For example, a stored procedure to update a customer record can check for update validity and inform the calling client if an error is detected.

- *Triggers* A trigger is a stored procedure that is initiated automatically by the DBMS when a defined event (e.g. data insertion, modification or deletion) occurs. Trigger procedures are invisible to clients and so provide an important mechanism for mandatory processing requirements which cannot be overridden by clients. Triggers are widely used to implement domain and referential integrity constraints. For example, when a new student enrolment record is inserted into the enrolment table, a trigger checks that student enrolment does not exceed the enrolment limit for a course.

9.3 TRANSACTION PROCESSING

A key concept in the development of robust, high performance, large-scale information systems is transaction processing. In Section 3.9.3. we introduced a form of RPC, known as transactional RPC, which was defined as a RPC mechanism that exhibits zero-or-one execution semantics. In the context of data protection and integrity, a transaction is defined as a unit of work which accomplishes a particular action with the following execution semantics:

- *Atomicity* all-or-nothing execution semantics, that is, the unit of work either completes successfully or aborts restoring any updated data to its state prior to execution of the transaction. A transaction which completes its execution successfully is said to be *committed.*
- *Consistency* the actions performed by a transaction must take data from one consistent state to another. The consistent states are defined by system designers. It is therefore the responsibility of application developers to ensure that state data changes and application logic are correct concerning data consistency.
- *Isolation* transaction execution has no effect on, and is not affected by, other concurrent transactions in execution.
- *Durability* any changes made by successful (committed) transactions must be permanent. Subsequent system failures must not cause the unrecoverable loss of changed data.

A transactional unit of work may involve a complex sequence of operations on data. The following transaction called Transfer transfers money between two accounts:

```
transaction Transfer{
        credit(accountA, amount, &newAbalance);
        debit(accountB, amount, &newBbalance);
}
```

In some circumstances, a transaction may decide that it wishes to *abort* the transaction after discovering an abnormal occurrence (e.g. accountB has insufficient funds). Several changes to data, however, may have occurred up to the point where transaction abortion is desired. Those changes must be negated (rolled back) if transaction abortion is successful, leaving all data in a consistent state. Transaction control can be implemented by a DBMS by means of three special commands: BEGIN TRANSACTION, COMMIT and ABORT (also known as ROLLBACK), which allow a client program to specify the nature of program termination so that the DBMS can either commit or abort database updates. The application determines the start of transaction control by executing the BEGIN TRANSACTION command which determines the scope of database recovery if the program aborts. Each transaction normally holds its own private instance of the data which may need to be committed and commit processing is effectively making the private changes permanent by writing it to the database. The transaction phase is terminated by execution of either COMMIT or ABORT commands. If COMMIT is executed or a program terminates normally, any data changes made after the BEGIN TRANSACTION command are made permanent. If ABORT is executed or a program terminates abnormally, any changes to data made after the BEGIN TRANSACTION command are negated. Transaction control is carried out by a server component known as a **transaction processing manager** (TPM) which responds to BEGIN TRANSACTION, COMMIT and ABORT commands by carrying out operations to ensure that data integrity can be maintained. A TPM can be an integral part of a DBMS or a separate component. Transaction processing using a TPM guarantees the integrity of data and has been the basis of on-line information systems (commonly known as on-line transaction processing (OLTP)) since the 1960s. Most OLTP systems were designed to be used on a centralized computer surrounded by dumb terminals. Ensuring data integrity in this environment is relatively straightforward since the application program, TPM and DBMS execute on the same computer.

An aspect of transaction processing relevant to DIS development is whether user interaction is within or outside the scope of commit processing. If a user interacts with a transaction after the BEGIN TRANSACTION command and may determine whether the transaction commits or aborts, the duration of the transaction and commit processing is dependent on user think time, the amount of screen I/O, etc. This type of transaction is known as a *conversational* or *long* transaction. A *non-conversational* or *short* transaction is one which does not involve user interaction within a commit scope. In a long transaction, TPM and DBMS resources are tied up indeterminately. Therefore short transactions are more efficient but limit the flexibility of user interactions, whereas long transactions could be very inefficient but are more flexible. Clearly, a DIS could be implemented using a single long transaction or many small, short transactions with user interaction phases in between. With the advent of graphical user interfaces (GUI), the notion of a transaction is becoming less clear because a GUI offers a user a wide range of control mechanisms which are difficult to map to the beginning and end of commit processing. Many GUI applications adopt the simple but dangerous approach of ignoring transaction processing altogether, requiring the user or application logic to cope with data inconsistency problems.

9.3.1 Concurrency control

Many transactions can be executing concurrently or simultaneously (e.g. in a multiprocessor system) some of which may be accessing the same data record. If a transaction is to achieve consistency and isolation properties, the TPM must ensure that no problems arise due to various transactions interfering with one another. Uncontrolled interleaving of sub-operations of concurrent transactions in execution can lead to four main types of problems (Hackathorn, 1993):

1. *Lost update*   This is illustrated in Figure 9.3(a). Transaction A reads the current balance value. Transaction B updates the balance from £500 to £600. Later, Transaction A imme-

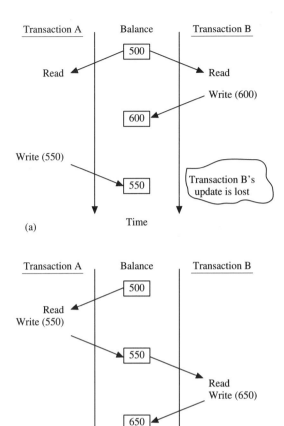

Figure 9.3 Transactional interference and serial execution. (a) Transaction B's update is lost. (b) Correct synchronization through serial execution.

diately updates the balance by adding £50 to the original value, increasing it to £550. The balance now contains £550 and B's update is lost.

2. *Dirty read* A data item (say, CURRENT_BALANCE holding the value £500) is updated to £550 by Transaction A. Subsequently, Transaction B reads the data item (value £550) as the customers current balance. Unfortunately, Transaction A aborts restoring the value £500 to the data item. Transaction B processed a 'dirty' value.

3. *Non-repeatable read* Transaction B reads the current balance which returns the value £500. Transaction A updates the data item to £550. Finally, Transaction B completes its processing by re-reading the current balance (expecting the same value as previously), but the new value £550 is returned.

4. *Phantom record* Transaction B processes all debit and credit transactions for a particular customer by initially reading all relevant rows from a table. While processing the rows, Transaction A inserts a new row corresponding to a new credit transaction. Finally, Transaction A re-reads all rows in the table as part of final processing. The number of rows in the initial read does not match the number returned in the final read.

None of the above problems would arise if all transactions were queued to ensure that they all execute *serially*. An example of this approach is illustrated in Figure 9.3(b). In reality, this approach is not practical because whilst avoiding the above problems, it minimizes the level of concurrency that is achieved. The key to meeting both aims is to serialize execution of only those transaction sub-operations which are operating on the same data items in a data-base and have conflicting operation semantics. If we serialize conflicting operations then we achieve data consistency. A TPM is responsible for using some strategy to achieve serializ-ability between conflicting transactions. A common strategy is to use a **locking** mechanism. Before data can be read or written to, a read or write lock must be requested by the application to obtain exclusive control of the data item. To maximize transaction concurrency where mul-tiple transactions wish to access the same data item, transactions can run concurrently if they all hold read locks to the same data item (sometimes known as a shared lock), but only a sin-gle transaction can run if a write lock (sometimes known as an exclusive lock) is held or if a read lock is held and other transactions are requesting a write lock. If the data item has already been locked by another transaction, the transaction may have to wait until the lock is released (by issuing an unlock command). The circumstances in which a transaction is required to wait for a lock are summarized in Table 9.3.

Table 9.3 Handling lock requests

Lock status of data item	Lock requested by transaction / Outcome	
No lock set	READ / Lock	WRITE / Lock
READ lock set	READ / Lock	WRITE / Wait
WRITE lock set	READ/ Wait	WRITE / Wait

Thus a lock is an effective mechanism for serializing access to the data item depending on the nature of the operation. A *lock manager* is responsible for processing lock and unlock requests. A TPM can also perform the lock manager function in addition to handling commit and abort requests. A lock manager must note whether a data item has been opened for reading, and if so by how many transactions, or for writing, in which case any subsequent requests to read or write should be refused. Transactions should be informed as to whether locks have already been taken out and if so, by whom. Transactions should also be informed of inappropriate use of locks, for example, using a read lock and subsequently trying to update the data item without first requesting a write lock. A *two-phase locking* approach is widely used to ensure that all pairs of conflicting operations of any two transactions are exe-cuted in the same order. Two-phase locking is so named because each transaction must acquire and release locks in two phases. In the first phase, a transaction acquires all locks, and in the second phase, locks are released. Thus, once a transaction releases locks it does not acquire any more locks. In *strict* two-phase locking, locks are held until a transaction commits (or aborts) and data is written to non-volatile storage which prevents dirty reads and other problems.

One major drawback of lock mechanisms is the possibility of *deadlocks*. An example of a deadlock is illustrated in Figure 9.4 using a graphing technique called a *wait-for graph* to depict waiting relationships between concurrent transactions. Transaction A holds a write lock on data item X and has a write lock request pending on data item Y. Transaction B holds a write lock on data item Y and has a write lock request pending on data item X. Both

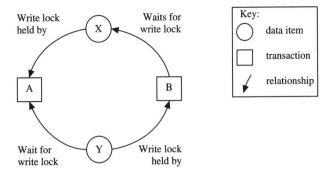

Figure 9.4 Deadlock detection using a wait-for graph.

transactions will wait indefinitely. This is the simplest case of deadlock. More complex cases can arise which involve multiple transactions. Three possible solutions to deadlock problems are prevention, avoidance and detection. In cases where the data items to be locked are known at transaction start time, a preventative solution is to lock all data items. However, this imposes a severe constraint on transaction concurrency and is unlikely to be appropriate for interactive information systems where often the data items required cannot be predicted. A similar technique with similar drawbacks is to order locks totally and require that each transaction acquire its locks in a defined order. An example of an avoidance mechanism is a *time-out*. When a transaction is waiting on a lock, after a fixed amount of time, a transaction must abort. If several transactions are in a deadlock situation, a single transaction timeout may lead to deadlock resolution without other transactions aborting. Detection methods maintain wait-for graphs in order to detect deadlock situations as they arise. Deadlocks are detected by searching for cycles such as illustrated in Figure 9.4. When a deadlock is detected, one or more transactions are selected and aborted in order to break the deadlock. This is an example of a server-initiated transaction abort.

There are alternative approaches to concurrency control which aim to reduce concurrency constraints, avoid deadlocks and lock maintenance overheads inherent in the two-phase locking approach. The **timestamp-based** approach attaches a timestamp to each transaction (for example, the transaction start time). All transaction commits are serialized (totally ordered) on the basis of timestamp order. When conflicts occur, transactions are simply rollbacked and restarted and given a new timestamp. Transactions are selected for rollback on the basis of the associated timestamp value. If a transaction attempts to read or update a data item, then the read or update will only be allowed to proceed if the last update on that data item was carried out by an older transaction; otherwise the requesting transaction is rollbacked and restarted with a new timestamp. This process ensures that transactions are completed in timestamp order when conflicts arise. No locking mechanisms are involved and therefore deadlocks cannot occur. The number of costly transaction restarts, however, increases significantly. Refinements to the basic timestamping method described above have been developed which reduce the level of restarts but usually at the expense of the degree of concurrency. An example of one method, known as conservative timestamping, is described in Bell and Grimson (1992).

The two-phase locking approach can be described as a pessimistic approach to concurrency control because it assumes that conflicts will arise and synchronizes transactions to avoid conflicts. **Optimistic methods** (Kung and Robinson, 1981), which are based on the assumption that in most applications the level of conflicts is low, allow transactions to execute without synchronization until a commit is attempted. At the commit point, a validation procedure is executed to determine whether any conflicts were encountered while it was running. The validation procedure decides whether changes to data items can be committed, if not then the operation must abort. Thus the concurrency control overhead occurs at the commit stage rather than at operation invocation as in the locking and timestamp methods. However, optimistic methods work well only when conflicts are relatively rare occurrences.

The granularity of locking is important. If the whole database needs to be locked if a data item is to be updated in order to ensure data consistency, this has a severe effect on the level of transaction concurrency that can be achieved. Transaction concurrency levels are improved by fine-grained locking mechanisms which lock a particular data record or data record attributes or sets of data records as they are physically stored on a storage device.

9.3.2 Transaction recovery

Where access to a database is critical to the operation of an important business process (e.g. flight reservation), some facilities must be available in the event that a transaction is aborted or a more serious failure occurs. In a distributed system, failures can occur in some parts of the system while the rest keeps on running. When a system is supporting multiple (concurrent) users, recovery from failure can be very complex. Transactional interactions help solve problems associated with concurrency and failure. The atomicity property means that each transaction appears to be indivisble with respect to failures by either completing successfully or not at all. The durability property means that the effects of committed transactions survive subsequent failures. In reality, transactions *do* fail in the middle of execution with potentially disastrous effects on critical data. However, programmers need not concern themselves about failures because the underlying DBMS or transaction management systems implement appropriate recovery mechanisms.

One essential recovery procedure is to regularly back up all databases. At least one copy must be held off-site for disaster recovery purposes. The frequency of backups is dependent on the importance of the data and frequency of updates. Important data is fully backed up daily. Less important data is fully backed up once or twice weekly, and daily changes (an incremental backup) are scheduled daily. This is not enough, however, to ensure atomicity and durability since partial failures can leave a database in a inconsistent state. A typical transaction processing system utilizes three types of memory (Weihl, 1993):

1. **Volatile memory**; all servers use this memory for temporarily holding data being accessed. This is normally small in volume but with very fast access and transfer times. The contents of this memory is lost after a crash. A typical volatile memory device is RAM.
2. **Non-volatile memory**; used to hold data not recently accessed. There is a much lower probability of data being lost from non-volatile memory. A typical non-volatile memory device is a hard disk.
3. **Stable memory**; memory that is assumed to retain data despite failures. Example stable memory configurations are disk mirroring, disk duplexing, server mirroring and RAID (see Section 7.6.3).

Weihl (1993) identifies four kinds of failures:

1. **Transaction abort**; in this case the operations performed by the transaction need to be undone.
2. **Server crash**; the active processes and contents of volatile memory are lost, but the contents of non-volatile and stable memory remain intact.
3. **Media failure**; some or all of the non-volatile memory is lost.
4. **Disaster**; the stable and non-volatile storage are both lost. Other essential components (e.g. the network, servers, workstations, etc.) may also be lost.

We review the recovery methods required for each of the above failure types.

Transaction abort recovery

Transaction aborts can be *transaction-induced* when an abort command is executed, *system-induced* (for example, when the transaction is aborted to break a conflict situation) or can be due to unforeseen circumstances (e.g. program failure due to a software bug). In these situations the transaction management system needs to record information to identify which transactions are affected and all data required to undo any previously updated data items.

A **transaction log** holds important information about all transactions against a database (e.g. updates, deletes or inserts) over a specified period of time. Data such as the transaction start and end time, and any updates can be used to undo transaction aborts. When a transaction requires an update, insert or delete operation to be carried out on the database, *before-images* and *after-images* will be placed in the transaction log file. The before-image is a copy of a record as it exists in the database before the operation is actioned, an after-image is the state of the record immediately after the operation is executed. Thus a transaction log contains:

- the transaction name;
- the name of the data item affected by the operation;
- the before-image prior to the operation execution (the **undo** record);
- the after-image which the data item will have after the operation execution (the **redo** record);
- other log management information relating to the transaction.

The log also contains log records of the type:

- {Transaction name, **start**} – the specified transaction has started.
- {Transaction name, **commit**} - the named transaction has committed. This signifies a partial commit since the transaction is not actually committed until all log records are written permanently to the database.

A marker or *checkpoint* is placed in the transaction log at a point when all outstanding updates in temporary buffers are written permanently to the database and all active transactions completed. The checkpoint data provides information concerning all transactions active at that point in time. The transaction log is absolutely vital for the ability of transaction processing management to implement transaction atomicity and durability, therefore, it should reside in stable memory.

Recovery from transaction abort depends on how database updates are carried out. There are two approaches:

1. *Write-through updates* in which updates to the database are applied synchronously to the actual database in non-volatile memory as a transaction runs.
2. *Deferred update* in which the update record is first transferred to a DBMS buffer in volatile memory. The buffered record is later transferred (asynchronously) to the actual database held in non-volatile memory (the buffer is said to have been **flushed**). Volatile memory is much faster, and delays associated with writing to non-volatile memory are avoided by minimizing synchronous writes to the database. This method of update introduces an additional failure condition; when a failure occurs while records are in a buffer but not yet flushed.

This gives rise to two transaction logging and transaction processing procedures which are summarized in Tables 9.4 and 9.5.

Table 9.4 Logging and processing for write-through update transaction processing

Type of transaction operation	Logging and processing procedure
Update	Record undo and redo records in the log; update the database.
Read	Read the desired data from the database.
Commit	Discard the undo record from the log.
Abort	Use the undo records in the log to back out the transaction's updates (in reverse order in which they were originally written to the log).

Table 9.5 Logging and processing for deferred-update transaction processing

Type of transaction operation/condition	Logging and processing procedure
Update	Record undo and redo records in the log; Redo record written to buffer.
Read	Read the desired data by combining the redo log and the database to determine the authoritative data.
Commit	Flush the relevant buffer.
Abort	Discard the transaction's redo record.
Failure occurs while records are in a buffer but not yet flushed.	Determine the status of the updating transaction at the time of failure: IF transaction issued a commit THEN apply the transaction's redo records from the log to the database to ensure that all updates have been committed. ELSE apply undo records from the log to the database to ensure proper abortion and rollback of any partial changes.

Server crash recovery

The transaction log is also used to recover from server crashes. Undo and redo records, checkpoints and other information (e.g. what transactions were active and their status) are used to recover a database to a previously consistent state. The last known consistent state is recorded at the last checkpoint. Using the transaction log, the recovery manager works through it deciding which transactions have to be undone (because they were active but uncommitted) and which have to be redone (because they were committed).

Media failure recovery

Recovery from media failure (e.g. a disk crash) is facilitated by duplicating transaction logs and databases. This ranges from archiving to magnetic tapes or optical disks, through to online duplexing or mirroring for fast recovery and fault tolerance.

9.3.3 Nested and distributed transactions

An extension of the notion of atomic transactions is the idea of a *nested* transaction which simply has subtransactions which can run concurrently. Each subtransaction can consist of other lower-level subtransactions thus forming a *transaction tree* of relationships between subtransactions and parent transaction. Subtransactions are serializable as part of the parent transaction, and failure of a subtransaction does not force the parent to fail. Thus structuring a transaction into a nested transaction can provide enhanced failure protection mechanisms. Concurrency control mechanisms need to be modified to support nested transactions. For example, in two-phase locking, the locking manager would need to ensure that no concurrent active transaction holds a conflicting lock at any level (subtransaction) of the transaction tree. When a subtransaction commits, its locks are 'inherited' by its parent; when it aborts, its locks are discarded (Weihl, 1993). The effects of a subtransaction are not permanent until the the the top-level parent (the root) of the subtransaction commits. If a nested transaction aborts, all effects of its descendants are undone.

When data is distributed across multiple servers, each transaction is divided into subtransactions, one for each server at which data accessed by the transaction is stored. Each subtransaction is executed at the relevant server and is treated as an atomic transaction by the server at which it is executing. Thus a subtransaction must be synchronized both with other transactions executing on the server and with other subtransactions belonging to the same nested transaction. We refer to this type of nested transaction as a **distributed transaction**. We will return to distributed transactions in Section 9.5.

9.4 DISTRIBUTION OPTIONS

Much of the discussion in the previous section assumed that all tables are located in a single database controlled by a single DBMS (i.e. a centralized DBMS configuration). In reality an organization is likely to create multiple databases some of which are remote from a user who wishes to access them. The controlled distribution of data over multiple servers possibly residing in multiple locations offers the following potential benefits.

- *Recognition of the distributed nature of organizational activities*   Many organizations operate on a multi-site basis. The data kept at the source site is often pertinent to the operation of that site only or the site is the one at which most of the processing involving the data is carried out. Local data, however, is often relevant to the overall operation of the organization and may be used for a variety of purposes. An organization may wish to permit local collection and updating of data and global shared access. This approach to data management places data closest to its source and data access performance is improved.
- *Increased reliability and availability*   In a centralized database configuration, DBMS failure means that the *whole* information system reliant on the data is down. In a distributed data management environment failure of a DBMS at one site does not necessarily prevent

other DBMSs or sites from operating. This can improve the overall reliability of an information system.

- *Local control of data*   One of the objectives of centralized databases is to impose centralized control of data to ensure that data consistency, integrity and security requirements are met for the organization as a whole. If data is distributed and controlled by end-user departments who are the primary source and users of the data, then those departments may have control of *their* data. Data can still be shared on a global basis by implementing remote data access mechanisms. This approach is compatible with the increasing trend towards local autonomy.

- *Increased performance*   Large centralized systems can be slow performers due mainly to the sheer volume of data and transactions being handled. If data were distributed in such a way that local sites could have quite small repositories of data, this results in faster local access minimizing the requirement to transfer large amounts of data over information networks. Appropriate distributed data design can minimize remote data access and large data transfers which can be slow due to the overhead of network access. Another performance advantage of distributing data is the support for parallel access (updates and retrievals) to distributed data.

Amongst the traditional data models, relational DBMSs provide the best foundations to support data distribution because of their ability to handle data partitioning and combine data partitions held at different sites into a single view to users. This is primarily because of the simple two-dimensional table structure in which data is held.

It is an accepted fact that large organizations have mountains of data stored in a variety of ways using a variety of data management products including DBMSs. This section analyses ways of managing the distribution of data in order to avoid excessive, uncontrolled duplication of data which often leads to loss of data integrity. It is not easy to decide where data should be held. There are five main approaches: partition, extract, replicate, cache and centralize. These are based on the three fundamental design approaches for distributed systems defined in Chapter 7: partition, replicate and cache.

9.4.1 Centralized data

A perfectly sound decision may be to centralize data by storing databases that service a community of users in one central place and directing all client requests to it. To reduce complexity, generally it makes sense to centralize data in certain circumstances, for example, if large quantities of data are frequently updated from multiple sites or departments or if most users access data equally and need to see the most up-to-date data values. This is illustrated in Figure 9.5. If a customer wishes to conduct business from any supplier branch, for example, and transaction data is required to be up-to-date then it is likely that a centralized server solution is applicable. This is a characteristic of reservation systems for hotels, flights, cars and so on. All SQL commands are serviced by a single database server. SQL commands are transferred to the database server via a remote data access service.

9.4.2 Partitioned data

Here the database is partitioned into several fragments and distributed across two or more servers. Thus, a single database is, without duplication, divided into smaller databases resid-

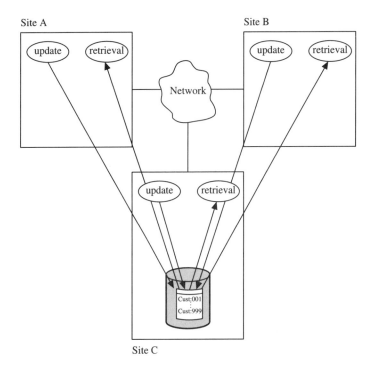

Figure 9.5 Centralization.

ing on multiple servers. The group of primary servers over which a database is partitioned has no data in common although some aspects of the structure of data are common. For example a primary server may be installed in each regional office of an insurance company and the customer database partitioned so that each regional server stores the records of all customers within that region. This is an example of **horizontal partitioning**, and is illustrated in Figure 9.6. Equally, the organization might have chosen **vertical partitioning** where all customer records are stored at each region, but the table columns are partitioned across each region such that no non-primary key column is duplicated. In effect, in vertical partitioning each region holds its own view of the database which does not overlap with the view of any other region. The insurance company, for example, may be structured functionally into pensions, life insurance, car insurance, etc., and each server will only hold attributes (columns) pertaining to the specific view of the data required by that business function.

If all customers in a region visit branches only in the same region (served by the same regional server) then all database reads and updates are confined to the region's database and no requests are directed to other primary servers. Partitioning in this case provides the best solution since each region can maintain its own data. If, however, customers are allowed to use regional and non-regional branches then the attraction of partitioning is determined by the ratio of local to remote requests (particularly updates) for each region. If only a marginal amount of requests flow between regions then partitioning could still be attractive but request handling is more complex requiring a request resolution protocol in order to determine which server can handle a given request and handle request routing.

The feasibility of partitioning is also determined by whether ownership of data can be

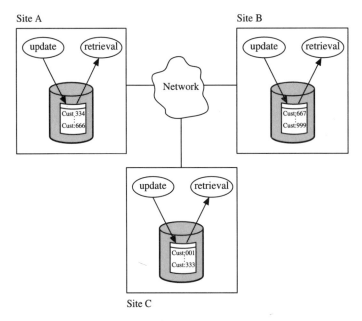

Figure 9.6 An example of horizontal partitioning.

clearly identified. An aid to identifying data ownership is to identify which events create, modify, read and delete an entity. Secondly, events need to be mapped to the location of user roles which trigger those events. Thirdly, remote access frequencies are required to determine the extent to which processing is related to data partitions. Remote access frequencies to other locations indicate the need for a request resolution protocol to ensure that requests are handled by the appropriate regional server.

The complexity of a client request is a factor when considering whether partitioning is appropriate. When a request is likely to update tables which are stored on different servers as a single unit of work, query processing is much more complex because of the need to handle partial failures. In general it can be seen that partitioning is attractive when ownership of data is clearly identified and requests are confined to the local site.

9.4.3 Extracted data

The second technique is to copy the data. For example, each regional server contains a copy of a database residing on a main server. If the data on the main server never changes then this is a simple and inexpensive technique. Extraction is illustrated in Figure 9.7. If the data on the main server changes frequently then data at the regional servers become rapidly out-of-date (i.e. a loss of data consistency). Loss of data consistency may not be a critical issue if, for example, applications using data at the regional servers are only interested in historical data for post-analysis (e.g. accounting data at the end of a period). There is never a need to update the historical data or keep it in step with the now changed data residing on a main server.

When a copy of data is generated with the intent that this data will not be updated it is called an *extract*. An extract is therefore a snapshot view of data at a particular moment in time. Hackathorn (1993) usefully defines several types of extract mechanisms. A *simple extract* mechanism is where an extract is carried out by the user using SQL SELECT statements and the result set stored in a local table for further processing. A *timestamped extract* mechanism performs an extract and associates it with a timestamp so that applications can make a judgement as to the currency or validity of the data. A *refreshed extract* is an automated extract mechanism which refreshes the extract periodically without the user explicitly requesting it.

9.4.4 Replicated data

Copied data with the intent that the data will be updated is known as a *replica* and is shown in Figure 9.7. The value of a replica depends on the data consistency among all copies and the level of data consistency required by an application. For example, a replica of a product database may not contain up-to-date data on product specifications but this may not pose a problem to some types of customer queries such as 'can you tell me how much product A costs?'. Maintaining data consistency is a significant challenge in the field of replicated databases. Clearly, the **replication control method** chosen must suit the purpose for which the data is to be used. For example, a strict consistency method such as primary-copy or primary-backup can be employed which guarantees that read requests return up-to-date data by applying updates immediately to replicas.

A strict consistency approach may be unsuitable, however, in configurations which require a large number of servers and where 100 per cent data consistency is not essential. Also, an update can fail if a replica is unavailable. If the probability that a replica is available is p, then the probability of n replicas being available is p^n which tends to zero as n increases. Ideally, in the interests of local autonomy, transactions which update the local replica successfully should not fail because one or more remote replicas are unavailable. A loose consistency method can be employed in which the local copy is updated first and other replicas are guaranteed to be updated but at varied times to suit the application. This *deferred update* approach

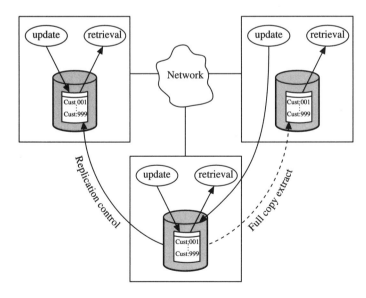

Figure 9.7 Replication and extraction.

reduces the complexity of replica control, improves transaction performance (providing the use of out-of-date data can be tolerated) and increases the practical limit for the number of replicas that can be employed. The replication control method determines how read and update requests are handled. Replication is certainly not the best solution for all applications. It may be an attractive method if storage volumes and update requests are low or if data availability is a relatively high priority.

9.4.5 Cached data

A cache is temporary (dynamic) replication of data. For example, in the insurance company scenario described earlier, one server acts as the primary server and regional servers temporarily make a local copy of data from the primary server to improve performance by reducing network load (or avoiding network access) and reducing the workload on the primary. An example configuration is given in Figure 9.8. Caches work very well when data is likely to be accessed frequently once referenced and the data is hardly ever updated (for example, when database tables are static lookup tables). As well as improving performance, caching is also an attractive technique because it does not change the essence of the underlying client/server interaction.

The main problem with caching is the need for a cache consistency mechanism to ensure that users receive up-to-date data as data is continually being updated and to handle ageing data being held in caches. Cache consistency approaches were detailed in Chapter 7.

9.4.6 Choice of approach

Six factors determine the choice of technique Hackathorn (1993), Renaud, (1992), Breu *et al.*, (1994).

1. Data ownership. Ownership is the degree to which a database can be partitioned into appropriate fragments and ownership of each fragment clearly identified. Ideally, each

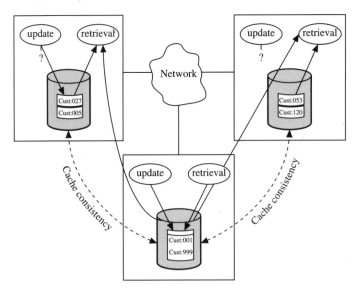

Figure 9.8 Caching.

fragment should map directly to a local site on which the owners of the data are located and where customer transactions are handled. Ownership can be classified as local, or non-local.

2. Locality of access. How often data is read or updated by remote sites. Affinity factors should be calculated for `read`, `update` and `total` requests to determine the extent to which remote `reads` and `updates` are confined to a single site.

3. Data volatility. The degree to which the database is updated during normal usage. The volatility of a database is measured in terms of size and flowrate. Suppose a database contains on average 200 000 records which are updated at the rate 100 000 records per month. The volatility is 100 000/200 000 = 0.5. The database is therefore 50 per cent volatile. In general, large volatile databases should be candidates for partitioning and small, non-volatile databases good candidates for replication.

4. Data currency. This is related to data volatility, but measures the business value of data and is an indicator of how important to the client that data is up-to-date. This gives an indication of whether a strict or loose consistency approach is appropriate for replication control should replication be seen as the most suitable approach. The refresh interval, in the case of replication using loose consistency, is dependent on this factor. In some situations, for example in airline reservation applications, temporary periods of data inconsistency (e.g. between refreshes) cannot be tolerated as double booking of a seat could occur. In this case a strict consistency control method should be employed. All time-critical data, e.g. reservation booking and emergency call-logging systems, are examples of systems which should employ strict consistency replication control methods.

5. Data volume. The storage size of the database compared with the typical storage capacity available. If the data volume is extremely large and cannot easily be partitioned, a centralized approach may be appropriate. Data volume can be described as high or low.

6. Data availability. A measure of the importance of the database to the information systems that use it. If availability is critical then some high-priority information systems cannot continue if the data becomes unavailable. Unavailability of non-critical data may lead to a degraded service that would be tolerated by users.

It is the combination of values for the above factors that lead to choice of a particular option. These factors may lead to a single option or a hybrid option (e.g. replication with caching).

9.4.7 Accessing distributed data – SQL extensions

Whether data is centralized, partitioned, extracted, replicated or cached, it needs to be accessed from application programs. In the spirit of transparency of access, that is, concealment of the distributed nature of the data, the mechanism used to access data should be independent of the DBMS product or hardware used or where it is located. An important consideration for relational DBMSs is how to process SQL commands when some of the data is distributed across the network. Essentially there are two options.

1. Move the data from the server to the client workstation executing the SQL commands (i.e. move the data to the command). This is achieved using a remote file access mechanism where tables are held in individual files, or using a remote data access mechanism where the contents of all selected tables are retrieved. The main drawback to this approach is the

potentially heavy network traffic which results from transfer of the contents of the database files from the server to the client workstation.

2. Move the SQL commands from the client workstations to the server where the data is (i.e. move the command to the data). This is achieved using a remote data access mechanism where the SQL commands are transferred to the server running the remote DBMS. The advantage of this approach is that accessing a variety of multi-vendor databases can be made transparent since all recognize virtually the same language interface: SQL. As long as the application (e.g. spreadsheet, database, word processor or programming language) can create and transport SQL statements to the DBMS and receive the results of executing the statement it does not need to know what or where the DBMS is.

The second option is generally the preferred approach mainly because it minimizes network traffic. Often DBMSs geared to this approach are known as 'SQL databases' or 'client/server databases' and provide, in addition to the basic DBMS functionality, the ability to allow applications running on client workstations to create SQL statements and transport them to the DBMS running on a remote server.

9.4.8 Achieving access and location transparency

SQL was originally defined as a relational data language in the days when centralized DBMSs dominated. It is therefore not surprising to find that the SQL standards do not define mechanisms and communication protocols for transporting SQL between client and remote server platforms. Unfortunately, although attempts have been made to standardize SQL and to extend it to incorporate mechanisms required for client/server DBMSs, there are many dialects with unique extensions peculiar to particular database products. This all serves to make interoperability and transparency difficult. In practice, integrating data from multiple data sources using SQL can be a very difficult exercise.

In the relational data model optimal access paths are determined by the DBMS. An SQL query statement specifies what data is required. Query optimization is the process of determining the optimum access paths to satisfy a data query. Although providing transparency for users reading data is simpler than for transactional transparency, distributed query processing is still complex due to the need to optimize access paths when tables may be spread across multiple servers. The optimization rules must take account of new factors, for example:

- the cost of accessing and transferring data across a network;
- the potential gain in performance of parallel processing of sub-queries.

There is also the issue of who carries out global query optimization in a distributed database environment. The process of query optimization is more complex in the case of distributed data because the optimum is selected from a greater selection of possibilities (often many times more than in a centralized system) all of which produce the same result. The main choices to be made by the optimizer are (Bell and Grimson, 1992):

1. the order of execution of operations;
2. the access methods for the relevant operations;
3. the algorithms (e.g. relational JOINs) for carrying out the operations;
4. the order of data movements between sites.

9.4.9 ISO remote database access (RDA)

The ISO remote database access (RDA) standard (ISO 9579-1) and the SQL Specialization (ISO 9579-2) are OSI standards to deliver remote data access protocol in an OSI environment based on the client/server model. Since OSI is designed to provide interworking in a heterogeneous environment, it follows that RDA is designed to operate with a multitude of SQL-based services. The client side is known as the RDA client and the server side, the RDA server. The network transport must be OSI compliant. The RDA standard defines comprehensive services to RDA clients as shown in Table 9.6 which lists the various services.

The SQL specialization standard maps the RDA services to SQL-based services. The current standard maps to SQL version 1.0. Work is progressing on future versions of the SQL standard. Another notable development to try to alleviate some of the difficulties of data integration at the data manipulation language level was the creation of a consortium of major database vendors called the SQL Access Group (SAG) who have attempted to define a comprehensive specification for a common interface for applications wanting to access various data sources. In terms of *de facto* standards, Microsoft produced its own specification, called open database connectivity (ODBC), based on the SAG specification.

9.5 DISTRIBUTED TRANSACTION PROCESSING

Data partitioned over two or more data servers introduces additional challenges. To illustrate these problems, three types of situations are considered:

1. A client invokes a *remote request* which is a single operation on data held on a single server.
2. A client invokes a *remote transaction* which contains multiple operations on data held on a single server.
3. A client invokes a *distributed transaction* which contains multiple operations on data partitioned over two or more servers. Each operation in a transaction operates on data held either on a single server or on multiple servers.

Remote requests

This is the simplest case as illustrated in Figure 9.9. The remote operation must be directed at the server which holds the data required. The server name may be specified by the client or supplied by the DBMS based on knowledge of where data is currently placed.

Remote transactions

An example of a remote transaction is shown in Figure 9.9. The server runs the DBMS, TPM and lock manager that together ensure transactional execution semantics. As with remote operations, the remote transaction must be directed to the server which holds the data required.

Distributed transactions

A distributed transaction involves multiple servers as shown in Figure 9.10. Transactional execution semantics is much more difficult to achieve simply because each operation can fail

Table 9.6 Remote database access and ODBC services

Type of task	RDA service element	Description	ODBC API	Description
Connect to data source	R-Initialize	Establish dialogue with RDA server	SQLAllocEnv SQLAllocConnect	Obtain an environment handle Obtain a connection handle
			SQLConnect SQLDriverConnect SQLBrowseConnect SQLSetConnectOption SQLGetConnectOption SQLGetStmtOption SQLSetStmtOption	Connect to an ODBC driver (server) Set and get connect options
Obtain information about data sources			SQLDataSources SQLGetInfo SQLGetFunctions SQLGetTypeInfo	Return information about data sources, driver functions and supported data types.
Prepare to send SQL request	R-Open	Open a data resource for access by subsequent operations.	SQLAllocStmt SQLPrepare SQLSetParam	Allocate statement handle. Prepare SQL statement. Assign parameter storage
	R-DefineDBL R-DropDBL	Define a stored procedure. Nullify a defined command.	SQLGetCursorName SQLSetCursorName SQLSetScrollOptions	Return cursor name. Specify a cursor name. Set cursor behaviour.
Submit SQL request to the server	R-ExecuteDBL	Execute a single query language statement	SQLExecute SQLExecDirect	Submit prepared SQL request. Submit a SQL statement.
Invoke stored procedure	R-InvokeDBL	Execute an already stored procedure		

Category	R- functions	Description	SQL functions	Description
Obtain result set	R-ExecuteDBL	Contained in the result parameters of the R-ExecuteDBL service element as defined in a specialization standard.	SQLRowCount	Return number of rows affected.
			SQLNumResultCols	Return the number of columns.
			SQLDescribeCol	Describe a column.
			SQLColAttributes	Describe attributes of a column.
			SQLBindCol	Assigns storage for column.
			SQLFetch	Returns a result row.
			SQLGetData	Returns a subset of column data.
	R-Status	Determine the status of an operation.	SQLSetPos	Set cursor position.
			SQLMoreResults	Get next result set if available.
			SQLError	Returns error or status information.
Transaction management	R-BeginTransaction	Begin a new transaction.	SQLTransact	Commit or rollback a transaction.
	R-Commit	Commit a transaction.		
	R-Rollback	Rollback a transaction.		
Terminate or cancel	R-Cancel	Cancel an operation.	SQLFreeStmt	Closes statement processing.
	R-Close	Close a data source.	SQLCancel	Cancels an SQL statement.
	R-Terminate	Terminate a dialogue.	SQLDisconnect	Close connection.
			SQLFreeConnect	Release connection handle.
			SQLFreeEnv	Release environment handle.
Obtain data dictionary information			SQLColumnPrivileges	Return privileges information
			SQLColumns	Return table column information.
			SQLForeignKeys	Return foreign key columns.
			SQLPrimaryKeys	Return primary key columns.
			SQLProcedureColumns	Return result set columns and parameters for stored procedure.
			SQLProcedures	List stored procedure names.
			SQLSpecialColumns	Return special table information.
			SQLStatistics	Return indexing and other stats.
			SQLTablePrivileges	List tables and their privileges.
			SQLTables	Return all table names.

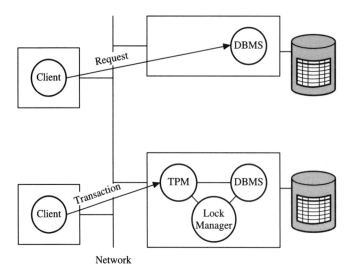

Figure 9.9 A remote request or transaction.

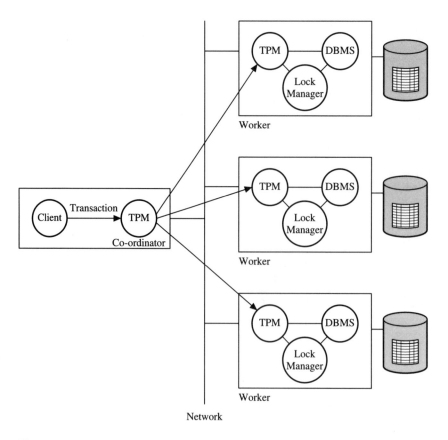

Figure 9.10 A distributed transaction.

independently. If the data changed by a distributed transaction is only reflected at some servers, the integrity and consistency of information will be lost. The technical challenge is to ensure that all servers commit or that all servers abort.

Distributed transactions introduce a more complex failure model. Failures can occur at the client end, at one or more servers, or in the network . A client failure will be noticed by the interacting user who can respond by resubmitting the transaction that was being processed. A system failure can result in a server losing all its variables in volatile memory that map to many active transactions. Media failure (e.g. hard disk failure) can occur at a server and result in permanent loss of data. Network failure results in lost messages. Under any failure condition, a server must be able to restart and reflect all committed or aborted transactions.

9.5.1 Two-phase commit processing

In a distributed system in which data is distributed over multiple servers connected by an information network, the concept of **global atomicity** is introduced, that is, the need to ensure that all the servers involved in a distributed transaction reach a consistent decision about whether to commit or abort the transaction. Data inconsistency will result if some servers are allowed to commit and some to abort the transaction. The most common solution to this problem is the **two-phase commit** (2PC) protocol which allows each server involved in a distributed transaction to co-ordinate their actions and collectively decide to commit or abort a transaction.

In the 2PC protocol, a client program is not concerned with the co-ordination of each server that it invites to complete a transaction, instead one server must act as the **co-ordinator**. This may be the first server from which a client requests a service in a distributed transaction. Each server that holds relevant data will become a **worker** (also known as a participant). Note that the co-ordinating server may also be a worker. Each worker will inform the co-ordinator when it joins the transaction. Every worker is responsible for local transaction recovery using its own transaction log and recovery mechanisms. The workers will execute local operations on behalf of the distributed transaction until the client informs the co-ordinator that it wishes to commit or abort the transaction. At this point the first phase of the two-phase commit protocol begins. Figure 9.11 shows how the co-ordinating server

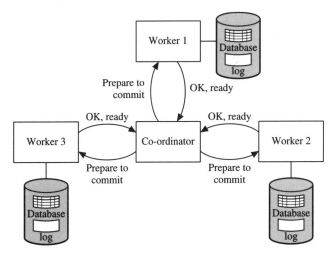

Figure 9.11 Two-phase commit: phase 1 – prepare to commit.

receives a request from the client to commit the transaction and begins its co-ordinating dia-logue with each working server. The co-ordinator asks each worker if they can commit. Each server replies 'yes' after writing all recovery information into a recovery-log stored on non-volatile storage. If a server encounters a problem, it responds negatively and the co-ordinator sends an abort command to all workers, and aborts the client transaction.

If all workers respond positively indicating they are ready to commit, the co-ordinator begins phase two of the protocol as shown in Figure 9.12. All answers received from workers are compared by the co-ordinator. If all answers were yes then the co-ordinating server will inform all workers that they can also commit by sending a 'global commit' message. They respond by making data changes permanent. Having committed their changes the workers inform the co-ordinator individually. The co-ordinator then removes all information about the location of each worker and the client is informed that the transaction has been committed as requested. If any of the servers (co-ordinator or worker) had not been able to commit their changes then the co-ordinator would have informed all workers to abort the transaction by send-ing a 'global abort' message. The client would also be advised of the abortion.

The two-phase commit protocol ensures proper co-ordination between relevant workers (servers). If a worker fails to respond, for example, due to network partitioning as a result of failed network links, the co-ordinator can detect this condition by means of a **time-out mech-anism**. If no response is received after a time-out has occurred, the co-ordinator will assume a failure condition and request all other workers to abort the transaction. Similarly, if the co-ordinator fails, a worker can detect this condition by time-outs. A client will abort the transac-tion after repeatedly attempting to receive a response from the failed co-ordinator. Techniques such as sequence control are required to ensure that if a client retries, transactional operations are not executed more than once. The 2PC protocol is summarized as follows.

1. The co-ordinator performs 'begin transaction' processing and asks all workers whether or not they are prepared to commit the local transaction.

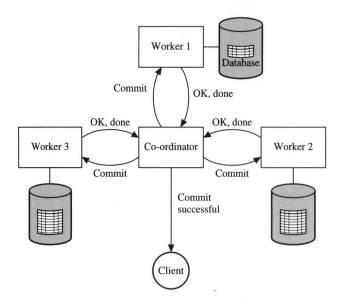

Figure 9.12 Two-phase commit: phase 2 – commit.

2. Each worker responds with either commit or abort acknowledgement.
3. If a worker responds with 'commit' acknowledgement, it waits to receive from the co-ordinator either:
   — a 'global commit' message (if all workers sent a 'commit' acknowledgement) in which case the worker performs local commit processing and sends an 'I have commited' acknowledgement;
   — a 'global abort' message (if one or more workers sent an 'abort' or the co-ordinator timed out) in which case the worker performs local abort processing and the co-ordinator performs 'abort transaction' processing.
4. If a worker responds with an 'abort' acknowledgement, it is free to abort the local transaction.
5. When the co-ordinator receives 'I have commited transaction' acknowledgements from all workers, it performs 'end transaction' processing.

The two-phase commit protocol described, is a **blocking protocol** because control will not return to the client until two-phase commit processing has completed. In particular, a client waits until operations are committed (or aborted) at all relevant remote servers and that all failure conditions are dealt with successfully. This can introduce a significant performance overhead particularly when the number of servers involved is large and concurrency limits are reduced because valuable server resources are held for longer. In the interests of local autonomy, performance and maximizing concurrency, it is desirable to implement a **non-blocking protocol**. Distributed systems with unreliable communications do not admit non-blocking solutions to the atomic commitment problem (Skeen, 1982). If reliable communication is assumed, a number of non-blocking protocols are possible as detailed in Skeen (1982, 1985) and Babaoglu and Toueg (1993). Skeen (1982) presents a **three-phase commit** (3PC) **protocol** which is inherently non-blocking in the presence of server or network failures (except when all servers fail or are isolated in other network partitions). The 3PC protocol enhances the 2PC protocol by introducing a **pre-commit** phase prior to the global commit/abort phase to reduce the uncertainty period while waiting for a 'global commit' or 'global abort' message from the co-ordinator. The 3PC protocol is summarized as follows:

1. The co-ordinator asks all workers whether or not they are prepared to commit the local transaction.
2. Each worker responds with either commit or abort acknowledgement.
3. If a worker responds with 'commit' acknowledgement, it waits to receive from the co-ordinator either:
   — a 'global pre-commit' message (if all workers sent a 'commit' acknowledgement), which indicates to the worker that all other workers have voted to commit and that it (the worker) will *definitely* commit in due course unless it fails. The worker responds by sending a 'pre-commit' acknowledgement;
   — a 'global abort' message (if one or more workers sent an 'abort' or the co-ordinator timed out) in which case the worker performs local abort processing and the co-ordinator performs 'abort transaction' processing.
4. If a worker responds with 'pre-commit' acknowledgement, it waits to receive from the co-ordinator either:
   — a 'global commit' message (if all workers sent a 'pre-commit' acknowledgement) in which case the worker performs local commit processing and sends an 'I have commited' acknowledgement;

— a 'global abort' message (if one or more workers sent an 'abort' or the co-ordinator timed out) in which case the worker performs local abort processing and the co-ordinator performs 'abort transaction' processing.

5. If a worker responds with an 'abort' acknowledgement, it is free to abort the local trans-action.

6. When the co-ordinator receives 'I have commited transaction' acknowledgements from all workers, it performs 'end transaction' processing.

Although both the co-ordinator and workers continue to experience periods of uncer-tainty, all local TPMs have been informed of a global decision to commit (signalled by the 'global pre-commit' message) prior to the first process performing local commit processing and can therefore act independently in the event of failure (Bell and Grimson, 1992). To pre-vent blocking, workers may need to communicate with each other and consider a large num-ber of system states in order to proceed with the correct global decision towards transaction termination. The main drawbacks of 3PC and other non-blocking protocols are that they are more costly (in time) and more complex to program and understand than a 2PC protocol. Alternatively, a non-blocking atomic commitment protocol based on 2PC and reliable broad-cast communication is described in Babaoglu and Toueg (1993).

Transaction management technology has evolved to the extent that it can offer good sup-port to organizations that wish to implement the various types of distributed transaction pro-cessing, concurrency control and recovery mechanisms discussed previously. There is a need, however, for a standard architecture to allow TPM, lock manager and two-phase commit functionality to interwork across many different server platforms and transaction processing environments. Transaction-based information systems will then be portable and interopera-ble. A common model for structuring distributed transaction processing systems is the X/Open distributed transaction processing (DTP) model developed by the X/Open consor-tium, as illustrated in Figure 9.13. It has been designed to meet portability and interoperability requirements by defining four standard components:

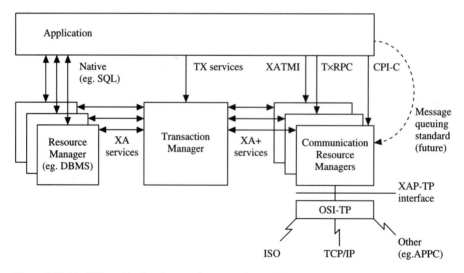

Figure 9.13 The X/Open distributed transaction processing model.

1. *Transaction managers* co-ordinate transactions by acting as the co-ordinator.
2. *Resource managers* which implement the 'worker' functions that provide access to the shared data utilized by transactions.
3. *Applications programs* which define transactions and commit units.
4. *Interface services* two service types have been defined:
   - *TX services:* the interface between applications and transaction managers. The main services are `tx_begin`, `tx_commit` and `tx_rollback`.
   - *XA services:* the interface between transaction manager and resource managers. The transaction manager issues an `xa_prepare` to relevant resource managers as part of the two-phase commit process. An `xa_commit` is issued by the transaction manager on receipt of confirmation that each resource manager can commit.

Many commercial distributed transaction processing products are modelled on the X/Open standard. The communications resource manager enables the integration of multiple transactional services, possibly using middleware such as RPC, message queuing and other mechanisms, through standard interfaces. For example, X/Open has defined a standard for transactional RPC called **TxRPC**. Communications resource manager to transaction monitor dialogue is supported by an enhanced form of XA services known **XA+**. Thus, with this standard, multiple resource managers and multiple middleware are supported through standard interfaces.

9.6 DISTRIBUTED DATABASE SYSTEMS

From the perspective of a database user, it is desirable to gain all the benefits derived from distributing data without worrying about where the data of interest is placed and how to construct the appropriate data manipulation language statements (e.g. SQL) to retrieve it from multiple server locations. A **distributed database** (DDB) can be described as a *logically integrated collection of shared data which is physically distributed across multiple servers connected by an information network.* A **distributed database management system** (DDBMS) is defined as the software to manage a distributed database in such a way that distribution aspects are transparent to the user. In general, a DDBMS supports the development of distributed databases which 'to the user, ...looks and behaves exactly like a non-distributed database' (Date, 1987).

If the database system is relatively small and is located on few servers, a client/server database solution using a remote data access service hides a lot of the complexity providing the SQL query is relatively simple (e.g. a remote operation or remote transaction). If the database system consists of large-scale (gigabyte) tables spread over multiple servers, then this complexity needs to be concealed from the user. Ideally, distributed data is presented to users based on a *global d*atabase (defined by a global conceptual schema) and a DBMS which automatically (transparently) maps global entities to entities in each local database (each defined by a local conceptual schema). The global database is visible to users and the mappings to local databases concealed to achieve distribution transparency. The data manipulation language used by users is based on the global conceptual schema and processed by that part of the DBMS that maintains the global database.

In the most strict interpretation of a DDBMS, full distribution transparency is implemented. Global database design, global schema definition, database fragmentation, mapping to local databases and distributed query and transaction processing are all integrated into the DDBMS. Date (1987) suggests that a DDBMS is characterized by:

- local autonomy and no reliance on a central site;
- continuous operation in the presence of failures;
- local independence;
- fragmentation (partition) and replication independence;
- distributed query and transaction processing;
- hardware, operating system, network and DBMS independence (heterogeneity).

Achieving all of the above is technically very challenging indeed. In the next section we outline various approaches to implementating a DDBMS.

9.6.1 Classifying DDBMS architectures

Different DDBMS architectures are created by different levels of integration of the components of a DDBMS and whether the same or different DBMSs are used at the local servers. There are three main factors which differentiate the various architectures.

1. The degree of **integration** between DDBMS components. A high degree of intregration is desirable because full distribution transparency is more easily achieved.
2. The degree of **local autonomy** or local control of data supported by the DDBMS. It is now frequently the case that servers which support DDBMS components are under separate and independent control. Administration authorities who control a database are often willing to let others share the data only if they retain control. Integration of DDBMS components is much more difficult where the degree of local autonomy is high. Sheth and Larson (1990) distinguish four types of local autonomy:
   - **design autonomy**, the ability of an administrative authority to design and implement the data model, database, storage structures and management and integrity mechanisms;
   - **association autonomy**, the ability of an administrative authority to decide whether and how much to share with others in the distributed system. This includes the ability to couple and uncouple from the distributed database system as they please;
   - **communication autonomy**, the ability of an administrative authority to decide whether and how to respond to a request to communicate with other DDBMS components;
   - **execution autonomy**, the ability of an administrative authority to decide whether and how to handle externally generated operations. For example, execution autonomy is exercised by treating an externally generated operation in the same way as local operations and to abort it if it is in conflict with a local transaction. An external system cannot enforce an order of execution of locally executed operations.
3. Whether a DDBMS is **homogeneous**; the use of the same DBMS at local servers (each may be running on the same or different hardware, software and communication systems), or **heterogeneous**; the use of different DBMSs. Heterogeneity in this context refers to differences in data models (hierarchical, network or relational) and at the system level (e.g. transaction management primitives and techniques, hardware and software requirements, and communications capabilities). One aspect of heterogeneity which is little understood and highly problematic is *semantic* heterogeneity which occurs when there is disagreement about the meaning, interpretation, or intended use of the same or related data.

We use the taxonomy shown in Figure 9.14 to compare the various DDBMS architectures (adapted from Sheth and Larson (1990), Özsu and Valduriez (1991) and Bell and Grimson (1992)).

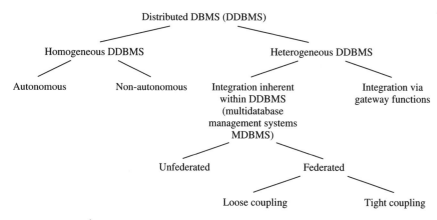

Figure 9.14 A taxonomy of DDBMS architectures.

As noted earlier, a homogeneous DDBMS is one in which the same DBMS is used at all local servers. Servers may consist of the same or different hardware, software and communication systems. A homogeneous DDBMS may be administered by a central authority (**non-autonomous**) or support local autonomy (**autonomous**). All users access the underlying local databases via a global interface described by a global schema and against which user views are defined. Since users access data through the global interface only, local DBMSs may or may not have local schemas. An example configuration is shown in Figure 9.15. The global schema is supported by two additional schemas: the **fragmentation schema** which details how each global relation is mapped amongst local databases; and the **allocation schema** which details at which server each fragment is stored.

A heterogeneous DDBMS uses different DBMSs at the local servers. Integration of the different DBMSs is achieved either through the use of external integrating agent software called **gateways**, or through special software subsystems inherent within the DDBMS itself. The latter form of heterogeneous DDBMS is known as **multidatabase management systems** (MDBMSs) and are usually associated with pre-existing database systems which require integration and support local and global users (i.e. via a global schema). Although MDBMSs can be unfederated (i.e. provides support for global users only) it is usually the case that MDBMSs are **federated** so that component DBMSs are autonomous (supporting local users) yet participate in a federation to allow partial and controlled sharing of their data.

Heterogeneous DDBMSs are inherently autonomous and there is no centralized control because component DBMSs enable local autonomy. Thus, federated MDBMSs represent a compromise between no integration (typified by the client/server SQL database approach in which users must explicitly interface with multiple autonomous databases) and total integration (typified by non-autonomous homogeneous DDBMSs in which autonomy is sacrificed so that users can easily access all data through a single global interface only). The main justification for federated MDBMSs is that often data is already distributed over multiple heterogeneous DBMSs before a federated MDBMS (FDBMS) is built, therefore a top-down approach is impractical. Like a gateway protocol, a FDBMS can result in loss of functionality because the full features of a particular local DBMS cannot be mapped to the global database features or vice versa. A federated MDBMS is further classified by Bell and Grimson (1992) as those that have a global schema (**tightly coupled**) and those which do not (**loosely coupled**). These

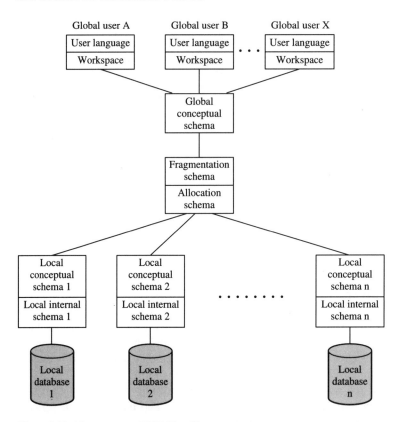

Figure 9.15 A homogeneous DDBMS architecture.

are illustrated in Figures 9.16 and 9.17. The global schema in tightly coupled federated MDBMSs consists of the amalgam of all data contributed by the local databases. In practice, the global schema is potentially large and complex since it represents the corporate shareable data resource. User views must be further constrained by defining constrained views on the global schema (for example, using the SQL CREATE VIEW statement).

In summary, we can distinguish between the various types of DBMSs in terms of the extent to which heterogeneity, local autonomy and distribution transparency are supported. Homogeneous DDBMSs offer the highest degree of distribution transparency at the cost of heterogeneity and to some extent local autonomy. Heterogeneous DDBMSs provide a high level of support for local autonomy and heterogeneity, but at the expense of distribution transparency (integration).

9.7 SUPPORT FOR MULTIMEDIA OBJECTS AND DATA STREAMS

Existing local and remote file systems provide the basic facilities to store and forward streams of multimedia data such as audio, video or animation. However, because of the time-based, stream-oriented nature of multimedia, traditional file systems by themselves cannot deliver such data to multiple users effectively in real-time on a large scale. In order to facilitate large-

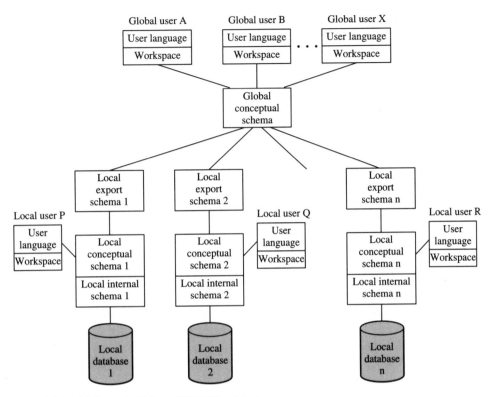

Figure 9.16 A tightly coupled federated MDBMS architecture.

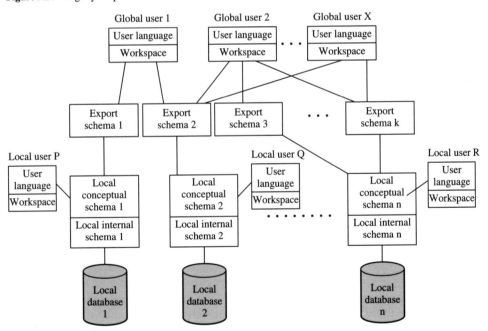

Figure 9.17 A loosely coupled federated MDBMS architecture.

scale shared access to data, multimedia file servers need to store large multimedia objects, and control real-time data streams, the media devices that store them, and the network protocols that distribute the data streams to and from user devices in real time. User processes must connect to the server making a request for one or more data streams. Multimedia servers also have to handle quality of service requirements so that user requests are accepted only if the server can guarantee that the request can be satisfied with quality of service required. Thus a scalable multimedia file server must exhibit the following features:

1. Optimization of the low-level (physical) and high-level (logical) data structures to support multimedia data stores. Due to the bit or byte orientation of current systems, software is used to, for example, map video frames into bit or byte objects and vice versa. Future server architectures must provide low-level support for the manipulation of non-textual information (traditionally in the area of image processing). Support for multimedia storage, retrieval and computation include:
   – video compression processors;
   – image processors;
   – media-to-media translation processors.
2. Improvements in sustained data rates and latency times of storage devices. Whilst processor and memory performance has doubled every two years, I/O transfer rates have not kept pace. Thus currently, the I/O subsystem is the main bottleneck and limits overall system response time. Disk storage densities are improving dramatically (at approximately 80 per cent per annum). Much higher I/O bus bandwidth is required together with increased opportunity for parallel operations (e.g. through the use of RAID I/O subsystem technology). The use of broadband network technology (such as ATM) will only exacerbate the problem in the future unless these issues are addressed.
3. Efficient synchronization and stream management. Multimedia are unique in nature compared with data and text objects because the incorporation of audio and video transforms a simple object into a time-based, continuous data stream that must be delivered at a constant rate with bounded delay between source and target in order to preserve human perception.
4. Network data transfer optimized for isochronous transfer requirements. Technology advancements which address this requirement are detailed in Chapters 4 and 5.

The main server functional components, data flows and control flows typical of a multimedia server is shown in Figure 9.18. Current multiprocessor architectures facilitate data and control flows via an internal bus and shared memory as illustrated in Figure 9.19. Performance is enhanced through the use of a two-level cache arrangement. Level one cache is on the processor chip, while the second level cache is on the multi-processor board. Cache consistency is maintained by maintaining a directory in each of the shared memory's modules to keep track of which processors have cached data and their status.

Rooholamini and Cherkassky (1995) proposed a novel alternative based on ATM cell switching technology. One or more ATM switches are used as the total system interconnect of a multi-processor multimedia server. An example configuration using this approach is shown in Figure 9.20. ATM switching technology and protocols have made it possible to build networks with speeds of several gigabits per second. This places a tremendous strain on end system architectures to match the data throughput required to ensure that they are not the major obstacle to implementing high-speed information services. ATM switching is being applied to all types of networks (LANs, MANs and WANs). A natural extension is to apply the same

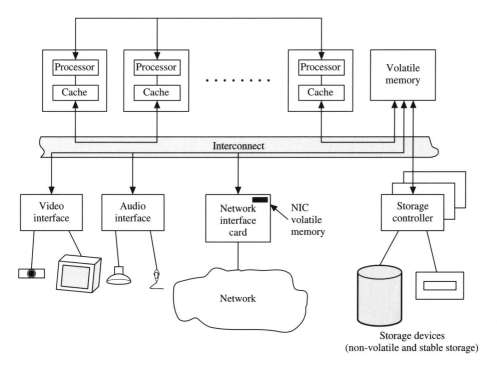

Figure 9.18 Multimedia server data and control flows.

concepts to the interconnection architecture of subsystems within a multimedia server. The attractions of this approach are:

1. A reduction in the need for multiple protocol and packet conversions as the same architecture may be used end-to-end.
2. High-bandwidth is achievable end-to-end because the high bandwidth network I/O can be matched with an equally high bandwidth interconnection system within the server.
3. High levels of parallelism because of ATM's inherent support for multiple physical connections.
4. The internal server interconnection architecture would conform to an international standard which is much more scalable than existing internal bus standards. Scalability is a key requirement of a multimedia server architecture.

PVC or SVC connections can be utilized depending on the urgency of communication. Most connections are likely to be PVCs. The majority of intrasystem communication is packet-based, therefore AAL 3/4 or AAL 5 protocols seem appropriate. The cost of memory is set to fall dramatically and the amount of memory on a chip to increase to gigabytes. Coupled with the need to transfer large multimedia objects, the unit of data transfer across an interconnect is likely to increase significantly. ATM offers a transfer size of a 48-byte cell.

Analysis by Rooholamini and Cherkassky (1995) shows that the latency exhibited by an ATM-based interconnect switching at 155 Mbit/s and 622 Mbit/s compares favourably with other bus-based technologies (such as Multibus-II and NuBus). Here latency is calculated as the time user data is ready for transmission until it is received at its destination. In the context of ATM-based intrasystem interconnects, latency consists of three components:

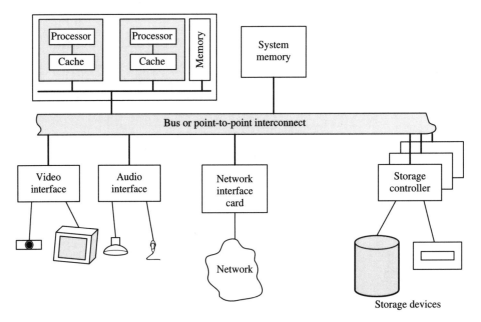

Figure 9.19 Current multi-processor architecture.

1. **cell processing time**, segmenting user data into cells;
2. **arbitration time**, to establish a connection with the destination subsystem;
3. **transfer time**, the transmission time and propagation delay associated with transmitting the cells to the destination subsystem.

An alternative example of a system designed to support multimedia storage and retrieval requirements is the multi-service storage architecture (MSSA) developed at the University of Cambridge Computer Laboratory (Bacon, 1993). MSSA runs above a microkernel for high performance services called Wanda (Bacon *et al.*, 1991) which offers multi-threaded processes and multi-processor thread scheduling amongst other performance-enhancing features typical of real-time microkernels. MSSA is a modular and extensible architecture comprising a two-level hierarchy of storage servers with value-adding service (VAS) layers above them. An access control mechanism extends through the VAS layers to support secure, accountable provision of services to user applications. The low-level storage service (LLSS) defines byte sequence storage abstractions to support a wide range of media types. The high-level storage service (HLSS) supports structured data objects such as flat files, structured files, compound multimedia documents and continuous media streams. Functions such as existence control and concurrency control are implemented at the HLSS level. An example of a value-adding service is IMP which provides support for multimedia authoring and presentation. It provides a scripting language for authoring multimedia presentations, and presentation services such as configuration control, synchronization, event management and the activation of presentation objects. The overall architecture of MSSA and IMP is illustrated in Figure 9.21.

In the database world, attention has been focused on the requirements of database systems to support complex data types associated with multimedia objects. Issues such as basic storage and access mechanisms, retrieving on the basis of content, query languages which incorporate multimedia objects, internal schemas appropriate to the physical storage of multimedia

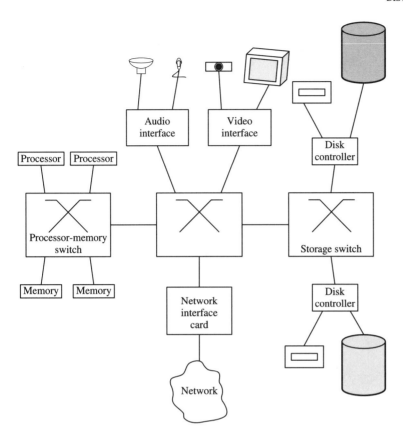

Figure 9.20 ATM-based multiprocessor architecture.

objects are typical research areas. Does a distributed multimedia database management system (MM-DDBMS) require extensions to the well-established relational data model or is a radically new approach required? Commentators in the database area generally agree that some sort of object-oriented technology is required. Whether this will evolve from current relational technology or be provided by something designed from a blank sheet remains to be seen.

A distributed object model and distributed object management rely on a distributed storage model that can represent and capture the clustering and fragmentation of objects (Khoshafian, 1989). This provides a straightforward mapping from a distributed object design to implementation using persistent objects. An **object-oriented DBMS** (OODBMS) combines object-oriented programming and database technologies in order eliminate the 'impedence mismatch' between objects in the object-oriented world and current relational, hierarchical and network DBMS technologies. An attractive feature of OODBMSs is that they support naturally the storage and retrieval of *multimedia and other complex data objects*. By supporting data classes, inheritance and encapsulation, OODBMSs can provide effective support for reuse. Although a very promising technology, the theory and practice of OODBMS has not yet matured. Even less developed is the concept of a **distributed OODBMS architecture**. Current offerings are centralized with no concealment of object location. The user is aware of non-local objects and must perform

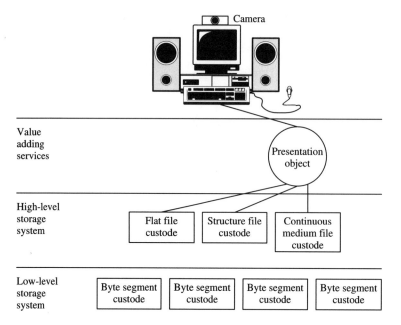

Figure 9.21 MSSA architecture.

remote accesses to the appropriate OODBMS server. Distributed OODBMSs are still in their infancy but represent a natural technology for implementing a distributed storage model particularly when involving complex data types. DISs are commonly designed using the distributed object model and therefore may provide the impetus for widespread adoption of distributed OODBMSs in the future.

Thus, the technology to underpin a MM-DDBMS already exists, such as high-speed networks, high-capacity, high-speed storage and memory technologies, and massively parallel server architectures. These technologies, however, need to be integrated and harnessed by appropriate MM-DDBMS technology which is currently still in its infancy in the reasearch domain.

9.8 DATA WAREHOUSE

Operational information systems are supported by operational databases, while MIS and SIS systems are supported by decision-support, informational databases. The differences between operational and decision-support environments are so large that it is logical to separate the two in terms of technology requirements. Table 9.7 (adapted from Inmon and Caplan, 1992) summarizes the main differences.

A **data warehouse** is a read-only repository of data to support decision-support systems such as MIS and SIS. Hackathorn defines it as 'a collection of data objects that have been inventoried for distribution to the business community' (Hackathorn, 1993). The key objective of a data warehouse is to give users the freedom to get the information they want.

The process of controlled transfer of data to the warehouse is known as **data staging**. This is illustrated in Figure 9.22. Data is 'cleaned up', filtered and transformed as part of the data staging process. Data staging is transparent to the users of the data warehouse, but is prede-

Table 9.7 Operational and decision-support environments (*adapted from Inmon and Caplan, 1992*)

Operational	Decision support
High data update load	Data loading and scanning with manipulation processes such as merge, sort, aggregate, etc.
Repetitive processing	Heuristic processing
Fast response times	Dependent on nature of query
Highly structured processing	Unstructured processing
Centralized processing	Distributed processing
Up-to-the-second processing	Long-term analytical processing
A few detailed records	Many records
Data which is accurate as of the moment of usage	Time variant data, relevant to one single moment in time. Every record requires timestamp
Little integration between applications (and data)	Data is integrated and accessed by multiple applications
Data is application oriented	Data is subject oriented
Low granularity of data	Different levels of granularity of data

fined as part of an information provision and data update strategy. The update characteristics of data warehousing are summarized in Table 9.8 (adapted from Inmon and Caplan, 1992). Clearly, data staging can be carried out at many different levels, for example, operational-to-warehouse, warehouse-to-workgroup server, and workgroup server-to-individual client.

9.9 SUMMARY

In this chapter we have reviewed key concepts associated with the distribution of data. The pressure to distribute data stems from the need to support local automony and for greater levels of performance, security and availability. Distributing data, however, introduces a number of new, complex problems such as distributed transaction recovery, distributed query processing and the need to hide complexity from the users. Distributed database management systems are broadly classified as homogeneous and heterogeneous. A sub-class of heterogeneous DDBMS known as multidatabase management systems (MDBMS) provide support for local autonomy and different DBMSs. Distributed object-oriented DBMSs and multimedia database management systems have the potential to provide much more powerful and flexible data handling than traditional heirarchical, network and relational DBMSs in widespread use today.

Although the discussion in this chapter was in the context of databases, many of the concepts and techniques relate to all types of data handling systems.

9.10 REVIEW EXERCISES

1. Describe using the ANSI/SPARC architecture the responsibilities of a database management system (DBMS).

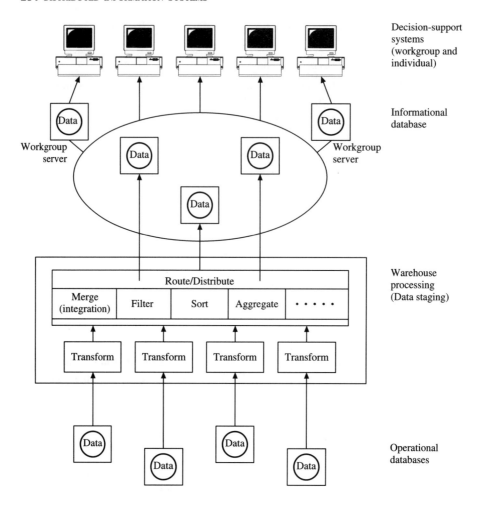

Figure 9.22 Warehouse processing (data staging).

Table 9.8   Update processing characteristics (*adapted from Inmon and Caplan, 1992*)

Operational	Data warehouse	Workgroup	Individual client
Transaction processing	Sequential load	Sequential load	Sequential load
Record at the time	Whole sets of data	Sets of data	Limited stets of data
Immediate update	Data staging, overnight	Data staging, hourly to overnight	Data staging or immediate access
Clerical staff	Data administration staff	Managerial staff	Managerial staff
Primitive data	Primitive and derived data	Primitive and derived data	Mostly derived data

2. Explain the differences between a hierarchical, network and relational data model.
3. What are the characteristics of relational database technology that make it suitable for implementing distributed databases?
4. Explain the term transaction. Discuss the role of a transaction processing manager.
5. Describe the five options for distributing data. What factors determine the choice of option?
6. What issues arise when a transaction involves data held on many servers?
7. Describe in detail the two-phase commit protocol. Why is it described as a blocking protocol?
8. Can SQL be used to implement a remote request or transaction? How might SQL be extended to provide the necessary functionality?
9. Describe the ISO RDA standard.
10. Describe Date's rules for defining a distributed database.
11. Discuss the differences between homogeneous and heterogeneous DDBMSs.
12. Describe the key features of a federated DBMS.
13. What requirements arise from the need to support the storage and access of multimedia data? Describe an example architecture designed to support multimedia data streams.

9.11 FURTHER READING

For an introduction to database concepts see Ullman (1988), Date (1990) and Korth and Silberchatz (1991). SQL is described in detail in Date and Darwen (1993) and Carter (1992). Distributed database concepts, and research and development results are presented in Bell and Grimson (1992), Öszu and Valduriez (1991) and Ceri and Pelagatti (1984). A comprehensive survey of distributed data management approaches is given in Sheth and Larson (1990). Query optimization issues are discussed in Ceri (1984). Database recovery issues are covered in detail in Bernstein *et al.* (1987)

10

SYSTEMS DEVELOPMENT AND INTEGRATION

10.1 INTRODUCTION

The degree of distribution and placement of presentation, processing and data components of a DIS are key considerations in design, development and implementation. It is no longer appropriate to assume that a distributed IT infrastructure is the exception rather than the rule when designing systems. The underlying IT infrastructure has moved from centralized to a very large number of powerful client and server computers, geographically dispersed and connected using very high bandwidth communications networks. There is now a wider range of options for the placement of DIS components. An increasing number of information services are accessible via a world-wide internet (see Section 8.12). In this chapter a number of approaches to DIS development are described. The main focus of the chapter is on moving from the logical design of a DIS through to implementation, taking account of rightsizing, transparency and other issues.

10.2 SYSTEMS INTEGRATION

In the early days when programming languages and operating systems were less functional, application programmers had to develop low-level functions such as basic input/output in addition to application-specific logic. As a consequence, applications were highly machine-specific and difficult to enhance. In time, operating systems and programming languages provided much more functionality to the extent that a single line of application code executed a complex OS function which previously required many lines of complex application code. Application programmers can now concentrate on providing application-specific functions and data presentation aspects. Visual application development tools allow application developers to design and generate a high proportion of data access, manipulation and presentation functions automatically by enabling the creation of user interface objects and flows of control using simple languages and design tools. Developers of distributed GUI-based applications can now concentrate on the design of the user interface and the linkages to reusable user interface objects, local and remote processing objects, and data objects. The linkages between objects are facilitated by local and remote IPC mechanisms (e.g. message passing, shared memory or remote procedure calls).

This approach to DIS development is consistent with emerging **rapid application development** (RAD) methodologies (Martin, 1991) which gained in popularity and maturity during the 1990s. RAD is a methodology covering systems development from business requirements through ongoing development. It can be classed as a 'toolkit' methodology and is open in that it can be adapted to projects, individual or organizational philosophy and can utilize a wide range of techniques and tools (Bates and Stephens, 1995). RAD focuses on achieving three main goals: high quality systems, fast development and delivery, and low costs. RAD moves away from emphasis on 'conforming to the written specification as effectively as possible' to 'meeting the true business (or user) requirements as effectively as possible at the time the system comes into operation' (Martin, 1991). In other words, RAD moves away from the concept of the frozen specification and places an emphasis on user involvement and responsibility throughout the development (Bates and Stephens, 1995).

RAD combines iterative prototyping with effective project management, testing, quality assurance, requirements specifications, reuse and so on. The DSDM consortium (DSDM, 1995), formed to promote RAD as a formal methodology, defined a number of principles of RAD projects which are summarized below (Bates and Stephens, 1995).

- Development teams are comprised of developers and users, who are empowered to make decisions.
- Business requirements are paramount.
- Developers and users keep in close communication through iterative development involving prototyping.
- Change is encouraged and all changes are reversible.
- All involved (developers and users) must be highly skilled and motivated towards business objectives – the focus is on delivery.
- Testing is done throughout development and reviewed by both users and developers.
- For larger projects, frequent deliverables should be scheduled.
- The high-level scope and purpose of the system must be agreed and fixed early in development.
- The relationship between vendor and purchaser must be one of co-operation.

The structure of RAD-based development projects is summarized in Figure 10.1 Business requirements analysis and systems analysis are carried out in joint application development (JAD) workshops involving key users, the client, some developers, a scribe (the documenter) and under the direction of a facilitator (Martin, 1991).

The migration from centralized, bespoke systems to distributed information systems using reusable components has given rise to three distinct roles concerning distributed information systems development:

1. **Fabricators**: responsible for specifying and building the infrastructure consisting of the

RAPID BUSINESS ANALYSIS
Initial Planning
Business Requirements Analysis
Scoping
Joint Application Development
Workshop

PEOPLE:
Users
Project manager
Workshop facilitator
Modelling expert
Scribe

PRODUCTS
Business objectives
Scope
Outline Business requirements
Priorities

- - - - - - - - - - - - - - - - · Strict Deadline (Timebox) - - - - - - - - - - - - - - - - -

INCREMENT
Build prototypes
Review prototypes
Change management
Dynamic priorities
Prototype evolves into product
Technical documentation
Testing
Quality assurance
Prototyping
Iteration

PEOPLE:
Users
Project manager
Developers (SWAT team)

PRODUCTS
Delivered increment
with
all necessary documentation
to
user satisfaction (priorities)

- - - - - - - - - - - - - - - - · Strict Deadline (Timebox) - - - - - - - - - - - - - - - - -

REPEAT for as many increments as appropriate with strict deadlines

Figure 10.1 RAD development structure (source: Bates, 1995).

essential (low-level) components required to build DISs. The analogy here is a manufacturer of PC add-in cards that package together low-level components (e.g. processor and memory chips) to provide a higher-level building block (e.g. a sound card). Examples of the basic tools for the fabricator are:

— generic services;
— corporate (horizontal) application and information support services such as corporate database systems;
— object class libraries and high-level application programming interfaces to enable rapid application development.

The emphasis is on building low-level, reusable components. Important decisions relating to maintaining data integrity, security and general systems management can be implemented and enforced to achieve an appropriate balance between flexibility and control.

2. **Builders**: responsible for packaging pre-fabricated components into a DIS. Depending on requirements, this could be done by personnel in a business unit or by highly skilled personnel in the central IT unit. Many end-users are quite capable of installing add-in cards to

a PC and configuring software to make use of the new functionality or performance level. Similarly, tools for GUI development, SQL database development and 4GL environments can be used by builders to develop new applications rapidly from lower-level building blocks provided by fabricators. GUI-based applications are much more difficult to develop than the traditional character-based, menu-driven systems, due mainly to the underlying event-driven processing mechanism and the greater need to understand a user's interaction requirements. Hence application builders require powerful tools that reduce complexity and which simplify design, implementation and testing.

3. **Users**: whose primary goal is to use existing IT resources effectively to support the business functions for which they are responsible. The use of a familiar GUI and other tools improve productivity and enable new applications to be assimilated easily. For some organizations operating in more dynamic business environments, many applications may need to be developed very quickly, used for a short period of time after which they are no longer required (so-called 'throw-away' applications). It is acknowledged that users utilize very little of the functionality of existing applications. Users are inhibited by a general lack of training and therefore make ineffective use of PC technology. Installing increasingly functional applications will not lead to dramatic improvements in user productivity unless they are appropriately trained (many users will just keep doing the same things they always did).

At present, more detailed methodologies, tools and techniques are required to help organizations develop the necessary skills in designing and building DISs.

10.3 MODELLING THE SYSTEM

Currently, there is a wide range of methodologies for information systems development. A common characteristic of these methodologies is the need to model three orthogonal views of the system:

- Data modelling, which is concerned with modelling the static structure of a system by showing the data and associations (relationships) between data in the system. A data model presents a static view of the system's underlying database.
- Functional modelling, which is concerned with the data processing in the system.
- Entity life history (or dynamic) modelling, which is concerned with modelling the time-dependent behaviour of the system. The emphasis is on how data and data relationships change over time in response to various events (external stimuli which results in some action by the system).

Most methodologies also adopt a life-cycle approach to describing the information systems development process in order to ensure that the final product meets cost, quality and timeliness objectives. The life-cycle approach usually encompasses separation of the logical and physical views of an information system. Focusing on the logical view avoids unduly constraining system design possibilities by considering technology issues too early. The required system is first viewed at a high level of abstraction which de-emphasizes the underlying physical IT infrastructure requirements and gives emphasis to modelling the real-world domain relevant to the system. The logical design is later transformed to a physical system using the chosen IT infrastructure and technology.

10.3.1 Structured methodologies

A criticism of many current development and multimedia authoring methodologies is the implicit assumption that the underlying IT infrastructure is centralized with all presentation, processing and data components of a multimedia information system residing on a centralized host computer in a centralized IT infrastructure (or stand-alone multimedia computers). Whilst there are many development decisions and modelling techniques common to the development of both centralized and distributed systems and de-emphasizing distribution during logical design can be helpful, ignoring distribution totally is not helpful and methodologies are being extended to consider issues such as component placement, distribution transparency and multimedia aspects when developing both the logical and physical views of the system. For example, when capturing system requirements during the logical view certain distribution aspects such as security, availability, performance and key volumetric data will need to be captured with the possibility that the underlying IT infrastructure may be distributed. In the physical view, the logical design which includes data, functional and entity-life history models will need to be transformed into candidate physical designs with issues such as distribution transparency and the relative placement of presentation, processing and data components fully considered.

It is beyond the scope of this book to compare current methodologies and detail the way in which they are being extended. A good example of how two current methodologies, SSADM and the BOS Engineering Method, can be extended is found in Breu *et al.* (1994).

10.3.2 Open distributed processing

Successful development of DISs requires more than the establishment of a distributed IT infrastructure and client/server development toolkits. There needs to be a radical re-think of methods, design processes and tools. A relatively recent development in distributed systems design approaches is the ISO reference model for open distributed processing (RM-ODP) which aims to extend the OSI drive for 'openness' from the development of communication systems to the development of distributed applications. Work first began in 1987 and submission for publication of the basic reference model started in 1991 (ISO 10746). Because there is a wide range of types of ODP systems (of which a DIS is one type) each with unique characteristics, the ODP standard does not attempt to specify the model in fine detail, but identifies several *interfaces* at which standardization may be required (Linington, 1992), such as:

- application program interfaces allowing access to a defined function (e.g. a data manipulation language or remote procedure call interface);
- human–computer interfaces;
- interconnection and interworking standards;
- multimedia storage and access standards to allow information exchange between systems. Issues to be addressed include how to handle complex data types, synchronization over a set of data streams and incorporating dynamic binding of related data streams using basic directory, trading and binding services.

ODP adopts the **distributed object model** because an object is a natural unit of distribution. Like most development approaches, ODP deals with the full complexity of distributed systems development by defining five viewpoints of a system each of which focuses on a particular abstraction representing an area of concern in order to reduce complexity. Each viewpoint describes an ODP system in terms of seven different *aspects,* or logical groupings:

1. Storage
2. Process
3. User access
4. Separation
5. Identification (naming and addressing)
6. Management
7. Security.

Each viewpoint emphasises one or more of the above aspects. The **enterprise viewpoint** focuses on the *purpose* of the system. This is the viewpoint of *users* and sponsors of the ODP system to be developed. Their prime concern is why (justification) and how the system is to be used within the enterprise. Important data include relevant business and management policies and processes and the user roles that impinge on the system and its environment. Thus this view models the activities and user roles which perform them in terms of human, organizational, social, political, economic, business and other perspectives. Use of the word *enterprise* recognizes that an ODP system may involve a number of distinct, interrelated organizations which constitute an enterprise or support inter-enterprise links. Enterprise modelling studies and models identify information such as:

- the organization's position in the relevant marketplace;
- the business activities for which an ODP system should be available;
- relevant critical success factors affected by an ODP system;
- organizational structure;
- organizational culture and management philosophy;
- user locations and user roles which define business tasks to be automated using an ODP system;
- security and management policies regarding access and use of information provided by an ODP system.

Enterprise models are used to make design, investment and migration planning decisions. The **information viewpoint** focuses on the *information aspects* of the system. This is the viewpoint of information managers, information engineers and systems analysts. This is concerned with information requirements, information flows and the *logical* partitioning of the information. If the enterprise model has defined data distribution requirements then this is reflected in the information model. The information model includes:

- structures of data elements that define the information needs;
- rules stating the relationships between data elements;
- data transformations as a result of data processing;
- data flows;
- the forms in which data and data processing are visible to users;

The **computational viewpoint** focuses on the computational aspects of the system. This is the viewpoint of application developers. This is concerned with the processing and associated data structures which provide the distributed processing functions. Here, programming functions (invocation, assignment, communication, etc.) and data structures are visible and therefore modelled. This viewpoint is independent of the computer systems and networks on which they will eventually run. If the enterprise viewpoint has definite and defined distribution requirements, then this is reflected in the computational model. In this viewpoint an application developer concentrates on the business problem to be solved and the logical system design, ignoring details of communication protocols, implementation languages, operating systems, etc. The computational model expresses:

- program invocations and related event triggers;
- synchronization between programs;
- inter-process communication requirements;
- data types that form the data to be processed, the processing operations associated with each data type and the results transmitted (either to another process or to an external agent). These requirements are expressed in terms of abstract data types or objects (in the object-oriented sense);

The **engineering viewpoint** focuses on the concrete mechanisms. This is concerned with mapping the computational model on to a concrete distributed system. Thus it includes:

- the IT infrastructure components to be used;
- the mechanisms used to provide the various transparency functions needed to support the ODP system described by the computational viewpoint;
- the mechanisms to support efficiency in terms of performance optimization (e.g., trading flexibility and portability for performance), robustness, reliability and other service-level requirements.
- the process of implementing the computational model using tools such as assembling programs and data, compilation and linking.

The objects visible from this viewpoint are processors, memory, information networks, control and transparency mechanisms, etc., that together enable efficient processing of programs and data whilst preserving the semantics identified in the computational model. Whilst these components are visible in the model, they are expressed independent of the physical artefacts that they represent. The engineering viewpoint is also concerned with improving the efficiency and ease in which distributed applications can be written and implemented through the use of specification languages and automated code generation tools. An engineering model thus expresses:

- distributed IT infrastructure component requirements such as processors, memory, information networks, storage, control and transparency functions, etc. The emphasis is on component functionality not the particular supplier products used to implement each component;
- placement of presentation, processing and data objects identified in the computational model;
- linkages between presentation, processing and data objects;
- the process of assembling, compiling and implementing the computational model using specification languages and associated tools.

The **technology viewpoint** focuses on the *conformance* issues in component selection and procurement. These are the views of programmers, system maintainers/administrators, and system managers and is concerned with the detail of the components and links from which an ODP system is constructed. They include hardware and software components such as client and server local operating systems, the input/output devices, storage, network equipment, etc. The technology model consists of configuration diagrams and descriptions (with justification) of standards and supplier products that have been selected to implement the engineering model. Technology components include:

- client and server hardware platforms, operating system, I/O devices, hard disk capacity, network type and equipment, etc.;
- generic services to be employed;
- network configurations and components;
- transparency functions to be employed.

The ODP framework for building DISs organizes these viewpoints to allow verification of completeness of each viewpoint model, and consistency between them. As we move from the enterprise through to the technology viewpoint we are moving from the highest to the lowest level of abstraction of an ODP system. At the highest level, real-world objects are modelled. At the lowest level, the technology viewpoint, we see the implementation of these objects and linkages between them. Veryard *et al.* (1995) proposed an enterprise modelling methodology for ODP (EMM/ODP) which provides some guidance on the chronological sequence in terms of possible start points, and endpoints for each viewpoint. It is illustrated in Figure 10.2. An EMM/ODP project is initiated by a driver for change, for example:

- problems with existing technology;
- new technology on offer;
- changes in policy which require organizational changes;
- changes in inter-organizational relationships;
- changes in the environment of the organization.

The ODP-RM does not prescribe the techniques used to carry out the modelling. Established techniques such as object modelling can be used.

Table 10.1 gives a view of how typical data-flow and object-oriented methodologies are aligned to the ODP-RM. In general, current methodologies offer a range of modelling techniques and diagramming paradigms for information, computational and, to some extent, enterprise modelling. The modelling areas which are less well developed are engineering and technology models. This is not surprising since the engineering model specifically addresses distribution, component placement and distribution transparency – issues which have not been a feature of older methodologies. This chapter focuses on developing an engineering model of a DIS and assumes that some methodology has been used to capture user requirements and the logical design. The next section outlines one approach to developing a *link model* which defines an engineering viewpoint of the DIS class of ODP system. The concepts, however, can also be applied to other classes of ODP systems. Chapter 12 presents an approach to developing the technology model from an engineering model.

10.4 THE LINK MODEL: AN ENGINEERING VIEWPOINT

Assuming a potentially distributed IT infrastructure, an engineering model of a DIS (a specific class of ODP system) emphasizes a view of the system as a network of associations between six fundamental types of entities (adapted from Domville (1992) and Hackathorn (1993)).

1. *Actor objects (AO)* An actor is an entity in the environment of a DIS which acts as a source and sink of a related set information within the domain of a DIS. An actor is normally a human user. The states and behaviour of an actor relevant to the associated DIS is represented by an actor object which relates to the specific role of the actor. In particular,

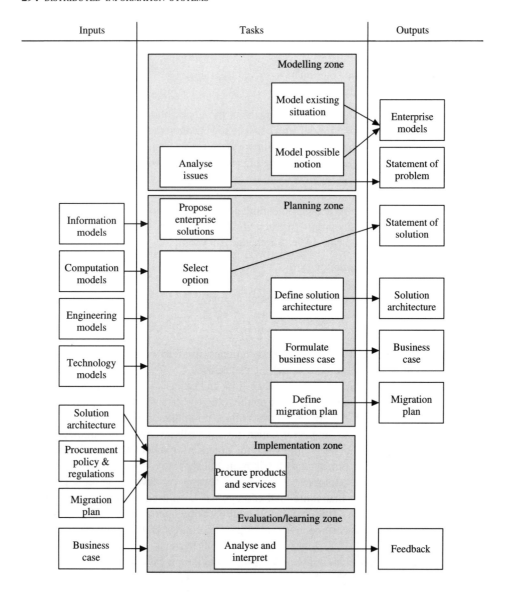

Figure 10.2 Extended EMM/ODP framework (adapted from Veryard *et al.*, 1995).

an AO will trigger events which a DIS is designed to handle. For example, in a banking system, a cashier is modelled as an AO with specific behaviours such as dispense cash, process transaction and verify account. Mobile actors, such as a salesman, are modelled as multiple AOs.

2. *User interface objects (UIOs)* A UIO is a processing object that handles events triggered by an actor object (i.e. an external agent in the real world). An actor represented by an AO interacts with a UIO through a defined interface (e.g. an ATM, a PC or a multimedia kiosk). The UIO is the means by which the functionality and behaviour of a DIS is made visible to the actor. An example of this interaction is where an actor interacts with the

Table 10.1 The alignment of dataflow and object-oriented approaches to the ODP reference model

ODP viewpoint	Focus	Modelling requirements	Data-flow oriented		Object-oriented	
			Model	Techniques	Model	Techniques
Enterprise	Purpose, scope and policies for the system	Identification of domains Federation requirements Roles played by the system Activities undertaken Policy statements about the system (administration, security, management, scope, etc.)			Object modelling?	
Information	Semantics of information and information processing	Static schema Dynamic schema Integrity constraints (invariant schema)	E-R model Data model	E-R modelling	Object model	Object modelling
Computational	Functional decomposition into objects which interact at interfaces	Interactions between presentation, processing and data objects of a DIS	Process model	Data-flow modelling Entire life history modelling	Functional model Dynamic model	Data modelling State transition modelling
Engineering	Mechanisms and functions required to support distributed interaction	Object placement Transparancy functions Linkage mechanisms between presentation, processing and data objects of a DIS	Few established models or techniques		Few established models or techniques	
Technology	Choice of technology	Generic functions for which standards and products must be sought Standards and product selection and/or build Procurement, implementation and management	Few established models or techniques		Few established models or techniques	

system via a PC with a GUI system. In this case, a UIO may utilize GUI components such as icons, list boxes, text boxes, command buttons and menus to present data and define an appropriate set of user control options. Actor actions generate events which are handled by the UIO. An actor may be presented with multiple UIOs in an environment (referred to as the actor's *workspace*) which affords an actor total control over which UIOs are initiated, terminated, activated and deactivated. A GUI usually offers activate/deactivate and initiate/terminate facilities. In addition, facilities for linking UIOs, so-called object embedding and linking, may be available.

3. *Processing objects (POs)* POs are the fundamental processing building blocks used to build a DIS. POs can represent, for example, a spreadsheet package, a word processor, a text editor, a graphics file viewer or a World Wide Web browser. A PO signals an event to another PO by sending a message with associated data. In this sense, a DIS can be viewed as a web of concurrent POs each responding to events and signalling events by passing messages to other local POs or remote POs over an information network.

4. *Data objects (DOs)* A DO encapsulates a particular type of data. A DO is described as *simple* if it is associated with a single media type and *compound* if associated with multiple media types. An example of a simple DO is a text file embedded in a file system. An example of a compound DO is one representing a mailbox of electronic mail messages where each may contain text, digitized voice and a video clip.

5. *User agent objects (UAOs)* User agents are required in the case when local POs or UIOs are linked to remote POs or DOs. For example, in a distributed application where a DO represents a relational database which may be remote from the client platform, a UAO may represent the client end of a remote data access protocol thus providing location and access transparency to the local PO. The UAO-to-remote-DO protocol transports SQL statements to the database server containing the DO and routes record sets back to the source PO. Other examples of UAOs are directory service agents, file and print service agents and remote information services agents.

6. *Link* A link is a connection between two communicating objects in a link model. A liaison may represent, for example, a remote procedure call or a remote data access protocol.

A user workspace may consist of multiple UIOs each representing a specific DIS or a part of a DIS, for example, an electronic trading system, an electronic mail facility, a videoconferencing system or World Wide Web browser. Each UIO responds to actor-triggered events (e.g. a mouse click or menu selection), manipulates one or more data objects (DOs) or signals events to POs. POs commonly perform the following types of processing tasks.

- *Editing*   which accepts user-generated events, presents data and may involve a change in the state of one or more DOs. Examples are text editors, word processors and spreadsheets.
- *Viewing*   which allow data (i.e. text, bitmaps, video, audio, animations, etc.) to be presented in its native format. Data is presented to a presentation device (e.g. the screen or a printer or speaker) but the data does not change state (i.e. read-only access). Examples of a viewer PO are a graphics file viewer and a sound or video player.
- *Browsing*   which presents an overview of a large volume of information. For example, a WWW web browser structures the shared information space available in the Internet as a set of hyperlinks between documents written using the HTML markup language. A web browser provides facilities for traversing hyperlinks.
- *Filtering*   which manipulates a data stream and passes the results to another PO, for example a compression/decompression filter program.

- *Searching*   which finds a set of information based on some search criteria (usually specified in terms of a query identifying specific attribute values of a DO type). This involves navigating DOs until specific DOs are selected according to the search criteria. An example of this is the selection of database records from remote servers. The user query is specified using one or more SQL statements. The SQL statements are directed to one or more remote servers and selected record sets are returned to the PO. Another example is World Wide Web, the Internet hypermedia system. Here the PO is a web browser and each DO represents a WWW document page, graphics file and so on. Starting from the home page DO, Internet-based information is navigated by following hypermedia links each of which can point to another web document page, a graphics file, etc. Users traverse links to navigate through the shared information space using a simple point-and-click metaphor.
- *Business logic*   which is embodied in one or more business operations developed by an application developer which encapsulate processing on a given set of data usually in response to an event. For example, a program written in a third-generation language to implement end-of-month processing on sales data held in a data file on a remote file server.

From the perspective of a specific user or organizational unit, we can emphasize ownership of any object by describing it as either private, personal shared or shared. A *private* object is owned by the user for private use only. A *personal shared* object is owned by the user but data can be shared with other users. A *shared* DO is one used by the user but owned by someone else. This emphasizes the *protection* mechanisms required to ensure that an object is completely secure from unauthorized actions and the level of concurrency control and data recovery mechanisms required.

A DIS will employ a network of different types of POs and DOs in order to implement the range of functionality required by an actor. Some POs and DOs are reusable components utilized by multiple DISs (e.g. a graphics viewer, video player, editor or a database). An important consideration is the linkages between the various local and remote objects which is explored in the next section.

10.4.1 Object placement: an infrastructure diagram

In order to consider alternative scenarios for the placement of various object types in a concrete distributed IT infrastructure, the various components of the infrastructure of relevance to object placement must be defined. An *infrastructure diagram* uses the following entities to model a particular IT infrastructure.

1. A *location type,* which defines a classification of location instances. For example, branch office or headquarters are location types.
2. A *location instance,* which is an instance of a particular location type at a physical location at which an object may be placed.
3. A *node type,* which defines a particular type of node which may be placed at a location instance. For example, client PC workstation and UNIX server are node types. A node type can describe the precise characteristics of the node in terms of software and hardware configuration, performance, capacity and other attributes.
4. A *node instance,* which is an instance of a node type at a particular location instance.
5. A *node link type,* which defines the type of connection between two nodes. The node link type describes the precise characteristics of the node link.

6. A *node link instance*, which is an instance of a node link of a specific type which connects two or more node instances. An ISDN link connecting a specific branch computer to a computer at headquarters is an example of a node link instance.

Any distributed IT infrastructure can be modelled using the above modelling entities since the above entity definitions do not assume any particular computational model. Each location, node and node link instance can be represented diagrammatically using any appropriate graphic so long as a key indicates what each graphic represents. A *link model* is produced from the computational model and infrastructure diagram (which represents a particular implementation scenario) by carrying out the following steps:

1. annotate the computational model indicating the type of each object represented (i.e. AO, UIO, PO, PO or DO);
2. define an object placement policy which defines rules for the placement of various UIOs, POs and DOs taking account of centralization, replication, partitioning, caching and service-level policies and decisions. POs should be separated into those which relate to the particular DIS (referred to simply as *processing objects* (POs) which may be local or remote) and those which are 'corporate' objects reusable across a wide range of systems within the organization (referred to as *corporate processing objects* (CPOs);
3. place the various objects on to the infrastructure diagram according to the object placement policy;
4. simulate the resulting link model using volumetric data (captured during the logical design phase) such as data volumes and workload characteristics in order to evaluate whether the link model meets functional and service level requirements.

10.5 CASE STUDY: AN AUTOMATED TELLER MACHINE INFORMATION SYSTEM

To illustrate how the use of an infrastructure diagram and link model can illustrate an object placement scenario, Figure 10.3 shows an infrastructure diagram for a typical ATM network. In this particular organization, an object-oriented methodology was used for the logical design of the system (the example approach, object modelling technique (OMT), is detailed in Rumbaugh *et al.*, 1991). The resulting object model is shown in Figure 10.4. Functional and dynamic (state transition) models were also produced but are not reproduced here. The resulting link model was derived by superimposing the object model onto the infrastructure diagram, taking account of the object placement policy adopted which can be summarized from the problem definition and statement of requirements as:

- ATMs placed at branch offices (of which there are 700 instances) owned by different banks;
- ATMs also placed in a number of strategic shopping malls (of which there are 70);
- an ATM accepts a cash card and communicates with the ATM server to process the transaction. The ATM dispenses cash, prints receipts and can provide the user with other (bank-specific) services. Banks are competing by providing a wide range of value-added services and will in the future provide services using ATM kiosks with very powerful, multimedia interfaces at the ATM. The infrastructure must take account of this future direction;

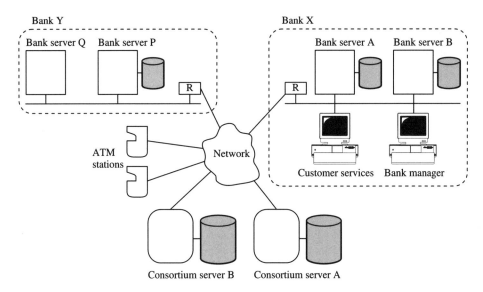

Figure 10.3 ATM IT infrastructure.

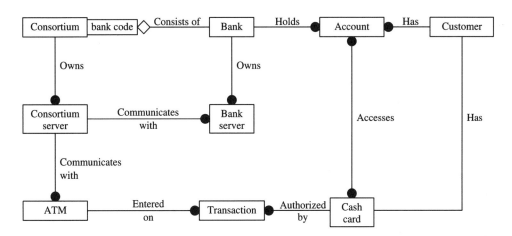

Figure 10.4 ATM object model (adapted from Rumbaugh *et al.*, 1991).

- ATMs communicate with an associated consortium server (owned and maintained by the bank consortium) which routes transactions to the appropriate bank server. The ATM server holds information concerning every bank in the bank consortium on whose behalf it is acting;
- a bank server (owned and maintained by a specific bank) maintains account objects and data stores for customers of the bank that owns it. All bank servers are able to connect to one or more consortium servers;
- the system must keep stringent records since the costs of the ATM service is apportioned according to the proportion of bank customers using it. Appropriate security mechanisms, such as secure authentication, must be implemented. The system must also handle concurrent access to accounts correctly;

- whilst each bank has its own information systems, the focus of this system is to implement the shared ATM service efficiently to the demanding functional and service-level requirements specified by the banks. In particular, the ATM service must exhibit 100 per cent availability and appropriate performance as defined in the service-level requirements specification. This means that whilst a particular ATM could be down (there are several ATMs per location), a consortium server must always be available and this requires a demanding fault-tolerance policy. The infrastructure should therefore feature, as a minimum, a replica server and backup network links between itself, bank servers and ATMs;
- each bank server has mature policies in the areas of maintaining security and integrity of all data sources.

Figure 10.5 illustrates an example link model which embodies the above object placement policy. Clearly the link model has to be tested using volumetric data and a simulation approach to evaluate it against the stringent performance and other service-level requirements. This will probably result either in adjustments to the link model or a completely new link model to be developed. The approaches to implementing links to various types of objects is an area which has not been developed fully and is the subject of the next section.

10.6 LINKAGES

A key aspect of a DIS is that POs and DOs can be local or remote from a UIO, and complex links between objects can be developed using appropriate linkages. Flexibility of access and integration (as perceived by an actor) are determined by the mechanisms available to implement links between UIO, PO, and DO. A link in this context is a directed path between two or more objects. The start of the link is anchored on the *source object anchor* and each object at the end of the link is known as *target object anchor.* A link must have only one source object anchor although a single object may be associated with several links. A *leaf object* is one which does not contain any source object anchors. Mechanisms are required to support many different types of linkages, such as the following:

- UIO to UIO
- UIO to PO
- Local PO to local PO
- Local PO to remote PO
- Local PO to local DO
- Local PO to remote DO
- DO to DO.

Links can be categorized into two types: static and dynamic. Static links are where the binding of source and target object anchors are established at the time when objects are created. Dynamic links are those where the binding between source and target object anchors are established at the time a user wishes to follow a link. This is analogous to the early binding (at compile time) or late binding (at run-time using a directory service) of program functions in program development.

Another aspect of linking is synchronization between source and target object. A synchronous linking mechanism is when the source object is blocked at the point when a user requests

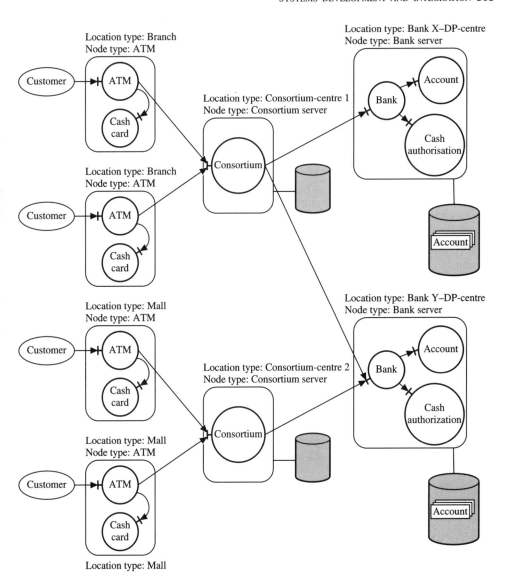

Figure 10.5 ATM: example link model.

link resolution until the link is resolved. In an asynchronous linking mechanism the source object is not blocked and is free to carry out other processing while the link is being resolved. These considerations are examined for each of the above linkage requirements.

10.6.1 UIO-to-UIO linkages

UIO to UIO linkages normally takes place on the client workstation. The linkage mechanism essentially supports the routing of actor events to the appropriate UIO, handling exceptions, handling I/O functions and providing a mechanism for inter-UIO communications. This functionality is usually provided by *presentation management* software (which is part of the presentation management layer) such as Microsoft Windows. A UIO is written using the presentation management's API which is a set of library routines and rules for performing functions such as creating window frames and handling various events in a GUI system. Actor event types which need to be routed to UIOs include:

- input events, such as mouse pointer movement into and outside of a window frame, a mouse button click, or when a keyboard key is hit;
- selection events, such as selecting a menu or toolbar item;
- window frame activation/deactivation, when, for example, a user double-clicks on an icon to activate it.

Processing actor events thus requires co-ordination between the presentation manager and a UIO. Either can exert overall control of event handling which leads to two models of event handling: the *event loop* and *event call-back* models (Berson, 1992). In the event loop model the UIO controls event handling. The UIO contains an event loop which calls a 'get event' presentation manager library routine which checks for any pending events. A UIO contains a specific event handling routine for each event type and it is this routine which is dispatched for each pending event. The event loop must dispatch event handling routines efficiently. The event call-back model moves event loop processing from the UIO to the presentation manager. A UIO registers all event handling routines with the presentation manager. The presentation manager is responsible for detecting events and calling the appropriate event handling routine.

An example of a presentation manager is the X-Windows system developed jointly by Massachusetts Institute of Technology, IBM and DEC in a project known as Project Athena (Champine, 1991). The X architecture splits the presentation management layer into client and server components using the client/server model. This configuration provides flexibility in the location of presentation management software in that both client and server software components can reside on the same client platform or split between client and server platforms.

The X model defines three main components: a display (i.e. a bit-mapped screen, a keyboard and a mouse interface), an X-server software component, an X-client software component (a UIO). A display provides the interface between an actor and the actor's workspace. The X-server component effectively provides an interface between the display and multiple X-clients (i.e. multiple UIOs) and controls each display element. The X model defines a protocol – the X protocol – for communication between X-clients and the X-server. The X-protocol defines various types of messages which generally indicate the type of event which has occurred (e.g. a mouse click or key depression). Once initiated, X-clients are suspended until an event occurs which is signalled by receipt of an X-protocol message from the X-server.

Whilst the X-server software component simply controls and manipulates display elements in response to X-client requests, it imposes no 'look and feel' rules. A window manager is a special X-client which imposes specific behaviour and appearance (look and feel) rules and generally handles the multiple window functionality such as window creation, resizing, activation, etc. An example window manager is Motif released by the Open Software Foundation (OSF) in 1989 and available on a very wide range of client and server platforms. OSF/Motif has a distinctive three-dimensional appearance. The availability of OSF/Motif across different platforms is particularly attractive in heterogeneous environments because it allows application developers to implement programs (written using OSF/Motif development tools) which support clients on different hardware platforms over a network but imposes the same user interface in terms of behaviour and appearance. OSF/Motif development package provides the following components which support the development and execution of UIOs:

- OSF/Motif window manager;
- widgets and gadgets (abstract objects such as scroll and button bars, menus, list boxes, etc.);
- user interface language (UIL), a macro language for describing the desired user interface and events to which a UIO is sensitive;
- a Motif application development environment for interactive user interface design and UIO development.

Another example of presentation management software is Microsoft's Windows which is the *de facto* standard for developing PC-based UIOs running on Intel microprocessor-based platforms. Although there are many presentation management systems, heterogeneity can be achieved by utilizing tools which define a common window manager API to which applications can be written and which can be compiled to run in a wide range of presentation management environments. It is then a simple matter to port an application to many different existing window managers and to those developed in the future.

10.6.2 UIO-to-PO and PO-to-PO linkages

In both types of systems there are two distinct linkages between POs: communicating POs reside on the local client platform and the case where some communicating POs reside on one or more remote servers. In the following sections any discussion regarding PO-to-PO linkages also applies to UIO-to-PO linkages unless otherwise stated.

10.6.3 Local UIO-to-PO or PO-to-PO Linkages

In Chapter 3 a number of local IPC mechanisms were introduced, namely:

- filter chains;
- file system or database with synchronization and concurrency control facilities;
- a shared memory facility;
- message queuing;
- a normal procedure call using dynamic link libraries.

All of the above mechanisms can be employed to provide linkages between local POs and UIOs. These mechanisms are usually provided by the native operating system and the presentation management software component via appropriate presentation management API calls (which are effectively procedure calls to dynamic link libraries). A good example is the *object linking and embedding* (OLE) mechanism supplied with Microsoft Windows (OLE, 1993).

10.6.4 Microsoft object linking and embedding (OLE)

OLE is an implementation of a defined object model (known as common object model (COM)) which is supplied with the Microsoft Windows presentation management software to facilitate inter-object communication across application and machine boundaries (i.e. across a network). Objects developed to COM are known as *component objects* and are interoperable with other component objects, perhaps written by different organizations or in different programming languages. Each component object has a set of properties (attributes) and an associated set of methods. OLE associates two types of data with an object: *presentation* data and *native* data. Presentation data is information required to render the object on a display device, while its native data are the object's internal attributes which are accessed via associated methods. COM ensures that objects behave in a consistent and well-known manner but places minimum constraints on how different objects are implemented and thus provides the 'plumbing and wiring' of OLE. This is achieved by defining a binary interface for objects that are independent of any programming language by making use of OLE object services. OLE services provide support for creating compound DOs as well as support for inter-object communication. Globally unique identifiers (GUIDs) are assigned to component objects, avoiding any possibility of an object naming conflict. OLE maintains an *object registry* which is a database of OLE-enabled component objects available on a system. It is updated whenever an OLE-enabled component object is installed or executed.

The *object linking* feature of OLE allows a UIO (acting as an *OLE client*) to be linked to data objects attached to an associated PO (acting as an *OLE server*) and any changes made to the data object by the PO are reflected in the UIO's view of the data object. The linking process places only the object's presentation data and a pointer to its native data in the UIO. For example, consider a UIO which represents a business report written using a word processor. Suppose the business report UIO contains an OLE link to a spreadsheet PO which displays some spreadsheet table. Any changes made to the spreadsheet data are automatically reflected in the business report UIO. Thus the UIO always shows the most current data. OLE maintains links between objects in common actions such as file move, copy and rename.

The *object embedding* feature of OLE allows a UIO (OLE client) to contain a data object without maintaining an active link to the associated PO (OLE server) which handles the native data. The embedding process places both an object's presentation and native data within the UIO. All information necessary to edit the embedded object is contained in the UIO. Thus any changes made to the original data object by the associated PO will not be reflected in the UIO since it does not contain a pointer to it. In effect the OLE server simply passes a copy of the relevant data to the OLE client. A major benefit of both object linking and embedding is that the OLE client does not need to understand how the data is encoded since the client simply asks the OLE server to do many of the common actions on the data such as displaying it on the screen or printing it. OLE also allows multi-level nesting of objects. Although embedding results in the UIO carrying more overhead data, it allows an object to be migrated to another computer and to be edited on a different computer since it contains no pointers to local data objects. In contrast, linked objects cannot be migrated outside the local file system, but linking is more efficient because a single instance of a data object can serve many different objects with each object viewing the latest data values.

The *OLE automation* feature allows a PO (an *automation object*) to expose methods that operate within and across other objects. This has the effect of *exporting* its services for use by other objects, then listening for messages (commands). For example, a user can invoke from a word processor PO a method that sorts a range of cells in a spreadsheet created by a different object. The word processor can then display the results of the sorted data by creating a spreadsheet graph and use the OLE linking feature to link it into the word processor document. Thus OLE automation allows component objects direct access to functionality provided by other component objects (as opposed to the data managed by a component object via object linking and embedding). OLE automation objects can listen for messages (commands) from other component objects. *Automation controllers* are software products or mechanisms for talking to OLE automation objects. For example a software product's macro language (or a third-generation language) may act as an automation controller, allowing users to send commands to OLE automation objects.

The *drag and drop* feature of OLE enables users to drag an icon representing a component object and drop it inside another icon which has the effect of sending a message from the dragged object to the object onto which it was dropped.

10.6.5 Linking to remote POs

Chapter 4 detailed two principle mechanisms for remote inter-process communications: message passing and remote procedure calls. Both of these mechanisms can be used in a DIS based on the distributed object model.

Microsoft OLE component objects executing within a single computer, communicate using a lightweight remote procedure call mechanism called Microsoft lightweight RPC (LRPC). OLE with distributed object support incorporates a full RPC mechanism based on DCE RPC (but with extensions to the DCE RPC interface definition language) to allow component objects to communicate across a network. In addition, security and name services are provided together with an interface definition language and support for stub generation through IDL pre-processing. Figure 10.6 illustrates the inter-play between Microsoft RPC and the OLE object system to provide distributed objects capability. The distributed OLE product was not yet announced at the time of writing.

An alternative example of a standard for which many supplier products are available which address the area of linking distributed objects is the common object request broker architecture (CORBA) developed by the Object Management Group (OMG) which was detailed in Chapters 3 and 8.

10.6.6 Linking to data objects

Chapters 4, 8, and 10 detailed many middleware mechanisms for inter-process communications including direct and indirect message passing, message queuing, remote procedure calls and transaction processing. All of these mechanisms can be used to link POs that are remote from each other. Many sytems utilize a RPC mechanism such as DCE RPC which provides good support for mission critical systems. DTP middleware also provides the basic services

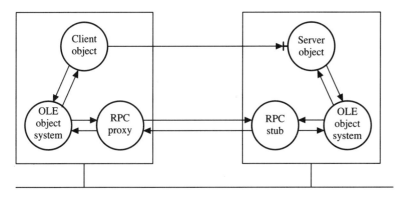

Figure 10.6 Microsoft distributed OLE specification.

required to implement mission-critical systems involving the interaction between local and remote POs.

Presentation management software, such as OLE by Microsoft, provide services for creating and maintaining compound (multimedia) documents. OLE provides features such as:

- **Visual editing**, which, instead of switching between POs to create parts of the compound document, enables users to work within the current context of their document. User controls are wrapped around the UIO corresponding to the compound document part which is to be worked on.
- **OLE linking and embedding** , and **OLE automation** features are used to create compound documents incorporating text, graphics, sound, animation, video and other diverse DOs.

10.6.7 DO-to-DO linkages – hypermedia links

When a DO represents a hypermedia object then its content may contain a pointer to another hypermedia object. For example the World Wide Web hypermedia system described in Chapter 8 defines a syntax, the hypertext markup language (HTML), for document formatting and embedding static hyperlinks in a web document (e.g. `<A HREF="http://www.wlv.ac.uk/"<A>` signifies a pointer to the Web server `www.wlv.ac.uk`) which points to another Web document. When a Web browser receives a 'user has clicked on a hypermedia link reference' event, it must send a request to the appropriate web server (in this case `www.wlv.ac.uk`) for the Web document. The web client to server protocol is the hypertext transfer protocol (http). Web documents can contain static links to other types of data objects, for example, a text file accessed using the FTP file transfer protocol, a graphics file, a gopher server, Usenet news and an Archie server. Thus a hypermedia DO is an example of a compound DO but with one or more target anchors to other hypermedia DOs as was illustrated in Chapter 8 (Figure 8.12).

A Web hypermedia DO does not need to exist on a Web server at the time that a browser sends a request for access. The URL can point to a file containing a script written according to the *common gateway interface* (CGI) mechanism described in Chapter 8. The CGI mechanism provides a standard way of running software on a web server to create a *virtual Web document* (documents created from a CGI script when a program is executed).

10.7 APPLICATION ARCHITECTURES

10.7.1 One-tier application architecture

A one-tier application architecture is typified by the traditional mainframe application. These applications are characterized by the tight integration of presentation, processing and data components into a single monolithic program running on a mainframe, minicomputer or PC server configured to support one-tier applications. It is often difficult to decouple these components. Applications are batch processes or online, accessed either using a dumb terminal or a PC with terminal emulation software as shown in Figure 10.7. The main advantages of one-tier architectures is that they take full advantage of the benefits of centralization: security, control and management. The main drawback is the high cost and relative difficulty of reusing application components.

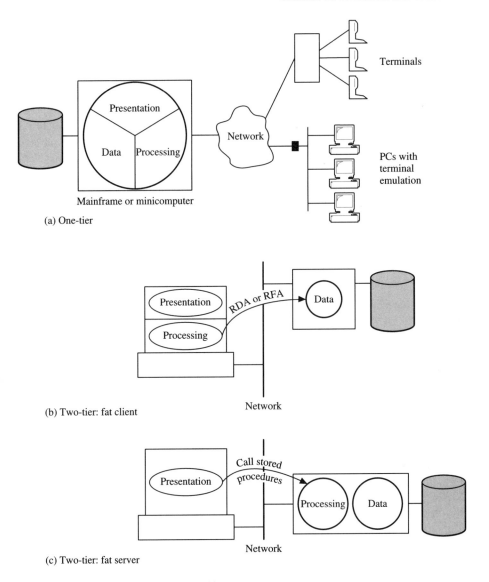

Figure 10.7 One- and two-tier application architectures.

10.7.2 Two-tier application architecture

In a two-tier application architecture, application components are decoupled and placed on to two IT infrastructure elements: client and server computers. This gives rise to two common configurations (see Figure 10.7):

1. The *fat client* configuration; where the presentation and processing components reside on the client, and the data component at the server. A classical example of this architecture is the file and the database server configurations in which application programs residing on the client send data requests to appropriate servers.

2. The *fat server* configuration; where processing and data components reside on the same server while the presentation component resides on the client. In this configuration, the server is commonly called an application server. This is a typical configuration for packaged software implementations with a GUI front-end.

Most implementations of client/server systems are simply two-tiered configurations. Both fat client and server configurations provide more flexible access to data compared with one-tier systems. The fat server configuration enables shared business logic and data which is more easily managed since it resides on a relatively small number of secure, reliable and scalable servers. DBMSs commonly offer good basic transaction processing services using stored procedures (commonly referred to as **TP-light** solutions). The use of SQL stored procedures, however, means that the processing and data components are quite tightly integrated and must normally be wholly contained in a single DBMS.

The main drawback is that it does not provide good support for a typical large organization which will need to develop business logic that manipulates data from a variety of SQL and non-SQL data sources (including legacy applications, possibly decades old).

10.7.3 Three-tier application architectures

The presentation, processing and data components are completely decoupled and typically reside on different computer platforms, forming a three-tier configuration.

- Tier 1 comprises client workstations each running the presentation component of an application.
- Tier 2 comprises **shared application services** which can be reused by multiple applications. Shared application services are replicated for enhanced availability and performance (when located close to tier 1 clients).
- Tier 3 comprises **shared data services** which may be widely dispersed geographically but can be accessed by application servers in tier 2. Distributed transaction processing (DTP) monitors (commonly referred to as **TP-heavy** solutions) are positioned as an attractive option for middleware because they offer a variety of low-level linkage mechanisms and provide database independence, security mechanisms, dynamic reconfiguration, centralized monitoring and management. An example three-tier architecture implemented using DTP monitors is shown in Figure 10.8.

Choosing the right application architecture is a rightsizing issue. Table 10.2 summarizes the strengths and weaknesses of each application architecture. In the ATM example which was illustrated in Figure 10.5, for example, a three-tier architecture was chosen as the basis for the link model. The ATMs are in tier 1, presenting an interface to customers. Tier 2 consists of the consortium servers. These are implemented using a DTP monitor and processing objects implemented as transactions. The third tier is formed by the various bank servers each of which holds customer account information for a specific bank.

10.7.4 The application development environment

The evolution of application development tools to support the development of distributed information systems has paralleled the evolution of application architectures from one-tier

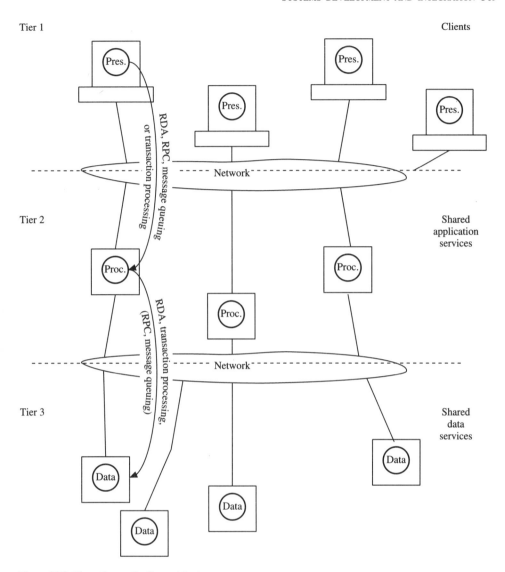

Figure 10.8 Three-tier application architecture.

mainframe systems to two-tier and finally three-tier. CASE tools evolved in the era when one-tier mainframe systems were dominant. A new breed of systems development tools were designed to support rapid development and deployment of two-tier client/server applications. These were characterized by their ability to easily generate GUI-based presentation components and simple business logic centred around accessing a local SQL database server. Second generation client/server development tools generally focus on the development of systems which adhere to the three-tier application architecture. Table 10.3 compares the typical features of these categories of tools.

Table 10.2 A comparison of application architectures

Feature	One-tier	Two-tier	Three-tier
Primary system type	Operational/transaction processing	Group/departmental operational/decision support	Enterprise-level operational/decision support
Scalability	Low (due to dependence on a single node)	Low–medium	High
Position in technology life-cycle	decline or re-positioning as high-end server	Growth	Growth
Design and implementation flexibility	Low	Low/medium	High
Implementation complexity	More difficult to implement	Easy to implement (good for prototyping)	More difficult to implement
Rapid application development and deployment	No	Yes	Possibly (dependent on the complexity of the application)
Security, performance and data protection	High (with OLTP and database recovery support)	Low-medium (dependent on use of stored procedures and transactional (SQL)	High (with DTP in tier 2 or alternative middleware with transactional semantics)
Ease of management	Good (due to centralization)	Good (small scale) Poor (large scale)	More difficult (due to increased complexity as a result of decentralization)

10.8 SUMMARY

In this chapter a number of methodologies and techniques for DIS development were outlined. A DIS is normally characterized by a sophisticated GUI presentation component with local and remote processing and data objects. The ODP model provides a framework for structuring systems analysis and design using the distributed object model. RAD offers a useful approach to ensure that user requirements are captured and quality systems are produced rapidly and cost-effectively. Object modelling techniques are a natural choice since many distributed applications employ the client/server or distributed object model.

An example approach for implementing a DIS from a logical (computational) model was detailed. One key issue is to consider the linkages between presentation, processing and data objects. A number of technologies for implementing linkages was described.

Table 10.3 Typical features of each category of distributed application development tools

Typical features	One-tier	Two-tier	Three-tier
Scale	• Mainframe application	• Workgroup application	• Enterprise application
Toolkit	• CASE tools with underlying assumption of a centralized IT infrastructure	• GUI front end and single SQL database server development tools	• Integrated development of all three-tier components
	• Centralized IT infrastructure assumed	• An existing RDBMS is presumed	• Distributed IT infrastructure assumed
	• Team development and centralized repository		• Team development and centralized repository
			• Configuration management/version control
	• Configuration management/version control		• Decoupled presentation, processing and data components
			• Flexible component placement options
Applications	Large-scale operational	Small-scale decision support	Large-scale operational and decision support
Support for building server-based business logic	Mainframe-based	Very limited (normally via stored procedures)	Yes
Support for GUI design	Limited (dumb terminals or PC with terminal emulation assumed)	Yes	Yes
Batch processing application development	Yes	Yes	Yes
Linkages/middleware	Terminal emulation protocol	• Local: DDE, OLE • Remote: RDA and RFA	• Local: DDE, OLE • Remote: RPC, transactional, message queuing, ORB
Design for reliability/ performance	Limited scope	Replicated database server	• Replicated shared application and data services • Load balancing • Dynamic reconfiguration

10.9 REVIEW EXERCISES

1. What are the goals and characteristics of the traditional systems development life-cycle approach?
2. Describe the main features of a prototyping approach to systems development. Is this approach appropriate to the development of distributed information systems?
3. What new perspectives does the ODP model introduce?
4. Describe the main issues of concern in the engineering and technology viewpoints in the ODP model.
5. To what extent do existing methodologies populate the ODP model with models and techniques?
6. Using the case study in Section 10.5, consider the needs of a bank manager. Extend the object model, infrastructure diagram and link model to consider a bank manager's needs. Include amongst bank manager requirements the need to utilize the World Wide Web to access certain financial information.
7. Discuss the linkage options available for implementing a DIS.

10.10 FURTHER READING

RAD approaches and issues are discussed in Martin (1991), Bates and Stephens (1995), Arthur (1992) and Clegg and Barker (1994). The Dynamic Systems Development Method Consortium, a consortium of leading industrial names has recently published a RAD method (DSDM, 1995). Many interesting papers on ODP can be found in de Meer *et al.* (1992). An approach to enterprise modelling is found in Veryard *et al.* (1995). An example object modelling approach is found in Rumbaugh *et al.* (1991).

PART FOUR

Management, Standards and Security

11

DECENTRALIZED MANAGEMENT AND CONTROL

11.1 INTRODUCTION

Chapter 2 highlighted the growing trend towards decentralized organizational structures primarily to improve operational flexibility and responsiveness to clients as a reaction to increased competition and an increasingly complex and dynamic business environment. We also identified that this trend was one of the main driving forces towards the widespread adoption of distributed information systems. In this chapter the relationship between organizational structure and the design, implementation and management of information systems and technology (IS/IT) is considered. The concept of local autonomy is described and various models used to balance autonomy and co-ordination explored. Systems for computer support for co-operative working (CSCW) are explored in the context of implementing co-ordination mechanisms in a decentralized organization. The contribution of workflow management systems to business process re-design is also explored.

11.2 ORGANIZATIONAL DESIGN AND INFORMATION SYSTEMS

Information systems requirements are greatly influenced by the management principles and associated organizational structure adopted. Therefore when developing distributed systems, it is useful to develop a perspective of the organizational culture and management philosophy of an organization because it can influence significantly a key decision, for example, the degree of distribution, administration and management domain hierarchies, etc.

Early ideas of management principles and organizational design regarded an organization as an instrument for making profits for the owners by converting inputs to profits by good management practice. *Scientific management* principles (Taylor, 1947), regarded shop floor employees as unsuitable to make decisions both in terms of their ability and motivation. Only 'higher-level' managers could carry out decision-making because it was thought that they had the best interests of the company at heart. Organizational tasks were subject to maximal fragmentation (i.e. a deskilling process), and work studies which were used as a basis for instigating payments by results (piecework) practices with the underlying assumption that people work as fast as they can (high productivity) to earn as much as they can. Inevitably workers became unsatisfied, bored, frustrated and antipathetic towards the organization. This simplistic model of an organization was later enhanced by the next phase of management science, known as *general management theory* (Fayol, 1949), which introduced the five elements of managerial work: planning, organization, command, co-ordination and control, which remain a feature of modern management theory and organizational design. It also introduced ideas such as delegation of authority (it was thought that authority was sufficient to get people to work effectively), creating a hierarchical organizational structure, management processes such as effective communications and motivation.

However, these classical organizational designs did not take account of the dynamic nature of organizations (i.e. change and how to cope with it) and the unpredictable, complex nature of people in terms of their interests, values, motivations and attitudes. The *human relations* perspective highlighted the importance of friendly supervisor–employee relationships, recognizing an employee's social needs (i.e. social status, social relationships and social norms), job satisfaction and enrichment. They criticized classical management principles on human terms in the sense that management should provide interesting and challenging work, and to some extent be responsible for the welfare of its employees.

The *systems approach* to organizational design places emphasis on the organization as a system which produces products or services that are attractive to customers in terms of factors such as functionality and price. The organizational system is sub-divided into inter-related sub-systems and which is itself part of a system. The assumption is that organizational goals are set, divided and passed down to sub-systems, and if sub-systems achieve their goals, the organization will achieve its goals. The information flows within and between systems; decision-making and control and co-ordination mechanisms are emphasized. However, the major contribution of the systems approach is its emphasis on the environment within which organizations operate and the introduction of monitoring and intelligence mechanisms for monitoring changes in the environment which may affect the long-term viability of the organization. In Section 11.3 an example approach is outlined: the Viable System Model (Beer, 1979) because it provides a useful perspective in determining information systems requirements and approaches to managing IS/IT.

In Chapter 1 it was highlighted that there is no permanent 'best-fit' in terms of organizational structure. The 'contingency' approach acknowledges that organizational structure and characteristics should reflect the organization's situation, taking into account situational factors such as age, size and the nature of the business environment. Thus the contingency approach is a development of the systems approach by examining the situational variables which affect sub-systems and inter-relationships between sub-systems. The relationship between organizational structure and these situational (contingency) factors is explored in detail by Mintzberg (1988), Galbraith (1988), Robbins (1989) and others, and can be summarized as follows.

- Larger organizations and those in stable business environments need more formalized structures. Standardization of activities is a mechanism for enhanced co-ordination especially where activities are routine in nature and the organization is too large to exercise centralized direct supervision.
- A large organization operating in a complex environment needs a higher degree of decentralization. This is because a centralized authority would find it difficult to maintain the expertise required to make timely and informed decision-making in this type of environment.
- An organization diversified in many markets needs a divisionalized (market-based) rather than functional structure. Diversification is a feature of large, mature organizations. A divisionalized structure reduces the co-ordination needed across units because each division is usually a separate functional structure with its own markets. However, even though divisionalization is desirable it is not always possible because some functions, for example, need to be centrally co-ordinated.
- An organization operating in a more dynamic business environment, i.e. when sources of supply are typically uncertain, needs a more organic structure to remain flexible to unpredictable changes in the environment. In an organic structure, co-ordination mechanisms are much less formally standardized.
- An organization operating in a 'hostile' business environment tends toward a centralized structure to gain tight co-ordination by direct supervision from top management, ensuring a quick and decisive response to the threats.
- An organization operating in an environment where external control (e.g. by a holding company or by government) is great, tends towards a centralized and formalized structure. This is mainly because these organizations are accountable to 'outsiders' and need to justify their decisions and behaviour.

The discussion above illustrates that we can expect a variety of organizational structures to be in use; there is no right way or wrong way to design an organization. Indeed, an organization may move from one structure to another in response to changes in size, product lines, the business environment, key personnel, and so on. Restructuring is now a normal activity in the life of an organization. Mintzberg (in Quinn *et al.*, 1988)suggests that analysis of contingency factors such as age, size, nature of the business and the business environment, leads to the identification of several natural structural configurations. To distinguish the configurations, Mintzberg defines an organizational structure in terms of five parts:

1. the strategic apex, consisting of top management;
2. the middle line, consisting of functional middle managers that control the technostructure;
3. the technostructure, consisting of staff who design and maintain the organization's rules and procedures;
4. the support staff, who are specialists providing support services (e.g. the legal, public relations, post-room and personnel departments) outside of the operating core;
5. the operating core, consisting of staff who do the basic work to produce the organization's products and services.

The main configurations identified are:

- a simple structure, characterized by a small organization which is highly centralized with little formalization;
- a machine bureaucracy, typical of a mass production organization which, by virtue of its age, size and mass-produced products, is bureaucratic with high formalization and concentration;

- a professional bureaucracy, where the nature of the product is such that professional staff make up the operating core with considerable control over their work (e.g. hospital consultants and academic staff);
- a diversified (divisionalized) structure, characteristic of organizations operating in a relatively simple and stable but diversified market. The organization is sub-divided into market-based, autonomous units. Each sub-unit typically adopts a functional structure;
- an autocracy, characterized by organizations operating in complex and dynamic environments. The operating core are highly trained, highly specialized experts handling non-routine, complex technologies. A good example is the pharmaceutical industry where products can take years to progress from concept to a marketable product. In such a market the use of creative project teams of experts in various fields is often the most effective organizational structure. This implies low formalization and concentration.

11.2.1 Political perspective

All of the management philosophies examined so far make the implicit assumption that management controls the business organization and have a right to set and control organizational goals. Lee and Lawrence (1985) argue that although this may be the position of managers in public, their actual private behaviour is in fact determined by their own interests and values. This *political* perspective characterises organizations in terms of different persons (actors) or **interest groups** who, as far as possible, will look after their own specific interests. In this perspective, no actor or interest group has the *right* to influence organization direction and activity although most actors share an interest in ensuring its survival (for selfish reasons). Actors are decision-makers actively pursuing their own interests and goals. Thus, an organization is viewed as a complex web of actors and interest groups competing and co-operating with the help of different resources at their disposal. Actors are able to achieve a different degree of influence in a given network of relationships based on their power base. With this perspective we can perhaps explain why conflict, coalitions and political activity are a normal feature of organizational life. The power needs of power-holders within an organization tend to generate structures with concentrations of authority (formal power), leading still further to excessively centralized structures. Put simply, people make organizations, and they create rules, policies, systems and procedures to help ensure that other employees behave in line with their wishes. A manager may adopt a particular leadership style or organizational structure irrespective of possible effects on profits or productivity but more likely to enhance his power base.

11.3 THE VIABLE SYSTEM MODEL

Beer (1972) approaches organization design and dynamics from a systems and cybernetic perspective (cybernetics is the science of control and communication) and serves as a useful model to determine information systems requirements and the influences on decision-making which may affect DIS development. Beer interpreted initial work by Ashby (1965) who applied cybernetic theory to the human brain and established the application of cybernetics to management science.

Ashby enhanced understanding of the complexity of systems and how to deal with it by proposing a precise measure of complexity: the *variety* of a system, meaning the number of

distinguishable elements (or states) of system. If a system has for example fifty distinguishable states, the variety of the system is fifty. Complexity is then defined as the number of different distinctions one can perceive. So although there are fifty possible variations, an
observer may, for some reason, find it difficult to observe more than about eight possible distinctions. Thus the observer cannot absorb all the variety of the system being observed.
Ashby's Law of Requisite Variety says that 'only variety absorbs variety'. In other words the
only way to control a complex system is with a control system which is at least equally complex. If the control system's variety is less than the variety of the situation it is trying to control, it cannot control it!

Information is an important factor in this context since the actual mechanism of control
involves information flows (e.g. commands and feedback information) between the controlling system and the system being controlled. However, other signals flowing around the system may cause undesirable changes in the state of the system (known as 'entropy' which are
signals that lead to undesirable changes to the state of a system). Thus information must be
purposely transmitted to defeat entropy in the controlled system. Organizations are complex
systems and the complexity of individual managers (each viewed as a control system) has to
be at least as complex as the complexity of the system (e.g. department) being managed. In
reality, the business environment has far more variety than managers can cope with. Can managers ever hope to be in control of the business environment which exhibits so much variety?
The problem is that managers can manage only if the variety of what is being managed is less
or equal to the variety of management. This apparent paradox which suggests that managers
can never be in control is resolved by recognizing the operation of two balancing mechanisms: *attenuators* (which reduce variety) and *amplifiers* (which increase variety) as shown in
Figure 11.1. Most of the time the main attenuator used by managers is ignorance! If managers
continue to be ignorant of key events and information, however, important decisions will not
be made. Thus if ignorance is the main attenuator then eventually this leads to a loss of
control of the system.

An organization can be viewed as a network of relationships (interactions) between people who carry out defined roles, working together for mutual benefit. It is these roles and relationships that remain relatively stable over time in the face of constant staff changes. The
organizational context in which these people operate either inhibits or supports problem solving from the perspective of a problem solver. The 'organization' might be perceived to be
rigid and inflexible, making it difficult for a problem solver to co-operate with others to

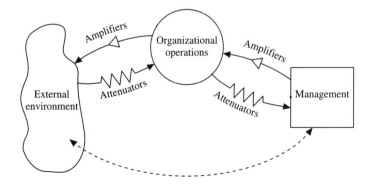

Figure 11.1 Amplifiers and attenuators.

achieve an objective. Organization design is about understanding how the organization works and how to develop an organizational context in order to foster creative problem solving (or increase the capacity for creative problem solving). Essentially, the organizational structure should improve the environment for problem understanding and debate which leads to better decision making.

At the heart of Beer's model is the concept of viability. An organization is defined from a cybernetic standpoint by Beer (1979) as **viable** if it is capable of maintaining a separate existence. This is more than an emphasis on long-term economic viability. It places emphasis on other factors which may influence long-term viability such as attitudes, values, levels of communication and co-operation, balancing short-term and long-term policy developments and so on. A viable system normally exists in a dynamic **environment** within which it maintains its separate existence (i.e. the business environment) and which may be a pre-condition of viability. For example, a human being will not live for very long without an environment which yields food and water. Similarly, an organization will not survive for very long without the means of production and a potential customer base. Environments are rarely stable and many organizations are competing for viability in an environment where changes are sometimes predicted, sometimes unforeseen or unexpected. Therefore a viable system must also be capable of maintaining a separate existence in the presence of unforeseen and unexpected changes in the environment. The main implication is that organizations must be adaptable but, at the same time, subject to effective control to ensure long-term viability.

An environment is typically complex, capable of exhibiting high variety. The environmental states are of a complexity which is beyond the ability of the individual manager to comprehend let alone manage. Indeed, the organization within which managers exert control is itself of high variety. Beer's *First Principle of Organization* (Beer, 1979) states that the sum of the varieties of each part must equate throughout the environment–organization–management trinity. Clearly attenuating and amplifying mechanisms are required to balance the differences in variety between environment and organization and between organization and management. Organizations and managers must not let this variety balance happen by chance (i.e. through sheer ignorance as the main attenuator) because it leads to loss of control which, in turn, leads to loss of viability. Typical attenuators and amplifiers are given in Tables 11.1 and 11.2.

Table 11.1 Balancing environment and organization variety

Attenuators	*Amplifiers*
Ignorance (let it happen by chance)!	Research and development
Market segmentation	Industry reports and analysis
Market research	Market trials and pilots
Moving out of a specific market (reverse diversification or 'back to the core' strategies)	New markets (e.g. opening operations in another country)
Self-help (or self-service) groups	Dealer networks and franchises Manufacturing under licence Advertising Takeovers to reach new markets and expand an existing customer base

Table 11.2 Balancing organization and management variety

Attenuators	Amplifiers
Ignorance (let it happen by chance)!	Enabling self-managed groups through delegation, policies and rules
Relevant information selection via computer-based information systems (e.g. management reports, accounts, etc.)	Participative decision-making
Information filtering by computer-based pre-processing of information using techniques such as statistical analysis and forecasting	Management by objectives
Use of appropiate indices which highlight when management attention or action is required	Organizational conversations which lead to commitments of others (getting other people to do things thus enabling more tasks to be carried out)
Organizational structure (e.g. functional structures)	Training
Pareto (80/20) analysis and action (i.e. identify and focus on the 20% of problems which accounts for 80% of the issues of concern)	Organizational structure
Company policy	Management teams
Organization conversations	

Espejo (1989) established the concept of *residual variety* which is defined as the disturbances that a system receives that require attention. An attenuation technique is effective if it minimizes the residual variety to such an extent that it is less or equal to the capacity of the system receiving it. For example, consider a pilot flying an aircraft from London to Edinburgh. The environment is represented by the flying environment which has disturbances such as the weather, the terrain, other aircraft and so on. An aircraft has complex electronics which deal automatically with a range of environmental disturbances (i.e. the aircraft handles much of the environmental variety itself). Any disturbances not dealt with by the aircraft (i.e. the residual variety not absorbed by the aircraft) must be actioned by the pilot. Hopefully the residual variety does not exceed the pilot's capacity to deal with the disturbances!

It is assumed that the aircraft reports information (through aircraft instrumentation) in a form that can be readily interpreted by the pilot. When information needs to be passed from one 'system' to another (in this case from the aircraft system to the pilot), effective *trans-ducers* are required which are mechanisms for translating or interpreting information from one form to another so that a receiving system is able to act upon it. Another example of a transducer is a business report produced by the accounts department for the manager of a business unit. The report acts as a transducer of financial information.

In organization–management variety balancing, managers have problems and have to manage the problems and tasks of concern demanded by the manager's role within the organization. Consequently they require relevant information and create the information needed to complete tasks and solve problems. Managers are therefore both transmitters and receivers of information and, as part of the problem-solving process, are **information managers**. Thus managers need to balance the variety of tasks and information processing requirements (high

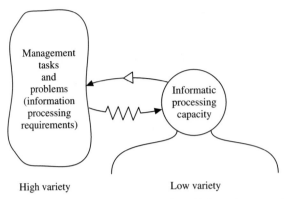

Figure 11.2 Balancing management tasks and information processing capacity.

variety) with their own information processing capacity (low variety) as illustrated in Figure 11.2 (Espejo and Watt, 1978). The main challenge for managers is how to utilize attenuation (e.g. reducing information needs) and amplification (e.g. delegating tasks to others) tools to balance the varieties and, at the same time, meet (by design rather than by chance) an organizationally defined acceptable level of performance.

Beer also introduces the notion of recursion in an organizational structure. His *recursive system theorem* (Beer, 1979) states:

> In a recursive organizational structure, any viable system contains, and is contained within, a viable system.

Thus an organization structured into autonomous subsidiaries (divisions) which themselves are structured in terms of autonomous departments is an example of a recursive structure. Individual managers are themselves 'viable' systems. Recursive structures are essential to ensure that an organization copes with the high variety of organizational tasks that have to be dealt with by distributing responsibility, discretion and autonomy in relation to tasks down to all levels. Each recursive level can be thought of as a **management domain** which exhibits a high level of autonomy, able to specify and implement its own policies. These policies can be as diverse as a strategic plan, a systems development policy, a security policy a procurement policy and so on. The principle of recursion emphasizes that *management is a distributed processing activity which requires a distributed processing system to support it.*

11.3.1 Five-system model

Beer's viable system model (VSM) recognizes that at any recursive level there is a collection of **operational elements** which carry out defined tasks and **metasystem elements** which ensure the long-term viability of operational elements. Five discrete systems (called Systems 1–5) are defined through which the various operational and metasystemic elements interact as shown in Figure 11.3 and summarized below.

System 1 – operational elements

These are the units that are to be controlled by the control, intelligence and policy metasystemic elements.

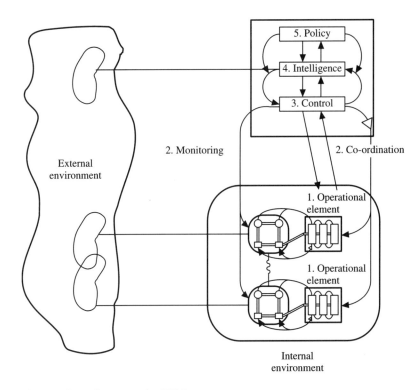

2. Monitoring

2. Co-ordination

External
environment

Internal
environment

Figure 11.3 The five systems in a VSM.

System 2 – co-ordination and monitoring

These are the information systems that facilitate decentralized decision-making within, and between the operational elements with respect to current needs, rather than by the metasystemic elements. Co-ordination by self-regulation rather than by intervention (i.e. by direct supervision) is the ideal. People operating at this level build their own **network of relationships with others** to make decisions and resolve problems. Example co-ordination mechanisms are annual budgets, the mission statement and strategic plans (which define relative priorities and implementations), timetables and planning life-cycles, and standard procedures and policies.

The monitoring channel is used to carry out investigations (audit) to validate or verify information received by the control metasystemic element from operational elements. Monitoring should be a public (explicit) process and sporadic to reduce the flow of invalid information.

System 3 – control function

This is the point at which operational elements connect to the metasystemic elements. System 3 is concerned with maintaining a stable internal state which is why it is appropriately labelled the control system. Policy directives are received from the policy metasystemic element and relayed downwards to the operational elements through the *command channel*. Resource negotiation involving operational elements is also managed through the *resource bargaining* channel. The more difficult the resource bargaining and control interactions between operational elements the more the control channel has to be used to resolve conflicts. To achieve a high level of synergy between operational elements the metasystem should seek to minimize use of this channel and maximize use of the co-ordination and monitoring channels.

System 4 – intelligence function

Whilst the control metasystemic element is focused on current internal operations and aspects affecting current internal behaviour (commonly referred to as the 'here and now' (Beer, 1979)), the intelligence metasystemic element is concerned with monitoring the environment and identifying behaviour and aspects likely to require changes to current internal behaviour. Thus the intelligence system monitors the environment to develop and adapt operational elements to exploit longer-term opportunities.

System 5 – policy function

There is a need to relate the short-term, internal perspective of the control function with the long-term, external perspective of the intelligence function. By ensuring good co-operation and interactions between intelligence and control functions, the policy-making process will be enriched by creative but realistic (in terms of the capacity of adaptation of existing operations to future needs) proposals and discussions about future possibilities. The output of the policy function is downward control (in terms of new policies, plans and goals) to operating elements via the control unit. Thus policy function decisions affect the whole of the viable system.

The recursive feature of VSM implies that the metasystemic elements at one level aggregate to a System 1 at the next recursive level.

Although Beer's VSM is a rich conceptual model which can be used to diagnose organizational problems and as a tool for organizational design, it can be intellectually demanding when applied to real problem situations. In practice, 'good' managers have a well-developed, intuitive understanding of problem-solving approaches articulated using the VSM cybernetic framework. Many managers are applying attenuation and amplification mechanisms without specialist knowledge of VSM because many of the techniques highlighted are widely accepted as good management practice.

11.3.2 Implications for information systems requirements

Although we have looked at models such as Mintzberg (1988) and VSM (Beer 1979, 1981, 1985; Espejo and Harnden, 1989) only briefly, the above discussion makes apparent the inter-related nature of management processes and information systems, and Beer's VSM identifies various classes of information systems which are applicable at all levels of recursion (i.e. all management domains):

1. *Co-ordination information systems* These are high variety information systems which supply information to enable co-ordination between operating elements. Base transactions of the business (such as accounting, personnel and stock) are recorded in accounting, personnel, stock control and other (transaction processing) information systems and provide the means of co-ordinating activities across the operating elements.

2. *Control information systems*   Operating elements in each autonomous system carry out a well-defined set of tasks. The metasystem controls and monitors the operating elements. Control ISs must provide information for the effective control (i.e. resource bargaining and decision-making at the operational level) and monitoring of operating elements in a particular autonomous system. Resource negotiations and operational decision-making are supported by group decision support information systems (GDSS) which seek to create the appropriate environment for resource bargaining and decision-making activities and satisfies the information needs of managers.

3. *Policy information systems*   At each level of recursion, the policy function tries to balance today's operation with tomorrow's needs and determines investment policy, future business strategy and so on. An effective policy function manages the interactions between intelligence (long-term, outward looking) and control (short-term, inward looking) functions so as to minimize (residual) information needs at the policy level and, at the same time, enhance the creativity and variety of proposals and options put forward and issues raised. Hopefully, management meetings at this level consist of interactions between policy-makers that result in balanced conversations and perspectives. Policy information systems are thus more concerned with communication issues and supporting the need to present proposals and debate issues with supporting information. Policy-makers also tend to require access to information quickly (for example as an idea is being developed) and in an unstructured, chaotic manner whilst meetings are taking place. Executive information systems (EIS) attempt to meet the information needs of policy-makers.

    GDSS technologies are also relevant to the policy function. It is often the case that policy-level conversations take place in 'board-rooms', therefore design considerations typically focus not only on user-interface and communications requirements but also on environmental issues such as ensuring that the meeting room is effective in terms of lighting, sound, space, comfort, furniture arrangement and so on.

Beer (1979, 1981) notes that the traditional development of corporate database systems to meet an organization's information needs leads to a centralized and rigid approach to information systems design together with a 'let's collect everything and process everything' approach to implementation. Distributed information systems afford an approach to information systems design which takes account of the information system's intended function and precise information requirements. An underlying distributed IT infrastructure can provide effective support for information distribution within and between management domains, and facilitate group conversations using GDSS technology.

11.4 BUSINESS PROCESS REDESIGN

IS/IT is an enabling technology for business process re-engineering (BPR). BPR involves the 'analysis of work flows and processes within and between organizations' (Davenport and Short, 1990), where a business process is defined as 'a set of logically related tasks performed to achieve a defined business outcome' (*ibid.*). The BPR process essentially examines current workflows with a view to identifying significant bottlenecks, discontinuities, and unnecessary or redundant steps that become candidates for deletion (Vaughn, 1994). Thus BPR is a streamlining process. Work flow models make use of rules to enforce correctness of dependencies and flows between work flow components. Workflow model rules define the conditions under which transaction dependencies can be resolved and their subsequent actions (Warne, 1994).

Workflow management systems are rule-based management software services that direct, co-ordinate, and monitor routine tasks arranged to form business processes (Warne, 1994). Workflows implement automated business rule enforcement and minimize manual intervention, manual co-ordination and paper flows. The use of workflow management systems results in increased throughput, reduced administration, reduced staff time tied up in day-to-day monitoring and tracking and an increase in time to concentrate on productive business tasks. A Workflow management system for a large organization is inherently a distributed system spanning multiple sites. In common with many distributed systems, distribution transparency, scalability, resilience, interoperability, performance and ease-of-use are key requirements. It is unlikely that these requirements can be achieved unless workflow DISs are developed utilizing the generic services described in Chapter 8.

11.4.1 Strategic information systems and distributed multimedia

In the context of strategic information systems, the goal of IS/IT is to support the achievement of sustainable competitive advantage. The main argument of BPR is that IS/IT can be used to effect the radical change in organizational structure and core business activities to achieve sustainable competitive advantage. Work at the Massachusetts Institute of Technology (MIT) defined five levels of business reconfiguration (Scott Morton, 1991; Darnton and Giacoletto, 1992) which are summarized in Table 11.3.

Research (Child, 1984; Rockart and Short, 1988) suggests that IS/IT has enabled a whole layer of management to be removed, creating *flatter organizational structures* with a much higher degree of discretion at the business unit level. IS/IT also supports integration across departmental and organizational boundaries. It can also facilitate team working, more effective horizontal information flows and planning and control activities at each level of recursion within an organization. Darnton and Giacoletto (1992) suggest that the key to harnessing IS/IT strategically is for organizations to determine the appropriate balance between corporate

Table 11.3 Levels of business reconfiguration

Level	Description	Characteristics
1	Localized exploitation	Emphasis on improved efficiency in the performance of a particular task.
2	Internal integration	Emphasis on improved effectiveness for an organization as a result of improved performance with respect to some objective.
3	Business process redesign	Emphasis on revolutionary changes in the design of organizational processes, necessary to exploit fully emerging technological capabilities for competitive advantage. Differential sources of competitive advantages in the marketplace.
4	Business network redesign	Exploiting sources of efficiency and effectiveness through linking with trading partners.
5	Business scope redefinition	Altering the scope of business proactively or in response to some change in the environment.

strategy, management skill and information technology. Some organizations have invested in IT but have not reaped the rewards simply because they did not possess the management skills and vision to leverage IT capabilities so that sustainable competitive advantage could be achieved (Scott Morton, 1991).

Many organizations have focused on the use of distributed multimedia technology to create strategic DISs which lead to new products and services, and enables an organization to change delivery channels to reach their customers (Dustdar, 1994). Dustdar details an example system developed by Barclays Bank based on a 'video-on-demand' model which they claim will transform the retail and wholesale banking market by replacing 'branch banking' with 'branchless shopping' using multimedia kiosks and interactive television accessible from the workplace, home or in public places (e.g. a railway station). Already, 'self-service' kiosk systems are having an impact on the provision of customer services in retail organizations. DISs employed strategically lead to the following benefits:

- Improved customer penetration, targeting and service (e.g. 24-hour availability).
- More effective use of the workforce (e.g. staff can concentrate on selling).
- Easy updating of information.
- The potential to exploit new delivery channels.

11.4.2 Information management and managers

As problem solvers, managers cannot solve all problems by sitting at their desks isolated from the rest of the organization, they must converse with others, discover possibilities, discover and assess complexity, gain the commitment of others and produce solutions. The information needs of managers are determined by their role which, in turn determine the set of tasks for which they are responsible. With an increasingly high variety of information sources at a manager's disposal, there is a constant need for the management of information. Every manager must determine whether they are in a situation of information overload or scarcity in relation to the tasks for which they are responsible.

Information management is the process by which a person balances his information processing capacity to his information needs. Balancing is achieved by reducing (attenuating) information needs without losing control of the situation and the use of information management tools to alert managers to situations which require attention. From the perspective of managers, organizational structure determines the pattern of information flows by specifying communication and control channels, and determines where in the organization specific tasks are carried out. The more effective the structure, the more evenly distributed are tasks and associated information needs. Excessively hierarchical structures lead to overloaded senior managers and underloaded lower layers both in terms of tasks and information needs.

GDSS technologies, sometimes known as **computer supported co-operative working** (CSCW) systems, allow managers to create organizational conversations easily and to participate in group conferences. CSCW systems can provide facilities to record the commitments established and manage conversations by highlighting broken commitments, negotiating extensions and so on. CSCW systems are discussed in detail in the next section.

11.5 COMPUTER SUPPORTED CO-OPERATIVE WORKING (CSCW)

Computer supported co-operative working (CSCW) attempts to exploit computer and communications technologies to support a decentralized organization where both formal and informal teams or groups of people (who may reside at remote locations) can interact and co-operate on projects and tasks using a variety of multimedia computer techniques such as messaging, computer conferencing and document co-authoring. CSCW as a design model encompasses a number of disciplines including psychology, sociology, organizational science and computer science since it addresses social, political and technical issues of co-operative groups.

The term 'CSCW' was originally conceived in 1984 to describe the interests of a number of researchers involved in the use of computers to support co-operative user groups. The area has evolved to combine the understanding of the nature of group working with the enabling technologies of computer networking, systems support and applications. There are many CSCW systems, both commercially available and research projects, that exhibit many of the different co-operation views that exist within the CSCW area.

Navarro *et al.* (1993) described two principal characteristics that can be used to identify CSCW systems.

1. *The form of interaction supported* A CSCW system is primarily used to support a number of computer users who wish to interact and co-operate in order to address and solve particular problems. The nature of the interaction and co-operation can normally be distinguished by the way in which people typically interact with each other. **Synchronous** communications involve two or more users at the same time and occur in 'real time'. An example of synchronous interaction is videoconferencing which provides live video and audio over a network between two or more users. Some products also incorporate live information or application sharing, and co-authoring of documents. **Asynchronous** communication occurs over a longer time period and does not require the simultaneous interaction of users. Most asynchronous systems tend to be based around the message system concept using store-and-forward messaging similar to electronic mail systems (which is an example of an asynchronous system).
2. *The geographical nature of the system* CSCW systems can be considered to be either remote or co-located. Remote systems are typified by sophisticated distributed applications such as multimedia conferencing systems. Co-located systems can include purpose built automated *meeting rooms* furnished with a large screen projector, computer network, controlling terminal and often makes use of multi-user software.

By expanding on these two characteristics, Williams and Blair (1994) have further identified four general classes included in co-operative systems :

1. *Meeting rooms* As described previously, the meeting room usually consists of a purpose built room or lab housing a computer network, projection screens, control terminal and possibly a number of input/voting terminals. The software used is normally multi-user and may encompass graphics and vote tally systems.
2. *Computer conferencing* This kind of system will usually consist of various groups known as conferences, each conference is made up of a set of members and some sequence of messages. These groups (or teams) can differ significantly in their nature: groups can differ in size, duration, objectives, formalization, and in many other aspects. An example of a computer conferencing system is the Internet Usenet system.
3. *Message-based systems* Most messaging systems are related to earlier electronic mail systems such as the Internet's SMTP system. More recent developments in distributed

networks and wide area networks have resulted in the widespread use of more functional, sophisticated messaging applications with features such as the ability to attach multimedia documents and to integrate meeting scheduling.

4. *Co-authoring*   Co-authoring systems aim to support and represent the negotiation and argumentation normally involved in group work. Co-authoring systems allow two or more users to co-author and edit shareable documents in real time. The document being edited is displayed in a window on all terminals, the user can participate in the editing procedures (according to the users status within the workgroup) or can passively watch as progress is made on the document.

CSCW applications increasingly involve distributed multimedia technologies. The term **groupware** has been described as CSCW technology that aids group collaboration to improve group productivity.

11.5.1 The human perspective

Understanding the human issues related to any IT implementation has traditionally been an area in which few computer professionals are involved. Many researchers have, however, analysed the impacts of these new interactive systems and have identified several important areas of human interactive behaviour.

Some social scientists hold the view that group work is not always necessarily co-operative. CSCW systems tend to assume a certain degree of equality between participants, this is not always the way a group will interact and may not be the appropriate approach to group work.

Groups or teams will differ greatly in respect of the dependencies that are exhibited between its members. Groups will also differ in their size, duration and objectives. It is seldom found that a group will consist of equally qualified individuals possessing similar rights and ambitions – co-operation can often be plagued by competition and the withholding of information in the interests of the individual or another interest group. A group will normally display three basic properties:

- the characteristics of the individuals;
- the relationships existing among the members;
- the attributes of the group as a whole.

There are two types of circumstances under which teams may come together:

- created deliberately to accomplish a task or objective by one or more people;
- created spontaneously by people who wish to participate.

Teams can be dynamic in their structure and involve a degree of evolutionary change. For a CSCW system to cope with such change and with the aforementioned group characteristics it must not be inflexible in its automation, rather, it should provide the type of process automation that is flexible to the human involvement, coupled with this a system must model the structure of the organization and its activities.

11.5.2 Standards and architecture

The majority of existing CSCW programs have been developed as standalone programs and as such are unaware of, and cannot 'talk' to other CSCW systems. At present much research is being channelled into the problems of compatibility between systems. Emerging from this research is the need for some kind of CSCW environment that will provide for the interoperability and harmonious integration of CSCW applications. As a precursor to the development of such an environment, Navarro *et al.* (1993) have identified certain general requirements for a CSCW system.

- **Information sharing**. Services must exist to allow the access and exchange of information between different application running on different platforms. A directory service must maintain a knowledge of users and system resources. There should also be a service to inform users of their current status within the co-operative work environment, this service should message the user about actions occurring in the shared application space. Current standards fail to address important problems related to CSCW applications such as access control and transaction locking.
- **Communication support**. Clearly, communication is at the core of all CSCW applications. Recent applications have relied on asynchronous standards such as X.400 which cannot fully cater for the demands that synchronous CSCW communications incur (i.e. real-time videoconferencing and document co-authoring). Communication support must provide support both for asynchronous and real-time group working, using a wide range of media types and allow for interchange across different communication media.
- **Organizational activities support**. By their nature, CSCW systems have strong ties with the organizational activities which they support. In order to manage these activities effectively, a set of services should exist that will allow for the management of members, resource sharing between activities, scheduling, monitoring and co-ordination of activities, mechanisms for negotiating roles, responsibilities and the division of activities. Workflow management systems provide support for routine activities. Ideally workflow management systems should interwork to enable inter-organizational workflow management. Less formal activities are support by electronic mail, meeting schedulers, conferencing systems, and so on.
- **Tailorability**. CSCW applications must be dynamic and tailorable to support the requirements of both developers and users. To these ends, the environment should supply some variation of a developer's toolkit and should also aim to break down some of the divides between user and developer.
- **Transparency**. Selective transparency mechanisms should be provided to facilitate the activities being carried out from different locations at different times using different interfaces. The complexities of the inter-organizational structures should be transparent to the user. Asynchronous and synchronous modes of working should be independent of the user's interaction. Unrelated objects that may disturb activities whether located remotely or locally should also be transparent to the user.

Given the general requirements above, a possible CSCW environment should be an **open** (non-proprietary) system to support the development of different CSCW systems. CSCW requirements are broadly similar to any distributed multimedia system and so should benefit from a similar set of open standards, for example, the open distributed processing (ODP) model (see Chapter 10). Robinson (1994) suggests that many problems of incompatibility between existing CSCW applications must be addressed from the viewpoint of the network providing suitable mechanisms to allow CSCW applications to interact fully and communicate. Clearly, a wide range of services to different CSCW applications are required which provide the information sharing and event synchronization services needed to allow CSCW applications to exchange information and interwork with each other. This is precisely the functionality that should be offered by generic distributed services discussed in Chapter 8.

11.6 DISTRIBUTED SYSTEMS MANAGEMENT

In Chapter 8 the need for systems management services was discussed. Clearly, automated systems management functions are required to cope with the complexity of management tasks that need to be carried out. Managing the IT infrastructure is no different from managing any other resource in the sense that it involves policy-making, intelligence gathering and control functions such as monitoring, control and co-ordination. Another well-defined technique is appropriate in the area of systems management, the *abstraction* of real resources into objects (known as **managed objects**) which is a representation of real resources for the purpose of systems management. Thus, a managed object is simply a resource object with a well-defined management interface. In a distributed system, real resources include network components, servers, user workstations, software components, peripherals such as printers and scanners. Any resource that may be monitored and controlled under the direction of a manager is a managed object. The term *manager*, in this context, is used to describe a human user, hardware or software process responsible for carrying out management activities. Managers must be aware of the **quality of service** requirements of systems. With the increasing use of time-sensitive systems, such as distributed information systems, this is becoming a critical issue (Hutchison *et al.*, 1994).

Logically, the collection of managed objects representing all real resources managed in a specific management domain is known as the **management information base** (ISO 7498-4). In reality, managed objects are inherently distributed physically, therefore it is appropriate to use the distributed object model to describe managed objects. A general architecture for distributed systems management is illustrated in Figure 11.4. Two main standards have emerged which address distributed systems management requirements: ISO/IEC OSI management model and standards, and the Internet simple network management protocol (SNMP) standards. These are described briefly in this section. The reader is referred to an excellent survey of distributed systems management issues by Sloman (1994).

11.6.1 OSI management model and standards

A comprehensive set of ISO/IEC standards has been defined for distributed systems management.

- An architectural framework (ISO 7498-4 and ISO/IEC 10040).
- A management communications standard known as Common management Information Services and Protocols (CMIS/CMIP). CMIS/CMIP (ISO/IEC 9595 and ISO/IEC 9596-1) define the services and protocols required to support communications between a managing and managed systems, as illustrated in Figure 11.5. All resources are managed using the services (which are expressed as a number of primitive operations) defined in CMIS.
- The following systems management functions, currently defined in ISO/IEC 10164:
  - (i) Object management (configuration management);
  - (ii) State management;
  - (iii) Objects and attributes for representing relationships and for access control;

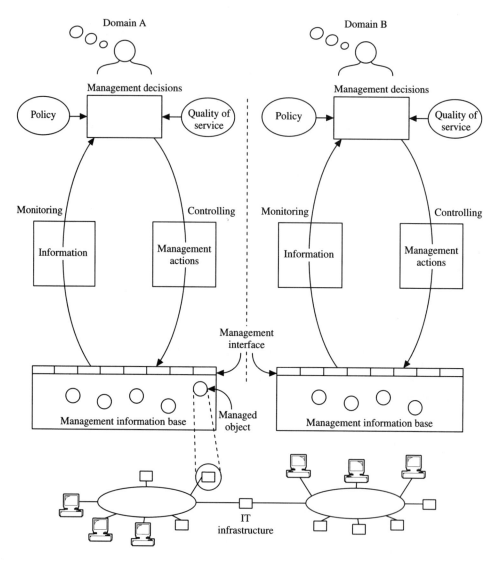

Figure 11.4 A general architecture for distributed systems management (adapted from Langsford and Moffett, 1993)

(iv)   Alarm reporting;
(v)   Event reporting;
(vi)   Logging;
(vii) Security alarm reporting and audit trails;
(viii) Accounting meter functions;
(ix)   Workload monitoring;
(x)   Test management;
(xi)   Measurement summarization.
- Guidelines for defining managed objects (ISO/IEC 10165-1 to 10165-6) which provide a practical aid to systems managers who need to define management information.

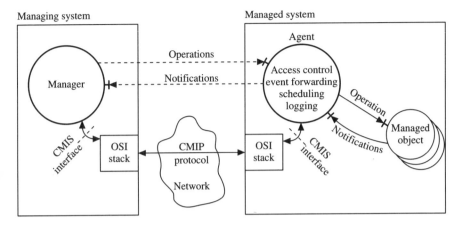

Figure 11.5 The use of agents in the ISO management framework.

A managed object constitutes four aspects, **attributes**, **operations**, **notifications**, and **behaviour**. Attributes are the visible interface to the managing system. Operations may be performed on it; how it reacts (i.e. what **actions** it takes) in response to operations being performed on it is defined as its behaviour. A managed object can report to a managing system by sending a notification. These four aspects describe the **capability** of management of a particular resource. Managed objects can be extensions of other objects through support for *inheritance* of attributes, operations and notifications. Objects are named according to the ITU-T X.500 naming convention.

Managing objects do not communicate directly with all managed objects because the volume of notifications and control actions would be prohibitive. Instead, an **agent** object is responsible for mediating between managing and managed objects, as shown previously in Figure 11.5. Normally, an agent is local to its managed objects, while the manager may be remote from the managed system. In this sense, the agent is a 'local agent'. Communication between managing, agent and managed objects can be modelled on the basic asynchronous request/reply or client/server paradigm.

11.6.2 Internet simple network management protocol (SNMP)

TCP/IP was developed without much consideration of how to manage a TCP/IP network infrastructure except for some very basic facilities such as Internet control message protocol (ICMP) which provides a mechanism for feedback on network problems. In 1987, the simple gateway monitoring protocol (SGMP) was developed for monitoring TCP/IP gateways (i.e. routers). Two subsequent standards emerged: SNMP and the ISO management protocol CMIP running over TCP/IP (known as CMOT). Both standards were approved by the Internet Activities Board (IAB). SNMP was viewed as a short-term solution; and the bridge to ISO standards, CMOT, the long-term choice (on the basis that organizations would eventually move from TCP/IP to OSI-based infrastructures). SNMP and CMOT were allowed to proceed independently with incompatible standards for the underlying MIB and service protocols. From the outset, SNMP was positioned as a relatively simple network management protocol that could be implemented quickly to allow experience to be accumulated concerning the management of networks. The original SNMP standard has been enhanced (SNMPv2) in the

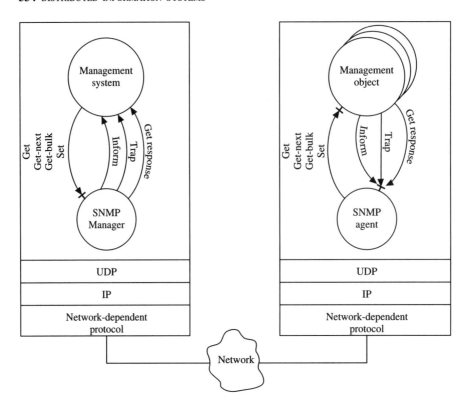

Figure 11.6 Internet SNMP architecture.

light of early experiences, providing better support for security and decentralized management. To some degree, SNMP can now be viewed as a mature and reasonably functional network management standard which competes with the rather more comprehensive ISO systems management standards. In terms of actual usage, however, SNMPv1 is the *de facto* standard; SNMPv2 should establish it as the market leader for the foreseeable future. The SNMP architecture is illustrated in Figure 11.6. SNMPv1 standards are documented in RFC 1155, 1213, 1157. SNMPv2 is documented in RFC 1441 to 1452.

To simplify SNMP implementation, only simple data types are defined. Both SNMP and OSI use the abstract syntax notation (ASN.1) for defining objects formally. SNMP uses a subset of ASN.1 with simple data structures which together reduce significantly the memory requirements to implement an SNMP system (at the expense of functionality). SNMPv2 operation types are compared with CMIS services in Table 11.4.

SNMP polls SNMP agents to initiate movement of data, whereas OSI management is event-driven which leads to lower traffic on the network (i.e. a scalable protocol). UDP and IP protocols are used to exchange management requests, notifications and data. UDP is a 'best-efforts' transport protocol which means that messages can be lost. SNMP defines a **proxy** mechanism for managing resources on non-UDP/IP networks. An SNMP agent can act as a proxy for non-UDP/IP environments by implementing a protocol conversion function. A *remote monitoring MIB* specification has been developed to support decentralized management. RMON defines additions to the basic MIB definition to allow managers to monitor at

Table 11.4 OSI CMIS and SNMP management operations

SNMP operations	CMIS operations	Description
GET-REQUEST	M-GET	Retrieve one value of an object
GET-NEXT-REQUEST	M-GET	Retrieve the next value of an object
GET-BULK-REQUEST (SNMPv2 only)	M-GET	Retrieve *n* values
SET-REQUEST	M-SET, M-ADD	Set the value of objects at the agent
GET-RESPONSE	Not required	Get a response from an agent
TRAP	M-EVENT-REPORT	Allows an agent to notify a manager of a significant event
INFORM (SNMPv2 only)		Unsolicited message sent from an agent to a manager
	M_REMOVE	Remove data from attributes
	M-ACTION	Perform action on objects
	M-CREATE	Create object
	M-DELETE	Delete object
	M-CANCEL-GET	Cancel Get operation

the sub-network level rather than at individual device level. SNMPv2 introduces an authentication protocol which can detect message alteration, insertion and replay. An encryption feature is used for data confidentiality purposes. Table 11.5 gives a comparison of OSI and SNMP features.

Although OSI and SNMP provide wide ranging facilities for distributed systems management, application and desktop device management functions are less well catered for. An industry consortium, known as the Desktop Management Task Force, has developed a desktop management interface (DMI) which attempts to capture basic information in a simple

Table 11.5 A comparison of OSI and SNMP management approaches

OSI management	SNMP management
Powerful and easily extendable	Simple
Flexible naming (based on X.500)	Restrictive naming
It uses the event-driven paradigm (efficient for large networks)	Uses the polling paradigm for manager–agent data exchange
Uses an object-oriented model	Simple data abstraction
Connection-oriented communication	Best-efforts connectionless
Powerful security	Good security (SNMP version 2)
Powerful scoping and filtering	It requires the name of the object (except for GET-NEXT)
Flexible complex data structures using full ASN.1 (large code and memory requirements)	Restrictive, simple data structures using a subset of ASN.1 (smaller code and memory requirements)
Transfer data lengths unlimited	484 octet data transfer limit
Optional negotiation	No negotiation

ASCII file to enable desktop devices to be managed. A more sophisticated mechanism, how-ever, is required for effective management in the future. Other areas requiring future develop-ment are software distribution and software and licensing management.

11.7 CASE STUDY: THE DEFENDER GROUP

The Defender Group consists of several companies grouped into the following business areas:

- parcel delivery;
- mobile communications;
- recruitment;
- hotel chains;
- security.

11.7.1 The parcel delivery business

The parcels industry is a $1.5 billion industry with the following characteristics:

- it is logistically complex (collect anywhere, deliver anywhere in the world – but usually by 9 a.m. the next morning to any US location);
- it is highly time critical;
- mostly involves low to semi-skilled operators;
- it is highly seasonal;
- there are numerous competitors operating in a price sensitive market;
- tremendous customer goodwill and loyalty (providing they are happy with the service). Contracted customers form 80 per cent of the customer base.

Defender Parcel's mission statement can be summarized as 'service excellence, on time, every time'. This translates to the following corporate objectives.

1. provide a competitive edge based on customer service;
2. provide a wide range of services;
3. high throughput of parcels;
4. provide a quantifiable return on investment.

In terms of Mintzberg's (1988) configuration, Defender Parcels is operating in a simple and stable environment (i.e. anyone can easily enter the parcels delivery business). The tech-nical system (i.e. the process of collecting and delivering parcels) is logistically complex but highly routine requiring non-professional staff in the operating core. This implies that Defender Parcels should be a machine bureaucracy where jobs and procedures are highly standardized. The organization should be structured on a functional basis (collection, deliver-ies, marketing, sales, personnel, etc.), with centralized control for tight co-ordination. Indeed, Defender Parcels is organized in this way.

Defender's business activities and user roles can be summarized by examining the life-cycle of a parcel which is first collected then delivered to its destination. This is illustrated in Figure 11.7. It is largely a manual process. Currently, a mainframe computer handles the accounting and personnel systems, and customer details and proof of delivery (POD) data. POD documents are microfiched for long-term storage. Dumb terminals are installed at each site to enable access to mainframe systems via an X.25 network. This is illustrated in Figure 11.8.

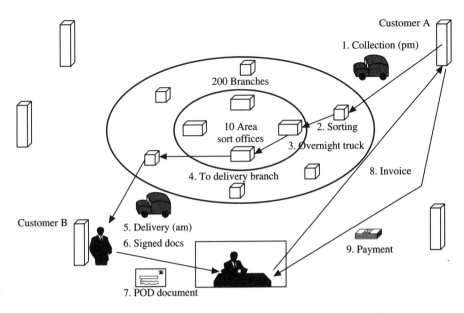

Figure 11.7 Defender Parcels: collect/delivery cycle.

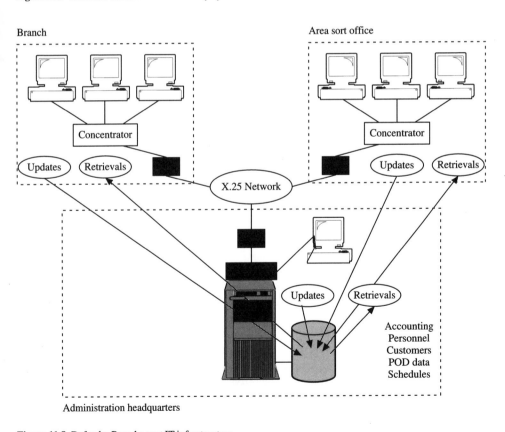

Figure 11.8 Defender Parcels: past IT infrastructure.

11.7.2 SWOT analysis

A SWOT (strengths, weaknesses, opportunities and threats) analysis provides an opportunity to evaluate the strength and weaknesses of an organization. SWOT analysis for Defender Parcels resulted in the following conclusions.

- *Strengths:*
  - long established reputation for reliability;
  - market leader (but facing stiff competition).
- *Weaknesses:*
  - immature/ineffective use of IT;
  - too much reliance on past reputation leading to a reluctance to innovate.
- *Opportunities:*
  - greater use of IT to reduce costs and offer new services;
  - maintain customer loyalty through improved customer services.
- *Threats:*
  - market share continually under threat by new entrants and existing competitors with a better cost base due to greater automation and use of IT.

11.7.3 Opportunities for new information systems

The evaluation above led to identification of the following information systems requirements:

- a parcel tracking system (using bar coded technology);
- use of EDI with larger contract customers;
- a vehicle tracking (using electronic communication), routing and scheduling system;
- customer services support system to handle sales calls, quotations, contracts and POD enquiries;
- a document image management system for handling POD and other documents;
- improved corporate-wide communications through the use of electronic mail and group communications technology.

The above applications portfolio formed the basis for identifying the future IT infrastructure requirements.

11.7.4 The new IT infrastructure

As illustrated in Figure 11.7, there are currently 200 branches, 10 area sort terminals and a central administration office and headquarters (which also houses the computer centre). In development phase one, service centres (one per area) were set up to handle all customer enquiries, quotations, orders and contracts (all previously handled by the administration centre). Customer service centres were equipped with computing facilities to enable an efficient customer-oriented service. At each centre, a UNIX server was dedicated to running a POD imaging system that enables POD images to be scanned, stored and viewed from a PC (running X-terminal emulation software). Another UNIX server runs the customer services support system to handle sales calls, quotations, contracts and POD enquiries. Both UNIX servers are accessible from desktop PCs. Each (486) PC runs Microsoft Windows and application software. Defender has standardized on Ethernet LANs throughout its sites.

Each branch and area sort terminal is equipped with a small UNIX server accessed by PCs (some equipped with bar-coding technology). Each branch collects data on parcels collected and sent to, or received from, area sort terminals. Branches also handle delivery schedules.

The computer centre runs a large mainframe handling enquiries and updates on the customer data and schedules as well as accounting and personnel systems. The 30 Gb database handles approximately 150 transactions per second over the peak three hours of the day (a UNIX server could not cope with this transaction load and database size). Thus data is largely centralized which makes sense in this case since large quantities of it are frequently updated from multiple sites and users, who access data equally and need to see the most up-to-date data values.

Information exchange between sites is facilitated by an ATM network (used by all companies in the Defender Group) over which TCP/IP traffic flows. A corporate-wide electronic mail facility is installed with interconnected local 'post-offices' to enable efficient global communications. The top-level IT infrastructure diagram is illustrated in Figure 11.9 and further refined in Figure 11.10. Defender Parcels evaluated a number of electronic mail and vehicle communication technologies.

One major problem that had to be overcome was a lack of sophisticated systems/network management tools. In the single mainframe-based computer centre numerous tools were available. Moving to a 200-site IT infrastructure demanded more sophisticated toolsets.

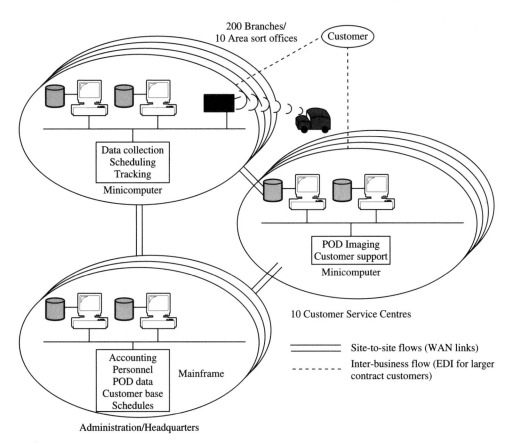

Figure 11.9 Top-level IT infrastructure design.

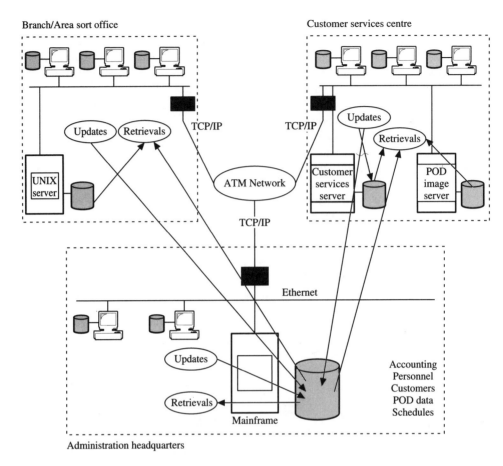

Figure 11.10 The new IT infrastructure.

Defender decided to commission a software company with specialist skills in developing distributed systems management tools to develop a custom system based on ISO CMIS/CMIP management protocols. ISO management protocols were chosen because it was a comprehensive framework using distributed object-oriented concepts which was felt to be appropriate to the complexity of the network being managed. A systems management agent runs on each UNIX server which manages a set of managed objects. The following conditions are typically monitored on an ongoing basis:

- processor over-utilization;
- disk full conditions;
- various class of errors;
- faulty PCs;
- local network faults;
- process faults and software errors.

Major notifications are relayed to a central management centre whose main task is to manage the backbone ATM wide area network. Individual systems and local area network management is devolved to regional management centres. Thus, systems management is decentralized.

11.7.5 Discussion points

1. Which classes of DIS have been implemented?
2. Can you see any additional opportunities for deploying IT?
3. Comment on the degree of distribution transparency that may be achieved with the new IT infrastructure.
4. Comment on the degree of distribution of the new configuration.

11.8 SUMMARY

Organizational structure and culture shape the design, implementation and management of distributed systems. This chapter briefly outlined a number of perspectives on organizational design and management. The viable system model (VSM) was used to illustrate the regulatory mechanisms and information flows associated with organizational structures, and the information systems requirements that arise. In particular, emphasis on workflow management and computer-supported co-operative working (CSCW) in addition to the more traditional information systems requirements.

Two main approaches to managing distributed systems were detailed: ISO management and Internet SNMP management. The ISO systems management standards are highly functional but complex. SNMP was initially designed as a simple protocol which was easy to implement, but has evolved into a reasonably functional specification that is now the *de facto* standard (also regarded as an open standard).

11.9 REVIEW EXERCISES

1. Explain why organizational structure and culture can have an impact on the way distributed systems are designed, implemented and managed.
2. How do managers cope with the complexity of dealing with the variety of activities, tasks and information associated with tasks for which he or she is responsible?
3. Describe the three types of information systems which are implemented to support organizational activities.
4. Why are graphics (and other media) and graphical user interfaces generally useful in decision-making?
5. What are the goals of business process redesign? What is the role of workflow management systems?
6. Part of the role of managers is to gain the commitment of others. How can computer-supported co-operative working (CSCW) systems help to achieve this goal?
7. To what extent is distributed systems management the same as any other management role?
8. What is a managed object? Describe a general architecture for distributed systems management.

9. Compare and contrast the ISO management standards with the Internet SNMP management standards.

11.10 FURTHER READING

A excecllent and very readable summary of organizational and management theories is found in Lee and Lawrence (1985). The viable systems model (VSM) is usefully summarized in Beer (1985) and Holmberg (1989). Espejo and Harnden (1989) contains some interesting papers on the VSM. Distributed systems management issues are comprehensively covered in Sloman (1994) and Langsford and Moffett (1993).

12

OPEN SYSTEMS AND STANDARDS SELECTION

12.1 INTRODUCTION

In Chapter 11 the Open Distributed Processing (ODP) standard was described and an approach to developing an engineering model detailed. The technology viewpoint is the lowest level of abstraction in the ODP reference model, and defines the underlying hardware and software products and standards that are used to implement an engineering model. This is the view of primary interest to those directly involved in implementing a DIS. A technology model consists of configuration diagrams and descriptions (with justification) of standards and supplier products that have been selected to implement the engineering model. Technology components include:

- client and server hardware platforms, operating system, I/O devices, hard disk capacity, network type and equipment, etc.;
- new horizontal application services;
- generic services;
- network configurations and components;
- transparency functions.

A key decision when developing a technology model is the choice of standards or products/services to fulfil the particular functional and non-functional requirements identified in the engineering model. The choice of standards for information technology may seem to be a relatively easy process to implement, but when a number of choices are available a considerable number of factors can impinge upon the decision regarding which standards to use in any particular context. In general, some guidance is required concerning:

- how to identify develop and specify, in a structured way, the standards applicable to each component in an engineering model;
- how to monitor and evaluate the use of standards;
- a framework which can be used to express the benefits of a particular choice of standards as a basis for justification.

In this chapter a framework is defined to provide guidance on the selection of products and standards to convert an engineering model into a technology model which details which products are to be used to build the DIS and IT infrastructure components (if necessary) to support it. It is rare that a DIS is implemented in isolation. Instead it makes use of the distributed, shared, reusable components of an IT infrastructure. Therefore, products and standards must be chosen which meet both the needs of the DIS being implemented and, in a wider context, the needs of other existing systems which also use infrastructure components. In almost all implementation situations, there are project-specific issues and strategic issues (i.e. issues relating to a wider context).

12.2 IS/IT STRATEGY, ARCHITECTURE AND INFRASTRUCTURE

There are in essence two distinct categories of standard that need to be considered when implementing a DIS or IT infrastructure. These are externally defined standard and internally defined standard. Externally defined standards are divided into five categories, which are as follows.

- **Closed**. This is a standard that is only used by specific organizations, not available widely and access to it is restricted to a small user base.
- **Proprietary.** This is a standard restricted mainly by the owner of the defining document or design. This is typically the type of standard sold by computer manufacturers who want to tie users into a specific product path.
- *De facto*. This is the type of standard that has achieved a wider user base and has become the pervasive standard by virtue of its use but is not supported by international standardization activity.
- *De jure*. These standards are those supported by the work of the international standardization bodies. This does not presuppose any actual use of the standard but only its derivation.
- **Open**. An open standard is one that has arisen in any way and is available to all interested users on equal terms without significant restriction

The various standards categories are not mutually exclusive in all cases, and this can cause some confusion. Thus the term *standard* is interpreted to encompass any external or internal standard types previously described. Where necessary, use of the term standard will be qualified by the type of standard (proprietary, open, etc.) being referred to.

Within any organization, standards will be defined at a number of different levels, dependent upon the focus or span of operation. Classically, standards might be defined at three levels (Moreton *et al.*, 1995):

- **strategic**: standards that should be used for all systems across an organization;
- **tactical**: standards which might apply for systems in a more limited context;
- **local**: standards chosen in restricted or exceptional circumstances to satisfy specific local needs in a particular organizational unit. These standards compromise to some extent the objectives achieved through implementation of tactical or strategic level standards, but offer short-term benefits.

This distinction is not always clear cut, and may be applied iteratively, dependent upon the context of use. For instance, a company will define its own strategic standards, or standards to support its information systems and technology (IS/IT) strategy. These 'strategic standards' will, of course, be defined in the context of the wider corporate group 'strategic standards'. The company standards will 'inherit' characteristics of the group standards. In order to be successfully promoted, IS/IT standards need to be formulated within the context of an IS/IT strategy.

It may be argued that in a rapidly changing business and technical environment, it is better not to have an IS/IT strategy. The need to respond rapidly to new business requirements is, however, the main reason for developing an IS/IT strategy. Without an IS/IT strategy that includes a flexible hardware and software architecture, there will inevitably be delays in implementing a DIS to meet new business requirements. It was noted in Chapter 2 that a complete IS/IT strategy has three main elements:

- The IS/IT architecture.
- IS/IT standards.
- IS/IT procurement.

Formulating an IS/IT strategy and architecture, selecting (or developing) standards for products and services, and the procurement of product and services are interrelated tasks in the process of developing a technology model.

12.3 DEFINING AND IMPLEMENTING THE IS/IT ARCHITECTURE

An IS/IT architecture comprises a coherent set of hardware, software and communications tools and building blocks that are used as the basis for developing specific applications. An architecture should include as many as possible of the common functions that will be needed to build a new DIS, so that bespoke development is reduced to a minimum. The architecture approach to IS/IT strategy has three main benefits: it provides the flexibility to respond quickly to changing business requirements; it helps reduce the variety of software in use and thus reduces costs; and it makes it easier to integrate applications. In essence, an IS/IT architecture consists of a list of IS/IT functions and a description of how they are to be provided. The components of the architecture will vary according to the type of business and the role that IS/IT plays in the business. In Chapter 2 we established that the IS/IT architecture can be divided into the following categories.

1. The **production architecture**, which establishes the hardware, software and communications standards, products and services to be used to support the production information systems.
2. The **development architecture**, which establishes the hardware, software and communications standards, products and services to be used to support information systems development activities.
3. The **information architecture**, which establishes the types and location of information which is utilized by the production information systems, and how (and from where) information is accessed by users and application processes.
4. The **service architecture**, which establishes the type and location of the range of user and application services.

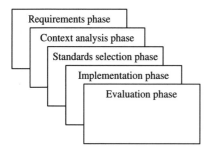

Figure 12.1 Standards selection and evaluation framework.

A particular IS/IT architecture is developed to meet either the long-term business goals of the organizational unit (in which case it is referred to as a **strategic architecture** (SA)) or the user requirements in respect of a specific information systems development project (in which case it is referred to as a **project architecture** (PA)). Clearly PAs should be closely related to the SA of the organizational unit which owns the project in order to realize longer-term benefits.

A framework to aid the selection of standards and appropriate implementation of an IS/IT architecture must take account of the temporality of technology and associated standards, and the variety of standards in a wide range of contexts. The framework used in this chapter consists of five phases, as illustrated in Figure 12.1 (Moreton *et al.*, 1995).

1. **Requirements phase**: determine user requirements and the business case.
2. **Context analysis phase**: determine the constraints and organizational issues likely to influence choice of standards.
3. **Standards selection phase**: develop the strategic or project architecture.
4. **Implementation phase**: develop or procure the necessary components and implement the system.
5. **Evaluation phase**: Evaluate the extent to which business and technical benefits have been realized.

Each phase of the framework will be examined in subsequent sections of the chapter.

12.4 REQUIREMENTS PHASE

The first step in migrating to a new IS/IT infrastructure is to define and agree on the architecture that the organization wants to end up with. Doing this will limit the migration difficulties because new systems can be procured to conform with the desired architecture. It is unlikely to be cost-effective to implement all of the architecture at once. This would normally require a large capital expenditure on items that would not be used fully for some time, until new applications have been built or old ones converted. SAs and PAs must relate to user requirements in terms of their contributions to achieving business benefits for a particular project. Users need IS/IT services to meet business requirements. SAs and PAs enable the implementation of IT services to meet specific user requirements thereby realizing business benefits identified for a project.

Benefits are expressed in terms of positive expected outcomes. These outcomes allow assessment of the *value* of moving from a previous solution to the new solution. The *cost* of making the change (a negative expected outcome) must also be tracked to allow evaluation of the extent to which benefits are realized. Example outcomes include:

- reduce the order/delivery cycle and quality of service information;
- improve the timeliness, availability, and analysis of information;
- reduce the overhead of collecting management information;
- reduce in error levels.

The process of defining SAs and PAs must start with identifying user requirements (in terms of business information systems requirements) which are then translated to IT and data requirements. IT and data requirements are then mapped to IT and data standards requirements which are expressed in terms of a strategic or project architecture.

The key to relating an SA or PA to user requirements and associated business benefits lies in defining a generic set of IS/IT functions and predicting the business and technical benefits expected of each service by the user. A user's IS/IT functional requirements can be expressed in terms of these generic functions, and the SA/PA based on it. The generic IS/IT functions define a set of common terms for communicating IT requirements, comprehensible to users and developers without the need to communicate the detailed technical standards used to implement them. IS/IT functions are defined so as to provide a link between user requirements (in terms of technical and business benefits) and the technical standards used to contribute to their achievement. Thus, standards requirements are articulated by relating them to one or more generic IS/IT functions. Table 12.1 presents an indicative list of generic IS/IT functions (adapted from work done in this area by BSI (1992)). A similar list should be produced to match the equivalent common terms used to describe these functions in the context of a specific organization.

In reality, an organizational unit will determine and express relevant generic IS/IT functions at an appropriate level of detail and which will evolve and be refined over time. In the framework for standards development, user requirements are articulated in terms of generic IS/IT functions and associated business and technical benefits. These functional requirements are then translated to standards requirements.

12.5 CONTEXT ANALYSIS PHASE

Projects are rarely in a position to select standards starting with a blank sheet. The organizational unit which owns the project will exert some influence over formulation of a PA for the project. This influence is typically manifested in the form of an IS/IT strategy and associated architecture which influences the shape of a project architecture in the interests of meeting wider business and technical goals requiring high levels of interoperability, portability and integration.

Standards are either mandated or recommended depending on the level of control which can be exercised on a project. The organizational unit itself may be influenced by other organizational units in its choice of SA. These hierarchical relationships in terms of the development of SAs and PAs can be modelled in terms of the following entities:

- An organizational unit has a **domain of influence** through the development of SAs and PAs. Its influence is exercised by specifying an IS/IT strategy and/or architecture which are inherited by all organizational units, community of organizational units or projects which it influences (hereafter referred to as *inherited context*).

Table 12.1 Generic IS/IT functions

Generic IS/IT functions	Description
Message distribution	Sending and receiving messages of limited structure.
Batched data transfer	Bulk transfer of structured data, e.g. files, within or between organizations.
Data exchange	Sending and receiving structured and unstructured information prior to presentation.
Integrated data query and update	Basic processing functions of `read, write, create, update, delete, compare, move and copy`, etc. for data items.
Source data capture	Collecting the required data prior to its input for processing.
Data storage and retrieval	Holding large quantities of structured and unstructured data.
Data and service safeguarding	Controlling access to data and its corruption or loss.
Executive information extraction	Providing business managers with flexible access to and presentation of information required for reviewing the business.
Mathematical calculation	Basic functions (and resources) required for intensive numerical processing.
Information management	Managing the information integration within and between information systems.
Information presentation	Presenting information to users using one or more media types (e.g. text, sound, video, graphics or image).
IT service management	Managing, integrating and accounting for the services, information systems and resources used by all other IT services.
Application development environment	Controlled development, distribution, maintenance and replacement of applications which realize the functionality of IT services.
Distributed systems environment	The need to support the possible distribution of processing and data across multiple remote processors and data storage and retrieval facilities.

- An organizational unit may belong to more than one domain indicating that it is influenced by multiple organizational units (each perhaps addressing a subset of requirements) which leads to the notion of multiple inherited contexts. For example, a hospital trust is an organizational unit which is influenced by national IS/IT standards and may also be influenced by standards defined locally by a community of organizations for mutual benefit.
- Every project belongs to the organizational unit that owns it (i.e. is responsible for the project).

Thus, every organizational unit can be modelled using the above concepts which serve to highlight the relative influence of organizational units in the process of standards development. An example is illustrated in Figure 12.2 which highlights the relationships between corporate standards and those developed by a group of (subsidiary) organizations (tactical standards) or locally by an individual organization (local standards). The process of SA development essentially consists of identifying the scope of user requirements being addressed by the architecture.

Most organizations, as noted earlier, are unable to start with a blank sheet when developing an architecture and implementing the associated infrastructure. For example, a large

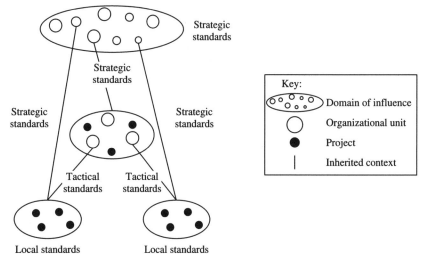

Figure 12.2 Domain of influence: an example.

organization with 10 or 20-year old legacy systems based on particular infrastructure products which have been in place for many years must recognize the problems of migrating from the current infrastructure to a new one. It may be that current infrastructure products are based on many proprietary standards. A new IS/IT strategy and attendant architecture must take account of what exists currently and the potential costs of moving to an alternative architecture (i.e., migration costs). Thus the organizational context has a significant influence on the type of standards (proprietary, *de facto*, open, etc.) which are appropriate. Therefore in order to ensure that an architecture focuses on *relevant* standards, the organizational context and issues likely to influence formulation of a strategic and project architecture in terms of benefits and constraints need to be considered at an early stage. The process of identifying inherited and organizational contexts is referred to as *contextual analysis*.

12.6 STANDARDS SELECTION PHASE

The main input to the process for translating user requirements to a corresponding architecture is the required set of IS/IT functions and associated technical and business benefits. The first step in this process is to identify the standards contexts and categories of technical areas for which standards must be sought. At the highest level, each context directly corresponds to the generic IT services. For each generic IT service a number of related technical areas (referred to as 'categories') can be defined. This is illustrated in Table 12.2. A particular category is likely to appear against more than one standards context. For example, the remote data access category is required both for the 'integrated data query and update' context and the 'executive information extraction' context. A single remote data access should cater for both needs. The next step is then to derive a single set of categories from the table of contexts and categories. This forms the specific set of technical areas for which standards must be sought. Intelligent selection of appropriate standards per category is facilitated by determining the status of standards in each category (see Section 12.10 which details techniques for evaluating the status of standards). The standards selected for each relevant standards category together form the SA or PA.

Table 12.2 Example/standards contexts and categories

Standards context	Example categories
Message distribution	Electronic mail, directory services.
Batched data transfer	File transfer, remote operation, remote file access.
Data exchange	EDI, electronic mail, text, graphics, sound, video and document interchange formats, directory services.
Integrated data query and update	Database access and manipulation (e.g. SQL), remote data access, data dictionary, distributed database, ISAM, directory services.
Source data capture	Keyboard, document scanners, OCRs, bar-codes, light pen, touch screen.
Data storage and retrieval	Data dictionary/repository, relational DBMS, distributed DBMS, object DBMS, disk storage devices, disk controllers, server platform.
Data and service safeguarding	Authentication and security management, backup, restore and archiving, user account management.
Executive information extraction	Database access and manipulation (e.g. SQL), remote data access, data dictionary, distributed database, data warehouse, decision support tools, directory services.
Mathematical calculation	Statistical and mathematics libraries, scientific oriented programming languages and tools.
Information management	Quality management integration management, interchange formats.
Information presentation	Terminal access, window services, GUI application programming interface and development tool kit, ergonomics, safety.
IT service management	Network management, systems management, service-level management, capacity management, problem management, accounting management, configuration management, directory services.
Information systems development	Data dictionary/model, programming languages, development methods and tools, development platform, operating systems, software portability.
Distributed systems environment	WAN/LAN remote procedure call, directory service, time service, network hardware components, base client workstation hardware and software, base server hardware and network operating system, cabling.

12.6.1 Dependencies

When a standard is selected for a particular category, it may require pre-requisite or co-requisite standards to be selected for proper implementation. For example, in the electronic mail standards category, choice of the Internet MIME standard determines that the Internet SMTP and TCP/IP standards are also selected. Thus when a standard is chosen, the pre-requisite standards, co-requisite standards or excluded combinations must also be documented to ensure that the appropriate combination of standards are selected when a number of choices are available. Relevant dependencies are identified during the context analysis phase.

12.6.2 Choosing the candidate standards

A single standard may not meet all potential requirements in a particular category. There may be a need to choose standards to match particular requirements and establish a mechanism for selecting appropriate standards given a set of requirements. This selection mechanism must be built into the SA and PA. Choice of a number of candidate standards can be articulated using the following selection structure which is defined for each category of standards.

1. **Strategic option**. The standard that should be used for all information systems across the organization. These standards map directly to the strategic architecture of the organizational unit in whose domain of influence this organizational unit or project is positioned.
2. **Tactical option**. An alternative standard which is appropriate in given circumstances. The strategic standard may offer the functionality required by the majority of applications, while the tactical standard offers specific features that are required by some projects but which are not found in the strategic standard.
3. **Local option**. These are standards or products chosen in exceptional circumstances. These exceptional circumstances need to be very well defined and the use of local implementations disallowed outside the immediate PA because to some extent they conflict directly with the business and technical requirements that the strategic options are positioned to satisfy. An example of a local option might be a specific (incompatible) PC-based electronic mail system installed for an isolated group of users to realize short-term benefits.

Using this structure, the selection process starts at the strategic option level by defining the strategic architecture which typically leads to long-term benefits or opportunities for the organizational unit and which imposes particular constraints on every project. Tactical or local options apply when the strategic option does not satisfy a particular requirement which may be met by the alternative option under specified circumstances. In terms of development timescales, it would be preferable for projects to choose strategic options which potentially lead to lower costs, greater availability of skilled staff, lower training costs and improved interworking with existing and future systems. Pre-requisite standards, co-requisite standards or excluded combinations are also documented to ensure that the appropriate combination of standards are selected when a number of choices are available. Figure 12.3 illustrates an example proforma for the specification of strategic, tactical and local standards and dependencies.

12.7 IMPLEMENTATION PHASE

In the next phase of the framework, a project architecture is used to establish a project plan for the development or procurement of products and services. Relevant procurement policies and regulations and project management standards are used to ensure that predicted benefits are realized through the effective and efficient implementation of the system.

12.8 EVALUATION PHASE

In the final stage of the framework, the effectiveness of standards used in a relevant strategic and project architecture should be assessed by evaluating whether the stated (user defined)

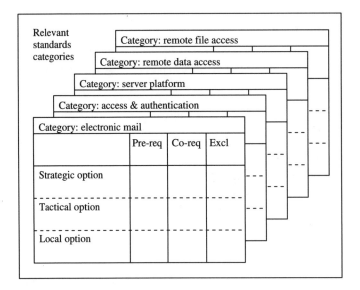

Figure 12.3 Defining the architecture.

business and technical benefits were achieved. In the user requirements phase of the framework, high-level business and technical benefits were expressed for each relevant standards context in terms positive expected outcomes. Often the value of a solution is derived by comparing it with the value of a previous solution or the tangible or intangible improvements as a result of implementation of the new system. Thus we measure the incremental or differential value of the designed change by analysing positive and negative outcomes (expected and unexpected). This phase establishes a *learning loop* which determines to what extent benefits were achieved by measuring outcomes, comparing with predicted benefits, and interpreting in order to improve organizational knowledge and the state-of-the-art. Finally, to close the learning loop, knowledge and good practice are disseminated.

12.9 A SUMMARY OF THE FRAMEWORK

The framework for standards development by an organizational unit or information systems development project was illustrated in Figure 12.1. Example processes relevant to each phase is illustrated in Figure 12.4 and summarized below (Moreton *et al.*, 1995):

User requirements phase:

1. Establish user requirements and the business case.
2. Identify relevant IS/IT functions and the business and technical benefits (in terms of expected outcomes) derived from successful implementation of each function.
3. Translate IT and data requirements to standards contexts and categories. Where possible, relate each standards context to the business and technical benefits to be achieved through successful implementation and use.

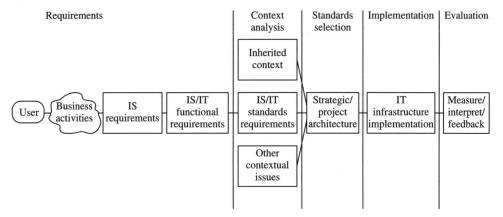

Figure 12.4 A summary of the standards selection and evaluation process.

Context analysis phase

1. Determine all relevant domains of influence which affect or are affected by the organizational unit and are related to relevant standards categories. This is summarized by one or more 'domains of influence' hierarchy diagrams. The main output of this stage are the identification of all relevant inherited contexts.
2. Determine other contextual issues which may affect the process of determining and selecting standards and developing the architecture. The main outputs from this phase are relevant contexts for standards selection, and any other constraints which will inform the standards selection process.

Standards selection phase

1. Where necessary summarize the status of standards for each category for which a standard must be selected (techniques which aid the selection of appropriate strategic, tactical and local options are detailed in Section 12.10).
2. Select appropriate strategic, tactical and (if necessary) local standards and implementations for each category. Each selection should be justified in terms of functional (business and technical) qualities which relate to the functional qualities specified in the user requirements. Collectively, the strategic, tactical and local standards across all relevant standards categories forms the relevant strategic or project architecture.

Implementation phase

Procure and implement products and services in accordance with the chosen architecture.

Evaluation phase

1. Evaluate the extent to which business and technical benefits have been realized. The business and technical benefits expressed for each standards context are used to determine the extent to which specific user requirements have been met and the contribution of related IS/IT functions and associated standards.

2. Disseminate information to relevant parties (particularly personnel involved in IS/IT standards development both at the strategic and project level) to provide feedback on the use of particular standards and to enable proper learning.

3. Apply any necessary adjustments to strategic or project architectures in the light of improved knowledge and technical changes and advances over time.

Having discussed the overall framework for development and selection of standards in this section, the next section illustrates the issue of domains of influence and highlights some techniques determining the status of standards within the appropriate organizational context.

12.10 STANDARDS TRACKING AND EVALUATION

In any application of standards to a particular area of work there is usually a choice of standards from the various groups of standards outlined previously. These will rarely be a perfect match for the particular application, organization or context in which they need to be applied. A useful approach to standards evaluation is to use a graphical representation to aid choice, a simplified example of which is illustrated in Figure 12.5 (Moreton *et al.*, 1995). This shows on the horizontal axis the degrees of **openness of standards** and on the vertical axis the level of the various functions that are relevant to each standard such as functionality, use, user base and other features. Use of this graphical method is particularly relevant to show what standards are to be investigated further. The relevant criteria for the evaluation of the standard are all plotted on the graph for each available standard and the most clustered group within the defined context should give the best fit for this particular application.

Figure 12.6 gives an example of the clustering of relevant standards for a few electronic mail standards and shows both some clustering and some widely divergent groups for the

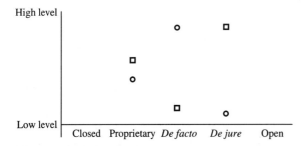

Figure 12.5 Standards graph – openness vs function. □ Functionality; ○ user base.

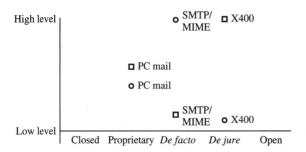

Figure 12.6 Standards graph – electronic mail example. □ Functionality; ○ user base.

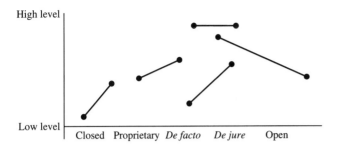

High level

Low level

Closed   Proprietary   *De facto*   *De jure*   Open

Figure 12.7 Standards tracking.

various standards. It should also be noted in some cases a standard that is not optimal can be justified based on existing (proprietary) systems already in place. This graphical method can also show how particular standards have developed over time (standards tracking), as shown in Figure 12.7. Here the various development paths of standards are tracked over a period of time (say, within the last two years), and the vectors show the dynamics of the standards process, the user uptake and other features. This can lead to a more informed decision about standards that are developing and those that are essentially stuck in process, or have been superseded. The standards movement is put into context when one considers the various routes that products or specifications can take towards success or obsolescence.

The life-cycle of standards is illustrated in Figure 12.8 (Moreton *et al.*, 1995). This links the various categories of standard in a comprehensive way and shows possible paths and developments that are not apparent in a simplistic approach. The diagram forms a state-transition record for the possible paths of different stages in the life of a standard. The events that trigger the change from the different possible states are shown next to the links, e.g. the move from an open standard to a need (the right-hand flow line) is occasioned by the use of the standard that shows that the current state of development of the standards does not satisfy the full range of (or developing) needs.

12.11 CASE STUDY: TWO COMPANIES MERGE

MyFirm Ltd with a history of using UNIX workstations in a client/server architecture has taken over the company YourFirm Ltd, that has been PC based for a similar time. The requirement is to recommend standards for the amalgamation process to form the IT infrastructure for the new banking organization – OurFirm Ltd! This has, therefore, defined a domain of influence for YourFirm Ltd inherited from MyFirm Ltd in the take-over. To illustrate the concepts described in this chapter, we will focus on the provision of a global electronic mail system and underlying network infrastructure for OurFirm Ltd. The issues apply equally to all other aspects of the take-over in terms of the development of a new IS/IT strategy.

The departments within MyFirm Ltd that currently use the UNIX workstations have relied on the UNIX mail utility with MIME extensions to exchange multimedia mail messages and TCP/IP based LAN connections as these provided a very cheap option for implementing a potentially global electronic mail service. MyFirm Ltd is connected to the Internet.

The groups within YourFirm Ltd have been competent PC LAN users for a number of

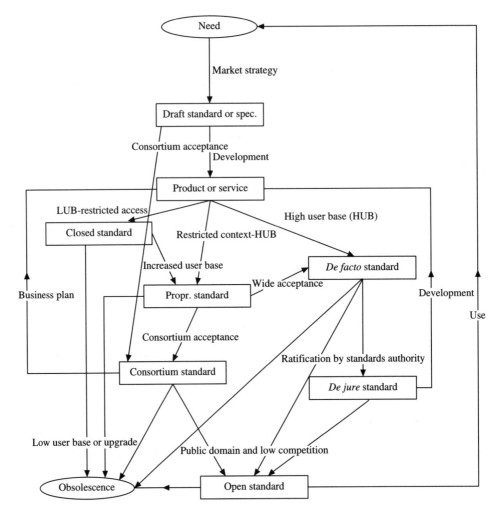

Figure 12.8 Standards life-cycle. LUB, lower user base; HUB, high user base.

years and have a range of applications in operation including a simple electronic mail package that is now out-of-date. The amalgamation has given the enlarged organization the opportunity to upgrade or change to a new system. The overall strategy for the new organization is to have a comprehensive mail facility that will enable all employees to exchange messages, allow electronic mail with external organizations and be a tool for communication with their customers and suppliers.

The UNIX network and the PC LANs are to be joined to form a complete internetwork for the organization in a number of buildings with various bridges and routers. Because MyFirm already have expertise in the implementation of TCP/IP and most of the equipment is already in place, the 'organizational context' is likely to heavily influence the IS/IT strategy towards implementing a TCP/IP internetwork for OurFirm Ltd. YourFirm, however, make extensive use of mail attachments which often consist of large multimedia documents, and have recently shown a keen interest in making extensive use of electronic publishing technology, principally World Wide Web technology. Consequently, existing network connections may need to significantly enhanced. Many of the mail messages that will be sent are departmental in nature and stay within the boundaries of the organization's network, but there are important messages that are sent over external networks.

No specific mail system is used by all suppliers and customers although there are various gateways to the different systems in use. Proprietary or *de facto* electronic mail standards can be used by customer or suppliers and internally as long as there are gateways available to a common transfer standard. At the strategic organizational level there is a limited choice of standard to which all other mail systems must interface: either ITU-T X.400 or Internet SMTP/MIME. This is illustrated in Figure 12.9. In the context of YourFirm Ltd, there is a wider choice of options ranging from X.400-based systems, Internet SMTP/MIME systems which directly interface to a UNIX server, and proprietary PC-based systems, as illustrated in Figure 12.10.

An X.400-based strategic level option has been adopted as most customers and suppliers interface to it and it provides high functionality. A tactical-level option of Internet SMTP/MIME or a specified PC-based mail system with an X.400 gateway. Most PC-based and UNIX-based electronic mail systems available incorporate both an X.400 and SMTP gateway. No local option is specified because it was felt that strategic and tactical options catered for all requirements. All electronic mail projects within OurFirm Ltd must now take account of the new strategic architecture outlined. One project may adopt a project architecture consisting of a PC-based mail system with an X.400 gateway, while another project may choose a different project architecture incorporating an Internet SMTP/MIME based mail system with an X.400 gateway. It should be noted that the analysis here has not been complete or

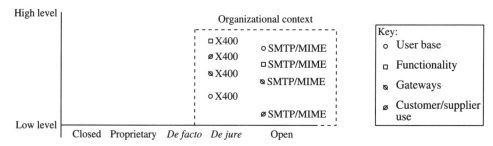

Figure 12.9 Example context – strategic level.

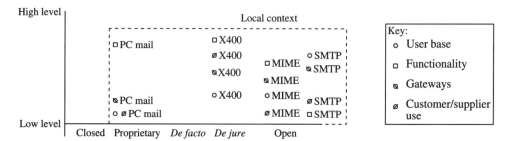

Figure 12.10 Example – local context (project-specific).

rigorous but merely indicative of the process described earlier. In particular, domains of influence in standards selection were taken into account, and informed decision-making concerning standards was facilitated by analysis of the organizational context and relevant standards.

12.12 SUMMARY

One of the most important aspects of implementing a DIS is selection of appropriate products and services based on internal and external standards. This is the area in which the technology viewpoint is focused in the ISO ODP model. In this chapter we have detailed a systematic approach to the evaluation and selection of standards, and development of an IS/IT architecture. The architecture is used to procure products and services relevant to the system to be implemented. Few systems are implemented in isolation. Standards selection is influenced by existing infrastructures and systems, and influences outside of the organizational unit which owns the project. Recognition of various domains of influence over standards selection is a feature of the framework. The main benefit of a structured approach is more informed decision-making based on a combination of local requirements and the needs of a wider user community (e.g. a group of companies).

12.13 REVIEW EXERCISES

1. Explain the differences between an IS/IT strategy, architecture and infrastructure.
2. Describe the technology viewpoint in the ISO ODP model.
3. What is the purpose of an IS/IT architecture? Can organizations implement distributed system successfully without an architecture?
4. Define the term 'standard'. Describe the various types of standards.
5. A specification has been developed by a consortium of companies. Products based on the standard have been implemented and are now widely used in the marketplace (i.e. it has become the market leader) implemented by many vendors. The specification is available across the Internet. How would you describe this standard based on the types described in Question 4? Comment on any ambiguities.
6. Choose a standards category and draw a standards graph for four competing standards in the area. Factors such as user base and functionality should be plotted.
7. Draw a standards tracking graph for two standards in a chosen standards category.
8. Produce strategic, tactical and local standards for client workstations in the case study of OurFirm Ltd.

12.14 FURTHER READING

Papers outlining ODP issues relating to the technology model are found in de Meer *et al.*, (1992). Technical computing and communications magazines and journals should be used to track relevant standards, products and services.

13

SECURITY

13.1 INTRODUCTION

In a traditional centralized system it is the operating system in the host computer that verifies the identity of all the users wishing to use system resources. In a large, multi-site distributed system with multiple administrative authorities, however, a centralized security service is impractical because it does not scale well, and there are also many more opportunities for intruders to maliciously corrupt systems and data. The need to employ more sophisticated security technology is paramount because many organizations have become highly dependent on networked information systems. Security mechanisms protect an information system from unauthorized usage or from unauthorized access. In this chapter some basic concepts in this area will be reviewed. In the context of security, the term **principal** (also referred to as *subject*) is used to describe a human user or information system entity (e.g. a process) who desires access to information or other resources. A principal invokes an object operation by sending a message to it, possibly over an untrustworthy network, which gives rise to four categories of security concerns:

- *Loss of Confidentiality* An object is revealed to one or more unauthorized principals.
- *Loss of Integrity* An object is corrupted either accidentally or deliberately.
- *Loss of Accountability* Principals act irresponsibly by falsely denying that an operation was carried out (or was attempted), or that a message was received or sent.
- *Loss of Service* A system was tampered with to the extent that a service is no longer available to the principals that wish to access it.

An information system with little or no security is open to a number of threats which may compromise confidentiality, integrity, accountability and availability. Some threats are immediately obvious, but most malicious threats are difficult to detect until the damage caused by them are visible. The following list are the ways in which an information system security may be breached.

- *Physical damage* The physical components of an information system are accidentally or maliciously damaged.
- *Forgery* Attempting to guess, or otherwise, information which can enable an unauthorized user to breach a security mechanism.
- *Interception* An unauthorized user modifies a communication channel unnoticed by communicating parties which results in messages being received by an intruder. This leads to loss of confidentiality.
- *Masquerading* A third party sending and receiving messages using the identity of an authorized user without delegation of authority. This may lead to loss of confidentiality, integrity and availability.
- *Modified* A message is modified or destroyed accidentally or deliberately. This leads to loss of confidentiality and integrity, and may also lead to loss of availability.
- *Replay* A message is first intercepted, copied and stored. At a later date the stored message is sent to the recipient. This leads to loss of confidentiality and may also lead to loss of integrity and availability.
- *Spoofing* An intruder masquerades as a trusted server.
- *Repudiation* False denial whereby either the sender denies sending a message or the recipient denies that it was received. Another form of repudiation is false denial of the use, misuse or abuse of resources.
- *Indirect infiltration* An information system is attacked by introducing an illegitimate program into the system unnoticed by users. Three types of mechanisms are common:
  - (i)   *viruses*   the program is attached to a legitimate program which is part of the information system and installs or reproduces itself whenever the legitimate program is run;
  - (ii) *trojan horses*   a program which offers some legitimate function, but also contains hidden additional software which is usually undesirable;
  - (iii) *worms*   the program exploits weaknesses in existing services to engage in illegitimate activity;
  - (iv) *logic bombs*   a trojan horse triggered when some event occurs;
  - (v)   *time bombs*   a logic bomb triggered by a date or time.

  Comprehensive anti-virus checking software is widely available to combat this type of attack.

An organizational unit is responsible for its principals and objects to the extent that it must ensure that an appropriate level of safeguards against attack is in place and the adequacy of safeguards can be demonstrated. An organization may be driven by commercial imperatives, legal requirements or customer demands. The appropriateness of security services is defined in terms of a set of rules; a **security policy,** which provides the benchmark against which security services are measured. Normally a security policy defines:

- procedures relevant to security management. In particular, what constitutes legitimate and authorized activity, security monitoring mechanisms, and so on;
- levels of responsibility. For example, under what circumstances and to whom responsibility is delegated;
- reporting requirements;

- which security mechanisms must be employed to ensure that the security policy is being enforced.

Normally, a security policy assumes that clients are untrustworthy until trustworthiness can be proven, and services are designed to be trustworthy. The network is assumed to be completely untrustworthy. Client and server computers must assume some responsibility for security in accordance with a security policy and therefore must be trusted to some degree. This can be the case only if appropriate security mechanisms have been implemented. Different organizational units may establish a different security policy and ensure that their clients and server objects obey it. Janson (1994), Sloman and Twidle (1994), and Moffett (1994) develop the notion of security domains and specifying a security policy per domain. A security domain is a set of principals and objects whose security is governed by a security domain policy defined by one administrative authority (Janson, 1994). Principals in a domain can be identified using a multi-component format which contains the unique name of the principal and the domain to which it belongs, for example:

Principal identifier = {name, domain-name}

In this scheme, the name field identifies a user or object uniquely. The domain name field identifies the domain to which the user or object belongs. An example of a principal identifier under the above scheme is {e.simon, scit.wlv.ac.uk} which specifies that user e.simon is registered in domain scit.wlv.ac.uk. Domain names are likely to be hierarchical, but any naming structure can be defined. Internet domain names or ITU-T X.500 structured names are likely candidates.

13.2 SECURITY MECHANISMS

In this section, the main security mechanisms which can be employed to meet the demands of a security policy are described. These are authentication, authorization, data confidentiality, non-repudiation and administration.

13.2.1 Data confidentiality

Data confidentiality is the process of ensuring that message contents are revealed only to authorized principals. The main technique used to prevent loss of confidentiality is *cryptography* which is the science of exchanging secret messages. *Encryption* is the process of transforming data into a form that cannot be understood without applying a second transformation using some shared secret called a *key*. *Decryption* is the process of applying a transformation using a key to recover the original data. The unencrypted form of the data is known as *plaintext*, and becomes *ciphertext* when encrypted. The notation used in this chapter to denote encryption of a message using key K is

$$\text{Ciphertext} = K[\text{Plaintext}]$$

Clearly intruders must not be able to access or forge key values. A *secret-key* (or *symmetric*) *cryptosystem* uses a single key for both encryption and decryption. In this approach the key is called a *secret key*. Thus, if K is a secret key

$$\text{If Ciphertext} = K[M]$$
$$\text{Then } M = K[\text{Ciphertext}]$$

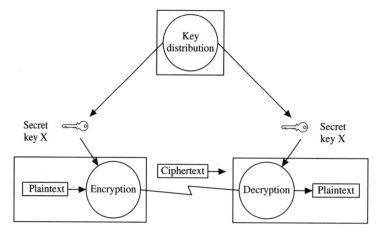

Figure 13.1 Secret key encryption.

Secret keys must be stored securely and distributed in such a way that intruders cannot obtain them. This is usually achieved by means of a third party: a *key distribution service*, an example of which is illustrated in Figure 13.1. An example secret-key cryptosystem is the Data Encryption Standard (DES) (DES, 1977). An alternative approach is a *public-key* (or *asymmetric*) *cryptosystem which* uses different keys for encryption and decryption. This eliminates the need for trust between principal and object and avoids the transmission of secret keys. One of the keys, the *public* key K_{pub}, is publicly known and the other, the *private* key K_{priv}, should be kept secret known only to the owner of the data. The public key is either sent directly to principals or stored in a database managed by a key distribution service which can handle operations such as 'give me the public key of principal X'. For example, the owner of message M encrypts it using the private key K_{priv} before sending it across the network. This is illustrated in Figure 13.2. Only those users who hold the public key K_{pub} are able to decrypt it. Thus

$$M = K_{pub} [K_{priv} (M)]$$

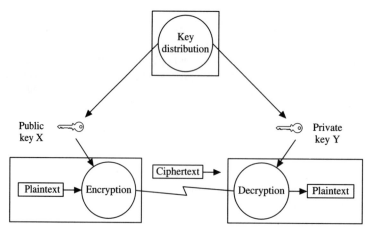

Figure 13.2 Public key encryption.

An example of this approach is the *Rivest–Shamir–Adleman* (RSA) algorithm, named after the developers (Rivest *et al.,* 1978). Both secret-key and public-key cryptosystems are secure approaches. The main problem with secret-key cryptosystems is the need to construct elaborate protocols to distribute secret keys securely over an untrusted network. The main problem with public-key cryptosystems is that sophisticated computations are required to produce mathematically related keys, which translates to less efficient (by a factor of 1000) and more expensive hardware implementations compared with secret-key systems. Key distribution, however, is much more straightforward in public-key systems since only the shared public keys are distributed. Some systems use a hybrid approach: a public-key system used for key distribution and a secret-key system for authentication.

Checksums are widely used in computer systems to verify that data has not been corrupted or modified, ensuring data integrity. Checksums are commonly used for security purposes to ensure that a message has not been modified by an intruder. This is a less expensive means of detecting modification in the case where it does not matter if the message is seen by others but it must not be modified. Whatever the technique employed, cryptographic techniques are fundamental to the implementation of data confidentiality, authentication and non-repudiation.

13.2.2 Authentication

Authentication is the process of establishing proof of identity. Two levels of authentication are required:

1. at client to server connection time. This addresses, for example, erroneous associations at connect or user login time;
2. for every message. This prevents message replaying and modification.

The most widely used authentication method is a simple password check at user login time. The system authenticates a user by comparing the password types at login time with a password hidden in a password file. In many systems, passwords are sent over the network leaving the system open to eavesdroppers who may be able to observe messages flowing over the network. Cryptographic-based authentication protocols avoid the transmission of passwords over the network and implement effective guards against various attacks. Another authentication mechanism is known as *message authentication* which verifies that the message came from its claimed originator and that it has not been altered during transmission. A common message authentication mechanism is the generation of a checksum, also known as a *message authentication code* (MAC), which is attached to a message before transmission. The receiver recalculates the MAC based on the message received, which reveals any alteration in transit, authenticates the origin of the message and the timeliness of message delivery.

13.2.3 Authorization

Authorization is the process of establishing which principals have the right to access a particular object. Once a user is authenticated, access control mechanisms are required to determine which resources a user can access and in what ways. **Access control** mechanisms have been implemented at various levels in a distributed information system, for example in the client and server operating system, and in a DBMS (e.g. using `Grant` and `Revoke` commands in

SQL). The most common access control mechanism is to associate with each object an **access control list (ACL)** that contains a list of {principal, access rights} or {principal group, access rights} pairs for every principal or principal group able to access the object. Access rights are typically read, write, execute, delete, owner, etc. An ACL-based protection mechanism can be usefully summarized in an *access control matrix* (Lampson, 1969; 1971). The rows of the matrix represent principal (or domain), and the columns represent objects. Each entry (i,j) in the matrix consists of a set of access rights which defines the set of operations principal (i) can invoke on object (j). This is illustrated in Table 13.1

Table 13.1 Example access control matrix.

	File X	*File Y*	*File Z*	Printer P
FSmith	read	owner execute		
JJones		execute		owner print
FRenaud		execute	read	
HBecker	owner read write		owner read write	

The use of ACLs are illustrated in Sections 13.3.3 and 13.3.4.

An example of another type of access control mechanism is a **capability** (Mullender and Tanenbaum, 1986) which is a special type of object that both names a principal and grants specific access rights to an object. In other words, access control information is attached to the principal rather than the object as is the case with ACLs. Each principal has an attached **capability list** which contains the capabilities of all objects to which it has access. To execute an operation on an object, a principal sends a request for execution specifying the capability for the object as a parameter. This protection scheme relies on the fact that a capability is granted to a principal and can never be altered by the principal. If all capabilities are secure, then all objects referenced by capabilities are also secure providing they cannot be accessed without specifying a capability. One attraction of capabilities is the ability to *delegate* a principal's access rights to another principal by simply passing the capability to it. For example, a user can request that a file be printed by sending a print request and the user's capability. The print server sends the user's capability with the read request to a file server.

In general, a principal has *privilege attributes* which specify the privileges associated with it. Equally, an object may have *control attributes* which define which principals can access the object and in what way. Access control also depends on the operation requested (e.g. read(x) suggests that a principal requires read access) and the context in which it is being requested (e.g. a file may need to be opened before it can be read). An access control mechanism enforces access control rules to decide whether a principal can access an object. When an operation is invoked, the decision whether to grant access is done by comparing a principal's privilege attributes with the target object's control attributes, given the operation, its context and the security policy to be enforced.

An issue relating to access control is the right to access an object across a network. Controlling access to networked objects can be achieved by blocking particular classes of messages to objects. A mechanism which blocks message delivery is known as a **filter**. A

security firewall is a set of components which together act as a filter for messages travelling in or out of a domain. A firewall is normally placed between an intra-organizational network and the outside world (e.g. the Internet). Cheswick and Bellovin (1994) suggest that internal firewalls may also be necessary to isolate security domains. In general, they suggest that a firewall should be positioned at the boundaries between security domains. An effective firewall is implemented by filtering every packet received from another security domain. This is known as **packet filtering** and involves setting up a special filter table which indicates which classes of packets should be blocked or accepted. An example filter table is given in Table 13.2.

Table 13.2 A firewall filter table fragment

Action	Our host	Our port	Their host	Their port	Comment
block	*	*	BadSite	*	dont trust BadSite
allow	main-gw	20	*	*	can connect to ftp server
block	*	*	*	*	default: block anything else

The filter rules are executed working from top to bottom. The example filter table blocks everything from a site called BadSite, everyone else can use only the anonymous FTP facility. A general firewall configuration is given in Figure 13.3. Additional firewall mechanisms can be built at higher layers (transport and application). Many application-level mechanisms rely on logging techniques and subsequent auditing. For an excellent discussion of firewall security and the Internet, see Cheswick and Bellovin (1994).

13.2.4 Non-repudiation

Non-repudiation is the process of authenticating the origin of a message. A principal must be able to be convinced of the identity of the sender or originator (*proof of origin*). In addition, a principal must be able to convince a third party of the origin of the message so that there can be no doubt or denial of origin. Conversely, non-repudiation of *receipt* is the process of proving to a third party that a message was indeed received by an identifiable principal so that there can be no doubt or denial that a message was received (*proof of delivery*). A good

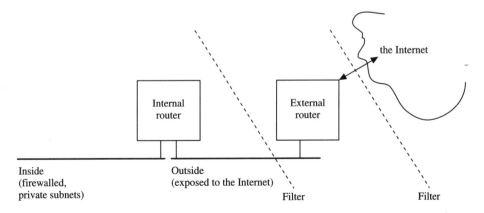

Figure 13.3 A firewall configuration.

example of repudiation is in an electronic data interchange (EDI) between trading partners. It can be advantageous financially if a customer can deny that an invoice was ever received! Non-repudiation mechanisms are employed to establish proof of origin and delivery.

Public-key cryptography can be used to enable the originator to *sign* a message before it is sent by encrypting it using the private key. Anyone with the corresponding public key can verify receipt of a message from the originator by decrypting it using the originator's public key. The use of a private key for this purpose is known as a *digital signature*. If the recipient can decrypt a message successfully then the originator cannot deny having sent it. In practice, a public-key based digital signature system uses only a portion of a message to form a digital signature so as to cut down on the number of computations required. To prevent replay, the message must include a timestamp or special sequence number to enable the receiver to detect the freshness of a message.

13.2.5 Security administration

Security administration is the process of managing the security environment and ensuring that the security policy is enforced and security is not being breached. There are four important aspects:

1. checking audit trails;
2. cryptographic and password management;
3. maintenance of security equipment and services;
4. informing users of their responsibilities in maintaining a secure environment.

An audit trail provides a record of what occurred in the immediate past and, when examined, an indication of whether a security system has been breached. A security administrator is required to examine audit trails regularly. Cryptographic management primarily involves managing the creation of keys and the storage of keys in a database for secure key distribution. In general, users are left to organize their own passwords. In some systems, however, users can be set up to enforce frequent changes to passwords and impose a minimum password length. Procedures such as physical security, data backup and recovery are required to ensure the security equipment and services are well maintained. Finally, users must be made aware of their role in maintaining security.

13.3 SECURITY TECHNOLOGY

An authentication service can be implemented using either secret-key or public-key cryptosystems. In this section an example of each type will be analysed: the Needham and Schroeder public-key protocol and the Kerberos secret-key protocol. The OSF/DCE security service is described as an example of a commercial implementation of authentication.

13.3.1 Needham and Schroeder public-key authentication

Needham and Schroeder (1978) produced initial work in the area of authentication protocols using a key distribution centre (KDC). Protocols for both secret- and public-key cryptosystems were produced. Table 13.3 describes the Needham and Schroeder public-key authentication protocol used to authenticate two principals: client c and server s. Each principal defines an additional data item, known as a *nonce*, which is used to tie together requests and replies to

Table 13.3 The Needham and Schroeder public-key authentication protocol

Direction: message content	Description
1. client→KDC: c, s	The client requests the public key for server s from the KDC.
2. KDC→client: $K_{kdc,priv} (K_{s,pub}, s)$	The KDC sends the server's public key $K_{s,pub}$ and server identifier, encrypted with KDC's private key. All valid principals hold the KDC's public key.
3. Client→server: $K_{s,pub} (nc, c)$	The client sends a message containing its nonce and identifier to the server, encrypted with the server's public key.
4. Server->KDC: s, c	The server requests the public key for client c from the KDC.
5. KDC→client: $K_{kdc,priv} (K_{c,pub}, c)$	The KDC sends the client's public key $K_{c,pub}$ and client identifier, encrypted with KDC's private key.
6. Server→client: $K_{c,pub} (nc, ns)$	The server sends its nonce together with the client's nonce, encrypted with the client's public key $K_{c,pub}$. This authenticates the server to the client.
7. Client→server: $K_{s,pub} (ns)$	The client returns the server's nonce encrypted by the server's public key $K_{s,pub}$. This authenticates the client to the server.

ensure that message requests and corresponding replies are fresh messages rather than replays of old messages. A nonce must therefore be non-repeating to avoid the possibility of replay. Nonces are generally timestamps or sequence numbers which are incremented after each request or reply in an authentication protocol.

The main weakness of Needham and Schroeder's authentication protocols is the possibility of message replay due to the fact that client and server principals must believe that the public keys supplied by the KDC are fresh. Old KDC replies could be stored by an intruder and replayed. This is easily overcome by adding a timestamp to the messages transmitted in steps 2 and 5.

13.3.2 Kerberos secret-key authentication

The **Kerberos** authentication service (Steiner *et al.*, 1988), developed at MIT, is a secret-key cryptosystem widely adopted as the basis of an authentication service in an unprotected network. The identities of principals are verified without relying on authentication by the client's or server's native operating system. It also does not trust host addresses and assumes that principal identifiers can be forged, and network packets can be intercepted, replayed or modified by masqueraders. Kerberos is based in part on Needham and Schroeder's trusted third party authentication protocol (Needham and Schroeder, 1978). This section describes the essential features of Kerberos Version 5 as detailed in Internet RFC1510 (Kohl and Neuman, 1993; Kohl *et al.*, 1994).

In Kerberos, each principal is uniquely named by attaching a principal identifier of the form {primary name, instance, realm}. Where the primary name is the name of the client or server (e.g. a userid or service name), the *instance* is either a null value or contains some particular attribute such as a machine name, and the *realm* (synonymous with security domain) identifies the security domain to which the principal belongs. Each realm is managed by an autonomous administration utilizing one or more authentication servers. Currently there are four types of realm name conventions defined: Internet DNS compatible, ITU-T X.500 compatible, 'other' names of example format: NAMETYPE: rest/of.name-without-restrictions, and reserved types which are undefined which will not conflict with any of the previous formats. For convenience, most currently operating Kerberos servers have chosen realm names that parallel their respective Internet domain names (e.g. athena.mit.edu). Thus Kerberos (version 5) supports the concept of multiple security domains with multiple naming conventions.

A basic Kerberos service consists of the following main components:

1. The **key distribution centre** (KDC). A third party trusted to hold a database of principal identifiers and their associated secret keys which is also known by each client and server registered in the realm managed by the KDC. The KDC is also involved in the *initial ticket exchange* process in which a client authenticates to a server for the first time (i.e. at connect time).

2. The **ticket-granting server** (TGS). A trusted third party which plays an active role in any *additional ticket exchange* process, for example if the client wishes to authenticate to another server subsequently. This process is logically separate from the initial ticket exchange process to avoid having to expose a client's secret key repeatedly as it authenticates to various servers during a session.

Kerberos uses two types of electronic *credentials* for passing authentication information: *tickets* and *authenticators*. A ticket is a record of assorted information which helps a client authenticate to a server. A ticket $T_{c,s}$ is passed between a client with principal identifier c and server with principal identifier s. A ticket is split into a plaintext part followed by a second part encrypted by the principal's secret key as follows:

Plaintext part

- *ticket version number*   the version number of the ticket format. Version 5 for this format;
- *realm*: the realm that issued the ticket;
- *server name*   the *primary name* part of the server's principal identifier.

Ciphertext part (encrypted using the private key K_x of principal x):

- *flags*   indicates which of various options were used or requested at the time the ticket was issued;
- *Key*   the session key $K_{c,s}$ shared by client c and server s and used to encrypt and decrypt messages passed between them;
- *crealm*   the name of the realm in which the client is registered and in which initial authentication took place;
- *cname*   the *primary name* part of the client's principal identifier;
- *transited*   records the names of the Kerberos realms that took part in the authentication process;
- *authtime*   the time of initial authentication for the named principal. The concept of 'initial' authentication arises because a ticket can be *renewed* by the TGS replacing a previous ticket which has expired. A Kerberos service could refuse to accept tickets for which the initial authentication occurred 'too far' in the past;

- $starttime$ the time after which the ticket is valid. If this field is empty then authtime is interpreted as the $starttime$ value;
- $endtime$ the time after which the ticket will not be honoured (i.e. the expiration time). This field together with the $starttime$ field determines the *lifetime* of the ticket;
- $renew-till$ the absolute expiration time for the ticket, including all renewals;
- $caddr$ the host addresses from which the ticket can be used. If there are no addresses, the ticket can be used from any location. In fact the decision by the KDC to issue a ticket to a principal in the case when $caddr$ is empty is influenced by the security policy in operation. The host address from which a message appeared to have been sent cannot be trusted. For example, it is very easy to send an IP datagram with an incorrect (but valid) source IP address – perhaps the address of the client whom an intruder wishes to masquerade as. The $caddr$ field cannot be tampered with without knowledge of the secret key $K_{c.tgs}$. Thus effective use of the $caddr$ field makes it harder for an intruder to use stolen credentials;
- *authorization data*   an optional field used to pass authorization data relevant to the associated service to which the principal is authenticated. The data in this field is specific to the end service and is therefore not used by the Kerberos service. This field contains the names of service-specific objects, and the rights to those objects. For example, when a client accesses a print server to print a particular file stored on a file server, the client can obtain a file server proxy to be passed to the print server. The client can store the name of the file and access rights in the authorization data field of the proxy. This ensures that the print server can use the client's rights only to print the file named in the authorization field. In general, if a principal obtains a proxy leaving the $caddr$ field empty and storing object names and associated access rights in the $authorization$ field, the proxy can be treated as a *capability*.

In Kerberos, an *authenticator* is a record sent with a ticket to a server s to certify the client's knowledge of the encryption key in the ticket. An authenticator A_c of client c is encrypted with the session key $K_{c,s}$ shared by client c and server s. An authenticator guards against message modification and replays by including a **checksum** and **timestamp** with the data. In public-key cryptosystems encrypting long messages can be very expensive. A checksum, using a small extract of the message, is used to detect if the data sent was forged or modified. The timestamp is normally the current time on the client's machine which is compared with the time the message was received to detect a replay of an old authenticator. A Kerberos authenticator contains the following information:

- *authenticator version number*   the version number for the format of the authenticator;
- $crealm$ functionally equivalent to the same field in the ticket;
- $cname$ functionally equivalent to the same field in the ticket;
- $cksum$ used to detect whether data has been forged or modified. A standard checksum algorithm (known as message digest or MD5) is used for this purpose. It should not be possible to modify the original data so as to produce a checksum that matches the original checksum;
- $cusec$ contains the microsecond part of the client's timestamp;
- $ctime$ contains the current time on the client's host. It is used in conjunction with the $cusec$ field to specify a reasonably accurate timestamp. The clock accuracy is dependent on how well clocks are synchronized in the distributed system;
- $subkey$ this is a key chosen by the client to protect this particular session. If this field is empty, the session key from the ticket will be used (unless an application specifies that it should not be used);

- `seq-number` used to detect replays (in which case it must be non-repeating even across session boundaries);
- *authorization data* this optional field is functionally the same as the field in the ticket.

The five-step authentication process (an optional sixth step is executed if the client requests mutual authentication) is detailed in Table 13.4 and illustrated in Figure 13.4. The client can be a process running on the users workstation, for example, a login program, or a process running on a server requiring access to another service.

Table 13.4 The Kerberos authentication process

Direction: message content	Description
1. Client→KDC: c, tgs, n	The client determines the user id c and requests ticket-granting ticket (TGT) for TGS specifying a nonce value n.
2. KDC→client: $K_c(K_{c,\text{tgs}}, n), K_{\text{tgs}}(T_{c,\text{tgs}})$	KDC supplies two data items 1. The session key for the client to TGS session and nonce, encrypted with the client's secret key. 2. The TGT $T_{c,\text{tgs}}$ encrypted with the TGS's secret key K_{tgs}. Only the client which knows the secret key K_c is able to decrypt to obtain the session key $K_{c,\text{tgs}}$. The user c is authenticated by prompting for a password then, using a secret transformation process, generating a key value to be compared with key K_c. Note that the TGT cannot be modified by the client since it does not know TGS's secret key K_{tgs}. If the user is authenticated by the client, the password can be deleted. K_c is used to decrypt the encrypted session key $K_{c,\text{tgs}}$.
3. Client→TGS $K_{c,\text{tgs}}(A_c, n), K_{\text{tgs}}(T_{c,\text{tgs}}), s, n$	Client sends to TGS its encrypted TGT along with its authenticator (encrypted with $K_{c,\text{tgs}}$) and request data identifying the server to which it wishes to connect.
4. TGS→client $K_{c,\text{tgs}}(K_{c,s}, n), K_s(T_{c,s})$	The TGS verifies the ticket, authenticator and request data, and replies with a ticket $T_{c,s}$ for a new server (s) (protected from tampering by encrypting it with the server's secret key K_s) and a session key $K_{c,s}$ encrypted with session key $K_{c,\text{tgs}}$.
5. Client→server $K_{c,s}(A_c, n), K_s(T_{c,s})$	Client sends its authenticator encrypted with the session key $K_{c,s}$ and also passes on the session ticket which was encrypted with the server's secret key by the TGS. The server authenticates the client by decrypting the authenticator and comparing it with the information contained in the ticket $T_{c,s}$.
6. Server→client $K_{c,s}[n]$	Optionally, if mutual authentication is requested by the client, the server sends a fresh message (e.g. the nonce n) encrypted with session key $K_{c,s}$. Receipt of the message [n] encrypted with session key $K_{c,s}$ is only possible if the server knows secret key K_s and was therefore able to obtain the session key $K_{c,s}$ from the ticket $T_{c,s}$ in order to encrypt the message [n] correctly. The server is authenticated.

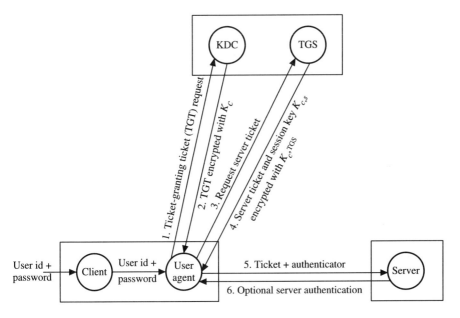

Figure 13.4 The Kerberos authentication process.

Subsequent message exchanges between client and server are encrypted (with the session key $K_{c,s}$ (i.e. $K_{c,s}$ [message]) since both client and server share this key and which has never been sent across the network unencrypted. Other features offered by Kerberos are:

- *authentication forwarding* the credentials of client c_i with credentials on one host can be forwarded to some other host and used by another client. This is particularly the case when a service (e.g. a print service) needs to request service from another server (e.g. a file server) in order to complete a client request;
- *inter-realm authentication* efficient inter-realm authentication is required because a federation of realms is a common requirement. Interoperability is implemented if two realms agree to share an inter-realm key or it shares a key with an intermediate realm that is itself interoperable with the realm containing the server (the destination realm). The number of key exchanges required to interconnect n realms is $O(\log(n))$. Key exchanges can be optimized by issuing a TGT to the nearest known realm to the destination realm (which may be determined using realm naming structure coupled with local information);
- *support for authorization and accounting* although Kerberos is not directly concerned with authorization and accounting issues it is viewed as a facility to enable these functions to be integrated into a Kerberos service opaquely. To support this, a Kerberos ticket has a special field; the *authorization data* field which can hold authorization and accounting information. Secure transmission of the information is the responsibility of the authorization and accounting services and is by means of encryption. The TGS always copies authorization data from a TGT to the session ticket. Thus upon decryption, this data is available to the server. The server must also be able to decrypt the authorization data (assuming it is encrypted). An example of its use is in the OSF/DCE system where it is used in conjunction with a privilege server to enable a client to validate a userid and test whether a user belongs to particular groups. This is detailed in the next section.

13.3.3 OSF/DCE security service

The OSF/DCE security service is designed to ensure privacy of confidential information and protect the integrity of communications in a DCE-based distributed system. In DCE each principal has a unique user identifier (UUID). To assist authorization, all principals with the same access privileges are defined as members of the same *group*. Every object in DCE can be protected by control attributes in the form of an access control list (ACL). The granularity of access rights are `read`, `write`, `execute`, `change-ACL`, `container-insert` (the right to add files), `container-delete` (the right to delete files), and `test` (the right to test for a value in a file without revealing its contents). An ACL specifies

- the default cell to which the ACL applies;
- the rights of each user in the default cell;
- the rights of particular groups defined in the default cell;
- the rights of everyone else in the default cell;
- the rights of users and groups in other cells.

Authentication and authorization are closely tied together in DCE and are carried out when a principal carries out a server login before generating DCE RPC calls. A Kerberos-based authentication method is implemented, where each DCE cell is a Kerberos realm. Inter-cell (i.e. inter-realm) security is via shared secret exchange as discussed in the previous section. The DCE registry service is used to create and maintain all secret key and other information for valid principals.

In addition to the Kerberos components: KDC and TGS, DCE defines an additional server known as a **privilege server** which is used to obtain the privilege attributes of a principal. KDC, TGS and privilege server components all execute on a single security server which is physically secured for increased protection. The authentication process detailed in the previous section is first used to authenticate a client to the privilege server. Privilege attributes are contained in a privilege attribute certificate (PAC), specifying the UUID of a principal and the groups to which the principal belongs. A PAC simply proves that an entity with the specified UUID is a member of each of the groups listed. The following additional steps are carried out once a client is authenticated to the privilege server:

1. The client asks the privilege server for the user's PAC containing the UUID and all groups to which the user belongs. The PAC is encrypted by the privilege server using the TGS's secret key K_{tgs}.

$$\text{Client} \rightarrow \text{Privilege server: } K_{c,p}(A_c, n), K_p(c, K_{c,p})$$
$$\text{Privilege server} \rightarrow \text{Client: } K_{c,p}[K_{c,tgs}, K_{tgs}(\text{PAC}, K_{c,tgs})]$$

2. The client asks the TGS for a PAC for use by the destination server s. The client does this by sending the encrypted PAC to the TGS. The TGS decrypts the PAC then reencrypts it with the secret key for server s, K_s which it obtains from the key database, along with a newly generated session key $K_{c,s}$. Before transmission to the client the session key $K_{c,s}$ is attached (to enable the client to read it) and the whole message is encrypted using the client-to-TGS session key $K_{c,tgs}$.

$$\text{Client} \rightarrow \text{TGS: } K_{c,tgs}(A_c, n), K_{tgs}(\text{PAC}, K_{c,tgs})$$
$$\text{TGS} \rightarrow \text{Client } K_{c,tgs}[K_{c,s}, K_s(\text{PAC}, K_{c,s})]$$

3. Finally, the client sends the PAC and session key to the server s together with an authenticator and nonce encrypted with the session key. The server s decrypts the PAC and session key using its secret key K_s. The session key $K_{c,s}$ is used to decrypt the authenticator which is used to authenticate the client. Finally, the server sends back the nonce together with a subsession secret key $K'_{c,s}$ known only to the client and server. The client decrypts the message and authenticates the server using the nonce. All subsequent message exchanges are encrypted using the shared subsession key $K'_{c,s}$ and the DCE RPC protocol.

$$\text{Client} \rightarrow \text{server } s: K_{c,s}[A_c, n], K_s[\text{PAC}, K_{c,s}]$$
$$\text{Server } s \rightarrow \text{Client}: K_{c,s}[n, K'_{c,s}]$$

The client can connect to additional servers by repeating steps 2 and 3 above using the original PAC and specifying the new server's to the TGS.

13.3.4 Novell Netware security services

Authentication in the Novell Netware network operating system is an example of the use of RSA public-key technology, as illustrated in Figure 13.5.

When logging into a network, a user is authenticated to establish that it is a valid user of network resources. Once authenticated, a user is subject to authorization controls based on access control lists (ACLs). After the user name and password is entered (assuming that the context has been set correctly so that the user object can be found in the Netware directory service (NDS)), the client login process sends the user name to the authentication server (this function is integrated into the NDS). The authentication sever responds with the user's private key encrypted using the user's password. The client login process then decodes it with the password typed in at login. If the password is correct then decryption is successful and the user's private key is revealed. After decryption, the user's password is erased from memory (thus, the password is kept for a very short period of time and is never sent over the network). With the private key the client process creates an authenticator which contains the user name, workstation address, lifetime value, session i.d., and so on, that acts as the user's *signature*. The client process encrypts the signature with its private key, forming the user's *credentials*. To authenticate the user, the client process creates a *proof*, which is the signature and login request message encrypted with the authentication server's public key. The proof is sent to the authentication server. The authentication server then authenticates the user to the network by decrypting the proof using its private key and the signature using the user's public key. Authentication occurs when the client data matches

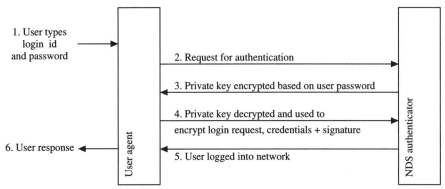

Figure 13.5 Novell Netware authentication process.

the authenticators, and the user is logged in to NDS. During a user session, the user's password and signature are never sent across the network.

To prevent the infiltration of forged packets during a user session, both client and server processes maintain information about the state of a session at any moment in time by independently deriving a 64-bit session key. In addition, a portion of a packet is altered intentionally by using an encryption-like algorithm (known as the MD-4 message digest algorithm) and used as a packet signature. The algorithm used changes dynamically with each additional packet sent since it relies on information regarding prior activity of the session.

A process known as *background authentication* occurs when a user tries to access an object in a partition outside of the partition to which the user originally logged in. In this case, NDS sends a message to the client process asking it to authenticate itself. The client process responds by constructing a proof and returning it to the NDS. If the proof matches those derived by NDS then background authentication occurs. Because the session key is never sent over the network, it is virtually impossible to forge a packet. This elaborate scheme avoids the overhead of encrypting the whole packet.

Authorization is based on ACLs. All resources in Netware are represented as objects in the Netware directory service (NDS) a directory service based on ITU-T X.500 (see Section 8.2.1). NDS defines two types of objects: *container* objects which can contain other objects, and *leaf* objects which represent actual resources such as users, servers, printers, and so on. Each NDS object contains an *object rights* ACL which is a list of NDS object ids that are allowed access to the object. The ACL also contains a *rights mask* that determines which types of access are allowable for each object contained in the ACL. The access rights are:

- **browse**. Grants rights to see an object (but not the object's ACL);
- **create**. Grants the rights to create a new object below this container object in the NDS directory tree (leaf objects cannot contain other objects). Granting create rights automatically causes browse rights to be granted;
- **delete**. Grant the rights to delete the object from the directory tree;
- **rename**. Grant the rights to change the name of an object;
- **supervisor**. Grant all access privileges to the object.

Every NDS object has information stored in it which is visible as a set of *object properties* (analogous to object attributes in ITU-T X.500). To see any of the properties of another object, an object must have the appropriate *property rights*. Each object property has an *object property ACL* which lists object ids and their associated rights to access the property. Property rights are:

- **read.** Grants the right to read the values of the property. The read right includes the compare right;
- **compare.** Grants the right to compare any given value to a value of a property. When this is done, a message states whether the compared values match or not, but the actual value of the property is not revealed;
- **write.** Grants the right to add, change, or remove any values of the property. It also includes the add self right;
- **add or delete self.** Grants a trustee the right to add or remove itself as a value of the property. This right is only meaningful for properties that contain object names as values, such as group membership and mailing lists;
- **supervisor.** Grants all rights to the property.

Object and property ACLs are the basis for Netware access control. By default, the object and property rights of a container object are *inherited* downward through the NDS sub-tree below the container object. This can be controlled, however, by blocking inheritance through the specification of a special property called an *Inherited Rights Filter* (IRF). An IRF acts as a mask that blocks the inheritance of object or property access rights downwards through a sub-tree.

A Netware server's file system has a separate access control mechanism also based on ACLs. Each directory and file has an associated ACL called a *trustee list* which contain object and associated rights mappings. Any object contained in the list is said to be a *trustee* of the file or directory. Possible trustee rights are supervisor, read, write, create, erase (a user can delete files or directories), modify (a user can modify a directory), file scan (a user can scan for files) and access (a user can change access control for trustees of the file or directory). Each file has an owner which initially inherits create file or directory rights. A file owner, however, is treated as a trustee with particular trustee rights. Each file or directory has a set of *file attributes* which can be used for security purposes because they can be used to inhibit (i.e. block) trustee rights. For example, if a rename inhibit attribute is set on a file, it cannot be renamed even if a user has rename trustee rights. The execute only attribute, for example, prevents unauthorized copying or modification of an executable file by a virus program.

Netware also provides auditing facilities and login restrictions such as disabling accounts, forcing the correct use of passwords, controlling workstations from which users can login, controlling the specific times of day users can login and automatic disabling of an account when a specific number of unsuccessful logins occur.

13.4 SECURITY LEVELS

The classification of information according to various levels of sensitivity (e.g. top-secret, secret, confidential and unclassified) is common practice in military organizations for implementing access controls. In this system, a user is assigned a particular **security clearance level** which allows him or her to access objects at that level and below. For example, a user with secret security clearance is allowed to look at objects classified as secret, confidential and unclassified (but not top-secret). This is known as a **multi-level security model**. In this system, it should not be possible for a user at a high security clearance level to simply copy secret data to users at a lower level, that is, information should only be able to flow upwards. This approach is an alternative to the implementation of authorization matrices.

A common framework for evaluating the levels of security offered by computer systems is the US Department of Defense's Orange Book on *Trusted Computer System Evaluation Criteria* first published 1983. It defines four general divisions of security from A to D, with A being most secure and D being the least. In addition, Division C is separated into two classes and B into three classes. Each security level includes all the functionality of the previous level. The security levels and major feature introduced at that level are summarized in Table 13.5.

The main trade-off is security level against system performance. Class A1 systems require significantly more resources to achieve the same system performance as Division D systems because of the high overheads required to execute the various security mechanisms. Therefore it is incumbent on an organization to determine exactly what level of security is required and to implement a security policy which reflects those requirements.

Table 13.5 US Department of Defense Orange Book security levels

Security level	Major feature introduced
Division D	Minimal protection
Division C	Discretionary protection
Class C1	Discretionary security protection, i.e. the user decides the level of protection required for objects owned by the user.
Class C2	Controlled access protection. Auditing is required so that users are accountable for their own actions.
Division B	Mandatory protection
Class B1	Labelled security protection. Every user has a security level (called a security clearance) and every object has a sensitivity level. The system decides whether a user can access an object based on comparing clearance and sensitivity values.
Class B2	Structured security protection. Rigorous design (using a formal security model), testing and proof of security
Class B3	Security domain. Further rigorous design and security assurance requirements. In particular, the security kernel of the system (the trusted computer base (TCB)) is rigorously designed, of a simple structure and is proven to be secure.
Division A	Verified protection
Class A1	Verified design. Formal analysis and mathematical proof that the computer system matches the system's security policy and its design specifications. Trusted distribution which ensures the security of the system while it is being shipped to the customer.

13.5 SUMMARY

Distributed systems need to be protected from unauthorized access, malicious destruction or modification, and accidental loss of data integrity. In this chapter the types of security breaches and security measures for combating attacks were detailed.

An important aspect of security is the definition of a security policy which is a management responsibility. The concept of security domains recognizes that there may be separate management domains each with different security policies. Security technologies mostly rely on cryptographic techniques. Example technologies such as Kerberos authentication and DCE authentication and authorization services were detailed. Implementing security can be expensive but few organizations can afford to overlook it.

13.6 REVIEW EXERCISES

1. Describe the security concerns for (i) a university, (ii) a bank and (iii) a small manufacturing business employing 50 people with a small LAN supporting order processing and accounting functions.

2. Discuss the types of security attacks an organization could be subjects to.
3. What security measures are typically implemented by (i) the operating system in the client workstation? (ii) the network? (iii) the operating system on a server computer? (iv) a database management system? (v) a file system? (vi) physical security systems.
4. What are the advantages and disadvantages of encryption?
5. Compare and contrast secret-key and public-key cryptosystems. Is there a case for implementing a hybrid system?
6. Explain the difference between authentication and authorization.
7. Compare and contrast capability and access control list authorization mechanisms.
8. What is a security firewall? Describe how security firewalls are implemented.
9. How can a system guard against repudiation of message origin or delivery?
10. Describe the Kerberos authentication process.

13.7 FURTHER READING

Security concepts are covered in many operating systems and communications texts, such as Silberschatz and Galvin (1994) and Coulouris *et al.* (1994). The DES algorithm is described in detail in Tanenbaum (1988). The RSA algorithm is described in Rivest *et al.* (1978). The Kerberos authentication protocol is described by Steiner *et al.* (1988). DCE security is described in Tanenbaum (1995) and OSF (1992).

14

FUTURE DIRECTIONS

14.1 INTRODUCTION

The preceding thirteen chapters described the concepts, techniques and technologies involved in the development and implementation of distributed information systems. With the continued evolution of underpinning technologies, users are going to be faced with an even more bewildering array of choices in the future. In the area of distributed information systems we will see more new concepts evolving, together with new types of technologies on offer which need to be integrated into a coherent system. Inevitably, the choice between implementing systems as soon as possible and postponing decisions in order to get more favourable conditions will become more difficult.

In this closing chapter, we look ahead based on the extrapolation of previous technology trends and current developments. There is no doubt that the next century will spawn new types of information systems and services as newer technologies appear that are much more suited to the support of distributed multimedia.

14.2 COMPUTER TECHNOLOGY

The performance of computer hardware continues to improve at a rapid rate while costs reduce to maintain very attractive price/performance ratios. Table 14.1 compares the CPU and display characteristics of a desktop PC in 1981, 1991 and 1995. The extrapolated profile of a desktop computer in early next century is also included. With this capacity on every user's desk, coupled with the likely advances in memory, storage and communications technologies, we will see a previously unimagined set of new information systems emerge in the near future.

Table 14.1 Comparison of the CPU and display characteristics of a desktop PC 1981–2000

	1981	1985	1991	1995	1997	2000+
Intel CPU	8088	80286	80486	Pentium	P6	P6+
Clock frequency	4.77 MHz	25 MHz	50 MHz	120 MHz	250 MHz	300+ MHz
Number of transistors	29 000	100 000	1.2 million	3.1 million	6–10 million	100 million
Typical real memory	128 Kb	1 Mb	2–4 Mb	8–16 Mb	32–64 Mb	64–128 Mb
Maximum real memory supported	256 Kb	4 Mb	64 Mb	256 Mb	2 Gb	n Gb
Display density	320 x 200	640 x 400	1024 x 768	1268 x 1024	1268 x 1024	1268 x 1024
Display colours	4	16	256 (8 bits per pixel)	16.7 million (24 bits per pixel)	16.7 million	16.7 million

Desktop (client) and server computers will continue to be dominant components of a distributed IT infrastructure designed to support information systems and services in the future. Powerful client computers will be incorporated in end-user devices such as kiosks in shopping malls and set-top boxes in homes to provide access to a wide range of services.

14.3 COMMUNICATIONS TECHNOLOGY

Users are making use of services which place increasing demands on the communications infrastructure. The infrastructure will need to offer an ever increasing range of bandwidths to support the types of widely-available services envisaged in the future (for example, interactive, full motion video and digital sound). ATM technology provides the capacity and scalability to meet bandwidth and latency needs for the foreseeable future. Like all new technology, the costs of installing ATM technology will continue to reduce dramatically as competition and usage increases.

Narrowband ISDN has enjoyed rapid employment as a digital, circuit-switched public WAN replacing the analogue public switched telephone network (PSTN). It is being used increasingly as the communications link to access on-demand information services incorporating video, images and text. Users employing distributed information systems eagerly await, however, the introduction of a broadband ISDN (B-ISDN) service based on ATM technology and gigabits-per-second fibre optic cabling. With the promise of high-speed, low-latency, 'bandwidth-on-demand' services, B-ISDN will open up a new generation of 'information-rich' wide area information services underpinned by a true global 'information superhighway'. Services will range from high-quality voice communications and video telephony, to high-definition television, digital video broadcast, and high-quality multimedia information services on demand.

The communications infrastructure will need to support a large number of mobile users each of which require transparent access to their 'local' environment no matter where they are physically located. Although support for mobile users is improving with the increased migration to digital cellular services, there are still fairly severe limitations, in terms of the speed and quality of communication, which constrain the range of information services that can be accessed. In particular, services which incorporate a significant amount of multimedia objects will need to provide alternative protocols and modes of interaction which are tuned to the relatively limited bandwidth and poorer quality-of-service available to mobile users.

The infrastructure should provide appropriate levels of security to ensure that personal, business and other potentially sensitive items of information cannot be accessed by unauthorized users. Security is no longer regarded as a secondary issue, sophisticated technology is being tightly integrated into the IT infrastructure and information systems to provide a high level of security to users.

14.4 MEMORY AND STORAGE TECHNOLOGY

Memory and storage technologies have been evolving at almost the same rate as CPU technology. Unfortunately, many different and incompatible storage technologies have been maturing for some time for which few standards exist. Within the traditional hard disk technology, physical size, access times and costs continue to reduce while storage capacity is rising rapidly. With the use of compression standards such as MPEG offering a compression factor of 50–100 (i.e. one minute of video is equivalent to 1 Gb uncompressed, and 20 Mb compressed) storage technology has evolved to cope with the demands of multimedia information storage and access. A desktop multimedia PC now incorporates gigabytes of hard disk storage with access times of much less than 20 ms and a transfer rate of much greater than 10 Mbytes/s (required for MPEG-2 video streams). Hard disks will remain as the primary storage device for frequently used, volatile data.

Optical storage devices offer greater storage capacity compared to hard disks because the amount of space needed per bit and the spacing between tracks is much smaller. Also, because reads are based on low power laser light, the recording surface is not degraded resulting in a long lifetime (provided the condition of storage and handling are appropriate). The current compact disk (CD) family of devices offer high disk capacity but with slower access times and transfer rates. CDs offer cheap, portable, large capacity and durable storage. Standard CD-ROMs provide 660 Mb of data storage with access times of typically 200–350 ms (the best optical devices achieve around 60 ms) and a transfer rate of 1.5 Mbytes/s. Multimedia information requirements demand higher disk capacity, lower access times and faster transfer rates. New developments, such as the Philips/Sony High Density CD (HDCD) and the Toshiba super density digital video disk (DVD), are increasing data capacity from 660 Mbytes to up to around 10 Gbytes (with transfer rates of around 10 Mbytes/s) by increasing the density of physically encoded disk data, introducing more compact error detection and correction code and using both sides of the disk. Thus optical devices will continue to offer high capacity storage but with performance characteristics comparable with hard disk devices.

Optical devices which support a write process have evolved from WORM (write once read many) drives to those which provide true read–write symmetry (i.e. erasable optical devices) and compare favourably with hard disks but with the ability to remove, interchange and transport optical disks easily. Thus jukebox systems of removable, erasable optical disks offer tens of gigabytes of on-line storage which can be used to hold on-line data and as a backup and archive medium. An example of an erasable optical device is the *magneto-optic* (MO) drive. A MO disk contains an active layer of magnetic material sandwiched between two protective layers. The polarity of a laser light source and the magnetic material can be varied by applying a magnetic field and heat, and it is these properties that can be used to represent a bit stream on an MO disk. Data is overwritten by first erasing it and, in the second pass, writing the new data. Data is read by analysing the polarity of the laser beam as it is reflected from the spinning disk. MO disks store around 200–300 Mb on a 3.5 inch disk and exhibit access times and transfer rates which are comparable to other optical devices. The choice of magnetic material largely determines the characteristics of MO drives. Current MO disks offer a long lifetime on shelf or in use and are available in 3.5, 5.25 and 12 inch disk units. Newer MO devices overcome the need to erase data before new data is written by employing a more sophisticated write and erase mechanisms using two active layers; a reference layer and a memory layer. Access times for these devices are reducing to around 20 ms and the data density is likely to at least double due to enhancements to the active layer material used and laser beam technology.

14.5 MULTIMEDIA TECHNOLOGY

Although many of the concepts of multimedia have been in the research domain since the early beginnings of computing, it was not until the mid 1980s when suitable computer, storage and communications technologies became available and affordable that users and vendors began to realize the technological and business opportunities. The industry then went through a phase where every other product launch was a multimedia product (no matter how tenuous the connection) and selling was a matter of technology push rather than market pull. Products were usually sold as a 'bolt-on' to existing technology not designed to support multimedia information systems. This resulted in increased complexity of software and hardware configurations and a perception that multimedia is a sound *card* or a CD-ROM (rather than focusing on information system functionality). There is now a greater realization that multimedia information systems cannot be implemented on a large scale without the availability of high-capacity, high-speed and low-cost underpinning technology which is closely integrated. This requirement stalled the market because the core technology and standards were evolving too slowly. The core technology is now at a level of maturity which adequately supports the implementation of large-scale multimedia information systems.

Three future developments are likely to have a major impact on the future design and development of multimedia technology. Firstly, mobile technology (such as personal digital assistants) are likely to make electronic information as portable as printed information. Secondly, the application of virtual reality concepts, which engage to a much greater degree the human senses, to the process of accessing and interpreting information. Although still a maturing technology, virtual reality is to some extent following the same path as multimedia technology in the sense that it has been in the research domain for a long time but is slowly moving into the commercial market. Virtual reality places great demands on the underlying core technology common to multimedia systems today. Thus, large-scale multimedia information systems are likely to incorporate virtual reality concepts when the core technology offers the required capacity and speed at a price affordable to those who implement information services and to those who use them. Thirdly, the application of artificial intelligence approaches in areas such as intelligent multimedia information access and retrieval.

14.6 INFORMATION SYSTEMS AND SERVICES

Distributed information systems are addressing the needs of business, academic and consumer markets. A potentially high-volume market, for which DIS is often positioned, is the home-orientated consumer business and entertainment-orientated market. In this and other markets, it is vitally important that applications have a good visual design. A common (i.e. consistent) user interface across many consumer services will assist usability. The price of using these services will need to be competitive with alternative information, services and entertainment delivery mechanisms (for example, 'video-on-demand' services versus a local video rental facility). Equally important is the fact that consumers will not want to use different devices to access different services. A single point of access to all services is desired. In the home environment, a candidate access point is the 'television' which is likely to evolve into an access point to traditional television services and other consumer services via a sophisticated set-top box (i.e. multimedia decoders with facilities to support user interaction) and remote control unit (a PC is not simple enough to be used by the average home user without significant training).

A feature of many current information services is that users feel overloaded by the quantity of information which can be accessed and received. This is because most information is received unfiltered. Use of Internet services such as the World Wide Web and Usenet newsgroups, for example, suffer from this problem. Information overload can be minimized by intelligent, automated filtering, and effective presentation of data (for example, using visual techniques). Intelligent filtering involves automating information search, selection and retrieval where information is spread across multiple information servers. Information services are likely to be augmented by the availability of sophisticated and automated filtering and presentation facilities in the future.

The availability of the core technology to implement distributed information systems will facilitate the implementation of a wide range of services in the future, delivering associated benefits to users. Example services and benefits are summarized in Table 14.2.

Table 14.2 Examples of services and benefits of multimedia technology

Type of service	Potential benefits
Multimedia-based electronic mail	A reduction in the potential for misunderstanding of the message content
Video conferencing	Reduced travel costs Increased time available for other tasks Reduced lost opportunity costs
Electronic publishing	The ability to provide up-to-the-minute information easily Reduced human intervention, resulting in quicker dissemination times and reduced staff handling and postage costs The ability to exploit new delivery channels The basis for tailored information services for different classes of users, thus achieving improved customer penetration, targeting and service
Electronic trading	Reduced human invervention, resulting in faster transactions and reduced staff handling costs Potential for increased capacity for handling transactions The ability to exploit new delivery channels The basis for tailored transaction and information services for different classes of users, thus achieving improved customer penetration, targeting and service
Multimedia information access	Access to up-to-the-minute information which is of high quality Ease-of-use through the use of intelligent and attractive visual designs Reduced need for human response to enquiries Improvement in the availability of complex information to a large number of users Ability to access the full range of information when mobile
Entertainment and other consumer services (e.g. video-on-demand, home shopping, home banking, group-based computer games and video messaging)	Reduced cost (and inconvenience) of travel More choice and control Easy access to up-to-the-minute information and services

14.7 SUMMARY

We have reviewed some of the technological developments which may impact the shape of future distributed information systems. Evolution to the next generation is dependent on each piece of the technological jigsaw puzzle maturing in relation to the other pieces to provide the overall IT infrastructure required. The emphasis is on the availability of low-cost pervasive technology to home consumers and business users for access to a very wide range of services. The various underpinning technologies are evolving to meet the stringent demands likely to be placed on them by distributed multimedia. With the potential developments that look promising at the time of writing, interesting times are ahead. It would be interesting to again review in ten years time the developments since this book was written and compare it with the speculations contained in this chapter. To what extent will information systems world reflect our current views? Watch this space!

GLOSSARY

Abstraction   The process of suppressing or hiding irrelevant detail to establish a simplified model, view or result.

Acknowledgement   A response to a communication. It can be positive or negative.

Adaptive routing   Intermediate routing nodes decide on a message-by-message basis which route a message takes towards its destination.

Address space   A private range of addresses available to a process.

Address   The unique identifier specifying the recipient or originator of transmitted data within a network.

Administrator   A human agent responsible for one or more management functions.

ADPCM (*Adaptive Differential Pulse Code Modulation*)   An ITU-T standard for voice encoding and compression to allow transmission within a 32 kbit/s digital channel.

Agent A software component that carries out work on behalf of another entity. For example, a *user* agent carries out work on behalf of a user (usually transparently).

Alternate routing   A safety technique enabling communication to continue despite failure of one or more links in a network or congestion. A network design based on alternate routing allows for alternate paths through the network to arrive at the same destination.

Amplifier   The recharging or reconstitution of a signal.

Amplitude   The maximum value of a wave or signal.

Analogue   A representation of a physically varying quantity using a continuously varying wave form (e.g. an electrical signal which represents speech).

API (*Applications Programming Interface*)   The way in which programs interface to a product or service. The programmer is aware of what services are offered and how services can be requested, but is not concerned with how the service is implemented. An API is often implemented as a library of functions.

Architecture   The structure of a system in terms of components and the interrelationships among its components.

ASCII (American Standard Code for Information Interchange)   A national variation of the International Alphabet No. 5 (IA5)   Which codes text characters using seven bits per character.

ASN.1 (Abstract Syntax Notation-1)   A formal language developed as part of ISO OSI standards for describing the representation of data object types and structures.

ATM (Asynchronous Transfer Mode)   A 53-octet cell-based data transfer technique which offers fast packet switching.

Atomicity   The property which describes anything which is considered not to be capable of further sub-division for a particular level of abstraction.

Attenuation   The weakening of transmitted signals as they travel away from their point of origin. Attenuation is usually caused by the inherent properties of the transmission medium.

AUI (Attachment Unit Interface)   The IEEE 802.3 cable and connector standard.

Authority   The legitimate power to perform an action.

Bandwidth   The range of frequencies that a channel supports, which ultimately determines the speed of the channel. For a digital channel this is defined in terms of bits per second. For an analogue signal it is dependent on the modulation technique used to encode the data. The terms bandwidth and speed are often used synonymously.

Base station   A fixed radio transmitter/receiver which electronically relays signals to and from mobile voice and data terminals or handsets.

Baseband   A network in which data is transmitted unmodulated as direct digital levels using the whole channel bandwidth. Since only a single channel is available, only one conversation can be supported at any given moment in time.

Basic Rate Access (BRA)   An ISDN service consisting of two 64 kbit/s 'B' channels and one 16 kbit/s 'D' channel, i.e. a '2B+D' configuration.

Baud   The number of signal changes per second. It is only equivalent to bits per second when one discrete signal change is used to transmit a single bit of data.

Binding Manager   An object which encapsulates the explicit binding mechanism and is visible to client and server processes.

Binding Object   See Binding Manager.

Binding   The formation of a relationship between two or more processing objects.

Bit   A fundamental digital quantity that can have a value of 0 or 1. The word 'bit' is a contraction of binary digit.

Block   A group of bits or characters which are treated as a single unit.

BPR   Business process re-design, the analysis and streamlining of workflows and processes within and between a business by identifying significant bottlenecks, discontinuities and unnecessary or redundant steps that become candidates for deletion.

Bridge   A device which interconnects two IEEE 802 LANs at the OSI datalink layer on the basis of MAC addresses. They control network traffic and security, filtering data frames where necessary to ensure that frames pass from one network to another only in order to reach their destination.

Broadband   A network in which multiple, independent and channels are used to carry multiple data conversations simultaneously over a single cable. Each data stream is modulated to the range of frequencies allocated to the particular channel associated with it.

Broadband ISDN   A high speed version of the ISDN service which supports speeds well in excess of 2 Mbit/s. It will provide a global high speed public switched network.

Broadcast   The simultaneous transmission of data across a network indiscriminately to all devices able to receive it.

Brouter   A hybrid bridge and router, which routes specific network protocols and bridges all other traffic.

Buffer   A temporary storage area for data to compensate for differences in transmission speeds or to hold data when there is a difference in timing of events.

Byte   A unit of eight bits. The alternative term 'octet' is also used.

Caching   The temporary storage of data locally to improve performance and availability.

Capacity   The amount of data that can be transmitted through a communications channel.

Carrier Signal   A wave used to modulate a signal. Modulation is used to impose information on the signal.

CATV (Community Antennae Television)   The cabling system used in cable television and telephony, broadband LAN and MAN technology.

CCITT (International Telegraph and Telephone Consultative Committee)   The former name for the ITU-T (International Telecommunications Union) a specialized agency of the United Nations. It is a major international standards-making organization.

Cell Relay   A generic term for a communications protocol based on the switching of short fixed length packets. Cell relay protocols provide a more efficient way of multiplexing different types of data (e.g. video, audio and data) onto the same channel. An example cell relay technology is ATM which uses fixed length cells of 53 octets.

Cellular radio   An interconnection of radio stations used to support two-way mobile telephone communications.

Channel   A single transmission path through a medium to enable communication. A single medium may be capable of supporting multiple channels.

Circuit Switching   A transmission technique in which a physical circuit is first established between sender and receiver before transmission takes place. When transmission is complete, the circuit is freed. The public switched telephone network is an example of a circuit switched network service.

Class   A template from which *objects* may be created.

Client/server   A model for structuring a distributed system. The system consists of two types of processes; clients which generates requests for service, and servers which receives requests, executes one or more operations and sends a result back to each client.

Cluster Controller   An IBM device type that allows multiple 3270 terminals to be linked directly to a host computer, or into an SNA network.

CMIS/CMIP (Common Management Information Service/Common Management Information Protocol)   The ISO OSI network management service and protocol. CMIS is an application layer service whereas CMIP is the peer communications protocol used to realize the service.

Coaxial Cable   A type of cable which is used in bus-based networks, such as bus topology LANs and CATV broadband MANs.

Coding   A representation of data.

Collision detection   CSMA/CD stations are designed to detect collisions instantly and attempt to recover by resending after a pseudo-random delay.

Collision   The result of two stations on a shared communications channel transmitting simultaneously normally associated with CSMA/CD LANs. Data is corrupted and both stations must retry their transmissions. The pseudo-random delay mechanism used by both senders results in a very low probability that another collision occurs between the two senders.

Communication   The effective transmission of information between sender and receiver.

Communications Server   A specialized network server that provides access to external networks and supports remote or mobile user access to local services. It is also commonly termed a remote access server.

Compression   A way of reducing the amount of data to be transmitted or stored by using techniques for representing repeated bit patterns. When the data is received or accessed it is decompressed into its original form.

Concentrator   A central chassis unit into which various modules can be installed each of which provides particular functions, such as a CSMA/CD or token ring LAN segment, bridging, network management, FDDI, etc.

Connection Oriented Service   A service which first establishes a connection between sender and receiver before data is transmitted. After data transmission is complete, the connection is terminated.

Connectionless Service   A service which transmits data without expecting an acknowledgement from the receiver. Full addressing information is attached to each packet so that it can be routed independently. It is particularly appropriate when the channel error rate is relatively low. This type of service is also commonly termed a datagram service.

Container   A class of object which encapsulates one or more other objects.

Context   The background which allows extra information to be carried implicitly during a particular communications session.

Control   A trigger of a predefined set of actions to be taken either by an information system or a user.

CORBA (Common Object Request Broker Architecture)   A standard developed by the Object Management Group for distributed object management.

Crosstalk   Unwanted interference from another adjacent communications channel.

CSCW (Computer Supported Co-operative Working)   The exploitation of computer and communications technologies to support interaction and co-operation between groups (formal and informal) of users.

CSMA/CD (Carrier Sense Multiple Access with Collision Detection)   An access control method typically used by bus-based LANs to detect and recover from data corruption due to two or more workstations transmitting at the same time causing a collision.

Data   Representations of facts or ideas.

Data Link   A direct serial data communications channel between two devices without intermediate switching nodes.

Data Rate   The amount of bits sent through a communications channel per second.

Data Transparency   The ability of a protocol to transmit any bit pattern.

Database Server   A remote data access (RDA) server. Clients generate requests using a query language, typically SQL.

Datagram Service   See Connectionless Service.

DCE (Distributed Computing Environment)   A suite of software and operating system extensions that is designed to support the development of distributed applications over a heterogeneous IT infrastructure. DCE provides an RPC mechanism and a number of generic distributed services.

De facto Standard   A standard by virtue of its widespread use, but not supported by international standardization activity.

De jure Standard   A standard supported by the work of an international standardization body. This does not presuppose any actual use of the standard but only its derivation.

Delay Jitter The maximum difference in the delay between different packets transmitted.

Digital Signal A signal which assumes only two discrete values representing 0 or 1, in contrast to an analogue signal which can assume a potentially infinite range of values.

Directory Service A service which maintains a distributed database of name-to-name mappings in both white and yellow pages form.

Discretionary Access Control An approach to access control which permits users to control the sharing of information.

Distortion Changes in a signal due to variable transmission conditions.

Distributed File Server A remote file access (RFA) server. Clients send file requests to the file server.

Distributed IT Infrastructure An IT infrastructure incorporating multiple autonomous processors that do not share local memory, but co-operate by sending messages over an information network. The IT infrastructure exhibits distribution transparency.

Distributed Operating System A single native operating system, resident in all network nodes, which inherently supports and manages network access to distributed resources in a globally coherent manner.

Distributed Processing The execution of co-operating processes which communicate by exchanging messages across an information network.

Distribution Transparency The extent to which distributed components are concealed (i.e. appear to be local) from users and application developers.

Domain A set of related entities which have been grouped for the purposes of administration and management.

Downsizing The migration of applications from a larger processor to a smaller (usually dedicated) processor configuration normally to improve performance or because it is more cost effective.

DS1 (Digital Signal 1) A transmission standard at T1 speeds (1.544 Mbit/s).

DS3 (Digital Signal 3) A transmission standard at T3 speeds (44.736 Mbit/s).

DSE (Digital Switching Exchange) A node in a telecommunications network.

DSU (Data Service Unit) Transmission equipment used to interface to a digital circuit at a customer site. It simply converts a local data stream (e.g. RS-232 or X.21) to the digital circuit standard (e.g. E1, T1 or primary rate ISDN).

Duplex A communications channel which supports two-way transmission of data.

Dynamic Routing See Adaptive Routing.

EIA/TIA 568 A widely used standard for structured cabling developed by the merged US Electrical Industries Association (EIA) and Telecommunication Industries Association (TIA). It specifies a star topology with a maximum horizontal cable run of 90 ms, allowing 10 m for hub and device attachment resulting in a total cable length of 100 m between each computer and hub. The related Technical Service Bulletins (TSB) 36 and 40 define three categories of cabling system: categories 3, 4 and 5.

EISA (Extended Industry Standard Architecture) A 32-bit adaptation of the original ISA bus architecture developed by IBM.

Electronic Data Interchange The exchange of structured business data between trading partners by electronic means.

Electronic Mail The electronic exchange of messages between users.

Emulation Hardware and software, or a combination of the two, that a device to behave like another type of device or program. For example, terminal emulation software allows a PC to emulate a dumb terminal.

Encryption   Use of secret codes to protect data from tampering or exposure to unauthorized users by rendering it unintelligible. Authorized users can recover encrypted data only if they know the secret code.

Error Control   A means of ensuring that data received across an information network is correct.

Error Correction   Technique to restore the integrity of data transmitted over an information network. Data is normally corrected by asking the sender to re-transmit the data packet in error.

Error Detection   A set of techniques for detecting errors in received data. Typical techniques are parity checks, block parity and cyclic redundancy checking.

Ethernet   Type of LAN introduced in the mid to late 1970s which was the basis of the IEEE 802.3 standard. It is commonly used to refer to all types of CSMA/CD LANs. It operates at 10 Mbit/s and is used to implement information systems that are not sensitive to stringent real-time constraints.

Explicit Binding   The ability of application processes to control the binding mechanism to ensure that user-specified quality-of-service requirements are satisfied.

Fast Ethernet   The IEEE 802.3 100baseT standard for CSMA/CD LANs which operate at 100 Mbit/s.

Fast Packet Switching   High speed networking technology which makes use of short fixed-length packets called cells and fast switching of cells to attain low latency. An example technology is ATM which defines 53 octet cells.

Fault Tolerance   The process of making a computer system or network resilient to component faults or breakdowns to avoid data loss and downtime.

Fax   Document and image transmission using facsimile techniques.

Fax Server   A specialized network server which services fax requests by sending and receiving faxes on behalf of fax users. Requests result in the fax pages being sent to the destination fax and (optionally) the subscriber charged a fee.

FDDI (Fibre Distributed Data Interface)   An optical fibre-based token passing LAN which employs dual rotating rings for fault tolerance. FDDI is a shared medium LAN operating at 100 Mbit/s.

FDM (Frequency Division Multiplexing)   A multiplexing scheme in which a single cable supports multiple channels by dividing the available frequency range into narrower bands. Each of these bands is used to carry a separate channel.

File Server   See Distributed File Server.

Flow Control   Procedures for controlling the rate of transfer of data between two devices in a network. Flow control procedures avoid data loss due to a receiver's buffer becoming full because the sender is transmitting data too quickly.

Frame Relay   A communications standard to provide high speed frame or packet delivery with minimum delay and efficient use of bandwidth. It is a slimlined version of the X.25 standard.

Frame   The unit of data transmitted over a data link.

Frequency   The number of cycles of a wave per second.

FTP (File Transfer Protocol)   The Internet (TCP/IP) protocol for file transfer.

Full Duplex   Simultaneous two-way transmission of data.

Gateway   An interworking unit which is responsible for the conversion between different protocol systems to provide a uniform applications environment. For example, a mail gateway is used to convert from one mail standard to another and vice versa.

Groupware   Hardware and software specifically designed to support CSCW.

GSM   The international digital cellular radio system to support digital mobile communications.

H.261   An ITU-T standard for video compression which defines a common algorithm for converting analogue video signals to digital at N x 384 kbit/s.

Half-duplex   A communications channel which supports two-way communications but can only be used in one direction at a time.

Handshake   A procedure to set up a communications channel.

HDLC (High-level Data Link Control)   The ISO protocol standard for error-free transmission of data over a data link. There are numerous subsets of HDLC in widespread use, e.g. LAPB (used in X.25), LLC (used in IEEE 802 LAN standards), and LAPD (used in Frame Relay).

Head-end   A special device in a CATV broadband cable network that receives signals on one set of frequency bands and re-transmits them on another. This allows signals to be sent and received over the same physical cable.

Header   Control data added to the beginning of a frame, packet, cell or message.

Hertz   One cycle per second of a wave form. It is a measure of the frequency of a wave (e.g. radio).

Heterogeneous   Support for products and services from different vendors.

HTML (Hypertext Markup Language)   The formal language used to create World Wide Web documents.

Hub   The central node in a star topology network or cabling system.

IEEE 802   The widely used IEEE standards for local area networks.

Information   Any kind of knowledge about things, facts, idea or concepts.

Infrastructure   The IT infrastructure consisting of all cabling, communications components, computers and other equipment which form the infrastructure to support distributed information systems.

Inheritance   The ability of one class of object to be constructed from other existing classes that are related (known as superclasses). This object-orientation concept facilitates software reusability and extendibility.

Intelligent Hubs   A network hub which can be configured as a managed device and which provides functions for fault diagnosis, isolation and resolution.

Interface Definition Language   A language defined to describe a server object interface by specifying the operations, parameters and data types required to implement the interface.

Interface   The definition of a well-defined set of services and a place where interaction takes place based on the services defined.

International Standard   A standard recommended or mandated by a recognized international body.

Internet (The Internet)   The world-wide internet which evolved from the Internet project in the mid-1970s by the US Department of Defense.

Internet   Abbreviation of the term internetwork which is an interconnection of separate networks. Each separate network is known as a subnet.

ISA (Industry Standard Architecture)   The 8/16-bit bus architecture originally developed by IBM for PCs.

ISDN (Integrated Services Digital Network)   The ITU-T standard for end-to-end digital switched public WANs.

IT Infrastructure   See Infrastructure.

Jabber   Data broadcasts occurring randomly on a CSMA/CD LAN as a result of a faulty network interface card.

JANET (Joint Academic Network)   The UK backbone WAN used by education and research communities.

Jitter   Slight movement of a transmitted signal in time or phase that can cause errors or synchronization problems.

Kilostream   A 64 kbit/s digital leased line service (originally used to denote a service offered by the UK network carrier BT).

LAN (Local Area Network)   A network covering a small geographic area normally within a building or building complex.

Leased Line a dedicated communications link between sender and receiver, usually leased from a network provider.

Legacy Systems   Information systems and technology which an organization already has in place. Use of the term generally refers to existing systems and infrastructure components which were implemented using older generation design approaches and technology.

Mainframe   A large multi-user computer designed to support a large number of users simultaneously.

MAN   Metropolitan area network, a type of network designed to cover an entire town or city, interconnecting multiple LANs.

Managed Device   One which can be controlled by a systems management centre normally using SNMP, CMIS/CMIP or a proprietary network management protocol.

Managed Object   An abstraction of a real resource for the purposes of systems management. More formally, it is an object with a management interface which is used for monitoring and control.

Manager   A human user, hardware or software process responsible for carrying out management activities.

Mandatory Access Control   An approach to access control which does not permit users to control the sharing of information. Instead, fixed access rules are implemented.

MAU (Medium Attachment Unit)   A transceiver device in an IEEE 802.3 network.

MAU (Multistation Access Unit)   An IBM token ring wiring hub.

Medium   The physical means by which signals are transmitted. For example, cable and radio.

Megastream   A 2 Mbit/s digital leased line service (originally used to denote a service offered by the UK network carrier BT).

Message   A unit of data for transmission over an information network.

Message Format   The structure of a message.

Method   Operations which are defined as part of an object and which operate on state data contained within an object.

MIB (Management Information Base)   The database (or set of variables) used to monitor and control a managed component.

Microwave   Wireless transmissions at very high frequency to deliver telecommunications services. It is dependent on line-of-sight transmission.

Minicomputer   A multi-user computer designed to support the needs of a medium-sized department of an organization. A minicomputer typically runs a single major application.

Model   A representation simplified for the purposes of description or calculation.

Modem   A device which allows connection of a computer on to the PSTN for data transmission.

Modem Eliminator   A device that can be used to replace a modem in particular instances of data transmissions over short distances.

Modulation   A technique for transmitting digital data using an analogue signal.

MTBF (Mean Time Before Failure)   Used to describe the reliability of a component.

Multi-port Repeater   A CSMA/CD wiring centre that allows multiple devices to be attached to at one point on a CSMA/CD segment.

Multicast   The transmission of data from one node to multiple destination nodes.

Multimedia Information System   One which enables users to share, communicate and process a variety of forms of information (media types) in an integrated manner.

Multimedia   The integration of a variety of media types (e.g. data, text, graphics, audio and video) within a single information system which supports user interaction.

Multiplexor   A device which can send multiple user data streams over a single communications channel. A similar device at the other end of the channel restores the original data streams (demultiplexing).

Multitasking   The concurrent execution of multiple processes or threads.

Name   A symbol identifying a resource or set of resources.

Name Space   Naming rules applying to a set of names.

NDIS (Network Driver Interface Specification)   A Microsoft device driver specification for supporting multiple protocol stacks concurrently using one or more network interface cards. NDIS separates higher-level communications protocols from actual PC networking hardware.

Network Address   A group of characters or bits which uniquely identifies a node on a network.

Network   Data sources and sinks interconnected by communications channels.

NIC (Network Interface Card)   A client workstation expansion card which contains the circuitry to connect a workstation to a network. The NIC fits into a workstation's expansion slot. A NIC is also known as a network adapter card.

Node   A device connected to a network.

Noise   The parts of a received transmission that were not part of the original message.

NOS (Network Operating System)   The software that extends the native operating system to provide support for network access to distributed resources.

Object   An entity with an interface described by a well-defined set of operations and state data, and which is invoked by sending a message to it. State data is completely protected and hidden from other objects and can be accessed only when necessary through an interface method.

Object Based   A programming language that supports objects as a language feature.

Object Modelling   A systems analysis or design approach based on object-oriented concepts.

ODBC (Open Database Connectivity)   A remote data access protocol specification developed by Microsoft which has become a *de facto* standard.

ODI (Open Datalink Interface)   A Novell specification for the interface between multiple protocol stacks and one or more device drivers for network interface cards. It is used to provide multi-protocol support in a computer with one or more NICs.

ODP (Open Distributed Processing)   An ISO reference model which describes how distributed applications can be developed in heterogeneous distributed environment.

OOP (Object-oriented Programming)   A programming language and environment that supports objects and inheritance as language features.

Open Standard   One which has arisen in any way and is available to all interested users on an equal terms without restriction.

OSI (Open Systems Interconnection)   An ISO architectural (reference) model and a set of standards which describe how communication is achieved across different vendors' systems. The reference model defines seven layers of function: physical, data link, network, transport, session, presentation and application layers.

Out-of-band Signalling   The definition of a separate channel, alongside user data channels, which is used to carry monitoring and control information.

Outsourcing   An integrated operations and maintenance service which is provided to an organization by a third party.

Packet Switching   A method of data switching whereby a message is first divided into small packets of a set maximum size and format. Each packet is then routed through a network of packet switching exchanges (PSE). Each PSE decides where to send a packet next on the basis of addressing and other information.

Packet   The unit of data transfer at the network layer of the ISO OSI reference model. Packets are routed through one or more switching or routing devices.

Partitioning   The fragmentation of a resource or service to improve performance and facilitate local autonomy.

PBX (Private Branch Exchange)   A telephone exchange owned by an organization.

PCM (Pulse Code Modulation)   A method of converting an analogue signal (e.g. a voice signal) to a digital signal. The signal is sampled at 8 000 samples per second each coded in 8 bits producing a transmission rate of 64 kbit/s.

Peer-to-peer   A model for structuring a distributed system in which all peer processes are clones with the ability to act as clients (requesting services from other peer processes) and servers (providing services to other peer processes).

Pixel   The minimum area of a static or moving image representing colour or shades of grey. Pixel is a contraction of picture element.

Port   An interface to a communications object.

Porting   Moving software from one operating environment to another incompatible one.

Print Server   A service which provides users with access to remote printers. Clients simply submit a print request to the print server. The print data is spooled and the request queued. The spool file is eventually sent to an appropriate printer.

Process   A logical representation of a physical processor that executes program code and has associated state and resources.

Proprietary Standard   A standard restricted mainly by the owner of the defining document or design.

Protocol   A set of rules governing communications.

Protocol Converter   A device which translates between two different protocols.

Proxy Agent   A network management agent which provides network monitoring and control facilities 'by proxy' for that device.

PSTN (Public Switched Telephone Network)   The public telephone network, probably the biggest network in the world.

PTO   An organization responsible for a public telephone network.

PVC (Permanent Virtual Circuit)   A fixed virtual circuit. It emulates a leased line connection.

Radio   Electromagnetic waves used as a medium for wireless communication.

Re-tries   The re-sending of data when no acknowledgement is received.

Recovery   The recovery of an IT infrastructure component after component failure.

Redirector   Agent software that translates operating requests into requests to a remote server.

Redundancy   Characters or bits which can be removed from transmitted data without affecting the meaning of a message.

Regeneration   A method of boosting a digital signal.

Relay   A generic term for an interworking unit.

Remote Access   A hardware and software component that supports user access to LAN-based services from a remote location through a public switched or leased line service.

Repeater   The interconnection of two LANs at the physical layer of OSI. The repeater simply regenerates (or amplifies) data signals.

Replication   The duplication of resources to improve performance or availability.

RFC (Request for Comments)   The working documents on the Internet which detail the design, implementation, standardization and experimentation activities associated with Internet protocols. Access to RFCs are easily obtained via the Internet.

Rightsizing   The placement of distributed information system components to fully exploit the underlying IT infrastructure cost effectively.

Ring Topology   An arrangement of nodes in a network whereby each node is connected to its two nearest neighbours. This forms a closed ring of interconnected nodes.

RIP (Routing Information Protocol)   A protocol for exchanging routing information between routers.

RJ45   Standard connector type for IEEE 802.3 10baseT networks.

RMON (Remote Monitoring MIB)   A MIB specification which defines additions to the basic MIB definition to allow managers to monitor and control at the sub-network level rather for each individual managed object within each sub-network.

Roaming   The ability of a mobile communications device to move freely from one mobile network to another.

Router   The interconnection of two networks through a common network layer protocol.

Routing Table   Information stored within a router which is used to select an appropriate path towards a packet's destination.

Routing   The process of delivering a packet to its destination across one or more networks via an appropriate path involving one or more routers.

RPC   Remote procedure call, a type of inter-process communication which emulates a local procedure call mechanism.

SDH (Synchronous Data Hierarchy)   An ITU-T standard for synchronous digital transmission over optical fibre. It standardizes transmission rates, signals and interfaces and is aligned with the SONET standard starting at 155 Mbit/s.

Segment   A term associated with the bus topology to describe an electrically continuous piece of the bus.

Sequence Control   The ordering of frames or packets so as to recover the original message when they are sent out of sequence.

Serial Interface   Hardware used to send and receive data one bit at a time.

Server   A node that processes requests for access to its resources.

Server Process   An instance of a service type on which operations can be invoked.

Service   An abstraction of a set of operations provided to clients which allows them to perform a particular function.

Session   A logical connection between two nodes or processes in a network.

SGML (Standard Generalized Mark-up Language)   An ISO standard for labelling (tagging) electronic documents so that they can be exchanged without losing structural information.

Shared Medium   A medium shared by multiple nodes. IEEE 802 LANs are examples of shared medium networks.

Simplex   One-way communication.

Sine Wave   A regular analogue wave which is generated by circular motion.

SMDS (Switched Multimegabit Data Services)   A connectionless data transmission service over high-speed MANs and WANs.

SMTP (Simple Mail Transfer Protocol)   The Internet (TCP/IP) standard for electronic mail.

SNA (Systems Network Architecture)   IBM's proprietary network architecture.

SNMP (Simple Network Management Protocol)   The *de facto* LAN management protocol defined for TCP/IP-based networks.

Sockets   A message-passing inter-process communications protocol commonly implemented in UNIX and Microsoft Windows environments.

SONET (Synchronous Optical Network)   A standardized set of transmission rates, signals and interfaces for optical fibre transmission developed by Bellcore. The basic transmission rate is 51.840 Mbit/s. SONET transmission rates grow in multiples of the basic rate into multi-gigabits per second.

Spooling   The process of directing prints to print queues for later printing when printers become available.

SQL (Structured Query Language)   A standardized data description and manipulation language for relational databases. It is widely used (with extensions) to implement remote data access (RDA) servers.

Star Topology   An arrangement of nodes in a network whereby each node is connected directly to a central hub. The hub implements a protocol standard for switching data frames between connected nodes.

State   Data about an object which determines its behaviour.

Static Routing   A routing algorithm where data messages always use the same path to the destination.

Store-and-forward   A method of transmitting data whereby messages are received and stored by each intermediate node before forwarding on towards their destination.

STP (Shielded Twisted Pair)   A type of twisted pair cabling.

Subnet   A self-contained network which is also connected to another network as part of a larger internetwork (internet).

SVC (Switched Virtual Circuit)   A non-permanent virtual circuit.

Symbols   The encoding system used for representing information.

Synchronous   Data transmission in which sender and receiver are permanently synchronized during transmission.

TCP/IP   A suite of protocols developed by the US Department of Defense which has become a *de facto* standard.

Telnet   The Internet (TCP/IP) remote login protocol.

Terminal Emulation   A software component that allows a PC to emulate a dumb terminal. This enables PCs to access traditional mainframe- and minicomputer-based information systems which are character-based. Typical terminal emulation protocols are DEC's VT100 and IBM's 3270.

Thread   A unit of scheduling and execution in an operating system.

Time-out   An event which occurs when a sending object does not receive an expected acknowledgement or reply within a specified time.

Token Passing   An access control mechanism that uses a special bit-pattern called a token to ensure that no two stations can transmit onto a shared medium at the same time.

Token Ring   A type of LAN promoted by IBM and the basis of the IEEE 802.5 standard.

Topology   The arrangement of nodes and links between nodes in a network.

TPM (Transaction Processing Manager)   A software component that supports transaction processing.

Trader   An object which performs trading.

Trading   Dynamically matching client service request types to servers which offers to service them. A trading service generally returns a reference to a server offering an appropriate service.

Transaction   Program execution semantics which exhibit atomicity, consistency, isolation and durability properties.

Transceive   Hardware and software capable of transmitting and receiving in CSMA/CD LANs.

Twisted Pair   A transmission medium consisting of a pair of copper conductors twisted around each other to improve noise immunity. It comes in two varieties; unshielded twisted pair (UTP) and shielded twisted pair (STP) which includes extra protective shielding.

Unique Identifier   A character or bit pattern which invariably and uniquely identifies a system entity or object.

UNIX   A type of operating system originally developed by AT&T which has become a *de facto* standard for operating system design.

UPS (Uninterrupted Power Supply)   A battery attached to computer hardware (e.g. a server) that provides backup power in the event that the main power supply fails. A UPS device gives enough power to enable orderly shutdown of a system.

Upsizing   The migration of an application to a larger processor usually to enhance performance due to a growth in the number of active users.

UTP (Unshielded Twisted Pair)   A type of twisted pair cabling which is the standard cable for telephone lines and some LAN technologies.

V.32   An ITU-T modem standard for up to 9.6 kbit/s over PSTN or leased lines.

V.32bis   An ITU-T modem standard for up to 14.4 kbit/s over PSTN or leased lines.

V.34   An ITU-T modem standard for up to 28.8 kbit/s over PSTN or leased lines.

V.42   An ITU-T standard for error control procedures.

V.42bis   An ITU-T standard for data compression in association with V.42.

Videotex   An ITU-T term used to describe TV equipment used to display computer-based data and to support user interaction, either transmitted via a telephone link (often known as Viewdata) or a broadcast channel (known as Teletext).

Virtual Circuit   A connection between two nodes which is connection-oriented.

Virus   Program code which attaches itself to another program and makes a copy of itself. It may or may not cause damage to a system but can be a serious nuisance.

VPN (Virtual Private Network)   A private voice and data network formed from a public switched network with intelligent public switches.

VSAT (Very Small Aperture Terminal)   Relatively small satellite dishes used by remote sites in a satellite-based network. A central office broadcasts or multicasts data to remote sites and two-way interaction can also be supported.

WAN (Wide Area Network)   A type of network designed to connect nodes over public highways spanning long distances (typically city-to-city, nationally and internationally).

Wavelength   The length of a wave. Calculated as the inverse of frequency.

Window   The number of unacknowledged data frames which is allowed by a particular protocol.

Wiring Closet   The location (e.g. a special room) in which cabling on a particular floor is terminated and which houses the wiring frame, hubs and other equipment.

Workflow Management   The definition and automation of workflows and procedures in an organizational unit. Also known as workflow automation.

World Wide Web An Internet-based distributed hypermedia information system.

X-Windows A standard developed by the Massachussetts Institute of Technology (MIT) for implementing a graphical user interface. It is widely implemented on UNIX-based operating systems.

X.25 An ITU-T standard for packet switching WANs.

X.400 An ITU-T standard for electronic mail.

X.500 An ITU-T standard for directory services.

X/Open An international standards making body for developing open systems technologies and standards.

Z39.50 An ANSI standard for information access and retrieval.

BIBLIOGRAPHY

Adie, C. (ed.) (1993) 'A Survey of Distributed Multimedia Research, Standards and Products', RARE Project 0BR (92)046v2, RARE, Amsterdam.

Anderson, D., Osawa, Y. and Govindan, R. (1992) 'A File System for Continuous Media', *ACM Trans. Computer Systems,* Vol.10, no.4, pp. 311–37.

Andrews, G. R. (1991) *Concurrent Programming Principles and Practice,* Benjamin Cummings, Redwood City, CA, USA.

Anklesaria, F., McCahill, M., Lindner, P., Johnson, D., Torrey, D. and Alberti, B. (1993) *The Internet Gopher Protocol,* Internet Request for Comment (RFC) 1436.

ANSA (1993) *The ANSA Application Programmer's Guide, Release 4.1,* APM Ltd, Poseidon House, Castle Park, Cambridge, UK.

Anthony, R. N. (1965) *Planning and Control: A Framework for Analysis.* Harvard University Press, Harvard, MA, USA.

ANSI/X3/SPARC (1975) 'Study Group on Data Base Management systems'. Interim Report, ACM SIGMOD, Vol. 7, no. 2.

Archer J. D. (1994) 'So you want to have corporate standards?', *Journal of Systems Management,* Vol. 45, no. 8, pp 28–31

Arthur, L.J. (1992) *Rapid Evolutionary Development, Requirements, Prototyping and Software Creation*, Wiley, Chichester, UK.

Ashby, W.R. (1965) *Introduction to Cybernetics*, Chapman and Hall, London, UK.

Babaoglu, O. and Toueg, S. (1993) 'Non-blocking atomic commitment' in Mullender, S.J. (ed.), *Distributed Systems 2nd edn*, ACM Press, New York, USA.

Bacon, J., Moody, K., Thompson, S.E. and Wilson, T.D. (1991) 'A multi-service storage architecture, *ACM Operating Systems Review,* Vol. 25, no. 4.

Bacon C. J. (1992) 'The use of decision criteria in selecting IS/T investments', *MIS Quarterly,* September 1992, pp 335–353

Bacon, J. (1993) *Concurrent Systems: An Integrated Approach to Operating Systems, Database, and Distributed Systems*, Addison-Wesley, Wokingham, UK.

Bacon, J. and Moody, K. (1995) 'Event management services in open object oriented distributed systems.' Proceedings of ANSAworks 95, APM Ltd, Poseidon House, Castle Park, Cambridge, UK.

Bal, H. (1990) *Programming Distributed Systems*, Prentice-Hall, London, UK.

Bannon, L. and Schmidt, K. (1991) *CSCW: Four characters in search of a context, Studies in computer supported co-operative work,* North-Holland, Amsterdam.

Bates, P.E., and Stephens, M.A. (1995) 'Rapid application development –concept, methodology or what?,' *Proceedings of New Directions on Software Development,* University of Wolverhampton, Wolverhampton, UK.

Bearman D. (1992) 'A user community discovers IT standards', *Journal of the American Society for Information Science,* Vol. 43, no. 8, pp. 576–578.

Beer, S. (1972) *Brain of the firm,* Allen Lane, Harmondsworth, UK.

—— (1979) *Heart of the enterprise,* John Wiley, Chichester, UK.

—— (1981) *Brain of the firm,* 2nd edn. John Wiley, Chichester, UK.

—— (1985) *Diagnosing the system for organizations,* John Wiley, Chichester, UK.

Bell, D. and Grimson, J. (1992) *Distributed Database Systems,* Addison-Wesley, Wokingham, UK.

Berners-Lee. T.J. Cailliau, R., Groff, J.-F., Pollerman, B. (1992a). 'World-Wide Web: the Information Universe,' Electronic Networking: Research, Applications and Policy, Vol. 2, no. 1, pp. 52–58, Meckler Publishing, Westport CT, USA.

Berners-Lee. T.J. Cailliau, R., Groff, J.-F. (1992b) 'The World-Wide Web', *Computer Networks and ISDN Systems,* Vol. 25, pp. 454–459, North-Holland, Amsterdam.

Bernstein, P.A., Hadzilacos, V. and N. Goodman, (1987) *Concurrency Control and Recovery in Database Systems,* Addison-Wesley, Reading MA., USA.

Berson, A. (1992) *Client/Server Architecture,* McGraw-Hill, New York, USA.

Bever, M., Geihs, K., Heuser, L., Muhlhauser, M., and Schill, A. (1993) 'Distributed Systems, OSF DCE, and Beyond', *DCE–The OSF Distributed Computing Environment,* A. Schill (ed.), pp. 1–20, Springer-Verlag, Berlin.

Bierer, D. (1994) *Inside Netware 4.1,* New Riders Publishing Indianapolis, IN, USA.

Birman, K.P. and Joseph, T.A. (1987) 'Reliable Communication in the Presence of Failures'. *ACM Transactions on Computer Systems,* Vol. 5, no. 1, pp. 47–76.

Birman, K.P. (1989) 'How robust are distributed systems?' In Mullender, S.J. (ed.) (1989) *Distributed Systems,* ACM Press, New York, USA;

—— (1993) 'The Process Group Approach to Reliable Distributed Computing.' *Communications of the ACM,* Vol. 36, no. 12, pp. 36–53.

Birrell, A. D. and Nelson, B. J. (1984) 'Implementing remote procedure calls.' *ACM Transactions on Computer Systems,* Vol. 2, pp. 39-59.

Bloomer, J. (1992) *Power programming with RPC,* O'Reilly and Associates, Inc, Sebastopol, CA., USA.

Borenstein, N. and Freed, N. (1992) 'MIME (Multipurpose Internet Mail Extensions)', Internet Request for Comment (RFC) 1341.

Borg, A., Blau, W., Graetsch, W., Hermann, F. and Oberle, W. (1989) 'Fault-tolerance under Unix', *ACM Transactions on Computer Systems,* Vol. 5, no. 1, pp. 1–24.

Breu, M., Aue, A., Hall, J. and Robinson, K. (1994) *Distributed Systems: Application Development,* HMSO, London, UK.

Brown, C. (1994) *UNIX Distributed Programming,* Prentice-Hall, London, UK.

British Standards Institute (BSI) (1992) *A Framework for User Requirements for InformationTechnology,* British Standard BSDD210, BSI, London, UK.

Budhiraja, N., Marzullo, K., Schneider, F.B. and Toueg, S. (1994) 'The Primary-Backup Approach' in Mullender, S.J. (ed.) (1993) *Distributed Systems 2nd edn,* ACM Press, New York, USA.

Buford, J.F.K. (1994) *Multimedia Systems,* Addison-Wesley, Reading, MA., USA.

Burrows J. H. (1993) 'Information technology standards in a changing world: the role of the users.' *Computer Standards and Interfaces,* Vol.15, no. 1, pp 49–56.

Burrows, M., Abadi, M. and Needham, R. (1990) 'A logic of Authentication.', *ACM Transactions on Computer Systems,* Vol. 8, pp. 18–36.

Cargill C F. (1989) *IT Standardization: Theory, Process and Organizations.* Digital Press, Bedford, MA, USA.

Carter, J. (1992) *Programming in SQL,* Blackwell Scientific, Oxford, UK.

Casavant, T.L. and Singhal, M. (eds.) (1994) *Readings in Distributed Computer Systems,* IEEE Computer Society Press. Los Alamitos, CA, USA.

CCTA. (1987) *Managing software maintenance,* HMSO, London, UK.

Ceri, S. (1984) 'Query Optimization in Relational Database Systems' in Bell, D.A. (ed.) *Infotech State of the Art Report on Database Performance,* Vol. 12, no. 4, pp. 3–20, Pergamon Infotech, Oxford, UK.

Ceri, S. and Pelagatti, G. (1984) *Distributed Databases: Principles and Systems,* McGraw-Hill, New York, USA.

Champine, G. A. (1991) *MIT Project Athena: A Model for Distributed Campus Computing,* Digital Press, Bedford, MA:., USA.

Checkland, P. (1981) *Systems Thinking, Systems Practice*, John Wiley, Chichester, UK.

Checkland, P. and Scholes, J. (1990) *Soft Systems Methodology in Action,* John Wiley, Chichester, UK.

Cheswick, W.R. and Bellovin, S.M. (1994) *Firewalls and Internet Security*, Addison-Wesley Reading, MA., .

Child, J. (1984) *Organization: A Guide to Problems and Practice*, Harper & Row, London, UK.

Clegg, D. and Barker, R. (1994) *CASE Method Fast-Track: A RAD Approach*, Addison-Wesley, Wokingham, UK.

Cochrane, P. (1995) 'Instant Gratification Technology', *ANSAworks 95 Proceedings,* April 1995, APM Ltd, Poseidon House, Castle Park, Cambridge, UK.

CODASYL (1971) 'CODASYL Data Base Task Group April 1971 Report,' ACM, New York, USA.

Codd, E.F. (1970) 'A Relational Model for Large Shared Data Banks,' *Communications of the ACM,* Vol. 13, no. 6, pp. 3773–87.

Comer, D.E. (1995) *Internetworking with TCP/IP.* Volume 1: Principles, Protocols and Architectures, 3rd Edition, Prentice-Hall, Englewood Cliffs, NJ, USA.

Comer, D.E. (1991) *Internetworking with TCP/IP.* Volume 1: Principles, Protocols and Architectures, 2nd Edition, Prentice-Hall, Englewood Cliffs, NJ, USA.

Comer, D.E. and Stevens, D.L. (1993) *Internetworking with TCP/IP,* Volume 3: Client-Server Programming and Applications, BSD Socket Version, Prentice-Hall, Englewood Cliffs, NJ, USA.

Corbin, J.R. (1992) *The Art of Distributed Applications,* Springer-Verlag, New York, USA.

Coulouris, G., Dollimore, J. and Kindberg, T., (1994) *Distributed Systems: Concepts and Design (2nd edn)*, Addison-Wesley, Wokingham, UK.

Cristian, F. (1989) 'Probabilistic Clock Synchronization,' *Distributed Computing,* Vol. 3, pp. 146–158.

—— (1991) 'Understanding Fault-Tolerant Distributed Systems', *Communications of the ACM,* Vol. 34, no. 2.

Crocker, D. (1982) 'Standard for the format of ARPA Internet text messages.', Internet Request For Comment (RFC) 822.

Darnton, G. and Giacoletto S. (1992) *Information in the Enterprise*, Digital Press, Bedford, MA, USA.

Date, C.J. (1990) *An Introduction to Database Systems* Vol. I, 5th edn, Addison-Wesley, Wokingham, UK.

—— (1987) 'What is a Distributed Database?' *InfoDB,* Vol. 2, no. 2-3, pp. 2–7.

Date, C.J. and Darwen, H. (1993) *A Guide to the SQL Standard,* 3rd edn, Addison-Wesley, Wokingham, UK.

—— (1982) *An Introduction to Database Systems, Vol II,* Addison-Wesley, Wokingham, UK.

Davenport, T.E. and Short, J.E. (1990) 'The new industrial engineering: information technology and business process redesign', *Sloan Management Review,* Vol. 31, no.4, pp. 11–27.

Davies, N.A. and Nicol, J.R. (1991) 'Technological Perspective on Multimedia Computing', *Computer Communications,* Vol. 14, no. 5, June.

DES (1977) 'Data Encryption Standard', Federal Information Processing Standards Publication 46, National Bureau of Standards, US Department of Commerce, Washington, DC, USA.

DIX (1980) Digital Equipment Corp.; Intel Corp. and Xerox Corp. *The Ethernet: A Local Area Network Data Link Layer and Physical Layer Specifications.* September 30.

Domville, I. (1992) 'The Distributed Application Environment - An Architecture Based on Enterprise Requirements' in Meer, de J., Heymer, V. and Roth, R. (Eds) *Open Distributed Processing.* Proceedings of the IFIP TC6/WG6.4 International Workshop on Open Distributed Processing, Berlin, Germany, October 1991, North-Holland, Amsterdam.

Douglass, D. P. and Walsh, L. (eds) (1992) *Basic principles for IT standards*, Butterworth Heineman, Oxford, UK.

DSDM (1995) *Dynamic Systems Development Method,* Tesseract Publishing, Farnham, UK.

Dustdar, S. (1994) 'The role of Multimedia Information Systems in Business Process Redesign: the case of Barclays Bank', Internal Paper, London School of Economics, London, UK.

Ellis, C., Gibbs, S. and Rein, G. (1991) ' Groupware –Some Issues and Experiences.' *Communications of the ACM,* Vol. 34, no. 1, pp. 38–58.

Espejo, R. (1989) 'The VSM Revisited', in *The Viable System Model: Interpretations and Applications of Stafford Beer's VSM,* Espejo, R. and Harnden, R. (eds), pp. 77 –100, John Wiley, Chichester, UK.

—— (1987) 'From machines to people and organizations: a cybernetic insight of management', in Jackson, M. and Keys, P. (eds.), *New Directions in Management Science*, Gower, Aldershot, UK.

—— (1983) 'Information and management: the complementary control-autonomy', *International Journal of Cybernetics and Systems,* Vol. 14, pp. 85–102.

Espejo, R. and Harnden, R. (1989) *The Viable Systems Model: Interpretations and Applications of Stafford Beer's VSM,* John Wiley, Chichester, UK

Espejo, R. and Watt, J. (1978) *Management Information Systems: A System for Design, Working paper 98,* University of Aston Management Centre, Aston, UK.

Etheridge, D. and Simon, E. (1992) *Information Networks: Planning and Design,* Prentice-Hall, London, UK.

Farmer, W. D. and Newhall, E. E. (1969) 'An Experimental Distributed Switching System to Handle Bursty Computer Traffic.' *Proceedings, ACM Symposium on Problems in the Optimization of Data Communications.*

Fayol, H. (1949) *General and Industrial Management,* Pitman, London, UK.

Fischer, M., Lynch, N., and Merritt, M. (1986) 'Easy Impossibility Proofs for Distributed Consensus Problems', *Distributed Computing,* Vol. 1, pp. 26–39.

Fowler, R.J., (1985) 'Decentralized Object Finding Using Forward Addresses,' doctoral thesis and Tech. Report 85-12-1, Dept of Computer Science, University of Washington, Seattle, USA.

Galbraith, J.R. (1988) 'Strategy and Organizational Planning,' in Quinn, J.B., Mintzberg, H. and James, R.M. (eds), *The Strategy Process: Concepts, Contexts and Cases,* Prentice-Hall, Englewood Cliffs, New Jersey, USA.

Garcia-Molina, H. (1982) 'Elections in a Distributed Computing System,' *IEEE Transactions on Computer Systems,* Vol. 31, pp. 48–59.

Gifford, H. (1979) 'Weighted Voting for Replicated Data', *Proc. Seventh Symposium Operating Systems,* pp. 150–162, ACM Press, New York, USA.

Gordon S. (1993) 'Standardization of information systems and technology at multinational companies', *Journal of Global Information Management,* Vol. 1, no. 3, pp 5–14.

Goscinski, A. (1991) *Distributed Operating Systems: The Logical Design,* Addison-Wesley, Sydney, Australia.

Gray, P. (1991) *Open Systems: A Business Strategy for the 1990s,* McGraw-Hill., London, UK.

Greenstein S. (1993) 'Markets, Standards and the Information Infrastructure. *IEEE Micro,* Vol. 13, No. 6 pp. 36–51.

Gusella, R., and Zatti, S. (1989) 'The Accuracy of the Clock Synchronization Achieved by TEMPO in Berkeley UNIX 4.3BSD,' *IEEE Trans. on Software Engineering,* Vol. 15, pp. 847-853.

Hackathorn, R.D. (1993) *Enterprise Database Connectivity,* John Wiley, New York, USA.

Halsall, F. (1992) *Data Communications, Computer Networks and Open Systems,* 3rd Edition, Addison-Wesley, Wokingham, UK.

Hammer, M. and Champy, J. (1993) *Reengineering the Corporation,* Harper Collins, New York, USA.

Handel, R., Huber, M.N., and Schroder, S. (1994) *ATM Networks: Concepts, Protocols, Applications, 2nd Edition,* Addison-Wesley, Wokingham, UK.

Harder, T. and Reuter, A. (1983) 'Principles of Transaction-Oriented Database Recovery', *Computing Surveys,* Vol. 15, no. 4.

Harrington, J (1991) *Organizational Structure and Information Technology,* Prentice-Hall, London, UK.

Hehmann, G., Salmony, M. G. and Stuttgen, H. J., (1990) 'Transport services for multimedia applications on broadband networks.' *Computer Communications,* Vol. 13, no. 4, pp. 197–203.

Helgert, H.J. (1991) *Integrated Services Digital Network,* Addison-Wesley, Reading, MA., USA

Herbert, A. (1994a) 'Real-time multimedia and objects', Architecture Report, APM Ltd, Poseidon House, Castle Park, Cambridge,UK.

Herbert, A. (1994b) 'CORBA Extensions for Real-time and Interactive Multi-Media', Architecture Report APM.1311.02, APM Ltd, Poseidon House, Castle Park, Cambridge CB3 0RD, UK.

—— (1995) 'ANSA Update.', ANSAworks 95 Proceedings, APM Ltd, Poseidon House, Castle Park, Cambridge, UK.

Hirschheim, R. and Smithson, S. (1986) *A critical analysis of IS evaluations,* Oxford Institute of Management, RDP 86/13, Oxford, UK.

Hodson, P. (1992) *Local Area Networks,* DP Publications, London, UK.

Holmberg, B.A. (1989) 'Developing Organizational Competence in a Business' in *The Viable System Model: Interpretations and Applications of Stafford Beer's VSM,*

Espejo, R. and Harnden, R. (eds), pp. 271–297, John Wiley, Chichester, UK.

Howard, J.H., Kazar, M.L., Menees, S.G., Nichols, D.A., Satyanarayanan, M., Sidebotham, R.N. and West, M.J. (1988) 'Scale and Performance in a Distributed File System', *ACM Trans. Computer Systems,* Vol. 6, no. 1, pp. 51–81.

Hutchison, D., Coulson, G., Campbell, A. and Blair, G. S. (1994) 'Quality of Service Management in Distributed Systems', in Sloman, M. (ed.), *Network and Distributed Systems Management,* Addison-Wesley, Wokingham, UK.

IEE (1992) *Radio LANs,* IEE Colloquium 1992/04, May. The Institute of Electrical Engineers.

IEEE (1985a) *Logical Link Control*. American National Standard ANSI/IEEE Std 802.2-1985, The Institute of Electrical and Electronics Engineers.

—— (1985b) *Carrier Sense Multiple Access with Collision Detection (CSMA/CD) Access Method and Physical Layer Specifications*. American National Standard ANSI/IEEE Std 802.3-1985,The Institute of Electrical and Electronics Engineers.

—— (1985c) *Token-Passing Bus Access Method and Physical Layer Specifications*. American National Standard ANSI/IEEE Std 802.4-1985, The Institute of Electrical and Electronics Engineers.

—— (1985d) *Token Ring Access Method and Physical Layer Specifications*. American National Standard ANSI/IEEE Std 802.5-1985, The Institute of Electrical and Electronics Engineers.

—— (1985e) *Draft IEEE Standard 802.1 (Part A): Overview and Architecture*, October, IEEE Computer Society.

Inmon, W. H. and Caplan, J. H. (1992) *Information Systems Architecture: Developments in the 90s,* QED Publishing Group, Wellesley, MA, USA.

ISO 7498-4 *Information processing systems –Open Systems Interconnection –Basic Reference Model – Part 4: Management Framework*. ISO/IEC 7498-4, International Standards Organization, Central Secretariat, Geneva, Switzerland.

ISO 8824 *Information Technology –Open Systems Interconnection –Specification of Abstract Syntax Notation One (ASN.1)*. ISO/IEC 8824, International Standards Organization, Central Secretariat, Geneva, Switzerland.

ISO 8825 *Information Technology –Open Systems Interconnection –Specification of Basic Encoding Rules for Abstract Syntax Notation One (ASN.1)*. ISO/IEC 8825, International Standards Organization, Central Secretariat, Geneva, Switzerland.

ISO 9579-1 *Information Technology –Database Languages –Remote Database Access –Part 1: Generic Model, Service and Protocol.* ISO/IEC 9579-1, International Standards Organization, Central Secretariat, Geneva, Switzerland.

ISO 9579-2 *Information Technology –Database Languages –Remote Database Access –Part 2: SQL Specialization.* ISO/IEC 9579-2, International Standards Organization, Central Secretariat, Geneva, Switzerland.

ISO 9595 *Information technology –Open Systems Interconnection –Common Management Information Service.* ISO/IEC 9595, International Standards Organization, Central Secretariat, Geneva, Switzerland.

ISO 9596-1 *Information technology –Open Systems Interconnection –Common Management Information Protocol –Part 1: Specification.* ISO/IEC 9596-1, International Standards Organization, Central Secretariat, Geneva, Switzerland.

ISO 9596-2 *Information technology –Open Systems Interconnection –Common Management Information Protocol –Part 2: Protocol Implementation Conformance Statement (PICS) Proforma.* ISO/IEC 9596-1, International Standards Organization, Central Secretariat, Geneva, Switzerland.

ISO 10040 *Systems Management Overview*, International Standards Organization, Central Secretariat, Geneva, Switzerland

ISO 10164-1 (1990) *Information Technology –Open Systems Interconnection –Systems Management Part 1 –Object Management Function*, International Standards Organization, Central Secretariat, Geneva, Switzerland

ISO 10164-2 (1990) *Information Technology –Open Systems Interconnection –Systems Management Part 2 –State Management Function*, International Standards Organization, Central Secretariat, Geneva, Switzerland

ISO 10164-4 (1990) *Information Technology –Open Systems Interconnection –Systems Management Part 4 –Alarm Reporting Function,* International Standards Organization, Central Secretariat, Geneva, Switzerland

ISO 10164-5 (1990) *Information Technology –Open Systems Interconnection –Systems Management Part 5 –Event Report Management Function,* International Standards Organization, Central Secretariat, Geneva, Switzerland

ISO 10164-6 (1990) *Information Technology –Open Systems Interconnection –Systems Management Part 6 –Log Control Function*, International Standards Organization, Central Secretariat, Geneva, Switzerland

ISO 10165-1 (1992) *Information Technology –Open Systems Interconnection –Structure of Management Information:* Management Information Model, International Standards Organization, Central Secretariat, Geneva, Switzerland

ISO 10165-2 (1992) *Information Technology –Open Systems Interconnection –Structure of Management Information: Generic Management Information,* International Standards Organization, Central Secretariat, Geneva, Switzerland

ISO 10165-4 (1992) *Information Technology –Open Systems Interconnection –Structure of Management Information: Guidelines for the Definition of Managed Objects,* International Standards Organization, Central Secretariat, Geneva, Switzerland

ISO 10746-1 *Basic Reference Model of Open Distributed Processing – Part 1; Overview*, ISO/IEC 10746-2, International Standards Organization, Central Secretariat, Geneva, Switzerland.

ISO 10746-2 *Basic Reference Model of Open Distributed Processing – Part 2; Foundations*, ISO/IEC 10746-2, International Standards Organization, Central Secretariat, Geneva, Switzerland.

ISO 10746-3 *Basic Reference Model of Open Distributed Processing – Part 3; Architecture*, ISO/IEC 10746-3, International Standards Organization, Central Secretariat, Geneva, Switzerland.

ISO 10746-4 *Basic Reference Model of Open Distributed Processing – Part 4; Architectural semantics*, ISO/IEC 10746-4, International Standards Organization, Central Secretariat, Geneva, Switzerland.

ISO 11172-3 *Information technology –Coding of Moving Pictures and Associated Audio for Digital Storage Media at up to about 1.5 Mbits/s –Part 3: Audio*, ISO/IEC 11172-3, International Standards Organization, Central Secretariat, Geneva, Switzerland.

ISO 11172-4 *Information technology –Coding of Moving Pictures and Associated Audio for Digital Storage Media at up to about 1.5 Mbits/s –Part 4: Conformance*, ISO/IEC 11172-4, International Standards Organization, Central Secretariat, Geneva, Switzerland.

Janson, P.A., (1994) 'Security for Management and Management of Security,' in Sloman, M. (ed.), *Network and Distributed Systems Managment*, Addison-Wesley, Wokingham, UK.

Kahle, B. and Medlar, A. (1991) 'An Information System for Corporate Users: Wide Area Information Servers', *Connexions –The Interoperability Report*, Vol. 5, November.

Kalin, T. and Barber, D. (1992) 'Has the OSI opportunity been fully realized?', *Computer Networks and ISDN Systems*, Vol. 25, no. 3, pp 227–239.

Khoshafian, S. (1989) 'A persistent complex object database language.' *Data and Knowledge Engineering*, Vol. 3.

Khoshafian, S. and Valduriez, P. (1993) 'A Parallel Container Model for Data Intensive Applications', *Proc. Int'l Workshop Database Machines,* pp. 156–170.

Kohl, J.T and B.C. Neuman, (1993) 'The Kerberos Network Authentication Service (V5)', Internet Request for Comment (RFC) 1510.

Kohl, J.T., Neuman, B.C. and T. Y. Ts'o (1994) 'The Evolution of the Kerberos Authentication Service', *Distributed Open Systems*, IEEE Computer Society Press.

Korth, H.F. and Silberschatz, A. (1991) *Database Systems Concepts (2nd Edn)*, McGraw-Hill, New York, USA.

Kung, H.T. and Robinson, J.T. (1981) 'Optimistic methods for concurrency control', *ACM Transactions on Database Systems,* Vol. 6, no. 2, pp. 213–26.

Lamport, L. (1978) 'Time, clocks and the ordering of events in a distributed system.' *Communications of the ACM*, Vol. 21, no. 7, pp. 558–65.

Lamport, L., Shostak, R. and Pease, M. (1982) 'The Byzantine Generals Problem,' *ACM Trans. Programming Languages and Systems,* Vol. 4, No. 3, July, pp. 382–401.

Lampson, B.W. (1981) 'Atomic Transactions.' in *Distributed systems: Architecture and Implementation. Lecture Notes in Computer Science 105.*, pp. 254-9, Springer-Verlag, Berlin.

—— (1971) 'Protection,' *Proceedings of the Fifth Annual Princeton Conference on Information Science Systems*, pp. 437–443; reprinted in *Operating Systems Review*, Vol. 8, no. 1, January, pp. 18–24.

—— (1969) 'Dynamic Protection Structures', *Proceedings of the AFIPS Fall Joint Computer Conference*, pp. 27–38.

Lampson, B.W., Abadi, M., Burrows, M. and Wobber, E. (1992) 'Authentication in Distributed Systems: Theory and Practice', *ACM Transactions on Computer Systems,* Vol. 10, no. 4, pp. 265–310.

Langsford, A. and Moffett, J.D. (1993) *Distributed Systems Management*, Addison-Wesley, Wokingham, UK.

Lansdown, J (1993) 'Interactive Multimedia: should we reexamine its rationale and principles?', *Multimedia in Higher Education: Portability and Networking,* December.

Lee, R. and Lawrence, P. (1985) *Organizational Behaviour: Politics at Work,* Hutchinson, London, UK.

Linington, P.F. (1992) 'Introduction to the Open Distributed Processing Basic Reference Model' in Meer, de J., Heymer, V. and Roth, R. (Eds), 'Open Distributed Processing', *Proceedings of the IFIP TC6/WG6.4 International Workshop on Open Distributed Processing,* Berlin, Germany, October, North-Holland, Amsterdam.

Linington, P.F. (1994) 'Multimedia and Streams.', ANSAworks 94 Proceedings, APM Ltd, Poseidon House, Castle Park, Cambridge, UK.

Marks, D. R. (1994)'ATM from A to Z' *Data Communications*, Vol. 23, No. 18.

Martin, J. (1991) 'Rapid Application Development', Prentice-Hall, Englewood Cliffs, NJ, USA.

Martin, J.L. (1993) 'Travels with Gopher.' *IEEE Computer*, Vol. 26, no. 5, pp. 84–7.

Martin, O.H. (1994) 'A Perspective on the shift/BETEL Project', *Speedup: 15th Workshop on Vector and Parallel Computing*, Vol. 8, no. 1, June.

McNurlin, B.C. and Sprague, R. H. (1989) *Information Systems Management in Practice,* Prentice-Hall, Englewood Cliffs, NJ, USA.

Meer, de J., Heymer, V. and Roth, R. (Eds) (1992) *Open Distributed Processing*, Proceedings of the IFIP TC6/WG6.4 International Workshop on Open Distributed Processing, Berlin, Germany, October, North-Holland, Amsterdam.

Metcalfe, R. M., and Boggs, D. R. (1976) 'Ethernet: Distributed Packet Switching for Local Computer Networks', *Communications of the ACM*, July.

Meyer-Boudnik, T. and Effelberg, W. (1995) 'MHEG Explained', *IEEE Multimedia,* Vol. 2, no. 3, Spring, pp. 26–38.

Michael, J.J. and Hinnebusch, M. (1995) *From A to Z 39.50: A Networking Primer*, Mecklermedia, Westport, CT, USA.

Mills, D.L. (1991) 'Internet Time Synchronization: the Network Time Protocol', *IEEE Transactions on Communications*, Vol. 39, no. 10, pp. 1482–93.

Minasi, M., Anderson, C. and Creegan, E. (1995) *Mastering Windows NT Server 3.5,* Sybex, San Francisco, USA.

Mintzberg, H. (1988) 'The Structuring of Organizations', in Quinn, J.B., Mintzberg, H. and James, R.M. (Eds), *The Strategy Process: Concepts, Contexts and Cases*, Prentice-Hall, Englewood Cliffs, New Jersey, USA.

MIT (1989) *Management in the 1990s Research Program Final Report,* Massachusetts Institute of Technology, Massachusetts, USA.

Mockapetris, P. 'Domain Names –Concepts and Facilities', Internet Request for Comment (RFC) 1034, Information Sciences Inst., Univ. of Southern California, Los Angeles, CA, USA,

Moffett, J.D. (1994) 'Specification of Management Policies and Discretionary Access Control,' in Sloman, M. (ed.), *Network and Distributed Systems Managment*, Addison-Wesley, Wokingham, UK.

Molka, J. A. (1992) 'Surrounded by standards, there is a simpler view', *Journal of the American Society for Information Science,*Vol. 43, no.8, pp 526–530.

Moore, K. (1992) 'Representation of Non-ASCII Text in Internet Message Headers.', Internet Request for Comment (RFC) 1342.

Moreton, R., Simon, E.S., and Sloane, A. (1995) 'Standards Implementation: Architecture and Context Analysis. Internal Report (submitted for publication), University of Wolverhampton, UK.

Mullender, S.J. (ed.) (1993) *Distributed Systems 2nd edn*, ACM Press, New York, USA.

—— (1989) *Distributed Systems*, ACM Press, New York,USA.

Mullender, S.J. and Tanenbaum, A. S. (1986) 'The Design of a Capability-based Distributed Operating System,' *The Computer Journal.*, Vol. 29, no. 4, pp. 289–299.

Mullender, S.J., Rossum, G. Van, Tanenbaum, A.S., Renesse, R. Van, and Staveren, H. Van, (1990) ' Amoeba: A Distributed Operating System for the 1990s,' *IEEE Computer*, Vol. 23, pp. 44-53, May.

Navarro, L., Prinz, W. and Rodden, T. (1993) 'CSCW requires open systems,' *Computer Communications*, Vol. 16, no. 5.

Needham, R. and Schoeder, M., (1978) 'Using Encryption for Authentication in Large Networks of Computers', *Communications of the ACM*, Vol. 21 (12), pp. 993-999, December.

Nelson, T.H, (1990) 'The right way to think about software design', in Laurel B. (ed), *The Art of Human-Computer Interface Design*, pp 235–243, Addison-Wesley, Reading, MA, USA.

Neuman, B.C. (1992) 'The Prospero file System: A Global File System Based on the Virtual System,' *Computing Systems*, Vol. 5, no. 4, pp. 407–432.

Nickel, W.E. (1978) 'Determining Network Effectiveness,' *Mini-Micro Systems,* Vol. 10, October.

OECD (1991) *Information technology standards: the economic dimension.* Information Computer Communications Policy, Report 25, OECD, Paris.

OLE (1993) *Microsoft OLE Today and Tomorrow: Technology Overview*, Microsoft Development Library, December, California, USA.

OMG (1994) *The Common Object Request Broker: Architecture and Specification'*, Object Management Group Inc., 492 Old Connecticut Path, Frameingham, MA., USA.

—— (1992) *The Common Object Request Broker: Architecture and Specification.* OMG Document Number 91.12.1, Object Management Group Inc., 492 Old Connecticut Path, Frameingham, MA, USA..

Orfalli, R., Harkey, D. and Edwards, J. (1994) *Essential Client/Server Survival Guide,* John Wiley, New York, USA.

OSF (1992) *Introduction to OSF DCE,* Prentice-Hall, Englewood Cliffs, NJ, USA.

—— (1991) *Guide to OSF/1: A Technical Synopsis,* O'Reilly and Associates, Inc., Sebastopol, CA, USA.

Oszu, M.T. and Valduriez, P. (1991) *Principles of Distributed Database Systems*, Prentice-Hall, Englewood Cliffs, NJ, USA.

Padovano, M. (1993) *Networking Applications on UNIX System V Release 4,* Prentice-Hall, Englewood Cliffs, NJ, USA.

Pan, D. (1995) 'A Tutorial on MPEG/Audio Compression', *IEEE Multimedia*, Vol. 2, no. 2, Summer.

Parker, M. M. and Benson, R. J. (1988) *Information Economics*, Prentice-Hall, Englewood Cliffs, NJ, USA.

Partridge, C. (1994) *Gigabit Networking,* Addison-Wesley, Wokingham, UK.

Patterson, D.A., Gibson, G. and Katz, R.H. (1988) 'A case for redundant arrays of inexpensive disks (RAID).' *ACM SIGMOD Conference,* pp. 109–116, Chicago, Illinois.

Perley, D. R.(1993) *Migrating to Open Systems: Taming the Tiger,* McGraw-Hill, London, UK.

Perlman, R. (1992) *Interconnections: Bridges and Routers,* Addison-Wesley, Reading, MA, USA.

Popek, G. and Walker, B. (Eds.). (1985) *The LOCUS Distributed System Architecture*, MIT Press, Cambridge MA, USA.

POSIX P1003.4a (1990) *Threads Extension for Portable Operating Systems,* IEEE, Piscataway, NJ., USA.

Postel, J. B. (1982) 'Simple Mail Transfer Protocol', Internet Request for Comment (RFC) 821.

Prinz, W. (1989) 'Survey of group communication models and systems' Computer Based Group Communication and AMIGO Activity Model, Ellis Horwood, Chichester, UK.

Pusztaszeri, Y-H., Hubaux, J-P., Goud, M., Biersack, E. and Dubois, P. (1994) 'Teletutoring over the BETEL Network', *Speedup: 15th Workshop on Vector and Parallel Computing,* Vol. 8, no. 1, June.

Quinn, J.B., Mintzberg, H. and James, R.M. (1988) *The Strategy Process: Concepts, Contexts and Cases*, Prentice-Hall, Englewood Cliffs, NJ., USA.

Ramanathan, P., Shin, K.G., and Butler, R.W. (1990) 'Fault-Tolerant Clock Synchronization in Distributed Systems', *IEEE Computer*, Vol. 23, pp. 33–42.

Rashid, R.F. (1986a) 'Threads of a New System,' *Unix Review*, Vol. 4, pp. 37–49, Aug.

—— (1986b) 'From RIG to Accent to Mach: The Evolution of a Network Operating System', *Proceedings of the ACM/IEEE Computer Society Fall Joint Conference*, ACM, November 1986.

Rederer, A. L. and Mendelow, A. L. (1988) 'Convincing top management of the strategic potential of information systems', *MIS Quarterly*, December , pp. 525–533.

Reed, D. P. and Kanodia, R. K., (1979) 'Synchronization with Eventcounts and Sequences', *Communications of the ACM*, Vol. 22, no. 2, February, pp. 3–23.

Reed, D.P. (1983) 'Implementing atomic actions on decentralized data.' *ACM Transactions on Computer Systems,* Vol. 1, no. 1, pp. 3–23.

Renaud, P.E. (1992) *Introduction to Client/Server Systems,* John Wiley, New York, USA.

Rieken, B. and Weiman, L. (1992) *Adventures in UNIX network Programming,* John Wiley, New York, USA.

Rivest, R.L., Shamir, A. and L. Adleman (1978) 'A method for obtaining digital signatures and public-key cryptosystems,' *Communications of the ACM*, Vol. 21, no. 2. pp. 120–126, February.

Rivest, R. L. (1992) 'The MD5 Message-Digest Algorithm.' Internet Request For Comment (RFC) 1321.

Robbins, S. P. (1989) *Organizational Behavior: Concepts, Controversies and Applications,* Prentice-Hall, Englewood Cliffs, NJ, USA.

Robinson, J. A. (1994) 'Communications services architecture for CSCW,' *Computer Communications*, Vol. 17, no. 5.

Rockart, J.F. and Short, J.E. (1989) 'Sloan MIT in the 1990s: Managing Organizational Independence', *Sloan Management Review*, Sloan School of Management, Massachusetts Institute of Technology.

—— (1988) *Information Technology and the New Organization: Toward More Effective Management of Interdependence,* Center for Information Systems Research, Sloan School of Management, Massachusetts Institute of Technology.

Rooholamini, R. and Cherkassky, V. (1995) 'ATM-based Multimedia Servers', *IEEE Multimedia*, Vol. 2, no. 3, Spring, pp. 39–52.

Rose, M. T., and Stefferud, E. A. (1985) 'Proposed standard for message encapsulation,' RFC 934.

Rumbaugh, J., Blaha, M., Premerlani, W., Eddy, F. and Lorensen, W. (1991) *Object-Oriented Modeling and Design*, Prentice-Hall, Englewood Cliffs, NJ, USA.

Sandberg, R. *et al.* (1985) 'Design and Implementation of the Sun Network File System,' *Proceedings of the Summer 1985 Usenix Conference*, Usenix, Berkeley, CA., pp.119–130.

Sandberg, R., Goldberg, Kleiman, S., Walsh, D., and Lyon, B. (1985)' The Design and Implementation of the Sun Network File System', *Proceedings of the Usenix Conference,* Portland, OR., USA.

Santos, A. and Tritsch, B. (1994) 'Co-operative mutimedia editing tool,' *Computer Communications,* Vol. 17, no. 4.

Satyanarayanan, M., Kistler, J.J., Kumar, P., Okasaki, M.E., Siegel, E.H. and Steere, D.C. (1990) 'Coda: A highly Available File System for a Distributed Workstation Environment.' *IEEE Transactions on Computers*, Vol. 39, no. 4, pp. 447–59.

Satyanarayanan, M. (1993) 'Distributed File Systems,' in Mullender, S.J. (ed.) *Distributed Systems,*: ACM Press, New York, USA.

—— (1990) 'Scalable, Secure, and Highly Available Distributed File Access,' *IEEE Computer*, Vol. 23, no. 5, May, pp. 9–21.

Schneider, F.B. (1993) 'Replication Management using the State-Machine Approach' in Mullender, S.J. (ed.), *Distributed Systems 2nd edn,* ACM Press, New York, USA.

Scott Morton, M.S. (ed.) (1991) *The Corporation of the 1990s: Information Technology and Organizational Transformation,* Oxford University Press, New York, USA.

Shank, J. K. and Govindarajan, V. (1992) 'Strategic cost analysis of the technological investments', *Sloan Management Review,* Fall, pp 35–51.

Sheth, A.P. and Larson, J.A. (1990) 'Federated database systems for manageing distributed, heterogeneous, and autonomous database systems', *ACM Computing Surveys,* Vol. 22, no. 3, pp. 183–236.

Shirley, J. (1992) *Guide to Writing DCE Applications,* O'Reilly and Associates, Inc., Sebastopol, CA, USA.

Simon, E.S. (1994) 'Client/Server Applications: Moving Towards Integration, Interoperability and Independence,' *Proceedings of New Directions on Software Development,* University of Wolverhampton, Wolverhampton, UK.

Simon, E.S. and Sloane, A. (1995) 'Electronic Tuition in a Conventional University Setting: Designing the IT Infrastructure,' 12th International Conference on Technology and Education, February.

Simon, E.S and Fosong, M.F. (1995) 'Fault Tolerance in a Distributed Systems Environment', *Proceedings of the 2nd Communications Networks Symposium,* Manchester Metropolitan University, Manchester, UK, July, pp. 269–272.

Singleton, J. P. (1989) 'Measuring IS performance: experience with the management by results system at Security Specific Bank', *MIS Quarterly,* June, pp. 324–337.

Sirbu, M. A. (1988) 'Content-Type header field for Internet messages.', RFC 1049.

Skeen, D. (1985) 'Determining the last process to fail.' *Transactions on Computer Systems,* Vol. 3, no. 1, pp. 15–30.

—— (1982) 'Non-blocking commit protocols,' in *Proceedings of ACM SIGMOD Conference,* Orlando, Florida, USA.

Sloane, A. (1994) *Computer Communications: Principles and Business Applications,* McGraw-Hill, London, UK.

Sloman, M. (ed.) (1994) *Network and Distributed Systems Managment,* Addison-Wesley, Wokingham, UK.

Sloman, M. and Twidle, K. (1994) 'Domains: A Framework for Structuring Management Policy', in Sloman, M. (ed.), *Network and Distributed Systems Managment,* Addison-Wesley, Wokingham, UK.

Smythe, C. (1995) *Internetworking: Designing the Right Architectures,* Addison-Wesley, Wokingham, UK.

Spring, M.B. (1990) 'Education in information systems standards', *Bulletin of the American Society for Information Science,* Vol.16, no.3, pp. 28–29.

Stallings, W. (1994) *Data and Computer Communications,* 4th Edition, Macmillan, New York, USA.

—— (1993) *Local and Metropolitan Area Networks,* 4th Edition, Macmillan, New York, USA.

—— (1990) *Local Networks,* 3rd Edition, Macmillan, New York, USA.

Stefani, J-B., Hazard, L. and Horn, F., (1992) 'Computational model for distributed multimedia applications based on a synchronous programming language, *Computer Communications,* Vol. 15, no. 2, March 1992, pp. 114–127.

Steiner, J. G., Neuman, B. C., and Schiller, J. I. (1988) 'Kerberos: An Authentication Service for Open Network Systems', *Usenix Conference Proceedings,* Winter.

Stevens, W.R. (1990) *UNIX Network Programming,Prentice-Hall,* Englewood Cliffs, NJ, USA.

Stokes, A. V. (1991) *OSI: standards and acronyms.* NCC Publications, UK.

Stonebraker, M.(1979) 'Concurrency Control and Consistency of Multiple Copies of Data in Distributed INGRES', *IEEE Trans. Software Eng.,* Vol. SE-5, no. 3, May , pp. 188–194.

Stuck, B. and Arthurs, E. (1985) *A Computer Communications Network Performance Analysis Primer.* Prentice-Hall, Englewood Cliffs, NJ, USA.

Siewiorek, D.P. and Swartz, R.S. (1992) *Reliable Computer Systems,* Digital Press, Bedford, MA, USA..

Tanenbaum, A.S. (1988) *Computer Networks,* 2nd Edition, Prentice-Hall, Englewood Cliffs, NJ, USA.

Tanenbaum, A. S. (1995) *Distributed Operating Systems,* Prentice-Hall, Englewood Cliffs, NJ, USA.

Tang, A. and Scoggins, S., (1992) *Open Networking with OSI,* Prentice-Hall, Englewood Cliffs, NJ, USA.

Taylor, F.W. (1947) *Scientific Management,* Harper and Row, New York, USA.

Ullman, J.D. (1988) *Principles of Database and Knowledge-base Systems,* Volume I and II, Computer Science Press. Rockville, MD, USA.

Vaughn, L.T. (1994) *Client/Server System Design & Implementation,* McGraw-Hill, New York, USA.

Veryard, R., Macdonald, I., Dobson, J. and Linden, van der R. (1995) *Enterprise Modelling Methodology* Report, APM Ltd, Poseidon House, Castle Park, Cambridge, UK.

Wallis, J. (1991) 'Toward a Cybernetic Approach to Information Systems', MSc thesis, University of the West of England, Bristol, UK.

Ward, J., Griffiths, P., and Whitmore, P. (1990) *Strategic Planning for Information Systems*, John Wiley, Chichester, UK.

Warne, J. (1994) 'Flexible Transaction Framework for Dependable Workflows', Architecture Report APM.1263.02, APM Ltd, Poseidon House, Castle Park, Cambridge, UK.

Weihl, W.E. (1993) 'Transaction-Processing Techniques', in Mullender, S.J. (ed.), *Distributed Systems 2nd edn* ACM Press, New York, USA.

Willcocks, L. (1992) 'Evaluating IT investments: research findings and reappraisal', *Journal of Information Systems,* Vol. 2, pp 243–268.

Williams, N. and Blair, G. (1994) 'Distributed Multimedia Applications', *Computer Communications,* Vol. 17, no. 2.

X/Open (1988) *X/Open Portability Guide (Issue 3): Networking Services,* Prentice-Hall, Englewood Cliffs, NJ, USA.

INDEX